ELLEN A. WILSON:
THE WOMAN WHO MADE A PRESIDENT

(A VOLUME IN THE
PRESIDENTIAL WIVES SERIES)

OTHER BOOKS IN THE
PRESIDENTIAL WIVES SERIES
Robert P. Watson, Editor

Dolley Madison
Paul M. Zall
2001. ISBN: 1-56072-930-9
(Hardcover)
2001. ISBN: 1-56072-937-6
(Softcover)

**A "Bully" First Lady:
Edith Kermit Roosevelt**
Tom Lansford
2001. ISBN: 1-59033-086-2
(Hardcover)
2011. ISBN: 978-1-61761-845-1
(Softcover)

**Sarah Childress Polk, First Lady of
Tennessee and Washington**
Barbara Bennett Peterson
2001. ISBN: 1-59033-145-1
(Hardcover)
2002. ISBN: 1-56072-551-1
(Softcover)

Frances Clara Folsom Cleveland
Stephen F. Robar
2002. ISBN: 1-59033-245-8
(Hardcover)
2004. ISBN: 1-59454-150-7
(Softcover)

**Edith Bolling Galt Wilson: The
Unintended President**
James S. McCallops
2002. ISBN: 1-59033-556-2
(Hardcover)
2011. ISBN: 978-1-61761-846-8
(Softcover)

Lucretia
John Shaw
2002. ISBN: 1-59033-349-7
(Hardcover)
2004. ISBN: 1-59454-151-5
(Softcover)

**Jackie Kennedy:
Images and Reality**
Mohammed Badrul Alam
2003. ISBN: 1-59033-366-7
(Hardcover)
2011. ISBN: 978-1-61761-840-6
(Softcover)

**Eliza Johnson: Unknown
First Lady**
Jean Choate
2004. ISBN: 1-59454-097-7
(Hardcover)

Caroline Lavinia Scott Harrison
Anne Chieko Moore
2004. ISBN: 1-59454-099-3
(Hardcover)
2009. ISBN: 978-1-60456-271-2
(Softcover)

Lou Henry Hoover: A Prototype for First Ladies
Dale C. Mayer
2004. ISBN: 1-59033-806-5
(Hardcover)
2011. ISBN: 978-1-61761-841-3
(Softcover)

Lucy Webb Hayes: A First Lady by Example
Russell L. Mahan
2004. ISBN: 1-59454-011-X
(Hardcover)
2011. ISBN: 978-1-61761-843-7
(Softcover)

Betty Ford: A Symbol of Strength
Jeffrey A. Ashley
2004. ISBN: 1-59033-407-8
(Hardcover)
2004. ISBN: 1-59454-149-3
(Softcover)

Dutiful Service: The Life of Mrs. Mamie Eisenhower
Robert E. Dewhirst
2004. ISBN: 1-59454-007-1
(Hardcover)

Grace Coolidge: Sudden Star
Cynthia D. Bittinger
2005. ISBN: 1-59454-473-5
(Hardcover)

Texas Bluebonnet: Lady Bird Johnson
David Murphy
2005. ISBN: 1-59454-556-1
(Hardcover)
2006. ISBN: 1-60021-259-X
(Softcover)

Nancy Reagan: The Woman Behind the Man
Pierre-Marie Loizeau
2004. ISBN: 1-59033-759-X
(Hardcover)
2011. ISBN: 978-1-61761-844-4
(Softcover)

Nancy Reagan in Perspective
Pierre-Marie Loizeau
2005. ISBN: 1-59454-695-9
(Softcover)

Ellen A. Wilson: The Woman Who Made a President
Sina Dubovoy
2007. ISBN: 1-59033-791-3
(Hardcover)
2011. ISBN: 978-1-61761-782-9
(Softcover)

Jackie Kennedy – Trailblazer
Mohammed Badrul Alam
2007. ISBN: 1-59454-558-8
(Softcover)

ELLEN A. WILSON: THE WOMAN WHO MADE A PRESIDENT

(A VOLUME IN THE PRESIDENTIAL WIVES SERIES)

SINA DUBOVOY

Nova Science Publishers, Inc.
New York

Copyright © 2011 by Nova Science Publishers, Inc.

All rights reserved. No part of this book may be reproduced, stored in a retrieval system or transmitted in any form or by any means: electronic, electrostatic, magnetic, tape, mechanical photocopying, recording or otherwise without the written permission of the Publisher.

For permission to use material from this book please contact us:
Telephone 631-231-7269; Fax 631-231-8175
Web Site: http://www.novapublishers.com

NOTICE TO THE READER

The Publisher has taken reasonable care in the preparation of this book, but makes no expressed or implied warranty of any kind and assumes no responsibility for any errors or omissions. No liability is assumed for incidental or consequential damages in connection with or arising out of information contained in this book. The Publisher shall not be liable for any special, consequential, or exemplary damages resulting, in whole or in part, from the readers' use of, or reliance upon, this material.

Independent verification should be sought for any data, advice or recommendations contained in this book. In addition, no responsibility is assumed by the publisher for any injury and/or damage to persons or property arising from any methods, products, instructions, ideas or otherwise contained in this publication.

This publication is designed to provide accurate and authoritative information with regard to the subject matter covered herein. It is sold with the clear understanding that the Publisher is not engaged in rendering legal or any other professional services. If legal or any other expert assistance is required, the services of a competent person should be sought. FROM A DECLARATION OF PARTICIPANTS JOINTLY ADOPTED BY A COMMITTEE OF THE AMERICAN BAR ASSOCIATION AND A COMMITTEE OF PUBLISHERS.

Full color presentation of graphics is available in the E-book.

LIBRARY OF CONGRESS CATALOGING-IN-PUBLICATION DATA

Ellen A. Wilson : the woman who made a president / editor, Sina Dubovoy.
   p. cm. -- (Presidential wives series)
 Includes bibliographical references and index.
 ISBN 978-1-61761-782-9 (softcover)
 1. Wilson, Ellen Axson. 2. Presidents' spouses--United States--Biography.
3. Wilson, Woodrow, 1856-1924. I. Dubovoy, Sina.
 E767.3.W64E45 2010
 973.91'3092--dc22
 [B]
                2010031969

Published by Nova Science Publishers, Inc. ✦ New York

"I owe everything to your mother--you know that, don't you?"[1]
Woodrow Wilson to his daughter Eleanor, [1924]

"...she quite literally as well as spiritually made him president."[2]
Ellen's brother, Stockton Axson

"Wilson once said that except for his father and his wife, he would never have reached the White House."
Ray Stannard Baker, Woodrow Wilson, Life and Letters.[3]

---

[1] Eleanor Wilson McAdoo, *The Woodrow Wilsons* (New York: MacMillan, 1937), 300.

[2] Stockton Axson, *Brother Woodrow: A Memoir of Woodrow Wilson* ed. Arthur S. Link (Princeton: Princeton University Press, 1993), 106.

[3] Ray Stannard Baker, *Woodrow Wilson, Life and Letters* (New York: Greenwood Press, 1927, 1968), v.4, 469.

In Erinnerung an meine liebe Mutter

CONTENTS

Foreword		**xiii**
Chapter 1	Youth	**1**
Chapter 2	First Love and a Wedding: Savannah and New York, 1883-1885	**31**
Chapter 3	Young Wife and Mother, 1885-1890	**67**
Chapter 4	Ellen in Princeton, the 1890's	**91**
Chapter 5	*Mater Familias*	**113**
Chapter 6	Travels, Trials, Tribulations, and Mrs. Peck, 1900-1910	**145**
Chapter 7	Politician's Wife, 1910-1912	**185**
Chapter 8	First Lady and Artist	**217**
Chapter 9	1914	**247**
Chapter 10	Epilogue	**257**
Index		**265**

FOREWORD

The role of Ellen Axson Wilson (or Ellen A. Wilson, as she always signed her name) in shaping or making Wilson president has never been examined. Perhaps it has just been overlooked, as Ellen herself has been. "She was a quiet, gentle, unassuming woman who avoided the limelight so successfully that she has been almost forgotten," wrote her daughter Eleanor in 1962. But for Eleanor's loving tribute to her parents in her two memoirs (*The Woodrow Wilsons* [1937], and *The Priceless Gift: The Love Letters of Woodrow Wilson and Ellen Axson Wilson* [1962]), the first and only biography of Ellen Axson Wilson did not appear until 1985, Frances W. Saunders' *Ellen Axson Wilson: First Lady between Two Worlds*. By contrast, Wilson's second wife Edith, to whom he was married only 8 years (compared to 29 years with Ellen), is well-remembered. She lived to the ripe old age of 89, and left posterity an autobiography. Books have been written about her, beginning in her lifetime, up to the present day.

As Woodrow Wilson lay dying in early 1924, he turned to his daughter Eleanor and said, "I owe everything to your mother." I dutifully made a note of this for my research, but it made no further impression on me. Not until I began writing did Wilson's statement take hold of me, and from then on, all the disparate pieces of Ellen's life--and influence--came together. I found it truly uncanny that right after becoming engaged to young Wilson in 1883, Ellen told her brother Stockton that he was "the greatest man in the world," when no one else thought so--not even his adoring father. Midway into the writing of her biography, I decided to change its title to reflect my view that without Ellen, Woodrow Wilson might well never have become president of the United States. Wilson scholars may disagree. For instance, historian John M. Cooper wrote in his *Warrior & the Priest: Woodrow Wilson & Theodore Roosevelt*,"...Ellen Wilson...had largely removed herself from her husband's academic and political concerns after the onset of a serious depression in 1905." [294]). However, I am certain that no one would agree with me more than Woodrow Wilson himself. And besides Wilson, also Ellen's brother, Stockton Axson. He had no reservations whatever about Ellen's contribution in making Wilson "literally" as well as "spiritually," the 28th president of the United States.

This biography is not solely about Ellen the first lady or the woman "who made Wilson president." It is revealing of Ellen the woman, the artist, the mother, the wife and lover of Woodrow Wilson. In turn we learn about their domestic life (finances, education of their children, health, socializing and travel), their married highs as well as lows (i.e., Wilson's six-year long infatuation with Mrs. Peck), and about their mindset and values. In many respects these were notably different from our own, in particular, their racial (i.e. racist) views.

Ellen was truly a gifted artist. Woodrow Wilson was consistently in awe of her artistic talent, declaring once that "there were very few people in America who could paint better than Ellen could." She was on the verge of making her own mark on the world as an artist before her untimely death, in 1914, at age 54. While I by no means neglect Ellen Wilson the artist, yet being neither a scholar of art, much less an artist, more could be said about this vital aspect of Ellen's life.

In the making of this book I owe personal, heartfelt gratitude to many people: everyone with whom I came into contact at Princeton University library and at the archives, especially archivist Tad Bennicoff--tirelessly helpful, with gentlemanly patience in the face of my impatience--as well as everyone at the Princeton Historical Society; the unfailingly helpful, diligent staff at the Manuscript Reading Room in the Library of Congress, and at the Smithsonian's Archives of American Art; and the countless individuals I phoned or e-mailed in Rome, Georgia and elsewhere in the south, in New Hampshire, and again in Princeton. My special thanks to Becky Watters of First Presbyterian Church in Rome, Georgia, Ellen's church.

Chapter 1

YOUTH

"'She never thinks of herself.'"[1]
Woodrow Wilson about Ellen.

"People say of him [a young man] that he is
as good and pure as a girl, though that is rather
an equivocal compliment."[2]
16 year-old Ellen to her mother.

When Ellen, or "Ellie Lou," as she was called in her youth, came into the world on May 15, 1860, in hot, sultry Savannah, Georgia, southerners were edgy over rumors of war. Her ravishingly beautiful mother Janie, or Margaret Jane, wrote frequent letters from Savannah, from the manse of her in-laws, to her absent husband Edward. Six months after Ellen's birth, their first child, 22 year-old Janie wrote: "The ladies in Charleston are already preparing lint bandages and I am afraid that will be the sad duty here soon."[3]

Though her mother-in-law "could not throw off the feeling of gloom" at the impending war, sunny Janie could not dwell on the negative. "I believe there are a good many who think I never am [sad], and in truth I am not often so," she had written calmly to her fiancé several years earlier.[4] Besides, this was baby Ellie Lou's first Christmas, celebrated southern style: no Christmas tree, but Christmas stockings stuffed with presents that hung from mantelpieces; on Christmas day, firecrackers, tin horns and heavy guns sounded in the streets, as though it were a fourth of July. There was no church service, and businesses were open as usual in the sober Protestant city of 14,000 whites, and 8,000 blacks.

The young and handsome, dark-haired Edward, or Reverend Samuel Edward Axson, was neither as sanguine nor as calm and even-tempered as his wife. As a young adult, Ellen would refer to her father's dinner-time tirades "against the times, the government, the Yankees, human nature, and things in general."[5] Edward Axson (preferring, like Woodrow Wilson, to go by his middle name) was, like Ellen's mother, a native of Georgia. Born in the tiny hamlet of Waltourville, in backwater Liberty County, on December 23, 1836, Edward Axson seemed destined to follow in his brilliant, handsome father's footsteps.

The fathers of both Janie and Edward had the reputation of being "eminent divines:" inspiring preachers and teachers of the Word. Both were Presbyterian ministers, belonging to that Calvinist creed brought south in the late 18th century by way of New England. Reverend Isaac Stockton Axson, Edward's father, had been born and raised in Charleston, South Carolina, and perhaps because of his Scottish parents, spoke with a decidedly un-southern burr to the end of his life. Somehow Isaac's widowed mother managed to educate her two sons. Isaac's brother became a physician, while Isaac graduated from the College of Charleston and in 1834, at age 21, from Columbia Theological Seminary in South Carolina.[6]

The perspicacious Englishwoman Fanny Kemble vividly described the 1830's Charleston of Isaac's youth. To the former English actress, it was a decrepit but charming city, filled with the "ruins and decays" of once lovely mansions: "...every house seems built to the owner's particular taste; and in one street you seem to be in old English town, and in another in some continental city of France or Italy. This variety is extremely pleasing to the eye..." Jarring to the uninitiated was the nightly curfew, "a most ominous tolling of bells and beating of drums," to summon indoors all persons of color.[7]

After his graduation from seminary, Isaac, like the Isaac of the Old Testament, married his Rebecca--Rebecca Longstreet Randolph--daughter of a prominent Charleston merchant. From then on, Isaac's professional star rose, taking him to various Georgia and South Carolina pastorates, to president of the Presbyterian-run Greensboro Female College in Greensboro, Georgia, until at age 44, in 1857, he accepted the call of the prominent Independent Presbyterian Church in Savannah, Georgia, a wealthy congregation.[8] For the next thirty-four years, Isaac Axson remained head pastor, becoming an anomaly in the church: a well-to-do clergyman, patrician lord of his small family flock, the stately "manse" adjoining the church his home, cared for by servants who, at least before the Civil War, were probably his slaves.

* * *

Of Isaac's three children, his son Edward appears to have been the most intellectually and spiritually gifted. The Presbyterian church of Edward's boyhood and youth, however, was drifting apart. Differences between the northern and southern churches ran deeper than slavery, an issue which also divided southern Presbyterians. Edward's future sister-in-law, Louisa Hoyt, married against her clergy parents wishes, not only because her husband was a Baptist, but because he owned slaves. In 1861, at a great meeting of southern Presbyterian clergy in New Orleans, the split between northern and southern churches became official. Slavery was neither approved nor was it condemned. Its eventual demise would bring about no reconciliation between northern and southern churches. After the war, the southern Presbyterian church continued on its more orthodox conservative course, shunning the growing popularity of the "social gospel," confining itself solely to the spiritual; some of its clergymen, like Woodrow Wilson's father Reverend Dr. Joseph Ruggles Wilson, went so far as to oppose the church's involvement in Sunday school: parents should teach religious fundamentals in the home, he insisted. When southern black Presbyterians began leaving their white congregations to establish their own, there was no attempt to woo them back, though white clergymen did not shun blacks. Ellen Axson, writing to her fiancé Woodrow Wilson in 1884, casually mentioned the marriage of a simple black couple in her grandfather's church, her grandfather Isaac Axson officiating. Such an event did not seem unusual to the race-conscious Ellen.

Ellen's father Edward, therefore, was destined to be a clergyman in this highly conservative denomination. What his childhood had been like, what he was like as a person, and how and why he died, will forever remain a mystery. His surviving correspondence bristles with intelligence, power of expression, great sweetness and humility. We learn from it and from Ellen's own letters that he was not given to athletics, did not even care for the southern man's passion for horseback riding, and never learned to swim (southerner Woodrow Wilson also never learned to swim, though he learned to ride well). As a grown woman, Ellen lamented that her father had no outside interests except his work. He enjoyed traveling, however, and a change of scene, though he seemed to have precious little opportunity for either.

There are few facts or anecdotes about Edward's youth. He seemed to grow up fast, engaged at 19, married at 21, already a full-time pastor, and at 23, already a father. His correspondence reveals a religiosity that was both intense and very personal. God was Father, a caring God, merciful and just. The severe Calvinist dogmas of predestination and of infants condemned to eternal hell fire if they died unbaptized, figured neither in his sermons nor in his other writings. In this he was not unusual. Perhaps because of the high level of education of its clergy,

Presbyterianism in the nineteenth century was beginning to shed its hard edge. In the late nineteenth century, the church would even renounce the harsh creed of unbaptized infants' eternal damnation (the one and only time in his life that Woodrow Wilson permitted himself a joke at his religion's expense[9]). Given the high incidence of infant mortality in the nineteenth century, Edward and his wife Janie still had no qualms waiting nearly a year after Ellen's birth to have her baptized.

In 1854, when Edward entered Oglethorpe College in Georgia, this 15 year-old already knew he wanted to be a minister. Writing to his fiancée four years later, from his room at Columbia Theological Seminary, he described it exultantly as "one of the best places in the world." He was not merely following in his father's footsteps, and as a pastor, he would not, as his father had done, seek out a more lucrative ministry. In 1880 he even considered leaving his pastorate in Rome for a lower-paying one in tiny Salem, Georgia, prompting one local wit to comment how "'...he wanted to hear that man preach who was thinking of going from a larger salary to a smaller one.'" This devout, intellectual man was well on the road to becoming an "eminent divine" before his life was cut cruelly short, at age 47.[10]

* * *

Compared to the sensitive, emotional Edward Axson, Ellen's mother Margaret Jane Hoyt was less brilliant, more restrained and serene. Sixth and youngest child of the eminent divine Reverend Dr. Nathan Hoyt, Margaret Jane, or Janie, was born on September 8, 1838, two years and three months younger than her future husband Edward. She grew up in Athens, Clarke county, in northeast Georgia, where for many years her father Reverend Hoyt presided over the First Presbyterian church. As the youngest child, Janie was adored and petted by her parents, and the playful favorite of her four brothers. Writing to her from his medical school in 1858, brother Will's reaction to his sister's imminent marriage would probably send tongues wagging nowadays:" ...it makes me almost sad to think of your getting married, to think that you will love a stranger better than me....I still hold title proper to that large part of your heart deeded to me."[11] Her relationship with her other siblings was no less affectionate and close-knit.

Janie's girlhood, her experiences coming of age in antebellum Georgia in the 1840's and early 1850's, are also an enigma. That her parents taught her to read and write in the manse is a near certainty. Otherwise, what her upbringing was like might be inferred to a certain extent from how she raised her own children. In this, as in other respects, she was nothing like her strict and unyielding sister,

Louisa. There could not have been a clearer contrast between Janie, born in 1838, and her older sister Louisa, born in 1830. Louisa's well-documented reputation as a ramrod puritan, "spare the rod and spoil the child" mother and disciplinarian, reflected the difference in upbringing of a child born second out of six, and a petted youngest child of older parents.

Glimpses of Janie's personality from her writing reflect a sunny young woman with a sense of fun, who enjoyed life. Unlike her future husband Edward, Janie loved horseback riding. According to her daughter Margaret, as a young woman she was used to riding cross-saddle rather than side-saddle; as a young married matron, on a sultry June day in 1858, Janie showed up for a visit in Athens with her hair cut short. In a letter to her husband Edward, she mentioned how the sight of her cropped hair "disturbed her parents" but that "other people thought it looked nice;" above all, "my darling likes it."[12] Given the mild reactions to her short hair, particularly from her husband, it could not have been viewed then as it would be nowadays: as a daring, rebellious act against an oppressive male culture. Indeed Janie's numerous long letters testify to the opposite, that she was happy (rightly or wrongly) in her sphere, bounded by church, her family and her friends.

As to Janie's preacher father, "'When it was known that Dr. Nathan Hoyt was to preach in Synod or Presbytery, the church was sure to be crowded.'" Yet this eminent divine apparently was no well-to-do clergyman. His four sons, however, managed to go to college, and each received professional training afterwards: William as a physician, Robert as a pharmacist, with sons Henry and Thomas becoming clergymen. Janie's letters reveal that her relationship with her mother was extremely close; so, too, would be her relationship with daughter Ellen. Otherwise Janie's mother remains a shadowy figure. That Mrs. Hoyt was highly literate, there can be little doubt. Nineteenth century Presbyterians, whether in the north or in the south, were zealous about educating their daughters.[13]

It is certain that Janie's parents would have taught their daughter at home. When she was 15, they enrolled her in nearby, Presbyterian-affiliated, Greensboro Female College.

The college did not award bachelor's degrees, though Janie apparently did "graduate," in what sense, we cannot be sure. The school, moreover, was probably tiny. (A few years later, Edward Axson described visiting a "large" female college, consisting of only 60 students.[14]) From all accounts, Janie distinguished herself at the school, winning numerous academic prizes, and upon graduating several years later, was snapped up as a full-time teacher (the teachers at the school were, however, referred to as professors).

Judging from the low opinion that both Ellen and Woodrow Wilson shared of southern girls' schools (and of southern girls' intellects in general), Janie's record as a student and her position as a "professor" may not have been as impressive as they seem. Nonetheless, for a woman to teach full-time as a "professor" in a female college was sufficiently unusual, in the south at least, to explain why her home town newspaper, when announcing her engagement, got her fiancé confused as the professor, rather than she.[15]

The president of Greensboro Female College during Janie's five years there-- three as a student, two as a teacher--was none other than Edward's father, Reverend Isaac Axson. It seems inevitable that sooner or later, Janie and Edward's paths would cross. Her gorgeous looks would have made her noticeable in any crowd; no one who knew Janie ever forgot to mention her outstanding beauty. Her daughter Margaret, also a beauty, heard her mother described as having "Great lustrous gray eyes, red-brown hair rippling back from a Madonna-like forehead," and a graceful, slender figure.[16] Coupled with her deep religiosity, young Janie must have been irresistible to the devout pastor-to-be Edward Axson, and just as importantly, to his parents, who adored her and were anxious to see them married.

Like Edward, Janie, too, had matured early and grown up fast: earning a living at 18, engaged at barely 19, and married at 20. She hardly fit the stereotype, which in some respects was true, of the wan and frail southern damsel. The same Fanny Kemble, on her tour of Georgia the year Janie was born, remarked that "The ladies that I have seen since I crossed the Southern line have all seemed to me extremely sickly in their appearance...," moreover, "they are languid in their deportment and speech." In short, Janie never belonged to that "two-thirds" of southern womankind whom her daughter Ellen would describe as "invalids to a greater or less degree." Neither would Janie's daughters, nor Woodrow Wilson's formidably educated sisters, also southern daughters of the manse.[17]

After a stiff beginning, the engagement letters of Ellen's parents revealed increasingly their mad passion for one other. At first, they hardly dared use each other's first names. "Mr. Axson, Dear Sir," wrote Janie at the outset of their engagement in 1856, "I was on the point of writing your Christian name but was afraid it might appear too bold in me as I had never called you by that name." She assured him that she was "not at all offended" that he, in turn, had omitted calling her "Miss" in his previous letter.[18] By now they had a two year courtship behind them. Edward soon was progressing to "my dearest little Pet," "my precious darling," endearments that could only lead to the sacred altar of marriage. That event took place at Janie's father's church in Athens, Georgia, on November 23, 1858.

Presbyterian weddings typically were starkly simple, perfunctory services, in this instance presided over by both minister parents. There probably was no reception or honeymoon afterwards. Edward Axson was the new pastor of what had formerly been his father-in-law's church in Beech Island, Georgia. The congregation must have been a poor one, for there was no manse for the newlyweds to settle in, nor could they afford a home of their own. Instead, they squeezed into a rented room without bath or kitchen, in the home of an elderly couple. They were so in love that they hardly noticed their surroundings. Edward, especially, seemed emotionally dependent on his wife, devastated when she was away, even when the separation was only a matter of fifteen miles. He wrote his "dearest little Janie" how he felt "lonely to kill....it will be impossible for me to see her face and enjoy her kisses for at least TWO days. I think I must take a big dose of Laudamon and sleep till Friday." The inconsolable Edward "almost felt just like lying down and dying" at the sight of their empty bedroom. Hinting at his state of mind if anything should ever happen to her, "I do not know what I would do."[19] In the light of his later breakdowns, these over-emotional outpourings might be signs of an emotional imbalance; or perhaps he was just teasing, although he was not much given to humor in his writing.

The couple was in fact much apart in the early years of their marriage. Edward was just too poor to support a wife who in the summer of 1859 discovered she was expecting. By the time daughter Ellen Louise came into the world on May 15, 1860, mother and daughter were living a peripatetic life, now spending months in Savannah at the home of Janie's in-laws, where Ellen was born, then months at her parents' home in Athens. Edward meanwhile struggled on as pastor in Beech Island, an insecure future hovering ahead because of the clouds of war. "Some persons may exult at the prospect of disunion but I cannot," wrote Janie in Savannah to her absent husband a few months before war erupted. "While I feel that our honor demands it, my heart weeps at the thought, and at times an almost irresistible sadness oppresses me." Baby Ellen relieved some of the gloom. "Oh she is a precious little treasure and if she becomes a spoiled child we will have only ourselves to blame," wrote Janie, "for she is the best child naturally I think I ever saw."[20]

War brought on even more dislocation and gloom. Edward Axson quit the Beech Island church in the spring of 1861, and shortly afterwards, joined a Georgia infantry regiment as chaplain. He must have witnessed horrifying scenes quite unsettling to his sensitive, emotional nature. By late 1863, after more than two years in the army, Edward succumbed, like so many men in the war, to a devastating illness. He recovered, and never returned to the army.

War's end found the little family of three living in Madison, northeast Georgia, where Edward had secured a position as pastor of the Madison Presbyterian Church. At last they were settled in their own home, albeit a rented one. They even conducted a school in their home, where little Ellen probably learned her A,B,C's.[21] Given the lack of a public school system in Georgia and the closure of most private schools during the war, the Axsons were providing a vital service, for which they, especially Janie, were well-qualified. Yet their stay in Madison was to be short-lived.

In late 1865, Edward Axson enthusiastically accepted a call to serve at the First Presbyterian Church in Rome, Georgia, a small city well over a hundred miles west of Madison. Rome, unlike Madison, had suffered severely in the war: its population depleted, its church, soon to be Edward Axson's pastorate, ruined. Financial considerations never paramount, Edward might have found the challenge of re-building and injecting new life into the church irresistible, compared to the more sedate ministry in Madison. To Edward, ministry was a vocation; when his ministry in Rome began to disappoint him, he wanted out. In the coming years, gilded age prosperity would change Rome's fortunes, deflecting parishioners, so it might have seemed to him, from spiritual to material concerns. No wonder that his growing restlessness led him to seek a new ministry in a simpler, more pioneer-like setting. Perhaps one that reminded him of his early years in Rome.

* * *

Hence by the spring of 1866, the Axson family of three were settled in Rome, in Georgia's upper northwest county of Floyd. In 1861, Floyd county's population had stood at 15,000, reduced by many thousands after the war. Rome's population, too, had sunk, and its economy was in shambles, thanks to rampaging Yankees. Eleanor Wilson McAdoo, in her memoirs of her parents published in the 1930's, recalled Rome as "a very small city. Gardens enclosed its stately old houses, tall trees sheltered the streets and no one was ever in a hurry." Her impressions of Rome were based on fleeting visits to the city in her youth. By then, the early twentieth century, Rome was beginning to transform itself into the graceful, progressive municipality of the present day.

An 1857 print of Rome, nine years before the Axsons arrived, likewise conveys a positive impression: of a thriving metropolis, steamboats plying its rivers, church steeples adorning its hills, industrious and prosperous.[22] Perhaps it was so. The city's economy, however, rested on agriculture, slave-based and backward. Despite being the county seat, Rome could boast neither schools nor a library, and its trains rarely ran on time. Long after the Civil War, when slavery had given way to inefficient sharecropping, agriculture still remained backward. A public library did not open in Rome until Andrew Carnegie generously donated one in 1911. Public schools arrived only in the 1880's. Hence when the educated Axsons arrived, there were no schools at all, public or private, except, ironically, the federally-funded Freedman's school of short duration.

In many respects, the depleted Rome after the war, and for many years thereafter, resembled a typical southern small town, the kind that Margaret Axson Elliott immortalized in her 1944 memoir. Though Margaret, Janie's youngest child, grew up in the small city of Gainesville, Georgia, rather than in Rome, she refused to make a distinction between her "grubby little town" and any other southern town, lumping them all under the rubric of "Illyria:" "To me, unaware of its unkempt dilapidation, it was a happy town," wrote Margaret. When she was 18, Ellen Axson mentioned a visitor's comment about Rome, that "'there isn't a house in Rome that is fit to live in,'" which she did not take seriously. Was it because Ellen, too, thought of Rome as a "happy town"? Postwar Rome also had its black slum typical of "Illyria." Described by Margaret as "... a scandal and a menace...Epidemics of all kinds started there--diphtheria, typhoid, a motley assortment of fevers....carried to the white population by their cooks, housemen, and laundresses."[23]

Postwar Rome was often a lawless town. In a state whose population after the war was almost equally divided between blacks and whites, anti-black feeling ran high. In 1868, less than three years after the Axsons settled in Rome, Romans, or perhaps the ill-famed Crackers who inhabited the backwoods, had committed, on record, 21 acts of violence against blacks, ranging from assault to murder. This was just two fewer incidents than in the much bigger town of Savannah. These, however, were only the recorded incidents. The Roman press, too, was unabashedly racist. In 1869, the city's *Weekly Courier* disparaged the recent establishment in Atlanta of Atlanta University, a school for blacks: "'We cannot see the object of the enterprise unless it is to more thoroughly indoctrinate the nigger into the peculiar principles (miscegenation, etc.) of Radicalism. It will, we imagine, be an odoriferous affair!'"[24]

Even remote Rome attracted its share of foreigners, however. Remarkably, Belgian immigrants lived in Rome, clustered on Mt. Alto. In 1874, there were even enough Jewish residents with the courage to erect a house of worship. Unlike Margaret's Gainesville, Rome was picturesque: "... the jassamine, the daffodils and the hyacinths are in bloom, the grass is green, and the town looks very attractive while the hills about it, veiled in a soft blue haze, are BEAUTIFUL" wrote Ellen to Woodrow Wilson.[25] Judging by Ellen's and her mother's panic at the thought of leaving Rome for Salem, Georgia, a hick town that needed a pastor in 1880, there were worse towns to live in, and not, as Margaret would have us believe, all of them equally bad.

This was the Rome into which the Reverend and Mrs. Axson and their five and a half year-old daughter Ellen ("Ellie Lou") settled for eighteen years, for the most part, happily.

* * *

The First Presbyterian Church in Rome had no official manse for the preacher and his family. For the first five years the Axsons lived an unsettled life in several rented homes. Finally, in 1871, they bought a lot and built their own house. The church, originally established in Rome in 1845, had been wrecked by Union troops during the war, and its members scattered. A church history reveals that "He [Pastor Axson] found the church building empty and forlorn, and only forty or fifty members of the congregation remaining. With great energy and consecration he devoted himself to the task of restoring and building up the church." Pastor Axson succeeded so well that the church grew steadily in membership, and consequently, in income. As poverty and hard times waned, and Pastor Axson's disillusionment and restlessness waxed, his popularity never suffered. Whether it mattered to him or not, the unworldly Edward was a success as a pastor. His salary grew correspondingly. The year they built their house, 1871, he received $1431, a decent salary for that time and under populated area; ten years later, this rose to $1750 (by contrast, Woodrow Wilson's Bryn Mawr College salary in 1885 was $1500).[26]

While Janie Axson habitually referred to daughter Ellen as a "poor preacher's daughter," the Axsons' poverty in Rome was far from grinding. Janie, like most women of her social background, was freed from common household drudgeries: cooking, heavy cleaning and laundry. White women, even marginally well off ones like Janie, customarily hired black women cheaply for these chores. The Axsons even hired a black nursemaid for Ellen. They bought silverware for their table, and books for their bookshelves. When Ellen finally went to school, they paid extra for art classes. The impetus behind their purchases, however, was most likely Janie. When a relative of Edward's sent him a handsome Christmas present, he was "very sorry she sent it," lamented Janie.[27]

Their home and their small luxuries, however, might not have been possible, or been fewer, had it not been for the help of Edward Axson's well-to-do parents in Savannah. The Axson's lot on east Third Avenue seems to have been a present from Edward's father, who might have helped pay for their new house. Because of her doting grandparents, Ellen grew up with more than a few luxuries: silk dresses, books, occasional jewelry, and pocket money. In a letter to her mother from Savannah, 17-year-old Ellen even gives the impression that she did not quite grasp the value of money. "Couldn't you scrape together twelve dollars to buy a cloak?" asked Ellen, commissioned to buying her mother a dress, when twelve dollars was more than a cook earned in a month. But then, during that same visit, her Uncle Randolph surprised her with a gift of coral jewelry worth 20 dollars, a small fortune, followed by expensive presents from her grandparents. Compared to her friend Janie Porter, who had neither silk dresses nor jewelry nor the chance to attend private school, Ellen grew up well off. Yet perennially, almost to the end of her life, Ellen imagined herself to be "poor" and economizing.[28]

Ellen's lifelong Rome friends, the Tedcastles, interviewed by Ray Stannard Baker in 1925, remembered the Axsons as "among the most prominent people in the town of Rome." The Axson home "was a home of books and religion, with a keen and decided intellectual life,"[29] surely mistaken hindsight. After all, Rome was no cultural haven like Princeton and Janie Axson, though intelligent, was no intellectual. Poor or not, white Presbyterian clergy did belong to the social elite in the south. More than likely Ellen grew up like her mother, a daughter of the manse, in a nurturing and highly literate family.

With no formal schooling until she was 11 and a half, Ellen most likely learned her letters at her mother's knee. By the age of 10, she was capable of writing the following charming letter to her father, describing a visit to a relative. She was accompanied by her little brother Stockton, 3 years old, and her mother Janie.

October 18, 1870 Brown's Bridge
Dear Father,
We got here safely, and are having a very nice time. I wish you would write to me. Give my love to Bettie, and all the rest. Stockton saw your picture in Mother's album, and cried out, That's Papa, that's Papa; he knew all the pictures in it. He is always talking about when he was to Rome. I am having a splendid time. We were gathering apples all day Friday. Saturday I was pieling[piling] up chips all the morning; in the evening, we were sweeping the yard, and then we went for Mother's clothes....but the clothes were so heavy that we stopped to rest by the mill dam, and oh Papa, it was so pretty, I could hardly get myself away. We got up on a big pile of hay and it was so nice we stayed ever so long playing on the hay. We did not go to church Sunday. Monday morning we went after Mother's trunk; we went in the wagon, and it jolted so, it gave me a headache. I got over it before night. Stockton says tell papa I cry and I love him; he says when he goes back to Rome, Papa will take him in his arms and hug and kiss him. Mother and all

the rest send love. Grandmother says she wishes you had come and preached for them...

Your loving Daughter, Ellie Lou Axson[30]

At age 10, Ellen was already showing signs of that power of expression that would make her as intelligent and powerful a writer as the far better-educated Woodrow Wilson.

Ellen's letter also reveals the warm relationships within her family and kin. Her brother Stockton (Isaac Stockton Keith, named after his grandfather) was born in Rome on June 6, 1867. By then Ellen was already seven. The family soon would be augmented by Janie's widowed mother. In 1876, when Janie was thirty-eight and daughter Ellen sixteen, Janie gave birth to her third child, Edward Axson, Jr. Ellen seemed destined to be a second mother to her siblings, doting on "Eddie" as though he were her own son.

Perhaps because the birth of Janie's children were spaced so far apart--her last, Margaret, was born when Janie turned 43--that the relationship between mother and oldest child Ellen was an intimate one. The Axson children, in particular Ellen and Stockton, were also very close to their father, who had the traditional view of the father as head of the household and disciplinarian to his children. Decades later, son Stockton confided in Ray Stannard Baker that: "Although Mr. Axson was a preacher, he did not preach much to me, trusted to his own example and occasional use of a leather strap to keep me on the narrow path."[31] As to Ellen, Edward might chide his daughter for her "strong opinions," perhaps teasingly, but to him, she was always "my gifted daughter."

While the Axson marriage was subject to strains, on the whole, it was a very happy one. Edward never forgot an anniversary. On the occasion of their 16th wedding anniversary, he wrote to his wife, "God has been wonderfully good to us...year by year we find that we are more and more dependent on each other and less and less able to get along without each other."[32] Whether this was really true of Janie or not, it certainly was true for him.

* * *

For the Axsons, strictly observant Presbyterians, religion was not only a system of belief but a regimen and way of life. "Sabbath day" (Presbyterians rarely called it Sunday) must have been as grueling for the Axson children as it would be for Ellen's own daughters. Two long services, with full sermons, were held on Sundays, one in the morning and one in the evening, neither one abbreviated for children; play, sports, or even light reading were proscribed.

Youth 13

Children not only had to learn the "Shorter Catechism," but to memorize it. Hence while work was disallowed, Sunday "rest" in this grim religion was far from relaxing. Weekly evening services, at least once a week, were expected of the Axson children, and most likely, daily family prayers as well, as in Ellen's own household. Some observant Presbyterians, like Woodrow Wilson's clergyman father, pushed the envelope as to what was proper, indulging in an occasional drink or game of billiards, and chain-smoking, even in bed. Yet they all frowned on dancing and card-playing, which smacked of gambling and lewdness.

Presbyterianism would grow more liberal as the nineteenth century waxed. Rarely, even in Ellen's youth, did religion infringe on all pleasure. When it came to food, there was never any fasting, or abstaining from meat on certain days, or any emphasis on plain dress or against wearing jewelry; sports were not frowned upon, except on Sundays, nor even novel reading, as in some Protestant creeds. But the moral code remained on an uncompromisingly high plane. If they could have, Presbyterians would have added an eleventh commandment: condemning selfishness. No sin short of murder was as loathsome. To instill unselfishness in their children, parents would go to many lengths. According to Eleanor Wilson McAdoo, her parents would never compliment their daughters on their appearance, or over-praise them. Both could lead to self-centeredness. Margaret Axson Elliott, a hater of "calvinism," recalled with gall how her guardian, Aunt Louisa, would rather have choked to death than pay her a compliment, "so firm was her belief that to tell a child she was pretty would spoil her."[33] Modern-day notions of "self-realization" and "love yourself first before you can love others," would have scandalized these nineteenth century "Calvinists."

Despite the sternness of religion in her youth, Ellen, unlike her sister Margaret, never rejected Presbyterianism, and observed "Sabbath day" nearly as sternly as when young. Though she was the type of person who would find Immanuel Kant "quite comprehensible" and who read Hegel easily, she, until the end of her life, loved the old hymns and relished a good sermon.

* * *

As far as raising girls was concerned, neither Janie nor Edward seem to have doubted the traditional Christian view at the time, that men and women had distinctly different, though not unequal, roles to play in life, a view that Woodrow Wilson also shared. This meant that neither parent would have encouraged Ellen to seek a career, though neither seemed in the least opposed to an unmarried woman earning her own living. But if she never married, a woman's living had to be earned, if she was forced to earn one, in a "womanly" career or job, usually lower-paying. This did not seem illogical or unfair to traditional Christians like the Axsons and to Ellen herself. Ellen in fact would follow in her mother's footsteps--though not so early in life--to seek a career for herself, out of her talent in art. Fortunately for her, art was a career that was, though open to men, also "womanly."

Although Ellen never learned to swim or ride a horse, or took up any other sport, such as hiking or biking, she was an excellent marksman with a bow and arrow (in her youth), and a good sailor. Her future husband Woodrow Wilson also never learned to swim, and was discouraged from learning to skate (and to smoke) by his anxious mother. By contrast, Ellen's youngest sibling Margaret, who was brought up by her strict, puritanical Aunt Louisa, described how she learned to swim, to ride horseback astride rather than side-saddle, and hiked and roamed the outdoors for hours on end. It is surprising to learn that as a girl growing up in the deep south, in the late nineteenth century, Margaret had complete freedom to spend the day before dark as she liked. Margaret, too, would earn a bachelor's degree in an era when few men or women did. Yet neither Margaret nor her sister Ellen ever pursued a career outside of marriage and motherhood, though both were well aware that there were women who did.

Ellen, like her mother, never cooked, cleaned or changed a diaper (the latter only by choice). Without having to prepare meals and wash up afterwards, and clean house, or work a full-time job, what did Ellen's mother do all day when Ellen was growing up? In 1861, Janie wrote her husband from Savannah how she was spending her spare time: there was company every evening, and going on visits all day long. Fifteen years later, daughter Ellen was writing her mother how she was spending her free time: "Last Monday I had eight calls. Tuesday I spent the day at Mrs. Peter's. Wednesday at Mrs. Harris. Thursday at Mrs. Phillips. While at Mrs. Phillips a lady....came to take us to the country, where they have a beautiful place, to spend several days."[34]

Visiting and going on visits was an important institution for women, north and south, which took up an enormous amount of their spare time.[35] Visitors usually dropped in, without announcing their visits ahead of time, or waiting for an invitation. As the wife of a pastor, Janie Axson could be called upon without warning from morning until night. While men also visited and were expected to return visits, theirs were less frequent and of shorter duration. In-between visits, Janie taught her children at home, just as Ellen would do, supervised the household, shopped, and engaged in the "feminine" occupations of church work, letter-writing and sewing. Only occasionally would she leave her narrow but important sphere to go on an extended visit to kinfolk.

Youth 15

Janie's letters reveal, just as Ellen's did later, a very busy life. But in the south at least, even among sober Presbyterians, there was no Yankee disdain for just having a jolly good time doing nothing. Even acquaintances called each other "sister," "brother," or "cousin," would sit on their verandahs for hours, chatting, laughing, and sewing, a way of life which Ellen's northern-bred daughter, Eleanor, would find so irresistibly appealing.

* * *

At age 11 and a half, Ellen finally went to school. Not that her parents were devotees of home-schooling. Yet had there been a public school in Rome, the Axsons still might have resisted sending their children there, especially their daughter. They were not apt to view "promiscuous" education--the mingling of boys and girls in the same school--very favorably. Moreover, formal schooling in that day and age, in the absence of mandatory schooling, was not always taken very seriously. Parents would enroll their children, boys as well as girls, at almost any age, and take them out for almost any reason. Teaching standards, as in the case of Ellen's mother Janie--hired to teach after only three years of formal education--were non-existent.

Rome Female College, the only school in Rome, had been forced to close its doors at the outset of the Civil War, along with many private schools in the south. They remained closed, apparently for financial reasons, until the fall of 1871. Though a private school, it was also affiliated with the southern Presbyterian church, and more likely than not, the Axsons were exempt from paying basic tuition. Two years later Baptists established Cherokee Baptist Female College in Rome (re-named Shorter College). Hence when Ellen was ready to start school, Rome had two schools serving the educational needs of girls, but none for boys.

Reverend and Mrs. John Caldwell--the Reverend having been a founding pastor of First Presbyterian church--returned in 1871 to head the girls school. As its dean, however, Mrs. Caldwell was the school's moving force. Perhaps she even wrote, undoubtedly approved, the 1881 college brochure, which promised "'to make earnest, thinking women, not automata'" out of its students.[36] Certainly in the case of Ellen Axson and not a few of her school friends, the brochure lived up to its promise.

The school was similar to Janie Axson's alma mater, Greensboro Female College. It was not a college along the same lines of a typical men's college, with a four-year curriculum leading to a bachelor's degree. Rather, it was a hodgepodge of primary, secondary and "advanced" learning. Graduation ceremonies were held every June, though it is unclear what milestone, if any, this marked. Students could graduate as young as Ellen did, at 16, after only a few years of formal education. Nor did graduation, as in Ellen's case, always signify the end of a girl's formal education at the school.

Still, at Rome Female College a girl could learn foreign languages, even Latin, traditionally not taught at girls' schools. In her first five years as a student, Ellen studied French (though she never acquired much familiarity with French literature), algebra, basic botany and natural history, philosophy as well as logic (though it is difficult to gauge what passed for "philosophy" and "logic."). As Ellen was known to have taught herself trigonometry during one summer,[37] the school apparently offered nothing in the way of advanced mathematics. What exposure she had to English and American literature, her forté, is unclear. She appears to have studied Shakespeare, whom she read voraciously, on her own, as well as all the prominent 19th century British and American authors (almost none of whom Woodrow Wilson had read, with the exception of Carlyle and Ruskin). Presumably she obtained her books from the school's library, since Rome had none. Ellen's formidable grasp of the poetic idiom, and of William Wordsworth in particular, was also self-acquired.

In short, learning at Rome Female College was for the most part basic and along traditional lines--by rote and class recitation. Fortunately, composition was part of a traditional girls' education, and at Rome Female College, Ellen must have acquired her mastery of the written word (though sadly, not penmanship; her script never advanced beyond a scrawl). Luckily for Ellen's future, the school offered art training by a competent teacher, Helen F. Fairchild, who had spent four years in New York studying art at the National Academy of Design.[38] New York's only art school until 1875, it was prestigious and well-regarded, in North America, at least.

Unlike Ellen's mother Janie, who dazzled her older brothers by the number of academic prizes she won in her three years at Greensboro, Ellen was not the best student at the school, nor did she consider herself very good. Did she claim this out of a sense of modesty or Presbyterian self-effacement? For such a brilliant girl as Ellen, with her wide-ranging, penetrating intellect, learning at Rome Female College must have been anything but challenging. Dynamic as Ellen was, she challenged herself, and after "graduation" at age 16, she stayed on for two more academic years to pursue her art training, and to soak up whatever further crumbs of knowledge the school could offer her.

* * *

Self-published author Ethyl Wilkerson, in her sentimental account of Rome Female College, no doubt exaggerated the "strong influence" which the school exerted on the cultural life of backwater Rome. In 1890, the school suddenly closed its doors for good, after a short life span of only nineteen years. In 1883, a much-needed public school system finally arrived in Rome, without the pretense of calling itself a "college."

In contrast to her mother's three years of formal schooling, Ellen would have at least two and a half times as much. Not that the difference mattered much. Ellen largely taught herself. But formal schooling did provide Ellen with a longer girlhood than her mother had enjoyed, who was engaged at 18 and married at 20. Though never doubting that she was a sober Presbyterian, Ellen could and did enjoy herself as a single young woman.

Ellen often reminisced to her future fiancé of the years she spent at school, at least seven in all, and the friends she made there, who became friends for life. She described schoolmate Anna Harris, a Rome judge's daughter, as "a girl with a 'masculine mind,'...She was decidedly the brightest girl in our school." Rosalie Anderson of Sewanee, Tennessee, was undoubtedly Ellen's oldest, best friend. "The eighteen years during which we have loved each other," wrote Ellen, during a visit to Sewanee," have given us endless memories in common." At the college "we were always famous schemers when together; the things which we are always going to do, and to read, and paint and study together...." When apart, they would write letters running fifteen to twenty pages in length.[39]

Rosalie often began hers with "my precious darling," an address that was also typical of Ellen's other best friend, Beth Adams (Elizabeth Leith Adams). 19 year-old Beth did not feel in the least self-conscious reminding Ellen of that time in school when they were in the parlor, "with my head on your lap, with my eyes looking straight up in your face...I can understand easily, dear, how I could have fallen so idiotically in love with you, but why did you fancy me..." and further on, "Do you remember Mamie's disgust at our 'sickening ways' because we exchanged one single kiss." (The kiss occurred when they were saying goodbye.) Months later, Beth wrote, "If I ever get the chance again to lay my head on your lap and look at you 'till I get my fill..."[40]

Such images of female intimacy might make most people wonder, in our time, if these girls had been clandestine lesbians, even though they married later on. In that case, Ellen might well have been a child molester. On a long visit to friends of hers in 1884, she referred to their seven-year old son as "my accepted lover in three days."[41] In our highly-sexualized times, it is difficult to imagine an era when "lover" meant sweetheart, "partner" an associate, "intercourse" a conversation, and a "gay" person was merely jolly. Could someone like Ellen, who one day would judge a young woman as "worthless" because she lived out-of-wedlock with an artist friend, really have had sexual contact with her school friends, and also with a child? Yet the present-day mindset might well believe so.

Ellen had many other school friends, and also a live-in girlfriend, Jane Porter ("Janie"). Daughter of a Presbyterian pastor in Savannah, he had left his children unprovided for after his death. 17 year-old Ellen generously invited Janie, a public school student, to live at her parents' home in Rome so that Janie might have the benefit of art and music classes at Rome Female College. This meant that Janie would share Ellen's room, be another mouth to feed, and one more person crowding the house, which besides Ellen and Janie, included Ellen's two parents and her two brothers. In 1879, Ellen bought Janie a beautiful broach as a Christmas present, "for the only article of jewelry she has except her cuff buttons is a little ugly old fashioned breast pin."[42]

During the stressful weeks preceding his near fatal stroke in 1919, President Wilson took time out to pay his respects to Janie Porter, by then a poor widow. No doubt she would have agreed with Wilson, who, as usual, best summed up Ellen's character: that she never thought of herself.[43]

* * *

When she was sixteen, and after five years as a student, Ellen "graduated" from Rome Female College in June, 1876. She promptly re-enrolled for another two years. There was no where else affordable for her to continue her art training, and her unfolding talents were formidable. Two years later, in 1878, the Paris International Exposition awarded Ellen in faraway Rome, Georgia, a bronze medal for a drawing which she executed of "a school scene." That Ellen would have been so honored was thanks to her art teacher, Helen Fairchild, who earlier had submitted a portfolio of her students' best work to the exposition. Of course this award must have fueled Ellen's ambition, which explains her and Rosalie's "scheming" to become art students in New York some day. Even with only one small art museum, New York City was becoming a mecca for artists nationwide.

At eighteen, when Ellen finally left her formal schooling behind her, she already was earning money as a portraitist, earning power that might have stood her in good stead in New York, where she also had relatives who might have taken her in. But Ellen chose to remain in remote Rome–most likely, she just was not ready to strike out on her own in a big city, with or without Rosalie.

The next five years turned out to be rich and rewarding ones. Ellen would gain a reputation in Georgia as a portraitist, and never lacked for work. She often copied from photographs, using either crayon or charcoal to draw. Her brother

Stockton recalled, "Her artistic gifts were really very great, and she had fully made up her mind to be a professional portrait painter...she worked extremely hard. And when she was perhaps twenty-two years of age she really contrived to earn a tidy sum of money each year...," enabling her to earn a living from her art;[44] nor would Ellen lose sight of her ambition to leave Georgia one day, for New York and eventually, Europe.

In the meantime she seemed to enjoy herself to the hilt as a single young woman, with hordes of friends and relatives. Moreover, the amount of traveling that Ellen did in these years is astonishing, not only for a young woman of that era, but especially, for a southern woman, who, like her mother and Ellen's friends, rarely ventured anywhere. "How CAN you resist an invitation to Savannah?" asked an astonished Rosalie in a letter to Ellen in the summer of 1877, referring to Ellen's reluctance to leave her drawing lessons at the college in Rome.[45] The furthest Rosalie had ever been, she wrote, was to Chattanooga. By then, Ellen had already traveled to Georgia's sea islands and seen the ocean, visited Atlanta, and spent every Christmas of her life in Savannah. This made Ellen the envy of her friends in Rome.

In July of 1880, 20 year-old Ellen had the opportunity to travel with Rome friends on a "glorious" trip, as she described it, to distant Canada, where they visited Quebec and Montreal, then headed for Niagara Falls. In her atrocious handwriting, she wrote her mother exultantly, "I can't feel grateful enough for this trip...I feel so much more self-reliant than when I left home."[46] Two years later, in the summer of 1882, she traveled alone to visit relatives in New York City and New England, a memorable sojourn of several months. Regrettably, no letters of hers survive describing her interesting journey, where she surely must have visited the art schools in Manhattan. Her father, however, followed her every change of scene and reported that "Ellie Lou" would be heading straight for Savannah upon her return from her travels. Perhaps this indicated a loosening of 22 year-old Ellen's ties to Rome. By then, she also was rebelling against her "compound name," signing her letters simply "Ellen Axson," a young woman with a pronounced identity of her own.

* * *

Unusual in her extensive and independent traveling, Ellen was also the opposite from Eleanor McAdoo's characterization of the south as a place where "no one was ever in a hurry." Ellen in fact wrote to a friend, Mr. Jones,[47] "I am a genuine American in one respect at least: I am always in a hurry...Possibly I have more irons in the fire than can well be managed by one 'girl'." She also described herself to fiancé Wilson: "'I am so self-willed, that when I can't have my own way I like to make myself believe that I have.'"

In that heyday of the women's movement, with feminist leaders such as Elizabeth Cady Stanton staunchly espousing radical equality between the sexes, twenty-something Ellen wrote of her feelings and thoughts on the "woman question." In the same letter to her friend Mr. Jones, who apparently wanted to know, and in her appalling script, Ellen explained herself. As to proponents of women's emancipation, "As far as I know, they have never had a follower among our Southern women," though she failed to explain why. She acknowledged "the many disadvantages under which woman labors" but regarded these not as "disabilities, for they cannot be removed by legislation," nor were they "wrongs" perpetrated on women, "for no one is to blame but mother nature herself, who so ordered it." Again she acknowledged that "We seem to be surrounded by barriers of every description, great and small, natural and artificial, constitutional and conventional. But I do not imagine that we have cause for complaint on that account...." because, once again,

> it was so ordained in the economy of nature. The eternal nature of things requires that it should be so...Neither [sex] can take the place of the other. What folly to attempt it! What smallness [?] to struggle against it--the law of creation!... Yet that is what these champions of their sex undertake. Because they imagine man's lot to be the more enviable one, they proceed to unsex themselves, and the result is a species of some kind of being resembling nothing human in heaven above and [on] the earth beneath.

Though Ellen's views on women's emancipation would surely be considered reactionary today, they were, rightly or wrongly, the product of a thinking, critical mind. Though she was well on her way to becoming a cosmopolitan, worldly woman and a liberal Christian, her belief that the "law of creation" created men and women to be different, though not unequal, would never alter in her lifetime.

How satisfied "Mr. Jones" was by her strong opinions on the "woman's issue" we will never know, since she appears not to have heard from him again. Judging from the length of her letter and her thanking him for "his favors," that is, his other letters to her, he may well have been a suitor. Surprisingly, despite Ellen's reputation in Rome as a brainy young woman, someone "who'd read all the classics," she never lacked for suitors.

At age 17 a young man "popped the question." This event, occurring during a visit to remote, semi-tropical Darien, Georgia, on a visit to her uncle, she described in detail to her interested mother. The young man in question was bothersome to her: "...Saturday [sic] after church he asked me to go to ride again that afternoon. I tried hard to get out of it, but there wasn't a hope...of escape." When the young man proposed, "in spite of all I could do...he was the most obstinate, persistent thing you ever saw." This "thing," she continued, "wouldn't take no for an answer, wouldn't stop talking and going on, in spite of all I could say. Of all the horrid things in the world, to be made love to is the most horrid." He, despite being "a real fine character" and an ordained deacon in the local Presbyterian church, wasn't "strong enough in the upper extremity, to be a real danger to me." Alas, this sissified young man was "just like his brother."[48] Other disparaging comments of men occasionally surface in other letters. At age 24, while engaged to Wilson, she received her last, even more desperate, proposal of marriage.

In her memoirs, Ellen's sister Margaret gives a vivid sketch of the white lawyers sitting on split-bottomed chairs outside the Gainesville courthouse, "...smoking, and I am sorry to say, chewing tobacco. They all got on their feet as Aunt Louisa passed and lifted their hats. Two of them broke off a hot argument and bowed deeply." This mix of exaggerated chivalry and uncouthness seemed typical of southern white educated men, as did widespread drunkenness and alcoholism. Ellen, though coming from a teetotaling Presbyterian family, was well aware, even as a young woman, of widespread drinking. ("I knew he *drank*," wrote Ellen of someone she knew in a little southern town, "as does everyone else in Morganton....")[49]

Is it any wonder that Ellen liked her male friends, but did not care for her suitors? By her early 20's, her extensive traveling, her artistic talent and wide reading had broadened her horizons over and above most young southern women. To add to her uniqueness, Ellen possessed a near photographic memory. She was known to quote Shakespeare by heart (unschooled Romans consequently referred to her as "a girl who had read all the classics") as well as reams of poetry, especially her favorites, Wordsworth, Lanier and the Brownings. "She knew more poetry than anyone else in the world, and could always find a poem to fit any situation," according to her sister Margaret. Ellen, writing to her fiancé in 1884, mentioned that it had taken her only seven minutes to memorize a whole page of poetry "perfectly" to her delighted nieces and nephews.[50] As already noted, she had a gift for the written word.

Though brainy, Ellen was also very pretty. Neither tall (five feet three inches) nor willowy (she described her "normal" weight as 115), she was trim, had deep auburn, naturally curly hair, which, until the end of her life, she had a flair for wearing attractively. Her ears were pierced and as a teenager, she wore "drop" earrings (as she called them), though no photos of her as an adult ever show her wearing earrings. Her cheeks were full, round and pink, which in middle age gave her a less attractive, jowled appearance. As a young woman in Rome, in an age when people had few changes of clothing, "she had evolved for herself an altogether charming costume to wear during the hot summer months," wrote her sister Margaret. This "cool" outfit consisted of "a long straight frock of white muslin with a fichu [shoulder scarf] knotted at her breast, white stockings and little black strapped shoes. She looked...as if she had stepped out of a Jane Austen novel." Throughout her life Ellen spoke a soft southern drawl, "a lovely Southern voice," according to ill-famed Mrs. Peck, who got to know Ellen in her middle years. Though an independent, energetic young woman with high aspirations, Ellen never came across as outspoken or "mannish," qualities she found hard to tolerate in a woman.[51]

Ellen also was good-natured rather than witty, and in modern-day parlance, "laid back" to a degree that exasperated her own even-tempered mother. Horrified to learn that a beautiful silk dress of her daughter's had been stolen, Janie Axson was annoyed at Ellen's complete nonchalance. A lost dress was not worth getting upset about.[52]

When Woodrow Wilson caught his first glimpse of Ellen in Rome, he was struck not only by her good looks but by "a face full of fun." Their early acquaintanceship in Rome was constantly interrupted by her being called away on picnics, boat rides, buggy rides, teas and long chats with friends on spacious verandahs (from where she, unbeknown to Wilson, got her first glimpse of him). It is a wonder that she found time for her extensive reading, voluminous correspondence, and her art work. Though never in love before she met Woodrow Wilson, dubbed a "man-hater" by her best friends, she did have a good time with both men and women.

* * *

Nonetheless Ellen's last few years in Rome, before she left for good in late 1883, were not cloudless, free of unease or of misfortune. Not that her life up until then had been free of unease or misfortune. In the nineteenth century, disease attacked suddenly and unexpectedly. Rarely did a letter of Ellen's or her parents and friends fail to mention premature death and sudden illnesses. In 1877, Rosalie Anderson wrote Ellen, "Rome has been so sickly this past summer." That was the summer when Ellen's own mother fell critically ill (though we know not of what). In the spring of 1883, Edward Axson mentioned to his sister-in-law Louisa, "We have had a good deal of sickness in our town lately--caused chiefly by measles...Last week there were eight of Mrs. Caldwell's boarders down at one time...I hear also of some whooping cough and some mumps."[53]

Youth

Still, seventeen year-old Ellen had no sympathy for a woman visitor to her grandparents' manse in Savannah, "a perfect monomaniac on the subject of diphtheria. She could talk of nothing else. She has three children, and her life is made perfectly miserable by the fear that they will have it."

> She says that when it [diphtheria] has been in a room, all the furniture, carpets, curtains and *every article* in the room must be *burnt*. If that isn't done, the disease will stay in the house *ten years*. Did you ever hear anything so absurd; and I have quoted her exact words.[54]

Yet when Ellen's own daughter contracted diphtheria in 1904, her letters reveal that she, too, could become a "perfect monomaniac on the subject of diphtheria." And no wonder. This frightening disease, if it did not kill, often resulted in heart disease and lifelong paralysis. Just as contagious but less virulent were scarlet fever, whooping cough, measles. Another constant menace was typhoid, not understood to be caused by contaminated water and food. Unluckily, Rome, though located in Georgia's upper northwest, was not far enough north to escape the deadly menace of malaria, common in the rainy spring and summer months. For this rampant fever there was no cure, because again no one, and no doctors, understood it. So like most Romans, Ellen drank "large doses of quinine" and took the precaution of sleeping with her windows shut tight to keep out "damp air," believed to be a cause of the disease, rather than mosquitoes. But sooner or later, everyone succumbed to the "chills and fever," even Ellen.

Resistance to disease might well have been compromised by a bland diet. Vitamin-poor, corn-based starches, such as hominy, were the mainstay of the majority--poor whites and blacks--where epidemics usually originated. They in turn, as Margaret Elliott noted, came into intimate contact with the white middle class as household servants and laborers. As if disease and epidemics were not threatening enough, Rome also was beset by torrential rains ("Rome weather") in spring and summer, and frequent deadly floods that wrecked homes and damaged bridges, railroads and businesses. Rome's climate, in short, was unhealthy and extreme. The heat and humidity in the summer months were so oppressive that Ellen's friend Rosalie Anderson found her home town in southern Tennessee "charmingly cool" by comparison.[55]

Hence despite what outsiders, such as Eleanor McAdoo, saw outwardly, life in the nineteenth century south, including Rome, was no idyll. Nor was everything always ideal in the Axson household. As the years in Rome passed by, Ellen's father Edward was increasingly subject to despondency, possibly even to deep depression. As the early years of struggle and hardship gave way to increasing prosperity, Pastor Axson seemed to detect a moral decline. Referring to her husband, Janie wrote that "He had become a good deal disheartened about his work here, felt as if he was not accomplishing much good, especially because of the poor congregations at night."[56] Instead of taking poor attendance at weekday evening services in stride, it bothered him unreasonably.

So frustrated did Edward become with his ministry that in the summer of 1875, he struck up a correspondence with Woodrow Wilson's distinguished father, Dr. Joseph R. Wilson, seeking advice. The world of the southern Presbyterian clergy was small and close-knit, so the older clergyman would not have been surprised to be solicited for advice from a younger one. "...it is a field particularly hard to cultivate," wrote Edward of his Rome pastorate, somewhat unfairly.[57] Dr. Wilson advised patience, which worked for awhile.

Five years later, Edward Axson referred in a letter to having had a "break down," but to no specific illness. For awhile that summer, Edward's father, Isaac Axson, even took over his son's pastoral duties in Rome. Edward's poor health, following on the heels of his decision to leave Rome for a smaller, poorer pastorate in Salem, Georgia, struck unease in the Axson household, especially in his wife and Ellen. Yet at no time did Janie try to talk her husband out of moving. No doubt she believed that a husband's will must override his wife's; Edward in turn admitted that his wife "has become very much wedded to her home."[58] It is a likely reason why he changed his mind in favor of staying. Janie was fortunate to have a husband who was both unselfish and reasonable. By late August, 1880, the crises were over. Six months later, Janie, at 42, found herself pregnant again.

For Janie, already a mother of a marriageable daughter and of a son barely out of infancy--four and a half year-old Eddie--and of a teenage son, Stockton, pregnancy must have been not only unwelcome but embarrassing. It certainly made her very sick. Writing a consoling letter to her mother less than a month before Janie gave birth, 21 year-old Ellen nonetheless was not unduly alarmed. She stayed on with her friend Rosalie in pleasant Sewanee, Tennessee, for several more weeks, where the two of them could sketch to their heart's content. Only after Ellen got word of the birth of her sister Margaret (Madge) did she return home. Janie had had no difficulty giving birth on October 10, 1881, one month after her 43rd birthday; it was the aftermath that endangered her.

The whole family anxiously watched over Janie. Lulled at first by the doctor who pronounced her remarkably well and recovering, who dismissed her low grade fever as something that would pass, Ellen and her father nonetheless became increasingly uneasy; unease turned to alarm one day when they discovered that Janie had fallen into a coma. It was inescapable, even to the

Youth 25

doctor, that Janie had succumbed to puerperal or "childbed" fever. Yet no one used the dreaded term.

This disease, by 1881, had a lengthy history of exhaustive study and research behind it.[59] Three years earlier the great French scientist, Louis Pasteur, had discovered the bacillus that caused the disease, and named it streptococcus. Decades before, the majority of European and British doctors had come to the conclusion that the disease, of which they did not know the specific cause, was transmitted by doctors and midwives; more often, however, by doctors, who also came into contact with wounds and cadavers. By 1850, the majority of doctors were aware of the necessity of washing their hands--even changing their clothes-- before attending a woman who might be stricken with childbed fever. By then, however, it was usually too late. For the majority of women, once stricken, the disease proved fatal.

Whether medical knowledge about the real cause of the disease had disseminated to the rural southern states by 1881 is uncertain. Childbed fever, in any case, was uncommon outside of maternity wards and hospitals. The bacillus, once it penetrated via the birth canal, almost always led to "intense shivering...followed by more attacks of shivering, a rapid pulse, and high fever." The fever often appeared to abate, though not disappear, as in Janie's case. ("Her fever is abating now," wrote Edward two weeks after his wife gave birth. "This morning the Drs. have pronounced her symptoms all better. She will probably be decidedly better tomorrow.") The hope that the fever had run its course was short-lived. Rather, brief recovery was usually a sign that the disease had taken a fatal turn. Janie's death struggle followed soon after she awoke from her coma. In the case of childbed fever, the end was usually very painful. "Death was almost invariably due to peritonitis or septicemia or a combination of the two."[60]

A year before her death, Janie had written her sister Louisa: "It is so sad to see a mother taken away just in the prime of life," referring to the sudden death of a neighbor.[61] When Janie herself died on November 4, 1881, three and a half weeks after giving birth to Margaret, she left behind a devastated family. Ellen's Aunt Louisa generously offered to raise the infant in her home in Gainesville. Meanwhile the tragedy of her beloved mother's death left Ellen angry at the world and at God. Assuming that her artistic talents were a gift from God, she vowed to give up art for good. Ellen was still young, however, and hope would surge again.

For the devout, suffering Edward, neither young nor sanguine, anger, if there was any, would not be turned against God. Six weeks after the tragedy he wrote to Louisa, "Don't imagine that I have allowed myself to repine. I have not. I would not have it otherwise than the wise and good Father has ordained: but the sense of loss and loneliness is almost more than the flesh can bear at times."[62] Never for a moment did either he or Ellen make Margaret feel unloved because of Janie's untimely death.

The family, consisting now of Edward, Ellen, five year-old Eddie and teenage Stockton, headed for Savannah to spend the Christmas holidays. "I can't say exactly," wrote Edward to Louisa, "how long our visit in Savannah will be protracted."

> Ellie Lou [Ellen] left Rome a half day before I and the boys did. This gave her the opportunity of getting a bird's eye view of the exposition which she enjoyed hugely. She says Stockton had no desire to visit the great show and I was glad of that; as he was not at all well when we left Rome."[63]

A pattern emerges of Ellen's returning high spirits, the onset of Stockton's lifelong physical debilities (real and imaginary), which no doubt had an emotional component, and of their father's inability to recover from his wife's premature death. Hence her mother's death was far from the end of Ellen's misfortunes.

Returning to Rome, "to the scene of our deep sorrow," as Edward had described it earlier, day-to-day life would never be the same. The dispirited family let Eddie's sixth birthday come and go without notice. Ellen's father succumbed to insomnia, and to what he mysteriously referred to as "My old troubles (but what they are precisely neither I nor the Doctor know) which never entirely quit me." Perhaps this was a reference to his attacks of depression, which he admitted "have returned of late in somewhat increased form."[64] Sparing his sister-in-law the nightmarish details, he suffered from night-time attacks of grief and depression so severe that he needed Ellen to hold on to as he paced his room, weeping and moaning.

If Edward had been dispirited by his ministry in the past, in 1883, he spoke often of relinquishing Rome altogether. Ellen was long of age, Stockton away in boarding school, and Aunt Louisa would eventually take in young Eddie. Ominously, Edward was not even considering another position. His thoughts turned to moving in with his parents in Savannah.

Never was there any doubt that Ellen would follow her father. Unquestionably, her father needed her. Besides, the prospect of departing Rome would be far different from a few years earlier. A move this time around would be to Georgia's largest, most cosmopolitan city, and not to some depressing, backwoods village.

Amid Ellen's nagging grief over her mother, the pain of her father's deterioration, and the depressing uncertainty of what lay ahead, hope appeared suddenly in that fateful year of 1883. A tall, slim lawyer, an outsider who had

Youth

come to Rome on some legal business, made a strong impression on her. Thomas Woodrow Wilson turned out to be the most extraordinary man Ellen had ever met: "'the greatest man in the world,'" she confided, soon afterwards, to a shocked young Stockton Axson.[65]

ENDNOTES

[1] Quoted in Mary Allen Hulbert, *The Story of Mrs. Peck* (New York: Milton, Balch & Co., 1933), 236.

[2] Ellen Axson to M.J.H. Axson ("Janie"), Aug.22, 1876. Presidential Papers, Series 2. Woodrow Wilson Collection, Princeton University Firestone Library (henceforth: *PP*-2).

[3] M.J.H. Axson to S. Edward Axson, Dec.31, 1860, Box 50, f.4. Woodrow Wilson Collection, Princeton University Mudd Manuscript Library. (henceforth: WWCol.)

[4] M.J.H. Axson to S. Edward Axson, Dec. 28, 1860, Box 50, f.4. WWCol. and M.J. Hoyt to S. Edward Axson, Oct. 6, 1856, *PP*-2.

[5] Ellen Axson to Mr. Jones, [1880-1884?]. *PP*-2.

[6] Frances W. Saunders, *Ellen Axson Wilson: First Lady Between Two Worlds* (Chapel Hill and London: University of North Carolina Press, 1985), 10.

[7] Frances Anne Kemble, *Journal of a Residence on a Georgia Plantation in 1838-1839* (Athens: Univ. of Georgia Press, 1984), 38-39.

[8] Saunders, 10, 12.

[9] "'Think of all those dear little babies that have been burning in hell so long; now they will all be released,'" quoted in Eleanor Wilson McAdoo, *The Woodrow Wilsons* (New York: Macmillan Co., 1937), 42.

[10] Saunders,10; S. Edward Axson to M.J. Hoyt, Dec.29, 1856, *PP*-2; quoted in M.J.H. Axson to Louisa H.Brown, April 13, 1880, Box 50, f.4. WWCol.

[11] William Hoyt to M.J. Hoyt, Nov.13, 1858. *PP*-2.

[12] M.J.H. Axson to S. Edward Axson, June [14], 1859. *PP*-2.

[13] Margaret Axson Elliott, *My Aunt Louisa and Woodrow Wilson* (Chapel Hill: Univ. of North Carolina Press, 1944), 9; Saunders, 9.

[14] S. Edward Axson to M.J. Hoyt, Oct.31, 1856. *PP*-2.

[15] *Idem.*

[16] Elliott, 8.

[17] Kemble, 101-102; Ellen Axson to Woodrow Wilson, April 16, 1885, in Arthur S. Link, ed., *The Papers of Woodrow Wilson* (Princeton: Princeton University Press, 1966-1996), v.4:494. (henceforth: *PWW*)

[18] M.J. Hoyt to S. Edward Axson, Oct.6, 1856. *PP*-2.

[19] S. Edward Axson to M.J. Hoyt, June 2, 1859, Box 50, f.11. WWCol.

[20] M.J.H. Axson to S. Edward Axson, Dec. 24, 28, 1860, Box 50, f.4. WWCol.

[21] Saunders, 13.

[22] Concerning 19th century Rome, see George Magruder Battey, Jr., *A History of Rome & Floyd County, Including Numerous Incidents of More Than Local Interest, 1540-1922* (Atlanta: Webb & Vary Co., 1922); and Ethel Wilkerson, *Rome's Remarkable History* (Rome: Georgia, [privately

printed], [1968].); Eleanor Wilson McAdoo, ed., *The Priceless Gift: The Love Letters of Woodrow Wilson and Ellen Axson Wilson* (New York: McGraw-Hill, 1962), 3.

[23] Elliott, 26, 87; Ellen Axson to M.J.H. Axson, Mar.18, 1878. *PP*-2.

[24] Quoted in Alan Conway, *The Reconstruction of Georgia* (Minneapolis: Univ. of Minnesota Press, 1966), 96, 174.

[25] Ellen A. Wilson to Woodrow Wilson, March 11, 1900. *PWW* 11:500.

[26] Saunders, 13-14,18; "First Presbyterian Church, Rome, Georgia (1833-1983): Our First Hundred and Fifty Years" (Rome, Georgia,[privately printed]), 8.

[27] M.J.H. Axson to Ellen Axson, Dec.26, 1879. *PP*-2.

[28] Saunders, 13; Ellen Axson to M.J.H. Axson, Feb.2, 1878. *PP*-2.

[29] Tedcastle interview, 1925. Ray Stannard Baker Papers, Library of Congress, Washington, D.C.

[30] Ellen Axson to S. Edward Axson, Oct.18, 1870. *PP*-2.

[31] Stockton Axson, *Brother Woodrow: A Memoir of Woodrow Wilson* ed. Arthur S. Link (Princeton: Princeton University Press, 1993), 51.

[32] S. Edward Axson to M.J.H. Axson, Nov.23, 1874. *PP*-2.

[33] Elliott, 86.

[34] M.J.H. Axson to S. Edward Axson, Jan.5, [1861], Box 50, f.4., WWCol.; Ellen Axson to M.J.H. Axson, Aug.22, 1876, *PP*-2.

[35] For a close study of 19th century women's lives and woman-to-woman relationships, see Carroll Smith-Rosenberg, "The Female World of Love and Ritual: Relations between Women in Nineteenth Century America" in *Women and Health in America: Historical Readings* ed. Judith Walzer Leavitt (Madison, University of Wisconsin Press, 1984).

[36] Wilkerson, 14.

[37] Saunders, 14.

[38] *Ibid.*, 15.

[39] Ellen Axson to Woodrow Wilson, Dec.10, 1883, Aug.4, 1884. *PWW* 2:575; 3:273.

[40] Elizabeth L. Adams to Ellen Axson, April 28, Nov.25, 1879. *PP*-2.

[41] Ellen Axson to Woodrow Wilson, May 1, 1884. *PWW* 3:154.

[42] Ellen Axson to M.J.H. Axson, Dec.18, 1879. *PP*-2.

[43] See Elliott, 298.

[44] Axson, 90.

[45] Rosalie Anderson to Ellen Axson, Sept.22, 1877. *PP*-2.

[46] Ellen Axson to M.J.H. Axson, July 6, 1880. *PP*-2.

[47] The following comments of Ellen Axson to Mr. Jones are taken from an undated letter of hers, most likely written between 1880-1884. *PP*-2.

[48] Ellen Axson to M.J.H. Axson, April 8, 1878. *PP*-2.

[49] Elliott, 87.

[50] *Ibid.*, 162; Ellen Axson to Woodrow Wilson, March 24, 1884, *PWW* 3:97.

[51] Elliott, 157; Hulbert, 235.

[52] Ellen A. Wilson referred to her stolen dress in a letter to Woodrow Wilson, Feb.17, 1889. *PWW* 6:102.

[53] Rosalie Anderson to Ellen Axson, Sept.22, 1877, *PP*-2; S. Edward Axson to Louisa H. Brown, March 27, 1883, Box 50, f.12, WWCol.

[54] Ellen Axson to M.J.H. Axson, Feb.2, 1878. *PP*-2.

[55] Rosalie Anderson to Ellen Axson, July 14, 1879, *PP*-2.

[56] M.J.H. Axson to Louisa H. Brown, April 3, 1880, Box 50, f.5. WWCol.

[57] S. Edward Axson to Joseph R. Wilson, Sr., July 14, 1875. *PP*-2.

[58] S. Edward Axson to Louisa H. Brown, Aug.25, 1880. *PP*-2.

[59] On puerperal fever, see Irvine Loudon, *The Tragedy of Childbed Fever* (Oxford & New York: Oxford University Press, 2000).

[60] *Ibid.*,5,8; S. Edward Axson to Louisa H. Brown, Oct.24, 1881, Box.50, f.13., WWCol.

[61] M.J.H. Axson to Louisa H. Brown, April 3, 1880, Box 50, f.5. WWCol.

[62] S. Edward Axson to Louisa H. Brown, Dec.26, 1881, Box 50, f.12, WWCol.

[63] *Idem.*

[64] S. Edward Axson to Louisa H. Brown, Feb.20, 1882. *PP*-2.

[65] Axson, 91.

Chapter 2

FIRST LOVE AND A WEDDING: SAVANNAH AND NEW YORK, 1883-1885

"Pray excuse this stupid scrawl."[1]
Ellen Axson, 1884

"...you have a gift of expression more delightful than I can say."[2]
Woodrow Wilson to Ellen, 1897

They first laid eyes on each other in Rome, most likely in early April of that eventful year, 1883. Ellen was a month and a half shy of her 23rd birthday; Woodrow Wilson was 26. Shortly after graduating from Princeton College he dropped his first name Thomas, preferring to go by his middle name Woodrow-- his mother's maiden name; Ellen in turn would soon be admonishing him not to call her "Ellie Lou"--she so disliked double names, so commonly southern. Their name changes, marking their passage from youth to adulthood, reflected their strong sense of personal identity. Wilson would always call her by a variety of names--never compounded--Nellie, Ellie, even Eileen.

Rome was most attractive in spring. It was the most glorious season of an otherwise intemperate, unhealthy climate. Everyone seemed to live out of doors, relishing the warm but unhumid weather, and fragrant, flower-laden breezes. Since the death of her mother a year and a half ago, Ellen had discarded her loose-fitting "Jane Austen" outfit, dressing herself in black mourning from head to toe. This dramatic change in attire made her appear slimmer, more mature. As a result, Wilson's first impression of her was that she was a widow. Her austere garb in no way dampened her youthful good looks: "A tip-tilted little nose, a perfect complexion, a sweetly curved mouth and hair like burnished copper."[3]

Ever afterward, their fateful first meeting seemed providential. Lounging on a verandah on a luscious spring day, as most Romans were doing, Ellen, at the home of her friend Agnes Tedcastle, noticed a striking-looking man walk by. According to Tedcastle, Woodrow Wilson "didn't see them" and therefore, would not have noticed Ellen asking her who that "fine-looking young man" was. Agnes, surprised, promptly replied, "'I don't know if I will tell you, you man-hater! That is Tommy Wilson.'"[4] What followed goes unrecorded, but it might well have been an afternoon's worth of gossip about "Tommy Wilson," an unmarried lawyer living in Atlanta, whose uncle was the father of Ellen's good friend Jessie Bones Brower, all of them Romans, and of course, solid Presbyterians. Sooner or later, Wilson and Ellen were bound to meet in that tightly-knit community of friends and kin.

Most appropriately, Woodrow Wilson first caught sight of Ellen in her father's church on the following "Sabbath." Stopping in Rome for several days to look after his uncle's legal affairs, Wilson of course would spend a Sunday in church; any kind of work, even reading a newspaper, would have been frowned upon. Not that Sunday was not work: rising early, digesting parts of the Bible before church, attending a long church service, then returning in the evening for another full service and sermon. According to Eleanor McAdoo, even meeting one's fellow parishioners after service for a little socializing was apt to be quick and subdued.

Seated in his uncle's pew, Wilson's attention was riveted on a petite figure veiled in black, seated close to the pulpit, who was bending now and then to whisper to a little boy, who Wilson assumed was her son. The boy was in fact Ellen's lively, no doubt intensely bored, brother Eddie. Was Ellen really oblivious to Wilson's presence in church that morning? She, whose interest in Wilson was piqued on that spring afternoon on the verandah, could have predicted he would show up in church, not that she would have divined his interest in her. Still, invisible antennae must have been elevated; meanwhile Ellen, swathed in the folds of her fluffy black veil, was looking her most attractive. "Woodrow stared shamelessly," wrote McAdoo. "What a bright pretty face! what splendid laughing eyes..." he thought as he stared at her. "...When the service was over he asked his aunt who the pretty girl in mourning was. 'Why, that's Ellie Lou Axson,' she said to him.' Miss Axson! Not a widow." Instantly he made up his mind to pay her father a visit; although the Axsons lived in the heart of Rome, to Wilson, their home was a mere "country parsonage."[5]

No one needed to tell Wilson about Ellen. He had heard of her "so often"--that she was an artist, and had "read all the classics." Despite what seemed to be her "laughing eyes," she had little to laugh about. Her brother Stockton's later recollection is doubtful: that on the eve of her meeting Wilson, Ellen had made up her mind to "go at least to New York, if possible later to Europe, and educate herself as an artist in oils." To leave her father, so long as he needed her, was unthinkable. Meanwhile, his mental health was deteriorating. To add to the strain, her father kept changing his mind about leaving Rome. "...I have extracted a good deal of amusement from Father's constantly changing purposes," she wrote, unconvincingly.[6]

Wilson, however, knew little of the underlying quandary within the Axson family when he showed up on their doorstep, that day or the next. He wrote down his own version of that first meeting.

Pastor Axson, with "unsuspected cordiality," duly received Wilson and ushered him into the parlor. Ellen, however, was no where visible. Edward might have felt a little flattered at this visit from the son of Dr. Joseph R. Wilson, a luminary in the southern Presbyterian church. Rarely lighthearted, Edward launched into a conversation about a matter that had bothered him deeply for years--"'Why have night congregations grown so small?' a question," Wilson noted with characteristic mirth, "that was much too big for me."[7] Anxious to change the subject, he asked after Ellen's "health."

This obvious signal somewhat surprised her father, who, however, did summon Ellen. What her impression of Wilson might have been in this brief encounter has gone unrecorded. It must have been positive, since she accepted her friend Jessie's--Wilson's cousin's--invitation to tea shortly afterward, knowing that he, too, was invited. She even let Wilson escort her home afterwards, "and I remember leaving you that afternoon," wrote Wilson later, "with a feeling that I had found a new and altogether delightful sort of a companion."[8] One suspects that the impression was reciprocal. Immediately afterward, he departed Rome for his (long despised) law practice in Atlanta.

Wilson was back in Rome two months later. Once again he returned to mind his uncle's legal affairs, using this "business" visit as an opportunity to court the woman he could not seem to get off of his mind. This was no easy task. Pulled in many directions by friends and relatives, Ellen had little free time to give to him. Besides, if Eleanor McAdoo is to be believed, "It was considered most unladylike to show the least sign of interest until a young man proposed."[9] In that case, how was a man to know if a woman was interested? In fact by the time Wilson left Rome, Ellen had made time to take solitary walks with him along lonely stretches of railroad track, shared a hammock with him at a picnic, and promised to write him. She was unmistakably interested.

A month later, Wilson revealed to a close friend that he had fallen in love "with a charming brown-eyed lassie" and that "the dear lassie has become learned without knowing it." Was this--Ellen's intellectual side--the clue to his deep attraction to her? Later he wrote Ellen--in that age when it was not politically incorrect to say such things--that "I had longed to meet some woman of my own age who had acquired a genuine love for intellectual pursuits without becoming bookish, without losing her feminine charm." He definitely did not want a wife such as John Stuart Mill's, who "knows as much as her husband of the matters of his special study, and furnishes him with opinion, ministering not to his love but to his logical faculty." Virtually in the same breath, however, he seemed to contradict himself: "a man...must be miserable if he have [sic] a study into which his wife cannot come as a close companion." Ellen did indeed become a "close companion" in his intellectual pursuits, someone he would turn to first when he needed an opinion.[10]

While his attraction to Ellen--a pretty, young woman artist with a bookish mind--is understandable, what was her attraction to him? By 1883 she had had numerous suitors and even marriage proposals, but not once had she felt the stirrings of romantic love. Yet according to McAdoo, Ellen felt "disappointed" when Wilson had not proposed to her before he left Rome. Her brother Stockton recalled his own impressions of Wilson: "You would have had to travel a long day's journey to meet a man with more winning manners, more friendly courtesy..." Wilson's was "a nature filled with loving kindness and sensitive consideration for the feelings of others."[11]

Loving kindness, lovableness, and learnedness, these resembled Ellen's father exactly, whether she was conscious of the similarity or not. A man like this could be no authoritarian, however much Wilson prized "manliness." Unlike her father and most southern men, however, Wilson was a true cosmopolitan. Always proud and self-conscious, like Ellen, of his southern identity, Wilson nonetheless disliked Atlanta for its provincialism and southern men for their boorishness. Wilson spoke without a southern accent, though he was born in Staunton, Virginia and grew up in such deep southern recesses as Augusta, Georgia and Columbia, South Carolina. It must have made a favorable impression on Ellen that Wilson had lived in and breathed the intellectual air of Princeton, New Jersey, where he graduated in 1879; that he was acquainted with New York, as she was, and was making up his mind that summer to abandon law and pursue a graduate degree in faraway Baltimore, at the prestigious Johns Hopkins University. His career, whatever it would be, would not likely bring him back to Dixie.[12]

First Love and a Wedding: Savannah and New York, 1883-1885

Given their mutual attraction, even love for one another, why had Wilson not proposed to Ellen in those steamy June weeks in Rome? He admitted later how close he came..."Had you not noticed my manner as I asked you to correspond with me during that delightful talk we had in the hammock?...how near I had come to telling you *then* that I loved you?" Telling a woman that you loved her-- and not proposing--of course was unthinkable, so he refrained. McAdoo claimed rightly that her father was poor, "He had nothing to offer her, he told himself--no money, no prospects and, in his opinion, a plain face and a difficult nature."[13]

Alas, neither Wilson nor McAdoo explained what he meant by his "difficult" nature, and his claim to plainness was surely made out of modesty: at 5 feet 10, he was lean, erect, dignified, with handsome features (despite his square jaw) and a beautiful voice. Indeed, despite being neither rugged nor much of an athlete, he exuded "manliness." Wilson's poverty, like Ellen's, was relative. His father, unlike hers, was a well-to-do clergyman, head pastor of the First Presbyterian Church in Wilmington, North Carolina. Ellen probably learned from Wilson that he was a struggling lawyer, unable to support himself and therefore, living off of his father's allowance. In an era without government student loans, his father also intended to support him and pay his tuition at Johns Hopkins University, where Wilson would soon enroll as a graduate student in comparative politics.

Poverty was surely a reason for not proposing, but so was lack of confidence. Unknown to Ellen--who would learn later, to her dismay--Wilson had recently been rejected as a suitor for the hand of his cousin, Hattie Woodrow, also an intelligent, cultured young woman. His suit had been ardent, and the rejection just as firm, though mainly on the grounds that he was her first cousin. Their engagement, had there been one, was doomed, as family pressure would have forced the couple to part ways. Presbyterians were opposed to marriage between first cousins, even though, now and then, first cousins, as Stockton Axson and his cousin Leila, tried to overcome it, unsuccessfully.

* * *

If Ellen was disappointed when Wilson left her "empty-handed," she was not the type of girl to bite her nails while waiting on edge for the hoped for proposal. Her best friends divined her feelings for Wilson, and knew that she was writing him. Jessie Bones Brower, Wilson's cousin--who had earlier invited them to tea-- had a photograph of him which she showed Ellen when they went out for a walk. She wanted Ellen to have it. "'Why, Jessie, I can't take that!'" exclaimed Ellen. But when Jessie casually threw it into a nearby strawberry patch, Ellen darted after it.[14] In the meantime Wilson was dissolving his law partnership with fellow lawyer Edward Renick. Afterwards he headed for Wilmington, North Carolina, to stay with his parents until the fall term commenced at Johns Hopkins.

Wilson wrote heartfelt letters to Ellen. "The Saturday [June 30] of my departure from Rome dragged along very tediously for me, and it seemed a cruelly long stretch from Rome to Augusta," where he was visiting relatives. In the weeks ahead, he finally got around to mentioning his side trip, a visit to a young woman, Miss Katie Mayrant, the daughter of his landlady at his boarding house in Atlanta. She and Wilson had become good friends while he boarded there, "Our relations *were* those of the closest intimacy," he wrote Ellen, but assured her that he never thought of marrying her. The tone of Katie's letters to him, however, bespoke a far greater intensity of feeling. His week-long visit to the small southern town that Katie and her mother had moved to probably excited Katie's own hopes of a marriage proposal. Yet "...she is not a woman of the sort most attractive to me. She has a frail beauty which is interesting in itself, and she is intelligent and affectionate...one could only shelter and care for her, as for a delicate flower, which cannot bloom in all weathers." What this Victorian turn of phrase meant exactly is unclear; Wilson seemed to prefer a woman who was more than delicate and needy. So why did he go out of his way to visit Katie? Perhaps his deep empathy made him feel for her, a young woman alone in a humdrum, remote little town, with little to look forward to. They never saw each other again.[15]

Hence Wilson had not been drawn to Ellen because there was no one else, because she just happened to cross his path when he, as he facetiously put it, "was in the market." Besides, Wilson had his own private fear before he finally proposed--that he was not making a good enough impression on Ellen. They, both mature adults, were lucky to have fallen in love with the right person.

* * *

No move from Rome was in sight, at least for that summer of 1883. Ellen planned to visit her close friend, Beth, in tiny Morganton, North Carolina. As usual---though unusual for a young woman in that era--she traveled alone, probably paying her own way. Unlike Woodrow Wilson, she was able to support herself. Was it out of consideration for his feelings that she almost never alluded to her earnings? In one letter to him she did. It was in the fall of that year, when she was staying with her friends the Tedcastles, her father being away. "I have, since I have been here, made some curtains, a set of hem stitched ties, and a jacket for Agnes, and fifty dollars for myself," she added breezily. In the same letter she noted, "I am occupied in the same way [as at home], viz. with sewing and drawing..."[16] Ellen's seamstress skills were formidable, but did she earn that much money merely from sewing for friends, or from her drawing? Fifty dollars was easily the monthly wage of a teacher. Earning a handsome fee, probably from her art, seemed to come more easily to Ellen than to Wilson, for whom lawyering had been an uphill struggle.

Ellen's trip to Morganton in late summer to visit Beth, now engaged to a Mr. Erwin, lasted several weeks. In some respects it was a trial for Ellen, who disliked Beth's clergyman husband-to-be. "Poor Beth, she is *always* on the defensive where Mr. Erwin is concerned, and she has need to be." Her visit ended abruptly when she received news that her father was ill--prostration, nerves, insomnia--and needed her. Early that September morning, a Friday, she left alone for the 150 mile train trip home, which would take an entire day and evening. Traveling through the Blue Ridge mountain country of western North Carolina, Ellen's route necessitated a stopover in Asheville, a small southern town which Wilson described as "horrid little Asheville." Since Ellen's train connection to Rome would not take place until evening, and since she seemed to have friends or relatives everywhere she went, she decided to wait out the day with friends.[17]

Meanwhile Wilson, on the eve of his departure for Baltimore, was visiting his parents in Arden, a vacation spot outside of Asheville. He had desired to rendezvous with Ellen when she was visiting Beth, but their letters--discussing a meeting--happened to miss each other. Wilson, however, was in Asheville that Friday on church business for his father--after which he would catch his train for Baltimore on Sunday. Unknown to Ellen, he had checked into an Asheville hotel, wholly unaware that Ellen, too, was in town. According to Eleanor McAdoo, who must have heard this account from her parents, he caught a glimpse of Ellen from his window just as she disappeared down the street. He immediately ran out of the hotel and caught up with her. Later they would both be enchanted at their "providential" meeting.[18]

Though dressed in black on that sultry day, Ellen, Wilson recalled later, looked fetching in her Kate Greenaway dress--Greenaway clothes, jewelry, and stationery being the rage in the 1880's--which she had sewn herself. Then and there Wilson talked her into staying the weekend so she could meet his parents. He also must have made up his mind that he would finally (at some point that weekend) "pop the question." And what about caring for her father in Rome? Probably right before she left Morganton, Ellen learned that her grandparents had headed for Rome to be with him, freeing her to spend a heady weekend in Asheville, most of it alone with Wilson. They both stayed at the same hotel.

The next day, Ellen had her first face-to-face meeting with Wilson's father Joseph and his mother Janet (nicknamed Jessie). "I was frightened beyond measure" when she headed out to meet them. However, "I think they must like me," wrote a surprised Ellen. Besides Wilson's mother, a shy woman who was born in Carlisle, England and emigrated to America when she was nine, two of her other children were present, Wilson's brother Joseph, ten years his junior, and her oldest child, Wilson's married sister Anne. Ellen was never destined to meet his remarkable sister Marion, also married and living in Arkansas, who "must have had a mental equipment comparable to Woodrow's own."[19] Seven years later, she was dead of tuberculosis, only months after her husband died.

This visit would mark the onset of a close friendship between Ellen and Wilson's father Joseph, who would outlive his wife Janet by many years. Though he never wrote a single book, Joseph R. Wilson was a scholar and an intellectual. Despite being a transplanted Ohioan and his wife a native of England, they both deeply identified with the south's culture and way of life, Reverend Wilson even staunchly defending slavery before and during the Civil War. Until Ellen came into Wilson's life, no one stood closer to him than his father, who died in 1902, with Ellen caring for him to the end.

Despite the success of this visit, Woodrow Wilson procrastinated proposing until the last possible moment, a Sunday--right before his train was due to leave Asheville for Baltimore. He proposed hastily, in the hotel lobby. After Ellen joyfully--and surely with relief--whispered "yes!," they kissed each other for the first time, in public view. There was not a minute to lose in discussion, however, leaving Ellen and Wilson with no idea of their wedding date, and no engagement ring.

Alas, few are the details of this, their first whirlwind weekend alone, aside from Ellen's visit with the Wilson clan. "Do you remember Mr. Bagehot about whom I talked to you one night on the verandah at Asheville?"--British intellectual Walter Bagehot being Wilson's favorite political thinker at the time.[20] Sitting together on the hotel verandah, admiring the majestic scenery, was probably as close to romance as the--still unengaged--couple ever got. Perhaps Ellen had never read the relatively obscure Bagehot, but she might have discussed the writings of her favorite British men-of-letters, John Ruskin and Thomas Carlyle, and several British novelists, including George Eliot, whom Wilson had never read.

Their engagement and wedding plans would be discussed in countless letters over the next twenty-one months. From Baltimore, Wilson worked out the following timetable: "I shall write you, dearest, every Tuesday evening and mail my epistles on Wednesdays. My letter will reach you, therefore, on Fridays; yours will reach me on Thursdays. What happy days Thursdays will be with me!"[21] Over a century later, postal mail would move no faster.

Ellen's engagement ring arrived in the mail. She found it exquisitely tasteful and the setting "chaste," and crowned, to her amazement, by a diamond. She gently chided Wilson, "You know it is not absolutely necessary to wear that particular sort of ring in order to 'feel engaged',"[22] guessing that he probably owed money to his parents for the extravagance. Several months later, he was borrowing train fare from a classmate to make a hurried visit to Savannah to see Ellen.

The engagement settled, they had no date for the wedding. It would not have occurred to them to marry and live together in Baltimore before Wilson finished his studies, living off of his father's allowance. Ellen's father and grandfather, and Wilson's own father, had married only after they had found employment, even if it was ill-paid; and this, too, was Wilson's and Ellen's unspoken plan. It meant that marriage was a long way off, which was more unsettling to Wilson, who began to hope for gainful employment before he finished his Hopkins studies, than to Ellen; long engagements--Ellen's mother's also lasted two years--were not at all uncommon in that age. (Ellen's contemporary, Sigmund Freud, was engaged for four years.)

* * *

Returning to Rome in mid-September, Ellen was now an engaged woman. Unbeknown to her, the next two and a half months would mark the end of her and her father's life in Rome. Her father still lay ill, her little brother Eddie was down with fever, and within a week, so was Ellen. All three--though her father also was suffering from other problems--were no doubt stricken with malaria. For several weeks Ellen was unable to write her fiancé in Baltimore, who became frantic, morbidly fearing that she had second thoughts about marrying him. When the longed for letter arrived, it even included a note from Ellen's father, congratulating Wilson on his engagement. Though now engaged, Ellen's letter began with "My dear Friend." Wilson responded wryly: "It was the sweetest letter ever written--and it seems to have been written with great rhetorical art for it observed the laws of climax, beginning 'My dear Friend'(as if I were nothing more!) and ending with confessions of love..."[23] He, of course, addressed her as "My own darling." From then on, Ellen switched to "My darling."

Ellen's always empathic father confided in his son Stockton, "'I could wish myself no better fortune than a son like that'," referring to Wilson. To know that Ellen's future happiness was secure was a source of relief to him who knew no relief from his own despondency. After convalescing that fall, Edward Axson finally made up his mind to resign his pastorate for "health" reasons. Ellen's concern for her father, who made no plans for the future, did not ease. Soon Ellen was writing Wilson: "The latest is that he will spend the winter 'quietly here, in his own home, where he can be most comfortable, and leave in the spring.'" However, "He changes his mind every day."[24]

Insomnia's ravages had something to do with her father's changeableness. He was liable not to sleep for four nights in a row; but when he could sleep, he seemed restored in health and mood, wrote Ellen. Word of Edward's mental health problems were circulating in Rome, making him vulnerable to ridicule. Almost in tears Ellen informed Wilson how she had gotten wind of unkind remarks that "one of Papa's best friends" had made "behind his back."[25] Despite her religious convictions, Ellen remained unforgiving; she was just as unforgiving years later, in the face of her own husband's enemies.

Edward Axson's resignation that fall brought a flood of well-wishers to the Axson home at all hours of the day. His parishioners loved him who had selflessly answered the call to restore their church to health and growth after the terrible Civil War years. On November 4th, Ellen was writing her fiancé, "We will probably go to Sav., as usual, for the holidays, unless he decides that there is too much malaria there for him to risk it."[26] Three weeks later, Ellen and her father were even discussing renting out their house, though Edward, by now chronically indecisive, could not make up his mind.

A sympathetic Wilson wrote his troubled Ellen, "I am grieved...because I know that to leave your long-time home will be a sore trial to you..." Considering all that had happened to her that year--meeting her future husband, their engagement, her father's resignation and decision to uproot their home--Ellen might well have felt a little dazed. Change was definitely in the air, but at 23, it was not dreaded. While she replied that "It is something so unprecedented in my experience to be all pulled up by the roots," this was no lamentation or "sore trial." In late November, at Thanksgiving time--though this holiday went unobserved in the south--father and daughter were packed and on their way to Savannah, having left little Eddie in the care of kin, probably Aunt Louisa in Gainesville. They locked their house, unrented for the time being; Edward Axson laid eyes on it for the last time.[27]

* * *

By November 28, Ellen was writing Wilson from "the manse" adjacent to her grandfather's church on south Broad Street, in the heart of Savannah, a city described by one Englishman as all "squares and leafy streets."[28] The manse was a stately square edifice of plastered brick or stone. "I must try to assist your imagination," wrote Ellen, "with a picture of our street, south Broad, and our neighbor the church:"

> Two of my windows look out on the street with the broad 'green' down the center and its four lines of live oaks. The others give a view of the garden[,]the church yard and the old mossy wall that divides them, which, with the leafy tracery, and tangled sunbeams on the soft grey stone of the church, is a pleasant enough sight in its way.[29]

She even mailed him "stereoscopic views"--double photographs that could be purchased like postcards--which were inserted into a stereoscope for viewing three-dimensionally, stereoscopes being quite popular with the middle class in that era.

Independent Presbyterian Church, still standing, was founded in 1755 and was an enormous church by Presbyterian standards. Its famous steeple, visible from afar, was a tourist attraction: from its highest point one beheld an unsurpassed view of the surrounding city, astride the picturesque Savannah River, over three hundred miles southeast of Rome. In the 1880's, ships, bulging with the south's cotton, packed the wharves. Long after the Civil War, cotton was still king, the city's economic mainstay. When its market value collapsed for good at the turn of the twentieth century, lack of economic diversity condemned Savannah to a steep and miserable decline. Until then, however, the city was an active, thriving metropolis of over twenty thousand people, boasting fine homes and with a cosmopolitan flair. Diverse creeds--even Roman Catholics had their own cathedral--and races mingled, though warily.

Residing in the manse when Ellen and her father arrived in late November were, besides her two grandparents, their married son Randolph, his wife and their five "unruly children," wrote a bemused Ellen, "whom no power on earth can repress."[30] Reverend Isaac Axson's wife Rebecca was the undisputed matriarch of this tribe, which included her strong-willed daughter-in-law Ella. It is unclear why Randolph Axson, a businessman, and his family chose to live with his parents, unless it was for financial reasons. Luckily in that household of eleven people, not including servants, Randolph, quite unlike his brother, was witty and light-hearted, and was close to his unfortunate brother Edward, and to his niece Ellen.

Amidst the usual horde of relatives and friends, and with deep roots in Savannah, her birthplace, the transition for Ellen was painless and even pleasant. Informing her girlfriends about her engagement occasioned much hilarity. Her close friend and former roommate Janie Porter "has been executing a sort of wild war dance accompanied with shrieks of triumph over my 'downfall'." Other friends were no less "triumphant." From all others who were neither close friends or relatives, Ellen wished to keep her engagement a secret, even wearing her engagement ring on her right hand. She was very averse to gossip, and Wilson agreed with her from the outset. "I would not for the world have you annoyed by having your engagement get to the itching ears of the Rome gossips," considering the limelight in which all pastors and their families lived. Not that close friends and relatives gossiped any less.[31]

Ellen settled into a busy routine. Her reputation in Savannah preceded her, and soon she was overwhelmed with requests for portraits and tinted photographs." ... I must *paint* while it is called day" because "its [sic] against my principles to waste day-light, writing letters," she wrote Wilson. Some of her portraits--usually she drew in crayon--were of Savannah notables: "Gen. Lawton and Mrs. Gen. L., Gen. Jackson and two of Mrs. Jackson, and Gen. Gilmon."[32]

Ellen and some friends were also taking lessons in "art needlework," which she had seen displayed, she wrote, at the Women's Decorative Art rooms in New York. As if this were not enough, Ellen worked for charitable causes. She did a "'plaque' for Mr. Johnson the Missionary, also a panel for Mr. J the M.--likewise a cherub's head--likewise some pin-cushions, etc. etc. all for Mr. J the M.!...It is a missionary *fair*, you understand."[33] Not once in her voluminous correspondence did she mention missing Rome.

At Christmas time, Wilson--to his later regret--decided to save the expense of returning home for the holidays and to spend them alone in Baltimore. "I send you several Christmas cards," he wrote Ellen, "of which the colored ones are curiosities because they represent the few simple, tasteful, pretty cards to be found amongst the thousands of ugly ones on sale in the stores of this much-stocked but not well-stocked town." Ellen in turn made him a hat band. Neither spent the holidays happily. His consolation was the prospect of marrying Ellen. A few days before Christmas, he wrote of his looking forward to the kind of wife Ellen would be for him: writing in the third person, she would be "..entering into his intellectual labors with keen sympathy and appreciation."[34]

Ellen's overriding concern that winter was her father. Unlike Ellen, Edward Axson was having a difficult time adjusting. Having resigned his position as pastor, he was neither looking for another position, nor working. Barely a week after their arrival in Savannah, Ellen wrote Wilson that her father had too much time on his hands. Boredom, however, was not his main problem. There was simply little understanding and no help for anyone suffering from mental illness. As much as Ellen loved her father, she, too, saw no deeper into his dilemma than that he needed some hobby to distract him, or some light reading.

Nor is it clear that Edward Axson suffered only from mental illness. No one seemed to know, least of all doctors at the time, what really ailed him. That there was actually some physical cause to his deterioration Ellen revealed in a letter she wrote in 1897, years after her father's death. She mentioned seeing a man in church who was wasting away from "catarrh of the stomach. I was struck Sunday by the poor fellow's wretched, wizened appearance. He seems to be shrivelling away. That is a dreadful disease; it is what Papa was supposed to have."[35] "Catarrh" usually referred to a perennially runny nose and sinus problems; stomach catarrh, on the other hand, might have referred to severe digestive difficulties. Her father's "wretched, wizened appearance" and his "shriveling away" would indicate that his problems, possibly his cause of death, were more than just mental. There was in fact a ghostly resemblance between his demise and Ellen's own, decades later, who was not much older than her father when she died. Despite the strides that medicine had supposedly made by then, doctors failed--until right before her death--to diagnose her fatal kidney disease, attributing her slow wasting away and feebleness to "over-work" and over-taxing herself.

Perhaps because holidays can depress people who have mental problems, Edward Axson declined rapidly during the Christmas and New Year's season. It is not known whether Edward's family in Savannah, aside from Ellen, had ever witnessed his night time attacks. Eleanor McAdoo described them vividly, perhaps having heard about them from her mother:"There had been terrifying nights when Ellen had heard him knocking his head against the wall of his bedroom and moaning pitifully. She had tried to comfort him, sometimes walking with him hour after hour back and forth across the room..."[36] No doubt these scenes, if they recurred in Savannah, would have terrified and shocked family members, for there is no other clue to explain why he was committed to the state mental asylum in Milledgeville, Georgia, probably on January 13, 1884. Ellen would never see him again.

The admission record, dated that day, described Edward as a "lunatic" whose "duration of insanity" had lasted approximately four weeks. Baffling for its vagueness and stupidity (perhaps an indication of the quality of care Edward would receive) was the statement concerning his health: "'General health has been failing for some time. Cause supposed from bad health,'" and his professional background: "'Patient is a Presbyterian preacher, and has been for quite a number of years, a devoted Christian.'" The admission record also stated that Edward "'is disposed to be violent occasionally.'" Did this indicate that he was violent towards others? Very unlikely. Or was this a reference to his night-time attacks? The admission record, again vaguely, referred to Edward's "suicidal tendency" as "slight," and that he was taking "chloral" to help him sleep at night. Chloral hydrate was used in this era as a sedative, and to induce hypnosis. Absent from the record is any reference to his "wretched, wizened" physical appearance and his "shrivelling away," Ellen's last memories of him.[37]

How and why Edward was committed to the Central State Hospital in Milledgeville may well remain a mystery. In his psycho-medical study of Woodrow Wilson, Doctor Edwin Weinstein made reference to Edward Axson's "acutely psychotic" condition. Psychosis, or mental derangement, was certainly not evident from Edward's letters from the asylum, which Ellen described as "perfectly lucid, affectionate and almost cheerful."[38]

Meanwhile, the man whom Eleanor McAdoo described as "gentle" and "over-sensitive" resigned himself meekly to his fate, as his few surviving letters testify. Edward rarely wrote about himself, or his treatment, and never complained or criticized. A month after being committed he revealed only that: "I had a bad night of sleeplessness last night and am this morning feeling badly in consequence. The Dr. however thinks I am improving," though what the doctor's diagnosis was, if any, is unknown, as was his treatment.[39] Ellen was to write Wilson, "We hear but little from the doctors--they have always been reticent in giving us--in Sav.--an opinion." Given that Georgia was a backward state not likely to have progressive treatment for "lunatics," and that the public was unaccustomed to challenging doctors and hospitals, Edward's prognosis was far from hopeful.

It is no wonder that Edward Axson died four and a half months later. Confinement in a depressing 19th century, public mental institution in a town that William McAdoo, Eleanor's husband, described as a "depressed little Georgia town" and "the poorest place imaginable,"[40] bereft of mental stimulation, company and visitors--no one in his family paid him a visit during his entire incarceration--was calculated to drive any intelligent person to despair, or madness.

* * *

The effect of Edward's confinement to a mental asylum, on Ellen and her relatives in Savannah, was traumatic. In that day and age, it was a social stigma to have a family member who was mentally ill or confined in an "insane" asylum. For that reason, Ellen even considered, and must have written Wilson, that she was breaking her engagement. A panicked Wilson dropped everything, borrowed train fare from a surprised colleague, and headed immediately for Savannah. There are no letters to document how he and Ellen spent their time together, except Ellen's allusion to his two days with her as "very wretched ones!"[41] Nonetheless, he rescued his engagement and, no doubt weakened by the stress and strain of his long, sad journey, was laid up sick for a week at his parents in Wilmington.

Ellen's letters to her fiancé, who was back in Baltimore by early February, reveal her troubling sadness over her father's condition, and her attempts to deal with it. She was "fighting the blues," she wrote, by means of "the best of all remedies, hard work." She then described completing a portrait and her work "at the machine," that is, the sewing machine. Sewing, including embroidery, seemed to be an important outlet for her, and she sewed maddeningly, "domestic, missionary and art needlework," she wrote.[42]

Ellen also went visiting, the all-important social institution for women, and a great comforter, even if she could not confide her father's condition. In her letters she never referred to religion, as some people do, as a consoler in a time of personal crisis. Rather, in a subsequent letter to Wilson, Ellen expressed frustration at her Maker. "We seem to accept, to follow His direction, not freely and joyfully, but only because we *must*...I want to be not merely *submissive* to his will, but gladly acquiescent," only to find that she was not.[43] It was not the first time for her, nor would it be the last, when religious consolation was found wanting.

Wilson's letters to Ellen rarely dwelled on her tragedy. Instead, they soothed and consoled by his funny way of describing day to day experiences, and his work at "the Johnny Hop," where he was making brilliant headway. He sent her a Valentine's card with the remark that "...there's no lover in the land who has more love to send his sweetheart by St. Valentine than I have to my Ellie.";[44] in another letter, he mentioned trying to grow his hair long enough to send her a "lock" of his hair (she had sent him one of hers), exchanging locks of hair being the sentimental Victorian custom of the day.

Over the next few months, Ellen's life on the surface returned to normal. Spring was in full bloom in Savannah, transforming the city into a haunting paradise, enticing Ellen to go on long walks in the moonlight. Of one such moonlit ramble she wrote, "I don't believe there is any other city in America with more of an almost solemn beauty than Sav."[45] Ellen attended lectures, even a rare one delivered by a woman, and took up her usual leisure reading, which included Henry James, of whom Wilson had never heard. Wilson mailed her reading matter--his recently published article, "Committee or Cabinet Government," and a book on "modern painters" by her favorite John Ruskin.

Still, by March, Ellen was confiding her inner torment that never left her for a moment. "I seem to be almost paralyzed by the uncertainly, the constant fear of 'something happening.'" She doubted that her father's reassuring letters from the asylum "meant much," and confessed again to "a terrible state of suspense." Keen as her suffering was, it seemed small compared to that of her friend Beth, whose uncle "had lost his mind from *intemperance*...what sorrows *can* be compared with those which come from *sin*?"[46]

There were other worries besides her father. Edward Axson was no longer supporting his three younger children, still minors, this burden devolving upon already over-burdened grandparents. Ellen foresaw having to care for her father in the event that he was ever discharged from the asylum, for, as she put it, "What future is there for one who, at best, has been the inmate of an insane asylum?" To support herself and her siblings, she simply was not earning enough money as a freelance artist (so much for Stockton Axson's memory of his sister earning a "tidy sum" from her art work). "I think I can make more at that [teaching] than at the crayon portraits," she wrote her fiancé, as she weighed the pros and cons of a teaching career; besides, she went on, she could still do portraits *after* school.[47]

That spring of 1884 found both Ellen and Wilson job-seeking. Desperate to be married and self-supporting, Wilson had applied for a possible opening as an instructor at Arkansas Industrial University in Fayetteville. On the surface, Wilson supported Ellen in her new plan to work. "Of course the mere chance of my securing a position at once ought not to be allowed to stand in the way of your taking a position as teacher of drawing...", though this might be a year-long, and quite unbearable, postponement of their marriage. "I think it very probable, dearest, that your dear father, were he consulted on the matter, would wish our marriage to come as soon as possible." But marriage was not on her mind. Expressing herself forcefully, Ellen responded "...how can I think of such things in the midst of this terrible suspense about Papa? How can I tell when or where he might need me? And my boys [her brothers] too need me now."[48]

Ellen went ahead with her job search. Some day she would express sympathy for struggling women, but she herself, without stress or strain, quickly secured a full-time position as an art instructor in a private school in Augusta, Georgia. She would begin in the fall, and was looking forward to it. Wilson, on the other hand, saw his one promising job prospect vanish. When a full-tuition fellowship at Johns Hopkins, including a stipend, was awarded to him at the end of May, he reluctantly gave up job-seeking. Alas, marriage had to be postponed another year, not that it occurred to either of them to marry while he was still a student, with Ellen teaching in Baltimore: so untraditional was it for a husband to be supported by his wife.

Mid-May found Ellen visiting Rome, staying at the Tedcastles, and working in her alma mater's art studio. Savannah had nothing to offer in the way of art studios or art training, even less than tiny Rome. On the side, Ellen once more was at work on crayon portraits, for which there seemed to be an insatiable demand. Weeks later, still in Rome, she enrolled in a decorative porcelain painting class. "I never felt any desire to learn it until I saw her work," referring to her teacher, a Mrs. Nance, having "seen so much daubing on china that I was rather disgusted."[49] But if Ellen was going to teach in the fall, she might as well learn it.

Ellen had earlier informed Wilson of her itinerary that summer: spending July with her best friend Rose and her husband in Tennessee, then dividing the rest of the summer between Rome and Gainesville, where her little sister Margaret and her brother Eddie were living. Her travels would end up taking her all over the state of Georgia. The degree of freedom and independence she exercised, as she traveled alone and at will, might not have surprised her as much as it surprises us today.

Wilson had no travel plans except to spend the long summer break with his parents in Wilmington. He proposed--and Ellen eagerly accepted--the idea of staying with him, for a few weeks at least, in Wilmington. To Wilson's astonishment, Ellen's prudish grandmother, matriarch of the Axson clan, was "violently opposed," as Ellen put it, to the plan. When seconded by Ella Axson, Ellen's aunt by marriage, Ellen relented under the pressure. "I have been obliged so often to give up things I had set my heart upon, that now I don't mind it much," she wrote with a streak of self-pity, notwithstanding her many advantages in life.[50] Yet obedience and duty were so deeply ingrained in both Ellen and Wilson that it would have been unthinkable for Ellen, and unacceptable to Wilson, to sneak in a visit while she was traveling alone that summer.

* * *

It was while visiting the Tedcastles in Rome that Ellen received the much dreaded news that her father had died on May 28. The tidings came not by way of Savannah, but from a letter sent to her maternal Uncle William Hoyt, a doctor in Rome. That the asylum in Milledgeville would notify him directly, instead of Ellen's grandparents, hinted that her uncle might have played a role in placing Edward Axson in the asylum, possibly after being consulted by the Axsons in Savannah. The news was heart-rending. "Oh my dear, dear father, the best, the purest, truest man I ever knew," lamented Ellen.[51] Too distraught to write Wilson, he received the tragic tidings from her young cousin; he made up his mind to visit Ellen in her time of trial. He arrived in Rome after the funeral and burial; Edward Axson, dead at 47, was laid to rest next to his beloved Janie.

Why neither Ellen nor any family member ever visited Edward at the asylum is difficult to divine, unless mental asylums prohibited such visits. Because the letter to Dr. Hoyt has been lost, the cause of Edward Axson's death may never be known. The asylum issued no death certificate, as this was not common practice in the 19th century. Wilson scholars, notably Arthur S. Link and Doctor Edwin Weinstein, have always assumed that Ellen's father committed suicide, for which the only telltale "evidence" is a passage in a letter of condolence, written to Ellen from a relative: "The place and manner of your father's death are inexpressibly sad; but you cannot doubt his acceptance in the Beloved." [52] Certainly suicide cannot be ruled out, but how did he commit it? Was he still taking chloral as a sedative and did he, one night, out of sheer frustration, take an over-dose? Or did he starve himself to death?

What Ellen wrote Wilson in early June was that "He seems to have sunk rapidly at the last; we had no warning whatever except that terrible letter to Uncle Will," which is not suggestive of suicide.[53] What it does not rule out, however, is that the hospital and staff, who seldom informed Edward's relatives of his treatment and care, were responsible, either through negligence or incompetence, for his untimely death.

As a suicide, would the Presbyterian church have allowed Edward a religious funeral and burial? Would his church in Rome have mounted a plaque in honor of his memory? Lastly, would an insurance company have made good on his life insurance? According to Frances Saunders, "Edward Axson left an estate of approximately $12,000 in the form of cash (largely from a life insurance policy)...."[54] The insurance money, a large sum in those days, must have come as a shock to Ellen, who exclaimed to her brother Stockton, "We're rich!" From then on, each of Edward's children received an annuity.

Not only had Edward provided for his family in case of his death, but he had also made, no doubt modest, investments in railroad stocks and bonds, which Ellen inherited. Ellen no longer had to teach to make a living. Informing the school in Augusta that she had changed her mind, she made plans to finally pursue her dream: to study art, full-time, at the Art Students League in Manhattan.

* * *

"The last part of my stay in Rome will be a turmoil of packing and breaking up, and selling out," wrote Ellen.[55] The renters, the Cranes, had been given notice. Not unusual for that day, they had been renting the house with all of the Axson's belongings still in it, from furniture to silverware. Ellen and Stockton, who was on his summer break from school, packed intensively ("the books are the worst of all...."), while Wilson was kept informed. He started for Rome on June 8 for a two

First Love and a Wedding: Savannah and New York, 1883-1885   49

week visit. Nothing is known of their time together except that he fell ill--it was malaria season--and was laid up at her friends, the Tedcastles, for nearly a week.

The excitement of imminent change, of having her beloved by her side, eased the pain over her father's death. Sadly, there was no denying that his end brought release from perennial anxiety, along with real financial relief. Ellen pursued her travel plans for the summer, that had taken her from Savannah to Rome. From Rome she would spend July with her friend Rose in Tennessee, and August at her Aunt Louisa's in Gainesville; what remained of the summer, before departing for New York, would be spent on a visit to Wilson at his parents home in Wilmington. Ellen's grandmother Axson had relented after all, thanks to a letter written by Wilson's mother, imploring her to allow Ellen to stay with them. On July 14, Ellen explained her grandmother's initial opposition: "local custom" in Savannah ridiculed any woman staying with a man who was not her husband, however innocuous her visit might be. Her grandmother, who had not personally opposed the visit, knew of examples to prove it.[56]

Much relieved, Wilson wrote facetiously, "When you come we can plan the best way for making New York and Baltimore very close together. We'll organize an inter-state Love League (of two members only, in order that it may be of manageable size)...I'll draw up a Constitution in true legal form, and then we can make by-laws at our leisure as they become necessary." He and his mother proceeded to fit up a room for Ellen's use as an art studio. She finally arrived in mid-September, her visit having been deferred because of a sudden recurrence of malaria ("...some of the *Rome* malaria, the doctor says, cropping out at this late date.")[57]

Ellen and her fiancé would spend nearly three weeks together. No letters inform us as to how they spent their time, though earlier Wilson had alluded to her desire to see the ocean. That wish, he wrote, he could grant her easily; otherwise, Wilmington, North Carolina had little to offer, being "an exceedingly dingy, uninteresting town...."[58] He intended to let her read the manuscript of his first book, *Congressional Government*, before sending it off to the publisher. She read it from cover to cover.

Surely they spent time discussing the current furor in their church over the theory of evolution that embroiled Wilson's favorite uncle, Dr. James Woodrow, a man of science. Notwithstanding that Charles Darwin, who had died two years ago, had been a staunch atheist, James Woodrow defended evolution at Columbia Theological Seminary in South Carolina, where he taught, causing dismay within southern Presbyterian ranks. When his pro-evolution article appeared in July in the *Southern Presbyterian Review*--Wilson immediately mailed Ellen a copy--it was the last straw. What followed was a barrage of angry criticism of his uncle and his views. Wilson, equating Darwin's theory with, as he put it to Ellen, "the indisputable facts of science," blindly accused the opposition of having a "precarious faith in God." Ellen, clearly bewildered, wrote back, agreeing with Wilson.[59]

Their heady days in Wilmington ending, Ellen and Wilson planned to travel to their destinations together. Leaving on October 1, they stopped en route for sightseeing in Washington, D.C., the first time Ellen laid eyes on the city which, thirty years later, became her home. Of course a visit to the Corcoran Gallery of Art was in order for Ellen, and a visit to the Capitol for Wilson; the next day, they boarded the train together for New York City. Today a matter of a few hours (or less), the trip in 1884 would take all night long. Consequently, they rode a sleeper train that would take them through Baltimore; Wilson preferred to stay with Ellen to ensure that she had a safe haven in Manhattan, before heading back to Johns Hopkins.

All told, Ellen would spend eight full months at the Art Students League in New York; these months were the most exciting of her young life. Deeply in love ("no other but yourself," she would write Wilson, "could have stirred my nature to its inmost depths"[60]), and plunging heart and soul into the maelstrom of American art, she was never happier.

* * *

The following months were also Wilson's initiation into the American art scene, of which, he admitted, he had not the faintest idea. "..and I must confess, with all contrition, that I don't know what the League is," when Ellen first broached the subject of studying at the Art Students League. WHY she desired to prepare herself so seriously for an art career when, as Wilson delicately put it, she would be putting it aside for him, was more difficult for him to grasp than he cared to admit. Wilson, however, felt "guiltily selfish" about her "sacrifice," referring to it not infrequently afterward. In their voluminous correspondence-- writing to each other every day--Ellen declared that she would never regret choosing marriage over a career. (Months later she wrote, "My experience and observation since I have been here have driven me to the conclusion that I *have* talent, above the average among the art-students. It is *barely* possible that my talent for art combined with my talent for work *might*, after many years, win me a place in the first rank among American artists--who don't amount to much *anyhow* you know!") She wrote vaguely about keeping up her art work during their summer vacations. [61]

First Love and a Wedding: Savannah and New York, 1883-1885   51

Frequently their correspondence reveals their opinions, especially Wilson's, on women and careers, marriage and the family. Wilson's rested squarely on a traditional biblical outlook: complementarity of the sexes, rather than equality. "Women are the best complement of men," wrote Wilson on one occasion, and neither one's lives would be complete without the other.[62] Hence it followed that a wife and mother pursuing a career outside the home was "unnatural," both to Wilson and to Ellen, and "selfish." A single woman doing the same might not be selfish, but, according to Wilson, she was probably not pretty.

"I don't wonder that you can have no sympathy with that false talk about 'a woman's right to live her own life,'" wrote Wilson, for a woman had about as much right to live her own life, he asserted, as did a man. "In my opinion, a woman proves her womanliness, a man his manliness, by longing for the companionship of marriage, and for all the duties and responsibilities that marriage brings."[63]

Marriage, however, was "supplementarity." "Their [women's] life must supplement man's life...This is not putting their lives in a position *subordinate* to the position allotted to men," he noted. Nor had supplementarity anything to do with a wife's subjection to the will of her husband, which Wilson called a "terrible" idea. "In a true marriage--a marriage, I mean, not of fancy but of genuine love--how could there be so much as a thought of a contest of wills, of the will of the wife bending, almost to breaking, under that of the husband!"[64]

Supplementarity as well as complementarity assigned the husband to be the head of the family, which Wilson fully intended to be. This meant that the husband, not the wife, would be responsible for sheltering, protecting and providing for the family's needs. Though the husband and not the wife would be the one to pursue a career outside the home, men as well as women, wrote Wilson, "can find their true selves only in love and devotion to family life," and not to a career.[65]

While Ellen expected to give up the professional pursuit of art after her marriage, she never for a moment considered her training in New York to be a waste of time or money. Quite the contrary. In addition to her intensive training at the League, she would add art classes at the Metropolitan Museum of Art's school, located on East 34th Street. "...I feel that nothing *counted* before this year," as though she were re-learning art from the bottom up.[66]

The Art Students League, located at 38 West Fourteenth Street in lower Manhattan, had always been Ellen's first choice. Its 1875 charter proclaimed: "The League will form and sustain classes for study from the nude and draped model, of composition, perspective, etc." at a time when art schools offered few classes "from life." Moreover, for the first time in American art history, women would fully partake in "life" classes, including the ones studying nude models (though these would be segregated by sex), and take a hand in running the school. Three years later, the League's widely-circulating prospectus read: "Three life classes daily, and a school in portrait painting, together with composition and sketch classes, are kept in continuous operation for eight months." The League, established by defecting art students from the National Academy of Design, was already claiming to be the most progressive training ground for budding American artists.[67]

By the 1880's, the Art Students League was attracting talent from all over the United States and Canada. When Ellen enrolled in the fall of 1884, approximately 500 students attended, and this number was growing rapidly. Leading artists would teach or learn at the League: Kenyon Cox (an 1880's photo shows him conducting the crowded women's "life" class), George DeForest Brush (Ellen's portrait teacher), Augustus St. Gaudens, F.W. Freer (a drawing teacher of Ellen's), Thomas Eakins (who also served on the board in 1885), Thomas Hart Benton, Frederick Remington, and later, Jackson Pollock. Though Ellen was disdainful of women's emancipation, she was only too glad to be able to participate in "life" classes, all but closed to women everywhere else. As Ellen's contemporary, Philadelphia native Mary Cassatt, put it, "'life classes for women usually meant having a live *cow* in the studio,'" referring to her training at the Philadelphia Academy of the Fine Arts during the Civil War years.[68]

* * *

After dropping Ellen off at her boarding house at 60 Clinton Place in lower Manhattan, Wilson wrote from Baltimore: "I cannot tell you how desperately heavy-hearted I have been ever since I left my precious little sweetheart in those dreary quarters amidst those horrid people."[69] The boarding house was crammed with forty-three women boarders, mostly from the working class. Ellen, by contrast, was easy-going, and quickly made friends in her shabby new surroundings. It was her first boarding house experience. In New York at least, rooms in boarding houses, as Ellen would discover, were often unheated, or poorly heated, and barely large enough to contain a cot. (Apartments being scarce, they were not an option for most renters.)

Crowded, with four other roommates, into a small room with only one window, Ellen soon was looking for better housing. Several weeks later she moved to 120 W. 11th St., three blocks from the Art Students League. She described her new abode as "a small house, only about 15 boarders, and Mrs. Beattie informed me that she takes 'no working girls, and no retail clerks.'" There

First Love and a Wedding: Savannah and New York, 1883-1885 53

were eight women and seven men, rent included board, but no bathing facilities, boarders having to make do with basins in their rooms. Though Eleanor McAdoo referred to her mother as having slender means, Ellen paid a high rent--eleven dollars a week, compared to five a week for her Clinton Place room--for a private room which she described as "beautifully furnished." This made her feel slightly guilty, as she always did when she spent money on herself. In addition, she paid twelve dollars a month for her classes at the League, which she considered a high fee. Ellen soon purchased a new, heavy winter cloak, for what would be her first northern winter. In short, Ellen was not forced to live in the squalor and penury of many of her fellow students at the League.[70]

For the first time in her life, Ellen, writing from her new room, said she was feeling lonely. A month later she changed her tune completely: "Really, instead of being friendless in the great city, I am getting to have too many friends!" There was, as usual, an array of relatives, living in or convenient to the city: a Cousin Hattie, Uncle Ben, Aunt Sallie and Uncle Tom, not to mention a saintly "Cousin Helen" who died in Hoboken, shortly after Ellen's arrival, and an army of other cousins besides. Ellen soon felt so much at home that she even dared the unthinkable: walking alone in the dark in Manhattan. She admitted to having had the misimpression of New York as crime-ridden. A fellow boarder, Mr. Marvin, however, "...laughs at our 'country' idea of N.Y. as such a dreaded place, says it is the *safest*, he knows of, in which to bring up children either boys or girls."[71]

Every week day Ellen walked the three blocks to the Art Students League. Though only five stories high, the academy actually towered over the neighborhood, which was a pleasant mix of small businesses and art studios. When she later enrolled in morning classes at the Metropolitan's school of art on East 34th Street, she compared the two schools: "The teaching there [the Met] is almost as good" and "the expense so much less."[72]

When Ellen began her classes at the League--October was the beginning of the academic year--she wrote that "We are all at sea about our work, for instead of crayon, they use charcoal entirely."[73] All of her training at the League involved drawing, painting or sculpting from live models. In her daily, detailed correspondence, Ellen dared not mention that some of the models she learned from were nudes, which would have shocked a squeamish Wilson; he never would have dreamed that his "Eileen" could expose herself to such an unmentionable. Wilson was not alone. Beginning in the 1880's, New Yorkers were in a growing huff over the League's "filthy" methods, and periodically, police would raid the premises, confiscating nude artwork to the outrage and hilarity of the Leaguers.

Anyone could enroll in the Art Students League; to "graduate" from class to class, one had to show real ability. In late November Ellen wrote elatedly that, on the strength of her portrait of Homer (clothed or unclothed?), she had been promoted to "head" class, presumably a more advanced portrait class. Moreover, her teacher, DeForest Brush, showered her with praise, as did another teacher, Mr. Weir. "He so seldom says anything *'nice'* that I scarcely knew how to take it." A week later, Wilson confided his own success: Houghton & Miflin had accepted his manuscript for publication, his first (by no means last) book. "*Dear* Houghton & Miflin!" wrote Ellen ecstatically," how I LOVE them!" For the next seventy-five years, Woodrow Wilson's *Congressional Government*--a lucid analysis of the inner workings of the legislative branch--would be a standard text in colleges and universities.[74]

November 1884 was also an exciting presidential election year, grabbing Wilson's attention more than Ellen's. However, when Democrat Grover Cleveland won, Ellen wrote melodramatically, "The League has been completely demoralized."[75] Why, is unclear. Perhaps because Republican rival, James G. Blaine, was a New Yorker; hence, Democrat Wilson warned, he represented "machine politics" at its worst.

That November, and for the first time, Ellen posed as a model in her "life" class. Besides hiring outsiders, students liked to take turns posing. It involved standing in front of one's classmates for an hour, with the poser dressed to suit his or her fancy. When it was Ellen's turn, she was coquettishly garbed in a Kate Greenaway outfit of her own creation. After fifteen minutes of standing, she felt herself growing faint; soon, she was swaying. Alarmed students rushed to catch her before she fell into a dead faint. She was by no means the first poser to faint, nor the last, she assured her fiancé. Such training was *terra incognita* to an appalled Wilson. Ellen certainly was no weakling. A few months later, after being knocked almost unconscious on the sidewalk (after bumping her head hard), she came to, got up with the help of two men who had rushed to her aid, and resumed walking to her classes.[76]

* * *

From time to time Wilson complained to Ellen about his "loneliness" in Baltimore, hacking away at studies that tried his patience, longing to have a real job and be married. By contrast, Ellen's life was a perfect frenzy of socializing, entertainment, and long, long hours of work. She often returned to her room at night too exhausted to light her stove, writing with freezing fingers instead of climbing into bed to sleep. Confiding in her Rome cousin Mary Hoyt, Ellen wrote that if she did not write every day, "'he gets a bad headache.'"[77] Her fiancé had an elaborate scheme for staying in touch: he regularly sent Ellen a box full of envelopes, each one laboriously typed with his address, and stamped. Such systematic ways impressed Ellen. Though an orderly person, she was by nature unsystematic in all she undertook, including raising children.

Being a sober Presbyterian did not preclude enjoying oneself. Ellen attended the theater every week, even giving in to the temptation--unthinkable in Georgia-- of going to burlesque shows at the "Bijou." When her guilty conscience admonished her to stop, Wilson was relieved: "A stage full of young women with scarcely any clothing on is not an improving thing to look upon," he gently chided, obviously unaware of the nude modeling going on at the League. Ellen also enjoyed sightseeing, taking her first walk across the newly-built Brooklyn Bridge, and seizing every opportunity to visit art exhibits, denied her in Rome and Savannah; moreover, as an art student, she attended them for free. Consequently she often frequented the high-priced exhibitions at the dinky, twelve year-old Metropolitan Museum of Art, which otherwise had little to offer in the way of a collection. New York having a paucity of "real art" from Europe, exhibits were usually private studio or art academy affairs. In 1882, League President Harper complained that New York was "'more poorly equipped for study than any fourth rate European city.'"[78]

Art galleries, specializing in the buying and selling of works of art, also were few. The famous Macbeth Gallery on Fifth Avenue, with which Ellen would transact business as First Lady, had not yet been born. The immense private fortunes that eventually would make fabulous art collections possible, were still being made. To native Georgian Ellen Axson, however, New York was art heaven.

Mailing her fiancé a portrait that a fellow student had drawn of her, she wrote, "That is the heaviest price one must pay at the League; - *some one* is *always* sketching one, on the sly."[79] With Christmas drawing nigh, she and Wilson began making plans for the holidays. But not before an unusual personal crisis occurred, involving Ellen and her church, or rather, her pastor.

Upon arriving in Manhattan, Ellen had tried out several churches (even guiltily attending an Episcopalian service at the Church of the Heavenly Rest), before settling upon a northern Presbyterian church--being more liberal than the southern--presided over by a Dr. Taylor. Ellen never missed her two Sunday services. On December 7, she wrote Wilson that her Uncle Tom (himself a southern Presbyterian clergyman) had recently revealed to her an alarming "fact": "Did you know that Dr. Taylor advocates marriage between white people and negroes?...Now isn't that perfectly disgusting?" This bothered her all week. The following Sunday, "I went to church resolutely last Sunday, saying to myself, 'I will conquer this feeling.'" As it turned out, "this feeling" was her antipathy for Dr. Taylor. "How can one respect a person holding such disgraceful, such disgusting views?" Unable to surmount "this feeling," she was considering leaving her church for another. Wilson, who would become the first U.S. president to introduce segregation in the federal government, wrote in response: "It is not made clear in your letter whether he made a speech whose object was to advocate intermarriage of the races in the South," but if it was, then "both his moral judgment and his political judgment are radically and utterly unsound...He has never seen the negro as we have seen him." Ellen forthwith left Dr. Taylor's church for the Scotch Presbyterian church, presided over by a Dr. Hamilton.[80]

While both Ellen and Wilson were thorough-going segregationists, neither one ever felt or exhibited anything close to the personal animus for blacks--for all people of color--of a Helen Bones, Woodrow Wilson's first cousin. Nor would racial prejudice blind First Lady Ellen Wilson to the disgraceful living conditions of poor blacks in the nation's capital, which she dedicated herself to improve, in the face of bitter criticism.

* * *

On December 21, Wilson was writing Ellen, in anticipation of his week-long visit to Manhattan, "Will you be ready to give him as many kisses as he wants? Will you do all you can to show him how thoroughly you belong to him?"[81] Less erotic than we would take it today, his ardent queries were the furthest removed from any suggestion of co-habitation. Wilson selected a boarding house nearby, and how many kisses--or what kind--they exchanged can only be imagined. Since no letters passed between them, precious little can be divined from their week together, except by inference.

Wilson must have discussed his interview for a history teaching position at Bryn Mawr College, a new "female college" near Philadelphia that aimed to be a "Johanna Hopkins." Several weeks later, the surprising news of his acceptance hit Ellen like a bombshell. Though the salary was considered very modest, $1500 a year, two could manage to live on it. Hitherto, the possibility that Wilson would continue for his doctorate at Johns Hopkins was not out of the question, prolonging their engagement; now Wilson was pressing Ellen--and not the other way around--to set a date for the wedding. A June wedding would be out of the question, wrote Ellen; she could not possibly be ready by then. Privately she had hoped to get trained in landscape painting over the summer. Two-thirds of American artists at the time were landscape painters. Landscape painting would

First Love and a Wedding: Savannah and New York, 1883-1885   57

be a wonderful pursuit during leisure hours. "...it must be one of the most delightful and healthful of recreations; and one for which I shall probably have some time, in summer vacations!" wrote Ellen to her fiancé in late March.[82]

She wrote no more of the matter. Wilson continued to prevail on a June wedding: they would have $500 (a gift from his parents) to enable them to spend a long honeymoon and rest before re-locating to Bryn Mawr.[83] None of this would be possible if they married late in the summer. Finally, Ellen agreed on a late June wedding at the home of her grandparents in Savannah. For the next twenty years art would be subordinate to her husband and children, but never, as her sister and brother Stockton maintained, was it shelved completely.

Hitherto not a soul knew of Ellen's engagement--neither at her boarding house nor at the League. Meanwhile she was seeing a good deal of a fellow boarder, a Massachusetts native named Mr. Goodrich. He had an interesting job as a representative of Houghton & Miflin, the very publishing company that was publishing Wilson's book. He was in the habit of escorting Ellen to theaters, they had discussed Emerson and Carlyle together, and found that they had numerous interests in common. Yet Ellen seemed blind to his advances. Wilson, however, was uneasy: "To go with him to the theatre on Monday, to prayer-meeting on Wednesday, and to the theatre again the next week is scarcely discouraging his attention--is it, little lady?," but, he added, "I know that you will do what is *right*." Hence out of sheer necessity, to calm her fiancé's fears, Ellen told Goodrich the news of her engagement. Once being told, she reasoned that Goodrich, because he was a civilized New Englander, would do nothing improper, and their friendship could continue. Wilson, however, was less confident about New England morals. And indeed, her news spurred Goodrich into a passionate declaration of his love for her, even pleading with an astounded Ellen to break her engagement and marry him instead. An anxious and outraged Wilson immediately headed for New York. Was it to "have it out" with Goodrich, man to man? Whatever took place, his two-day visit had little effect. Shortly afterwards Ellen wrote that she herself had finally "'had it out'" with the hapless Goodrich: "Such a scene!" she declared. The next day, at breakfast, "he was an object ghastly to behold--ate nothing." He soon fell ill. Wilson, however, had no sympathy for the "third-rate melodrama" of the unhappy Goodrich, the "poor, dangerous baby." Illness--or despair--seemed to put an end to the "melodrama."[84]

* * *

Life was getting increasingly hectic. Moreover, Ellen wrote that she was feeling guilty. "I feel I am leading a very selfish life here, doing only my *own* work all day long." Hence despite her heavy schedule--she had just added classes at the Metropolitan--and her preparations for her upcoming wedding--she decided to volunteer as a teacher at the Spring Street Mission School on Sundays, though what she taught is unclear. Charitable work was, after all, permitted on "Sabbath" days. On February 8, she wrote her fiancé, "I was rather pleased with my first experience of a city mission. It is a big room-full of noisy bright very clean and respectable looking little darkies, - did I tell you it was a colored school?" In time she would have a favorite, a bright little black boy. This experience led to no speculation on larger issues, however. Nor was Ellen ever a conscious reformer. "She was compassionate," recalled her brother Stockton, "less given to reforms than to quietly performed acts of mercy."[85] Ellen continued to work in the school every Sunday, until she left New York for good.

Writing of her work in the mission school reminded Ellen about something else: "By the way, all this reminds me of our model for the week; who is a little 'darkie'--not *very* dark, however. She is really pretty and exceedingly picturesque, with the most remarkable pre-Raphaelite hair." Soon afterward, Ellen's turn to pose came again. Her "ordeal" was successful this time, in part because she was allowed to sit. "...it certainly is a strain to have fifty people stare at you for an hour." Two weeks later she informed Wilson, "We had a great time in sketch class this afternoon; --the model [a man] fainted 'dead away' at the end of the first quarter."[86]

* * *

"Art is a severe mistress; she demands long and constant service before she will give the smallest reward, and I am the merest beginner now." Despite being the "merest beginner," Ellen was rewarded that spring when she got admitted to painting classes at the League, which, she emphasized, had very "tough" standards for admittance. Since painting would be held in the mornings, Ellen was forced to give up her classes at the Metropolitan. She was sorry to do so. Surprisingly, she even admitted to preferring the Met to the League, if "they [the Met] only had models. But I *must* paint from life."[87]

Ellen's disillusionment with the League was gradual, and had nothing to do with its training. Rather, it was the environment, an atmosphere of radical freethinking and the championing of radical lifestyles, that profoundly disturbed her. She was shocked to hear of the atheistic "Society for Ethical Culture" in Manhattan, to which some Leaguers, men, women and at least one professor, belonged. ("What a terrible faith, or no-faith!" she exclaimed.) Judging from numerous references in Ellen's and Wilson's letters, feminism also was widespread at the League, along with the view that marriage cost a woman her

First Love and a Wedding: Savannah and New York, 1883-1885   59

identity and was a better deal for men than women. One who personified this view, though married, was a Mrs. Powell, also a native southerner. Ellen was horrified to discover that this woman Leaguer lived only three months of the year with her husband and small child, and the other months pursued art studies full-time at the League. When asked how she could neglect her family for so long, she smiled, "'I married a *very unselfish* man, and I myself am *very* selfish.'"[88]

"At the League," wrote Ellen, "I feel sometimes as though all the world were turning aside to infidelity, and I am really disheartened." As a consequence, church attendance became more meaningful, for "it serves to keep my courage up...." Decades later, Ellen discouraged her talented daughter Eleanor from enrolling in the League. According to Eleanor, "...some of the 'new thought' she [had] heard at the Art Students League made her feel that the very foundations of society were in danger." Wilson could not have agreed with Ellen more.[89]

Ellen's new roommate that spring, Leaguer Antoinette Farnsworth, a "Yankee" from Michigan, poked fun at Ellen's traditional notions. When Farnsworth informed Ellen of her own engagement that summer, she made it clear that she had no intention of having an engagement or marriage limit her freedom.

> ...I shall not give up art. Not one bit! It will be useless to tell you so but I *can* and *will* show you. I don't agree with you any more than I did on a woman's duty - sphere[,] etc.

Furthermore,

> I go everywhere with all the young men just as I used to with the exception of two evenings in the week which I keep for Mr. Drew....I am to be a gay Bohemian. Not a simple home girl at all. I wasn't made for one.[90]

Ironically, by choosing marriage to Woodrow Wilson over her own career, Ellen did more for herself as an artist in the long run than did Farnsworth (Mrs. Drew), who outlived Ellen by many years.

* * *

Fine spring weather would find Ellen and fellow Leaguer Antoinette sketching outdoors in Central Park. As her wedding drew near, Ellen's and Wilson's letters grew more ardent. A letter of May 17, five weeks before their marriage, was wholly devoted to the subject of kissing. Their joy in shared values and interests constantly surfaced in their correspondence. In late March Ellen wrote,

I too have an ever-deepening sense of the inborn sympathy there is between us in all matters of importance; we look at life in the same way, our ideals and aspirations are in harmony, and our thought is so often the same...

To both Ellen and Wilson, such harmony made it "a great and sweet though solemn privilege to live."[91]

Moreover, quite often they read the same books, understandably relishing novels and stories set in Dixie. Incredibly, Ellen's daunting academic and social calendar, her church work and daily correspondence, did not preclude a steady fare of reading (and sewing). One book especially struck both her and Wilson's fancy: *The Prophet of the Big Smoky*, whose pseudonymous author, Charles Egbert Craddock, was in fact a woman, a Miss Murphee. Ellen was sorry that Murphee had revealed her gender at last, she wrote Wilson, for people were bound not to think her work that good anymore. Replied Wilson magnanimously, "There is certainly not a single touch in the story that reveals a woman's hand."[92]

The date for their wedding, June 24, had only been firmly set in early May. As late as April 13, Ellen insisted that no date be set for the wedding--until she had seen a "doctress." "I will find out all about myself and if I am not quite sound I'll break off my engagement!" Wilson took her literally, "...there came crowding in upon me thoughts of my own precarious health. Had I a right to ask you to marry me?" To Ellen, this was nonsense. Her concern in fact was not her general, but her gynecological health. The "doctress" apparently pronounced her sound, that is, able to bear children. Surely this came as no surprise to Ellen. Did the doctor also--as some women doctors used to do--inform her of the "facts of life"? While traditionally mothers were encharged with this task, that was far too often not the case. Ellen's contemporary, writer Edith Wharton, had to beg her mother to tell her "'what will happen to me'" on her wedding night. Even then, her mother shrugged her off, "'You can't be as stupid as you pretend,'" she replied. Similarly, Wilson's future "boss" at Bryn Mawr, Martha Carey Thomas, did not learn the facts of life until she was 21 and had read about them in one of her father's medical books. Ellen, who had so many married girlfriends, might long have known. Sex and procreation, however, were certainly not topics of conversation between her and her fiancé, who must have wondered how much Ellen actually knew. On the other hand, there is nothing to suggest that Wilson had lost his virginity before he married at age 28. By the same token, one has the impression that he knew very well what "the marriage act" was all about.[93]

The closer the wedding date, the more harried Ellen became, trying to plan a Savannah wedding long distance from Manhattan. Her frugality did not prevent

First Love and a Wedding: Savannah and New York, 1883-1885   61

her from hiring a seamstress, not only for her wedding gown but for a whole new wardrobe (she was still, up until then, wearing mourning). As the wedding was going to be simple in the extreme, one wonders what the fuss was all about. There would be no wedding in church ("that sort of thing isn't 'my style'"[94]), Ellen preferring an intimate family wedding in the manse's ample parlor; no formal wedding invitations, no photographer, no music, singing or service, only the perfunctory exchange of wedding vows; no bridesmaids or best man, and unhappily, no reception, not even a wedding cake afterwards for the many guests and their children. Alas, this was not an unusual wedding scenario for nineteenth century Presbyterians.

* * *

On May 21, just a week before Ellen planned to depart for Savannah on a steamer, she wrote of her utter exhaustion after a long day. "I think I will take a dose of morphine to keep me awake (it would do it most effectually) and spend a whole night writing;"[95] for besides Wilson, she still owed letters to many people long neglected. Since Wilson's response to her letter included no allusion to the morphine, it must have been an innocent enough, over-the-counter remedy against sleepiness. Both Ellen and Wilson, moderate in their intake of food and drink, were far from being drug addicts.

Wilson had already left Baltimore for his sister's abode in South Carolina. Soon Ellen was packed and on her way, traveling alone as usual, for a memorable trip back to Savannah. It was a perfect voyage on a steamer from New York harbor, arriving in Savannah on June 1.

In keeping with her spartan wedding, Ellen's dress would be, not surprisingly, "...very simple...a plain long skirt, with no fussiness about it, looped up on one side to show a lace short skirt." Moreover, it did not occur to her to wear a veil. A kind person--perhaps a relative--gave her one. "...I was a little dubious about it, being very much afraid of looking too much 'dressed up.' But it was given to me, and I suppose I must wear it." It was, however, "immensely becoming."[96]

When the day of the wedding arrived, Wilson and his wedding party had already spent the previous night in a Savannah hotel. His parents, his married sister Anne Howe, her little son Wilson, and teenage brother Joe accompanied him. The manse's parlor, where the wedding would take place at seven o'clock that evening, was crammed with Axson clan. When the time came, Ellen's grandfather and Wilson's father took turns reading the marriage ceremony, the bride and groom looking so radiantly happy that all the women guests started crying. Immediately after the brief ceremony, the couple stood together to receive the congratulations of the guests, most of whom Wilson had never met. Since their honeymoon in Arden Park, North Carolina, was not due to begin until July 1, they had plenty of time to prolong the wedding; however, they were anxious to be off that evening, on the night train departing for Wilson's sister's home in Columbia, South Carolina. Wilson could hardly wait to have Ellen all to himself. Writing Ellen two weeks before the wedding, he had asked: "I may see you a *little* while by yourself--mayn't I--before the ceremony? I want to hear from your own sweet lips of your readiness for that act which is to crown our lives with a happiness such as we are only *waiting* for." He found the waiting harder than Ellen. "To be sure," responded Ellen, "you may see me, darling, before the ceremony--and hear from my lips of my readiness for that act which will make me *all yours* " though she wondered, "surely I cannot make a gift of myself more entire than it is already."[97]

Immediately after the marriage ceremony a ruckus began. Ellen's little brother Eddie had taken an instant dislike to his cousin Wilson Howe. The two started fighting like wildcats, right on the parlor floor. While Ellen was horrified, her new husband thought it was hilarious. After all, it was the only entertainment in an otherwise lackluster wedding.

The congratulations over, bride, groom and groom's family headed for the railroad station. Someone had alerted the train engineer that a bride would be boarding that evening. The wedding party arrived punctually. Ironically, no one recognized the bride (Ellen, without a veil, being her usual understated self), hence the train waited and waited, until someone tipped off the conductor that the bride and groom had long since boarded.[98]

The couple's mood can be guessed. After a nearly two year engagement, they were finally man and wife. Ellen's love for her husband was touching: it "dignified, enobled, *glorified* my life!" she wrote in a love letter shortly before her wedding. "...what new *meaning* it has given to life--to womanhood! It has made it seem an inexpressibly sweet and blessed thing to *be* a woman."[99] Ellen's love and devotion to Woodrow Wilson would dominate her life up to the day she died, twenty-nine years later.

ENDNOTES

[1]   Ellen Axson to Woodrow Wilson, Nov.13, 1884. Arthur S. Link, ed., *The Papers of Woodrow Wilson* (Princeton: Princeton University Press, 1966-1996), v.3:431. (henceforth: *PWW*)

[2]   Woodrow Wilson to Ellen A. Wilson, Feb.28, 1897. *PWW* 10:177.

[3] Eleanor Wilson McAdoo, ed., *The Priceless Gift: The Love Letters of Woodrow Wilson and Ellen Axson Wilson* (New York: McGraw-Hill, 1962), 4.

[4] Tedcastle interview, 1927. Ray Stannard Baker Papers, Library of Congress, Washington, D.C. (henceforth: RSB papers)

[5] McAdoo, ed., *The Priceless Gift*, 4; Wilson's reference to the Axson home as a "country parsonage" in a letter to his friend Richard Heath Dabney, *PWW* 3:27.

[6] Stockton Axson, *Brother Woodrow: A Memoir of Woodrow Wilson* ed. Arthur S. Link (Princeton: Princeton University Press, 1993), 90; Ellen Axson to Woodrow Wilson, Nov.12, 1883, *PWW* 2:525.

[7] Woodrow Wilson to Ellen Axson, Oct.11, 1883. *PWW* 2:468

[8] *Ibid.*, 469.

[9] McAdoo, ed., *The Priceless Gift*, 10.

[10] Woodrow Wilson to Robert Bridges, July 26, 1883, *PWW* 2:393; Woodrow Wilson to Ellen Axson, July 16, Oct. 18, 1883, *PWW* 2:389, 480-483.

[11] Axson, 34, 215.

[12] On Wilson's background, see John M. Cooper, *The Warrior and the Priest: Woodrow Wilson and Theodore Roosevelt* (Cambridge: Harvard University Press, 1983); John M. Mulder, *Woodrow Wilson: The Years of Preparation* (Princeton: Princeton University Press, 1978); Henry W. Bragdon, *Woodrow Wilson: the Academic Years* (Cambridge: Harvard University Press, 1967).

[13] McAdoo, ed., *The Priceless Gift*, 10; Woodrow Wilson to Ellen Axson, Oct.16, 1883. *PWW* 2:481.

[14] Axson, 52.

[15] Woodrow Wilson to Ellen Axson, July 4, 1883. *PWW* 2:378, 381-383.

[16] Ellen Axson to Woodrow Wilson, Oct.15, 1883. *PWW* 2:476.

[17] Ellen Axson to Woodrow Wilson, Oct.2, 1883, *PWW* 2:452; McAdoo, ed., *The Priceless Gift*, 13.

[18] McAdoo, ed., *The Priceless Gift*, 11.

[19] Woodrow Wilson to Ellen Axson, Jan.1, 1884.*PWW* 2:641; Margaret Axson Elliott, *My Aunt Louisa and Woodrow Wilson* (Chapel Hill: Univ. of North Carolina Press, 1944), 107.

[20] McAdoo, ed., *The Priceless Gift*, 42.

[21] Woodrow Wilson to Ellen Axson, Oct.14, 1883. *PWW* 2:474.

[22] Ellen Axson to Woodrow Wilson, Oct.2, 1883. *PWW* 2:451.

[23] Woodrow Wilson to Ellen Axson, Sept.27, 1883. *PWW* 2:444.

[24] Axson, 52; Ellen Axson to Woodrow Wilson, Nov.5, 1883. *PWW* 2:519.

[25] *Ibid.*, 518.

[26] Ellen Axson to Woodrow Wilson, Nov.5, 1883. *PWW* 2:519.

[27] Woodrow Wilson to Ellen Axson, Oct.18, 1883, *PWW* 2:483; Ellen Axson to Woodrow Wilson, Nov.27, 1883, *PWW* 2:553.

[28] *Savannah Revisited: History & Architecture* (Savannah: Beehive Press, 1994), 186.

[29] Ellen Wilson to Woodrow Wilson, Nov.28, 1884. *PWW* 2:554.

[30] Ellen Axson to Woodrow Wilson, March 24, 1884. *PWW* 3:97.

[31] Ellen Axson to Woodrow Wilson, Nov.29, 1883, *PWW* 2:555, Woodrow Wilson to Ellen Axson, Sept.22, 1883. *PWW* 2:437.

[32] Ellen Axson to Woodrow Wilson, March 10, 18, 1884. *PWW* 3:77,90.

[33] Ellen Axson to Woodrow Wilson, March 18, 1884. *PWW* 3:90.

[34] Woodrow Wilson to Ellen Axson, Dec.22, 1883. *PWW* 2:597,601.

[35] Ellen A. Wilson to Woodrow Wilson, Jan.31, 1894. *PWW* 8:446.

[36] McAdoo, ed., *The Priceless Gift*, 28.

[37] Admission record quoted in full in Edwin A. Weinstein, *Woodrow Wilson: A Medical and Psychological Biography* (Princeton: Princeton University Press, 1981), 67 (fn. 33).

[38] *Idem*; Ellen Axson to Woodrow Wilson, Feb.18, 1884, *PWW* 3:30.

[39] S. Edward Axson to Ellen Axson, Feb.16, 1884. Presidential Papers, Series 2. Woodrow Wilson Collection, Princeton University Firestone Library. (henceforth: *PP-2*).

[40] William Gibbs McAdoo, *Crowded Years: The Reminiscences of William G. McAdoo* (Boston: Houghton Miflin Co., 1931), 12, 25.

[41] Ellen Axson to Woodrow Wilson, Feb.6, 1884. *PWW* 3:6.

[42] Ellen Axson to Woodrow Wilson, Jan.28, March 10, 1884. *PWW* 2:664-665; 3:77.

[43] Ellen Axson to Woodrow Wilson, Feb.4, 1884. *PWW* 3:7.

[44] Woodrow Wilson to Ellen Axson, Feb.12, 1884. *PWW* 3:19.

[45] Ellen Axson to Woodrow Wilson, Feb.11, 1884. *PWW* 3:16.

[46] Ellen Axson to Woodrow Wilson, March 19, 31, 1884. *PWW* 3:93,117.

[47] Ellen Axson to Woodrow Wilson, Feb.4, May 6, 1884. *PWW* 3:7,162.

[48] Woodrow Wilson to Ellen Axson, May 8, 1884, *PWW* 3:166-167; Ellen Axson to Woodrow Wilson, May 6, 1884. *PWW* 3:162.

[49] Ellen Axson to Woodrow Wilson, March 31, July 14, 1884. *PWW* 3:106,246.

[50] Ellen Axson to Woodrow Wilson, March 31, 1884. *PWW* 3:106.

[51] Ellen Axson to Woodrow Wilson, June 2, 1884. *PWW* 3:201.

[52] Type-written letter of Ben Palmer to Ellen Axson, June 12, 1884. *PP-2*.

[53] Ellen Axson to Woodrow Wilson, June 2, 1884. *PWW* 3:201.

[54] Frances W. Saunders, *Ellen Axson Wilson: First Lady Between Two Worlds* (Chapel Hill & London: University of North Carolina Press, 1985), 48.

[55] Ellen Axson to Woodrow Wilson, June 5, 1884. *PWW* 3:206.

[56] Ellen Axson to Woodrow Wilson, July 14, 1884. *PWW* 3:244-245.

[57] Woodrow Wilson to Ellen Axson, July 15, 1884, *PWW* 3:248; Ellen Axson to Woodrow Wilson, Sept.8, 1884, *PWW* 3:322.

[58] Woodrow Wilson to Ellen Axson, Dec.8, 1883. *PWW* 2:571.

[59] Woodrow Wilson to Ellen Axson, June 26, 1884. *PWW* 3:217-218; McAdoo, ed., *The Priceless Gift*, 72.

[60] Ellen Axson to Woodrow Wilson, April 3, 1885. *PWW* 4:448.

[61] Ellen Axson to Woodrow Wilson, June 2, 1884, March 28, 1885. *PWW* 3:201, 4:429.

[62] Woodrow Wilson to Ellen Axson, March 6, 1885. *PWW* 4:339.

[63] Woodrow Wilson to Ellen Axson, March 1, 1885. *PWW* 4:316.

[64] Woodrow Wilson to Ellen Axson, March 1, May 20, 1885. *PWW* 4:317,609.

[65] Woodrow Wilson to Ellen Axson, March 1, 1885. *PWW* 4:318.

[66] Ellen Axson to Woodrow Wilson, March 28, 1885. *PWW* 4:429.

[67] Marchal Landgren, *Years of Art: The Story of the Art Students League of New York* (New York: McBride & Co., 1940), 18-19, 28; see also the more recent work by Raymond J. Steiner, *The Art Students League of New York: A History* (Saugerties, NY: CSS Publications, 1999), chapter 1.

[68] Quoted in Steiner, 53.

[69] Woodrow Wilson to Ellen Axson, Oct.4, 1884. *PWW* 3:330.

[70] Ellen Axson to Woodrow Wilson, Oct.11, 1884. *PWW* 3:357-358.

[71] Ellen Axson to Woodrow Wilson, Nov.3,4, 1884. *PWW* 3:399-400.

[72] Ellen Axson to Woodrow Wilson, March 10, 1885. *PWW* 4:350.

[73] Ellen Axson to Woodrow Wilson, Oct.6, 1884. *PWW* 3:336.

[74] Ellen Axson to Woodrow Wilson, Nov.29, Dec.3, 1884, Jan. 17, 1885. *PWW* 3:497,510, 618.

First Love and a Wedding: Savannah and New York, 1883-1885   65

[75] Ellen Axson to Woodrow Wilson, Nov.5, 1884. *PWW* 3:407.

[76] Ellen Axson to Woodrow Wilson, Nov.13, 1884, Feb.19, 1885. *PWW* 3:434-435;4:270.

[77] Mary Hoyt interview, Oct.1926. RSB papers.

[78] Woodrow Wilson to Ellen Axson, Oct.30, 1884, *PWW* 3:388; Harper quoted in Landgren, 40.

[79] Ellen Axson to Woodrow Wilson, March 15, 1885. *PWW* 4:369-370.

[80] Ellen Axson to Woodrow Wilson, Dec.7, 1884, *PWW* 3:523-524; Woodrow Wilson to Ellen Axson, Dec.11, 1884, *PWW* 3:532.

[81] Woodrow Wilson to Ellen Axson, Dec.21, 1884. *PWW* 3:567.

[82] Ellen Axson to Woodrow Wilson, March 28, 1885. *PWW* 4:429.

[83] McAdoo, ed. *The Priceless Gift*, 147.

[84] Ellen Axson to Woodrow Wilson, Feb.1, 6, 8, 1885, *PWW* 4:210-212, 219-220, 226; Woodrow Wilson to Ellen Axson, Jan. 24, Feb.10, 1885, *PWW* 4:4-5,233,242.

[85] Ellen Axson to Woodrow Wilson, Feb.8, 1885, *PWW* 4:225; Axson, 104.

[86] Ellen Axson to Woodrow Wilson, Feb.10,27, March 9, 1885, *PWW* 4:234,306,347.

[87] Ellen Axson to Woodrow Wilson, March 10, 28, 1885, *PWW* 4:350,429.

[88] Ellen Axson to Woodrow Wilson, Nov. 15, 16, 1884. *PWW* 3:436, 442.

[89] Ellen Axson to Woodrow Wilson, May 18, 1885. *PWW* 4:604; McAdoo, ed., *The Priceless Gift*, 123.

[90] Antoinette Farnsworth to Ellen A. Wilson, Nov.30, 1885. *PP*-2.

[91] Ellen Axson to Woodrow Wilson, March 29, 1885. *PWW* 4:434.

[92] Woodrow Wilson to Ellen Axson, March 19, 1885. *PWW* 4:385.

[93] Ellen Axson to Woodrow Wilson, April 13, 1885, *PWW* 4:485; Woodrow Wilson to Ellen Axson, April 15, 1885, *PWW* 4:488; R.W.B. Lewis, *Edith Wharton: A Biography* (New York: Fromm International, 1985), 53; Leila J. Rupp, "'Imagine My Surprise:' Women's Relationships in Historical Perspective" in *Women and Health in America* (1984), 91.

[94] Ellen Axson to Woodrow Wilson, June 6, 1885. *PWW* 4:689.

[95] Ellen Axson to Woodrow Wilson, May 21, 1885. *PWW* 4:614.

[96] Ellen Axson to Woodrow Wilson, June 6, June 10, 1885. *PWW* 4:689,700-701.

[97] Woodrow Wilson to Ellen Axson, June 10, 1885, *PWW* 4:703; Ellen Axson to Woodrow Wilson, June 12, 1885, *PWW* 4:706.

[98] Mary Hoyt interview. Oct., 1926. RSB papers.

[99] Ellen Axson to Woodrow Wilson, June 7, 1885. *PWW* 4:690.

Chapter 3

YOUNG WIFE AND MOTHER, 1885-1890

"...I am more affected by your opinions than by those of anybody else."[1]
Woodrow Wilson to Ellen, 1884

"Under Mrs. Wilson's gentleness, there was inflexible steel."[2]
Stockton Axson

Just as Wilson had picked the day of the wedding, he also arranged the honeymoon. "...sweetheart," he wrote Ellen from Baltimore in May, "we shall be due at Arden Park on the 1st of July." Located ten miles south of "horrid" Asheville, North Carolina, where he first proposed to Ellen, Arden Park was a secluded, densely-wooded eden nestled in the mountains, popular with vacationers, including Wilson's parents. Because he was partial to spacious living quarters, Wilson reserved not one room but at least two in an eight-room cottage, enshrouded in a fragrant pine forest. Ellen would have agreed to any honeymoon or to no honeymoon; according to Eleanor McAdoo, she liked Arden Park in part because it was cheap: "Woodrow had only five hundred dollars to get married on," reminds McAdoo, stressing her parents' slender means. Even in the likelihood that Ellen's private annuity ended upon her marriage to Wilson, $500, in 1885, was at least double what a live-in servant would earn in a year.[3]

Their married life commenced at the pleasant, rose-bedecked cottage of Wilson's sister Anne, a doctor's wife, in Columbia, South Carolina. By the time the couple arrived at Arden Park several days later, they surely had consummated their marriage.

Even before they were engaged, Wilson was teasing Ellen about her first impression of him--as "undemonstrative." Their engagement in fact unleashed a frenzy of passionate feeling on Wilson's part, who often mentioned how "frightened" he was at the "intensity of my love for you." A week after his engagement he wrote her of a dream with obvious erotic overtones: "You might be scandalized by the number of kisses and caresses to which you submitted in that dream-meeting with your lover."[4] But he knew that Ellen would not be scandalized.

Though more reticent than he to express her physical desire for him, it was plain from Wilson's numerous references that Ellen's intensity matched his. "You did not tell me till just the other day, precious," wrote Wilson, "that you are fond of being *petted.* You had several times said, in Rome and in Wilmington last summer, that you liked me to kiss and caress you." For Wilson's part, "you can *never* give me as many kisses as I want!" Almost a year after their marriage, Wilson remarked: "Won't you be afraid to see me (three weeks from next Saturday) since you must know that I'll be so hungry for the *full* privileges of love-making that I'll be ready to eat you up," revealing an Ellen who was probably far from frigid. After a two-year courtship and engagement, there is little doubt that the newlyweds' pent-up passion for each other found full expression during their honeymoon. The timing was also "right:" Ellen became pregnant several weeks after her wedding.[5]

Eleanor McAdoo described her parents' honeymoon in Arden Park as "idyllic," and lasting two weeks. In fact, for the first two weeks, constant rain battered their honeymoon cottage, and with the rain, came the cold, as well as ill-health. Wilson and Ellen, worn down almost to skeletons--on the eve of her wedding Ellen complained of dress patterns "for a girl of fifteen, being too large for me!"--arrived exhausted from weeks of feverish preparation, and hundreds of miles of travel. Wilson's mother wrote a concerned letter, commiserating with them for having to be "shut up by rain in the mountains...The idea of your studying German! That sounds very unromantic..." But she hoped that "you will both be able to gain flesh in the mountains. Do try to get well, dear."[6] Ellen was boning up on the German language to assist her husband with his second book, *The State.*

When the weather finally cleared, the newlyweds decided to prolong their stay four more weeks. They hiked all day in the deep woods (though in that era they called it "walking") and reveled in each other's company. "'We are out of doors most of the time," wrote Ellen to her cousin Mary Hoyt, "'walking together and reading unless I coerce him into singing, for he has a beautiful voice.'"[7] Ellen could not even carry a tune.

Now a forgotten past-time, "reading" meant taking turns reading aloud, a pleasurable entertainment in that pre-electronic era. Ellen and her girlfriend Beth had read George Eliot's *Middlemarch* to each other, pausing now and then to squeal in excitement; Ellen's brother Stockton read aloud Lewis Carroll's *Through the Looking Glass* in snatches, when the two of them were in the throes of moving out of their home in Rome; in the two weeks Ellen and Wilson spent in Wilmington, they took turns reading aloud his favorite novel, R.D. Blackmore's *Lorna Doone*. For their anticipated honeymoon, they would not have forgotten to pack their treasured books. Wilson again read more of his favorite Bagehot to Ellen, rather deep intellectual fare, but they also took turns reading Dicken's *Martin Chuzzlewit*. Noticeably absent on Ellen's part, however, was any mention of sketching, or any other artistic pursuit, during the whole of that summer.

Whether Wilson managed to "gain flesh" during his six-week honeymoon is unknown; Ellen, one month pregnant when they left Arden Park, must have. They left their honeymoon paradise for nearby, dinghy Morganton, to pay a long visit to Ellen's friend Beth Erwin. Holed up in the remote outskirts of Morganton with her young children and uncompanionable spouse, perennially pregnant Beth was still Ellen's intimate friend. Ellen had been appalled at Beth's marriage to a clergyman who shared none of Beth's interests and who, as it turned out, made her life miserable. It was the last time Ellen laid eyes on her beloved girlfriend, who died young, leaving her six children in the care of a negligent father.

* * *

If their honeymoon gave rise to fantasies of what their married life would be like--"peaceful and serene" on Ellen's part--while Wilson envisioned having Ellen at his side, painting, reading poetry aloud, doing research for him--the reality was turning out differently. Severe morning sickness, lasting all day, left Ellen feeling a wreck all winter long. Wilson, anxious and fearful, was left to nurse Ellen as though she were an invalid. Their rented rooms in Mrs. Wildgoss' boarding house in Haverford, into which they moved in mid-September, proved unsatisfactory, and were soon abandoned for a tiny, college-owned cottage on Bryn Mawr's campus. Wilson found teaching history (or any subject) at a woman's college distasteful, and his "boss," Dean Martha Carey Thomas, disagreeable. Nonetheless, despite life's tribulations, Ellen echoed her husband's feelings when she referred to "this beautiful, blissful year," their first year of married life.[8]

Bryn Mawr, too small to qualify as a village, lay but a few miles from the heavily-Quaker enclave of Haverford, a suburb of Philadelphia, located a mere ten miles away. Although a commuter rail connected Haverford to Philadelphia (the "main line," the first commuter rail in the country), in the 1880's, Bryn Mawr was an isolated, peaceful nook. It enchanted the two southerners, Ellen and her husband, who, by the same token, would probably have found a comparable setting in the south quite intolerable.

Quakers, who were fast abandoning their quaint garb and speech, established and ran the new college for women. In fact, Wilson's superior at the college (the same age as himself), Dean Thomas, daughter of middle class Quakers, was worldly, sophisticated, and at 27, a Ph.D.-educated freethinker, and ardent feminist. At 21, Thomas had referred to "marriage, love, all" as "useless and false sentiments," and in old age, to babies as "disabilities." Nor would Thomas'views ever mellow: on the eve of her death in 1935, along with her championing the radical equality of the sexes (she was an early supporter of the Equal Rights Amendment), she had embraced racist Margaret Sanger's birth control and population control theories.[9]

In short, Thomas represented just about everything that Ellen and Wilson disliked about the "new woman." Alas, Thomas was not even pretty, another handicap in Wilson's eyes; nor did it help that she wore her hair severely parted in the middle (in contrast to Ellen, with her head of soft curls), and looked older than her years.

It is no wonder that Wilson, who once wrote Ellen of the "chilled, scandalized feeling that always comes over me when I see and hear women speak in public," found Thomas too "aggressive" and did not admire her; on Ellen's part, she found it "absurd" and "unnatural" for him, probably for any man, to have to answer to a woman (unless it was his mother): "...the idea of any *woman* assuming airs of superiority over *you*," she'd written her fiancé.[10] Yet Bryn Mawr College throve under Thomas' capable leadership. She in turn admired Wilson and, as one of America's foremost educators, attended his inauguration (Wilson had invited her) as president of Princeton in 1902.

After perusing the new college's catalogue, Ellen had been duly impressed: "Truly they have a masculine standard 'sure enough,'" and conceded, "I couldn't get in," an indirect admission of Rome Female College's slipshod standards.[11] Even so, Wilson disliked the college; the fact that it was so new and so small--only two buildings, 42 students and half a dozen faculty members--did not help matters.

The hospitable Wilsons never seemed to invite students to their home, even after they moved into a roomy house, as they often would do in Princeton. It must have unnerved the two of them to see women students living on their own, governing themselves, and allowed to smoke in public, right on campus. A class photograph of 1886, taken outdoors, even revealed students wearing short hair--

Young Wife and Mother, 1885-1890   71

and many not bothering to wear a hat at all (including Dean Thomas), a clear affront to etiquette. While Ellen enjoyed "mothering" male students at Princeton, Bryn Mawr students were an entirely different breed.

By the end of his second academic year at Bryn Mawr, Wilson had had enough. "When I think of you, my little wife, I love this 'college for women,' because *you* are a woman; but when I think only of myself, I hate the place very cordially." Shortly before their marriage, Wilson confessed, "Had I had independent means of support, even of the most modest proportions, I should doubtless have sought an entrance into politics...I have a strong instinct of leadership, an unmistakably oratorical temperament, and the keenest possible delight in affairs." Six months after moving to Bryn Mawr, Ellen and her husband, according to Eleanor McAdoo, were weighing the pros and cons of his earning a Ph.D. degree, which might improve his career chances. Before they married, Ellen feared that getting a doctorate would be a strain on his health; now, she encouraged him and fed his ambition.[12]

* * *

Writing from Baltimore to his fiancée in Manhattan, Wilson had insisted that they rent not one room but two in Bryn Mawr, "...it would be unhealthful, as well as uncomfortable and inconvenient, to 'live' and sleep in the same room," though countless Americans did just that. "We must have a work room," he continued, "and it must be *your* shop as well as mine," knowing that Ellen felt comfortable painting and sketching with people about her;[13] in fact, Ellen liked having close friends and family around her at all times.

As letters on the subjects of housing and income flew back and forth between them that spring of 1885, it was clear that Ellen intended to work after her marriage: "My only *comforting* thought is that I too can work, and will, if I can find the work to do,"[14] another indication that her annuity would cease after her marriage. Wilson had referred to Bryn Mawr as an "outrageously expensive place to live": two furnished rooms averaged, with board, around twenty dollars a week for a couple. On Wilson's expected salary of $1500, that meant an outlay of close to a thousand dollars a year on room and board. However, considering that they did without servants and had few other domestic expenses, it should have left them enough for small luxuries, even savings (Wilson was earning more than Ellen's father did only two years earlier, who supported children as well as servants).

Not until Wilson became U.S. president, however, did he and Ellen ever feel that they had enough money, and in all those years they saved little. While Ellen was perennially obsessed with economizing, they actually spent liberally--on themselves, on relatives, friends, and on charity.

In the first two years of their three years at Bryn Mawr, Ellen was pregnant most of the time and far too unwell to work, even paint. When she did feel well, her free time was devoted to helping her husband with his work. After all, she had an abundance of leisure time. Faculty members choosing to live in the tiny college cottages (dubbed "the Betweenery)," where Ellen and Wilson lived for two years, were not expected to clean their abodes or cook. All meals were taken in common in an on-campus dining room. Hence, besides laboriously translating the dull German sources Wilson needed for his second book, Ellen also helped him prepare his class lectures.

When Ellen informed her brother Stockton and her Uncle Randolph in Savannah--that she had enrolled that spring in cooking classes at Mrs. Rorer's famous Philadelphia Cooking School--"her uncle's astonishment knew no bounds."[15] Ellen, after all, had never had to cook a meal in her life, and never showed an interest in cooking (in contrast to sewing). Mrs. Sarah T. Rorer, author of a best-selling cook book in 1886, and future author of a dozen more cook books and manuals, trained middle-class women to cook well and to manage their cooks, a mission seemingly at odds with that of Dean Martha Carey Thomas. But Rorer herself was a self-made woman (who, moreover, laid the foundation of modern dietetics), though with a less extreme agenda.

Throughout her marriage, Ellen never needed to cook. Even on a modest professor's income, she was freed of household drudgery. Traveling to Philadelphia twice a week for her cooking classes, on the other hand, might have relieved her from the monotony of life in tiny Bryn Mawr, although she and Wilson enjoyed the area they lived in. Besides, she did acquire excellent cooking skills, according to her daughter Eleanor.

When her confinement drew near, Ellen was seriously at odds with her husband over where the baby would be born. Wilson could not persuade her to have the baby at home in Bryn Mawr. She would not have a child of hers, she told him, born north of the Mason-Dixon line. She would go "home" to Georgia for her lying-in, and have the baby at her Aunt Louisa's in Gainesville.

As she later admitted to her daughters, Ellen actually lied to her husband. She really had not cared where the baby was born, but she cared about her husband-- facing the burden of Ph.D. exams at Hopkins that spring--desiring to spare him the distractions and worry of childbirth, as well as the expense. Ellen reasoned that having her baby in Gainesville would be cheaper than at home. But what with the expense of train travel for her, and later for her husband who would fetch her and the baby home, and the allowance (always generous) he was committed to

Young Wife and Mother, 1885-1890

sending her for the weeks she spent in Georgia, it would in fact have been less expensive to have stayed in Bryn Mawr. Defeated, Wilson guiltily accompanied a visibly-pregnant Ellen to Washington, D.C. in late April, two weeks before the baby was due. There she transferred to the train for her long journey to Gainesville; unbeknown to Ellen or her husband, she was dangerously close to giving birth, alone, on a grimy southern train.

* * *

Ellen, who always kept her private fears from her husband (unlike Wilson, who needed her reassurance), would never have admitted her fear of facing childbirth. But according to Eleanor McAdoo, her fright was real: not just about the impending birth, but its aftermath. Would she succumb to childbed fever like her mother? Would she, like so many southern women of her acquaintance, end up a lifelong invalid, confined all day to a sofa, unable (or unwilling) to minister to husband and child?

Just hours after her arrival in Gainesville, Ellen went into labor. A Doctor Bailey, as well as her capable Aunt Louisa--for whom nature was an open book-- were at her side when Margaret Woodrow Wilson saw the light of day the following morning of April 16, little knowing, or caring, that she was named after her mother's own mother. Though the birth was two weeks early, it had been quick and unproblematic for mother and child, though the mother was not a little disappointed that Margaret--was not a Woodrow, Jr. This disappointment was far less keen than later--when daughters 2 and 3--appeared on the scene.

"I never saw any lady bear the pangs of labor so heroically as the dear child did," wrote her Aunt Louisa to Wilson immediately after the birth. "She did not let a groan escape her and would smile sweetly between the pains and kiss me affectionately." Such stoicism touched Wilson to the quick. "Oh, my darling, my darling," he began writing Ellen after receiving Louisa's note, ending with "Oh, I love you, I love you, I love you--and I love the baby almost as much as you..." From then on until his arrival in Gainesville eight weeks later, each of their letters exuded passionate love. Once again he sent Ellen a box full of stamped, addressed envelopes for her daily correspondence.[16]

Ellen's birthing and recovery were typical for southern women who could afford doctors. While Aunt Louisa was at Ellen's side, Louisa's women friends, who barely knew Ellen, gathered downstairs, patiently waiting until the birth was over. Men seemed entirely absent. Nor were they invited up to see the new mother and newborn. Ellen's four-and-a-half year old sister Margaret, who was convinced that Ellen was her mother, jealously slapped her infant niece when she was brought in to see her, causing Ellen to burst into tears.[17]

Unlike today, Ellen leisurely recovered from childbirth. Writing Wilson on the tenth day after giving birth, "I can't walk or stand yet, that is I can't take more than two or three steps,--but I can sit two hours or more without fatigue..." Moreover, she avoided going outdoors for at least another month. When one of her eyelids became slightly infected, Aunt Louisa frightened her with tales of women going blind after giving birth, wrote Ellen. So she took care to avoid reading, but not scribbling letters. Altogether it must have been a thoroughly boring recovery, mitigated only by the excitement of her new baby and the expected coming of her husband in June. Gainesville, wrote Ellen after her second confinement, was "a sordid little country town" and "a wretchedly dull place," which she never would have said about Bryn Mawr.[18]

"I haven't any pains or disorders of any sort; except the inevitable trouble with my breasts--raw and tender nipples," wrote Ellen to her husband, two weeks after giving birth. "Baby's meals involve a not very mild form of torture for me." She and Wilson were not at all reticent about discussing intimate physical problems. Her sore breasts, she continued, "will toughen...Then I have the very welcome trouble of an excessive flow of milk--that is more than baby can manage yet--so that they have to be rubbed & 'drawn' & fussed with generally," she admitted frankly.[19] She also spent time sketching her newborn.

Ellen meanwhile felt an intense longing for her deceased mother, in the same way that her own daughter Jessie would feel for her, in 1915, after giving birth to her first child. Ellen's thoughts turned increasingly to Rome, 90 miles away, which she had not laid eyes on for two years. Word reached Gainesville in early May of horrific flooding in Rome, "a dreadful calamity," Ellen wrote Wilson. Her Uncle Will's family had sustained serious losses. The Axson homestead in Rome was still unsold. She learned that her parents' books, which she and Stockton had so laboriously packed, were water-damaged beyond repair. "Am sorry we must go to Rome, but it seems necessary to spend a few days there to see about the books and things; to gather up the fragments that remain."[20] And to visit her parents' graves in Rome with her newborn.

By the time Wilson arrived in Gainesville in the second week of June, Ellen was up and out, in blooming health, having remained indoors for longer than a month, at the insistence of her cautious Aunt Louisa. Ellen in fact was determined to have another child as soon as possible, which dismayed her husband, who knew how much suffering her pregnancy had cost her. She thought his fears were absurd. She wrote before he arrived: "If I were too exquisite a creature to be a wife and mother, I would have died in the budding beauty of young maidenhood

(!) and been laid away 'under the violets'..." Besides, "it is a great thing to be the wife of such a man!" as her husband. To serve him well (and present him with a son) was her ambition. She wrote,

> You don't know how I *glory* in your splendid gifts, your noble, beautiful character, that rare charm of manner and "presence."....how much greater is my delight in your triumphs than it could ever have been in any little success of my own.[21]

Wilson was no less worshipful of his wife. He had just completed his Ph.D. exams and wrote Ellen ecstatically, "You are the centre of my life and no fulness of that life can find expression but in love for you! That's the delight of it all! I won the degree *for you*. I don't care for it for myself."[22]

* * *

Delighted to be parents, Ellen and Wilson departed Gainesville with their baby for Rome and other southern points in what would be a leisurely summer, one of the most important perquisites of the teaching profession, after all. Wilson's academic teaching positions, even at tiny, raw-boned Bryn Mawr, afforded him and his family a leisurely, genteel way of life, in stark contrast to the lifestyle of most of their fellow Americans, then as well as now; college teaching, even at Bryn Mawr, also paid more than preaching. Certainly Ellen and Wilson did not appear to be hurting for money that summer. The newly-minted Dr. Wilson found time, even with the distractions of a new baby and the fierce southern heat, to work on *The State*, a profound study of the origins and evolution of government.

After surveying the flood's ravages in Rome, the Wilsons decided to keep renting the still intact Axson home (for $250 a year). The happy reunion with old Roman friends and relatives was overladen with sadness: Ellen's middle-aged uncle, Robert Axson, a Rome pharmacist, had recently committed suicide after being in declining health for some time. From Rome they headed north to the new home of Wilson's parents in Clarksville, Tennessee. There Ellen and baby Margaret remained, while her husband headed out to Little Rock, Arkansas, for an overdue visit to his older sister--the brilliant Marion Wilson Kennedy--wife of a tubercular clergyman. Together with four young children, the Kennedy family was eking out a living in their parsonage on only $1000 a year, a third less than Ellen and Wilson had to live on. Wilson promptly fell ill in Little Rock;

meanwhile, Ellen wrote that the temperature in Clarksville was hovering in the nineties--at night.[23]

By early September, the family was back in their cool, comfortable two-room cottage in Bryn Mawr. One would have thought that, with little to do except assist her husband in his studies, Ellen could look after Margaret full-time. Instead, she hired a part-time nurse to free her from the rigors of 19th century child care. Nor did she bother sewing all of her baby's clothes. Writing her husband from Gainesville during her second confinement, Ellen referred to the "Wanamaker's bill for the baby's shirts," Wanamaker's being the most important department store in Philadelphia.[24] Moreover, husband and wife were increasingly dissatisfied with life in their tiny cottage.

Wilson, despite telling Ellen that his doctorate meant little to him, felt it stoking his ambition. The thoughts of this future enemy of the German state turned to the idea of studying in, of all places, Berlin. Was this a sign of some subtle rivalry with Dean Thomas, who had earned her prestigious doctorate from the University of Leipzig? Wilson could not look forward to a leave of absence on salary, but the prestige of studying abroad, in those days, far exceeded what it does nowadays (a friend of Wilson's even went to Germany for his Ph.D.--in English) and could advance his career. The only money which the Wilsons had to finance such an expensive venture--came from Ellen. She volunteered to use money from her inheritance (though this was not the house in Rome) for their year (or two) abroad. Aside from the excitement of going to Europe and improving her German, Ellen had little to gain from uprooting herself for at least a year, baby in tow, far from friends and relatives, and Wilson was duly appreciative of her sacrifice.

Another pregnancy deferred their, or rather, Wilson's German fantasy; part of their trip money went instead to purchase furniture for the eleven-room house they intended to rent that spring.[25] Years later, in all of their European travels, either alone, together, or with their children, neither Ellen nor Wilson ever managed to set foot in Germany.

* * *

Ellen loved children, and was more than ready to be a mother. Writing her fiancé from Savannah back in 1884, she made the unusual observation that Savannah's greatest beauty was its children. Her volunteer work among poor black youngsters in Manhattan demonstrated that race was no barrier to her love of children. Mothering her siblings doubtless prepared her for her new maternal role. With the prospect of living in a large house before her, Ellen now insisted on having her eleven-year old brother Eddie live with them. And why not her cousin Mary Hoyt from Rome? Though referring to herself as "without much education," Mary Eloise Hoyt, a teacher in Rome's new public school system, yearned to study at Bryn Mawr, but could ill afford to pay room and board. Ellen generously invited her to live with them if she passed the college's grueling entrance exams.[26] It was a testament to Ellen's broad-mindedness that, despite her reservations about Bryn Mawr and its students--neither she nor Wilson recommended the college to their own daughters--she offered a struggling cousin a way of studying there. An 1890's photo of Mary Hoyt, who graduated from Bryn Mawr and never married, revealed a woman of striking good looks--and wearing short-cropped hair.

The Woodrow Wilsons' 11-room rental was a former Baptist parsonage that stood on Gulph Road, which ran behind the college's only two buildings. It was surrounded by dense woods, a serene haven that offered the privacy both Ellen and Wilson craved. Eleanor McAdoo, as usual, emphasized that her parents chose the house because the rent was cheap, since "it was an old house badly in need of repairs." Apparently this made no impression on Wilson's parents. "...whatever can you want with *eleven* rooms!" exclaimed Wilson's mother Janet. "Why we have only *six*--and have abundance of room!" Wilson's parents never understood their son and daughter-in-law's proclivity for ever-more spacious living.[27]

Ellen and her husband relished not only spacious--but eventually, gracious living as well. Their household, which in upcoming years would include an ever-growing number of hired help, was an expansive one, and they liked it that way, too. Yet neither one ever gave up the notion that their lifestyle--even after they moved into their luxurious new home in Princeton--was anything other than "plain" and "simple," to use their favorite terms.

One reason for indulging in the luxury of a commodious house of their own (albeit rented) was Wilson's salary raise. His new, 3-year contract with the college stipulated an annual salary of $2000, a generous increase of 25% over his previous salary, although he had only been teaching for two years. In addition, he was given permission to absent himself from the college every spring semester, to deliver a six-week course of lectures at his alma mater, Johns Hopkins, for which he also would be paid; moreover, regular royalties from Wilson's first book were finally augmenting the family income. Although their income mushroomed, and by middle class standards was comfortable, it was far from enough. Wrote Ellen to her husband on the eve of their moving into their rented house, "...if we get hard up this month we can borrow from *Eddie* instead of some one else,"--referring to her little brother's annuity (from their father's inheritance) of approximately $200. Five months later, Wilson was borrowing money from his father.[28]

Before they took possession of their new home, Ellen went south once again (not alone this time, but with her husband) to have her new baby, with little Margaret in tow. It is unfathomable why she insisted on giving birth in Georgia once again, at the height of malaria season. Unlike the year before, Wilson was not facing Ph.D. exams, and Ellen, after all, had no love for Gainesville. But her family was there--her two brothers and her little sister Margaret--whose welfare concerned her deeply. She ended up nursing Stockton, in Gainesville for the summer, through a severe bout of malaria; and she returned to Bryn Mawr with Eddie, who regarded her as his mother. Aunt Louisa still clung to little Margaret, who was like her own child.

This time Ellen took no chances, arriving in Gainesville in early July, six weeks before the baby was due, and remaining there until mid-October. Though she badly wanted her husband with her, she pressured him to return to Bryn Mawr for his own good. She knew that Bryn Mawr's civilized surroundings and nearness to major libraries were more conducive to intellectual work than backwater Georgia.

To Ellen, her unborn child was the "little fellow;" that is, until, on a grueling hot day in late August, he once more turned out to be a she. Jessie Woodrow Wilson, named after Wilson's mother Janet Woodrow (who in turn was nicknamed "Jessie"), would grow up to be a devastating blond beauty, and their most gifted child.

This time Wilson returned to Gainesville in time for the birth, but returned north during Ellen's leisurely, six-week recovery. Although Ellen's delivery was unproblematic and she recovered swiftly, she was no longer eager for another baby. Her second pregnancy had made her more ill than the first, and even she referred to it as a "sickness."

As long as Ellen was in Gainesville, Wilson could not bear living all alone in their new rental. He went to the trouble of sub-letting it for the summer, while he secured a boarding house room at $10 a week, canceling any profit he and Ellen might have derived from the sublet. Ellen, meanwhile, who hired a full-time nurse to look after one-year old Margaret, was living part of the time in a boarding house in Gainesville ("a dinghy boarding house" which was, moreover, "full of intensely commonplace people," and hence "much worse than no people at all..."[29]), perhaps because her Aunt Louisa was short of space due to a son's upcoming wedding. Train fares, boarding house expenses, and the sordidness of Gainesville might partly explain why Ellen would have her last child at home, cheaply and conveniently.

* * *

By mid-October, the Woodrow Wilsons, together with Eddie Axson and Mary Hoyt ("Cousin Mary"), were at last gathered in their 11-room Gulph Road house in Bryn Mawr. Wilson's classes usually let out by afternoon, freeing him to go home and "stoke the furnace, pump water from the well with a hand pump and clean the yard," according to Eleanor McAdoo.[30] Ellen could not do without a nurse for the babies, and a cook, who also pitched in to do housework.

Ellen was intensely happy in her role as *mater familias*. Besides her own babies, her brother Eddie and "Cousin Mary"--Stockton and Wilson's young brother Josie would also join them for the summer--she and Wilson welcomed visitors with warm southern hospitality. Her marriage, moreover, was a partnership in which she and Wilson shared in decision-making. For his part Wilson was deeply dependent on his wife. "He needed her admiration, as a man needs water in a desert," noted Eleanor.[31]

Despite signing a new 3-year contract, Wilson was no happier at the college. "Lecturing to young women of the present generation on the history and principles of politics," he noted in his diary, "is about as appropriate and profitable as would be lecturing to stone-masons on the evolution of fashion in dress." He admitted, however, that the general "absenteesim of mind" on the part of his students might be due to "undergraduateism, not all to femininity." He and Ellen spent the fall and upcoming spring of 1888 casting their net for a better position. For awhile, the University of Michigan looked promising. "Just think!--they have never filled that vacancy yet;" wrote Ellen to her absent husband in April. "[They] have absolutely *no one*--not even an 'instructor' in political science."[32]

The Woodrow Wilsons planned to defer a summer vacation until they knew what lay ahead for them. Instead, Wilson's brother Josie and Ellen's brother Stockton, both 21, traveled to Bryn Mawr to spend their vacations in the ample, welcoming household. Decades later, Stockton Axson vividly recalled that summer of '88. He and Wilson, both great walkers and intimate friends, despite their age difference, enjoyed hiking the ten miles to Philadelphia and back. One night, Wilson, Stockton and Josie grabbed their guns and ran outdoors, convinced that they heard an intruder. Yet they saw no one. "Several nights we three men stayed on a back porch for several hours" and "hid behind a huge water cask...", Stockton recalled. Then "one night we thought we heard him; and Mr. Wilson fired and then was terribly anxious lest he might by chance have hit somebody." They never found the culprit, but learned afterwards that he was some "maniac" escaped from the local "insane asylum."[33]

The climax of that uneventful summer was Wilson's appointment as professor and "Chair of History and Political Economy" at Wesleyan University in

Middletown, Connecticut. He was offered a salary of $2500, or 20% higher than he was currently earning at Bryn Mawr. Technically co-ed as of 1868, only a sprinkling of women attended Wesleyan, which had a student enrollment of 215.

Wilson gratefully tendered his resignation from his woman's college on June 29, and wormed his way out of his 3-year contract. The rest of the summer would be a frenzy of packing, as well as anxiety over where they would live in Middletown, no easy task done from a distance of over two hundred miles. Resigned to living temporarily in a boarding house with the whole family, at last Wilson heard of a commodious house rental, owned by a preacher and his wife. On August 30, Wilson was able to inform his publisher that: "My address after Sept. 1st will be *Middletown, Conn.*" in a house on High Street, overlooking the Connecticut River.

Relieved that they would be moving into a house of their own, Ellen and Wilson still abhored moving. It fell particularly hard on Ellen. Each move was a wrenching pulling-up of roots, of endless packing (she always put herself in charge of hiring the movers and organizing the move) and the misery of re-locating and unpacking. This would be their third move in three years of marriage, and they had enjoyed the Philadelphia area. In all their married life, they never lived longer than eight years in any one place. But since the moves were for the sake of her husband's career, Ellen never once complained.

* * *

Compared to Bryn Mawr, Middletown definitely was remote. Perhaps because it lay in the center of the state, Middletown was aptly named; incorporated as a town in 1651, it was ancient compared to Bryn Mawr, or even Rome. Middletown had a public school system in place, including a high school, long before the Civil War, and a free library was established in 1875. Pious Methodists had established Wesleyan College in 1831 (a university by the time Wilson taught there), the town's only noteworthy institution.

Wilson, unlike Ellen, felt typical Presbyterian disdain for Methodists ("Baptists who can read"), and in a short time, felt a similar disdain for the quality of its undergraduates, even though they were, at long last, men. Still, to be teaching men--and coaching their football team--was its own reward to Wilson. Despite the mediocre quality of its student body and Wesleyan's humble reputation, teaching at a nominally co-ed, overwhelmingly male university still was more prestigious--especially if one was chair of a department--than in a woman's school.

Young Wife and Mother, 1885-1890

Middletown was distant from big city libraries, a handicap to someone like Wilson who was still working on his seminal work, *The State*, and regularly churning out articles and book reviews. Middletown was also too far from Baltimore to allow Wilson to return home on weekends when he was teaching there six weeks a year (a dispensation which Wesleyan had generously granted him), a hardship for both Ellen and Wilson; and the wild New England winters bore down hard on Ellen's soft southern frame. Yet they were happy in Middletown, with its leafy residential streets, surrounded by high hills, and a Presbyterian church that they liked.

Indeed Middletown, a prosperous burg of nearly 12,000 inhabitants in 1880, was a pristine, pleasant haven compared to its slovenly southern counterparts. "Southerners of those days who visited the North always returned raving about the villages of New England," noted Ellen's sister Margaret. "'So white!' they would say. 'So clean!' It wasn't to be wondered at if they lived in towns such as Illyria," Margaret's prototype of the Southern Town.[34] Moving away in two years time again would be painful for the Wilsons.

They set up house in September, 1888, two weeks before Wilson's term at the university was set to start. Their rented home on High St. had been described to them as "large"--a two-story, four-square colonial--with ample front and back yards, shade trees, no electricity, but with a real bathroom and indoor plumbing, which must have been a pleasant change from Bryn Mawr. Four months later, Ellen once again found herself pregnant. This time, she "felt sorry" to find herself with child.[35] With each pregnancy getting harder, this third one would be the hardest yet.

With twelve-year-old Eddie and two babies to care for, Ellen faced a servant problem. Only Maggie the cook had agreed to accompany the Wilsons to Connecticut, and servants were hard to come by in Middletown. "If I could only *get* a good white one I would take her in a hurry," wrote Ellen, hoping to stave off hiring a black one. With none forthcoming, Ellen settled for a Mary from Philadelphia, an African-American who would be nurse as well as all-round housekeeper. Despite Ellen's initial misgivings, Mary turned out to be such a fine, caring servant, that they were anxious to bring her with them to Princeton.[36]

Live-in servants were paid $12-$14 a month in those days, in New England at least. This expense seemed exorbitant to frugally-minded Ellen, who felt guilty about it. "There is so much cause to worry about expense," she wrote typically, though it did not stop her from hiring servants.[37] Notwithstanding her husband's much-higher salary at Wesleyan, and the proceeds of the sale of Ellen's house in Rome coming in that winter, in addition to their other sources of income, they spent nearly all that they took in. A year later, they had enough to consider building a summer house in South Carolina (though nothing ever came of if), indicating that their savings were just deferred spending. Although neither Ellen nor Wilson was a spendthrift, Wilson seemed guilt-free about spending money, compared to Ellen.

In contrast to Bryn Mawr, Middletown was a thriving city with a rich social life. Ellen and her husband arrived in Connecticut with misgivings about "cold" New Englanders, only to find them surprisingly warm and welcoming. Soon Ellen's social life took on the contours of her life in the south, centering on the all-important institution of visiting.

Female visiting was as customary in New England as in Dixie, though the visits might be shorter. A few months after moving to New England, Ellen was "complaining" about having an average of four or five visitors a day; as in the south, these were drop-in "guests." Ellen, too, was expected to dress in her best and return visits. Although she frequently complained about how much time they took, it never occurred to her not to go. Some of her visitors in Middletown were members of a Miss Mansfield's sewing circle, of which Ellen became an active member. The pastor of the Wilsons' church in Middletown, Azel Washburn Hazen, and his wife Mary, also became Ellen and Wilson's intimate friends. During her long, painful pregnancy, Ellen would find Mrs. Hazen on her doorstep almost daily, bringing her fresh flowers, or ice cream, and staying for a visit. "...she *won't* be put off," wrote Ellen.[38]

* * *

Frequent, persistent attacks of nausea in January had been the only clue Ellen needed to divine that she was pregnant for the third time. As the days passed, she felt more and more ghastly. "There is no use trying to blind myself to the fact that I am getting steadily--for the last day or so--rapidly worse," she wrote in mid-February. By then she felt not only ill but, rare for her, with nerves stretched thin. Nothing else could explain the desperate letter she penned to her husband, who was absent for his lecture series at Johns Hopkins:

> I have done *so* little to make you happy. When I look back over my married life I am oppressed with a sense of failure so great that it seems to me my heart must break. How much of the time I have been a mere dead weight upon you--perfectly broken down with sickness.[39]

By "sickness" she meant her pregnancies, which frequently incapacitated her. "Oh, I am not fit to live!" she wailed.

Young Wife and Mother, 1885-1890

What shall I do! What *shall* I do!...and what will be the state of my nerves at the end of the ordeal. Already I feel as if every particle in my body were a separate living organism--and every one in convulsions! It is a *horrible* feeling; no one who has not felt it can form the slightest conception of it...Oh my darling pray for me--pray *hard*.[40]

For someone like Ellen, who never complained or focused attention on herself, such an extraordinary outpouring of personal misery must have panicked Wilson. He canceled a week's lectures to rush home and be at her side. On February 24, back in Baltimore, he alluded to their resolution--not to have any further children.[41]

But until then, Ellen's ill-health continued far longer than she anticipated. A day after her anguished letter (she never again wrote in such a vein), she calculated--no doubt based on her last pregnancy--how long her "illness" would last: "I will be sick at the shortest calculation eleven weeks more--most probably thirteen...", indicating that her second pregnancy had made her ill longer than her first. As it turned out, thirteen weeks later--in May--Ellen was still feeling ill; by late summer, she was traveling to New York City to consult a specialist, possibly an obstetrician. Despite her suffering, "I wouldn't have a miscarriage for *anything*," she wrote. But if only "it" were a boy: "...*wouldn't* I be exultant in spite of nausea & nervousness!"[42]

Pre-natal care was not customary in the 1880's, unless the expectant mother was having problems. For her worsening nausea, Ellen consulted not her family doctor, a man, but the town's female doctor, Florence Taft. Ellen took to Doctor Taft immediately ("...I like her--her manner etc.--extremely"). Though Taft plied her with "a thousand questions," she apparently was no specialist in obstetrics, submitted Ellen to no physical exam or tests, merely assuring her that she could remedy Ellen's "sickness" with the prescribing of some, as it turned out, ineffective pills. Though Ellen's nausea continued, even grew worse, Taft apparently never advised her to seek a specialist, nor did she seem to allude to any serious, underlying problem.[43]

Edith Wharton's early twentieth century novella, *Summer*, depicted the small city, New England woman doctor unflatteringly as outwardly charming, but slyly performing illegal abortions on the side for exorbitant fees, neither an upstanding nor an honest person. Too little is known of Doctor Taft to ascertain whether she resembled Wharton's unsavory Doctor Merkle, and whether she, too, plied a lucrative abortion trade, of which Ellen, sheltered as she was, would have been ignorant. Ellen continued to see Taft from time to time, even though she offered no relief from her sickness. On her own, Ellen read the-then popular expert on childbirth, Doctor Chavasse, seeking answers she never found, and procured other pills she had tried before, or heard of, through her husband.

On October 16, 1889, Ellen finally gave birth, in her home on High Street, to her third child, alas, yet another girl. This daughter never forgot a conversation she overheard, not meant for her seven year-old ears, in which her mother related how much she had cried when Doctor Taft announced the baby's sex. "The third girl brooded secretly for years over her misfortune." Wilson, who had suffered nearly as much as his wife during her long ordeal, insisted that the child be named after Ellen. Unassuming Ellen protested that she had never liked her name. So "Ellen" became "Eleanor," Wilson's favorite child.[44]

Ellen might have felt fortunate to have survived three pregnancies in a row. Not only was childbirth hazardous in her day, but pregnancy as well. Contagious diseases abounded that infected pregnant women. Ellen, while pregnant, nursed her young brother Eddie through a bout of mumps, wondering whether she, too (who had never had mumps), might become infected. Unlike most women in her day, however, Ellen had kind servants to help out at home, as she remarked in a letter, and plenty of leisure time in which to rest in bed, all day long, if necessary.

As it turned out, even well-cared for Ellen was not spared the hazards of 19th century pregnancy. Several months before Eleanor was born, Ellen traveled to New York to consult at least one specialist. He subjected her to a physical exam and a urine test, which in turn revealed albumin in her urine, a symptom of kidney damage. Perhaps because the doctor (and other doctors whom Wilson consulted about her albumin problem) did not take it seriously--one specialist merely advised avoiding foods with a high albumin content--her condition went untreated, or perhaps there was no treatment. According to medical historian Doctor Edwin Weinstein, albumin in Ellen's urine revealed that "she may have had an upper urinary tract infection or a toxemia of pregnancy with kidney damage. Either could have led to the chronic nephritis [i.e., kidney inflammation] from which she died in 1914."[45]

"My children cost me very dear--there is no denying that--" admitted Ellen, "but I pay the price *most gladly*..."[46] Indeed her children may have cost her her life in the long run; though Ellen lived another twenty-five years, death claimed her in her prime.

* * *

Wilson, who was again away at Johns Hopkins in the spring of 1890 for his lecture series, waxed lyrical in his daily letter to Ellen, in mid-February: "The minute I begin to think about you your sweet image and all your sweet ways rise up to dominate my whole mind--and straightway I fall down and adore you..." For Ellen's part, any slight criticism of her husband offended her deeply. "Once and again," continued Wilson, "when you are angry with some one whom you suspect of not appreciating me, you burst into a passion of love-making which makes my heart leap all day with uncontrollable joy..." That he needed the nourishment of her love is unmistakable. "Oh, Eileen, you will love me so when I come back to you, wont [sic] you--and you will promise it once and again, wont you, in your letters by giving free vent to your love for Your own Woodrow," he concluded.[47] Now and again, when he worked in his study, she would silently enter, embrace and kiss him. According to her brother Stockton's memoir, their marriage for many years was romantic and idyllic.

As to Ellen, with three babies in her care, a young brother and soon, Stockton coming to live with them and study at Wesleyan, her time was full to the brim. Conscientious but unsystematic, bills were not always paid on the dot. (Doctor Taft was not paid for nearly three months after delivering Eleanor.) "I am afraid I must begin with business tonight and disagreeable business at that...I allude to Camp's bill," she wrote her husband in early March.

It came just after you left and was for *two* months $70.26(!), and I have been intending ever since to ask you if that was correct--if the 'bill rendered' before was really unpaid. Now it has come again today--for 3 mos. & has grown to $104, and I suppose it ought to be attended to. Is there enough money in bank for such a huge bill though?[48]

According to Eleanor, her mother was always in charge of family finances, which Wilson found distasteful. In reality, however, he managed their monies and, according to the above quote, even paid the bills. On one occasion when he was away again at Johns Hopkins, Ellen had no way of opening their safe, having to ask him for the combination numbers. Increasingly, as Wilson became a more important public figure, Ellen did take over the management of their financial affairs until, when he entered politics, she put herself in charge of all of their investments.

Ellen had far more to worry about that spring than a "huge" bill of $104. During the Christmas holidays, only weeks after the ordeal of her pregnancy, Ellen scalded her foot in the kitchen after upsetting a pot of boiling water. Why she was moving pots on the kitchen stove when she had a cook in the kitchen beside her is unclear (unless it was "Sabbath day," when no Wilson servant ever worked), but the burns were severe. Typically, the family doctor made a house call, dressed the burns, and Ellen recovered slowly at home, unable to walk for many weeks. From her cheerful daily letters to her husband--who had to be away at Johns Hopkins shortly after her accident--one would not divine her pain, or her misery. There is also an unmistakable hint of boredom: unable to shop (an important activity for Ellen, which she performed with utmost gravity) or to visit, she took to sewing all day long, a stationary activity. "What I have done has been of the pleasantest, easiest sort--dresses for the children," she wrote her concerned husband, who feared she was over-working. "I have enjoyed every stitch of it; and it has really been a great resource," she assured him.[49] No mention of any sketching or painting.

As if her injury were not distracting enough, everybody was thrown off-balance in early spring when Wilson received an offer to teach at his *alma mater*, Princeton College. Princeton was incomparably more prestigious than Wesleyan, and Wilson was happy to accept. With the publication of his second book, *The State*--with its extravagant tribute to Ellen--and his numerous other publications and speaking engagements, it appears that Wilson no longer had to apply for teaching positions. Princeton wanted him badly. As professor of jurisprudence and chairman of "political economy," he would be paid $3000, or 20% more than at Wesleyan, all told, a handsome salary. In five years of teaching, Wilson's annual salary had doubled. Meanwhile, hundreds of dollars of royalties flowed yearly into the Wilsons'bank account, not only from Wilson's books, but also his magazine articles.

From a letter of Ellen's that spring, however, one would never guess that they were prospering. Regarding possible living arrangements at Princeton, Ellen recommended stringent frugality:

> Suppose we try 'light housekeeping' for a year....Did you not tell me that the hotel there,--University Hall?--is used as an apartment house? We might get four rooms there (or elsewhere) and have them serve our dinner while we prepared the other meals on an oil stove. We could keep one good servant, -- Mary, if possible, who would sleep in a corner of the room in which we did our light cooking, with a screen partition. The sitting-room would also be the dining-room and we could wheel some of the cribs in it at night...We must if possible, by one means or another, 'live cheap' next year.[50]

But Wilson continued to hunt for a roomy house, and shortly afterwards, found an impressive two-story, white frame home, close to campus, at a rent of $42 a month. The owner, aged Professor Hunt (or "Granny Hunt" to his students) even agreed to Ellen's request to renovate it from top to bottom, at his expense, and according to Ellen's suggestions. She wanted "blue and bronze" wallpaper for the parlor, and just the right shade of woodwork, "a rich walnut," for the dining room and study. In addition, "I should like the paper in the big double bed-room

Young Wife and Mother, 1885-1890

downstairs a good warm colour as much as possible like that in our guest room; -- I send sample." And as to the bathroom, "Will you please look at the bath-tub particularly and if it is a horrible black thing like this [in Middletown], which *no* scrubbing can improve, insist upon having it renovated."[51] Few tenants then or now could ever hope for such an indulgent landlord.

Their new home was a far cry from a primitive, bathless apartment. Moreover, its setting was peaceful and bucolic, surrounded on two sides by meadows. In a few years, the Wilsons would purchase the lot adjacent to them, on which they would build their dream home. In the meantime, the "Hunt House" came with a big barn which contained rooms that the Wilsons could rent out, and did, to students.

Moving again, so soon after moving out of Bryn Mawr, would again be wrenching. But there was no question that Wilson was making a strategic career move. "I go to Princeton with very high hopes of opportunity for effective work," he wrote a friend. "My teaching will lie exclusively within the particular fields in which I most want to study and write..." which would eventually make Wilson's reputation known well beyond academic circles. Wilson's sister Marion, who had never met Ellen in person, divined: "If the society of Princeton is anything like as intellectual as I have always understood, Ellie will be pleased too." She was right on the mark.[52]

ENDNOTES

[1] Woodrow Wilson to Ellen Axson, Dec.18, 1884. Arthur S. Link, ed., *The Papers of Woodrow Wilson* (Princeton: Princeton University Press, 1966-1996), 3:554. (henceforth: *PWW*)..

[2] Stockton Axson, *Brother Woodrow: A Memoir of Woodrow Wilson* ed. Arthur S. Link (Princeton, Princeton University Press, 1993), 223.

[3] Woodrow Wilson to Ellen Axson, May 6, 1885. *PWW* 4:565; Eleanor Wilson McAdoo, ed., *The Priceless Gift: The Love Letters of Woodrow Wilson and Ellen Axson Wilson* (New York: McGraw-Hill, 1962), 147.

[4] Woodrow Wilson to Ellen Axson, Oct.23, 1883. *PWW* 2:487.

[5] Woodrow Wilson to Ellen Axson, May 17, 19, 31, 1885. *PWW* 4:601, 676; 5:242.

[6] Ellen Axson to Woodrow Wilson, June 9, 1885, *PWW* 4:697; Janet Woodrow Wilson to Woodrow Wilson, July 13, 1885, *PWW* 5:5.

[7] As quoted by Mary Hoyt to Ray Stannard Baker, Mary Hoyt interview, Oct., 1926. Ray Stannard Baker Papers, Library of Congress, Washington, D.C. (henceforth: RSB papers)

[8] Woodrow Wilson to Ellen Axson, Jan.23, 1885, *PWW* 3:634; Ellen A. Wilson to Woodrow Wilson, May 11, 1886, *PWW* 5:217.

[9] Marjorie Housepain Dobkin, ed., *The Making of a Feminist: Early Journals and Letters of M. Carey Thomas* (Kent, OH: Kent State University Press, 1979), xiv, 146.

10. Woodrow Wilson to Ellen Axson, Oct.31, 1884, *PWW* 3:389; Ellen Axson to Woodrow Wilson, Dec.8, 1884, *PWW* 3:526; McAdoo, ed., *The Priceless Gift*, 148.
11. McAdoo, ed., *The Priceless Gift*, p.137.
12. Woodrow Wilson to Ellen A. Wilson, Feb.24, 1885, Oct.10, 1887. *PWW* 4:287, 5:605.
13. Woodrow Wilson to Ellen Axson, May 9, 1885. *PWW* 4:575.
14. Ellen Axson to Woodrow Wilson, Jan.20, 1885. *PWW* 3:626.
15. Axson, 91; on Mrs. Rorer and her recipes, see Ted Meredith, ed., *Mrs. Rorer's Famous 19th Century Recipes: Recipes by Sarah T. Rorer* (Kirkland, Washington: Nexus Press, 1981).
16. Louisa Cunningham Hoyt Brown to Woodrow Wilson, April 16, 1886, *PWW* 5:158-159; Woodrow Wilson to Ellen A. Wilson, April 17, 1886, *PWW* 5:159-160.
17. Margaret Axson Elliott, *My Aunt Louisa and Woodrow Wilson* (Chapel Hill: Univ. of North Carolina Press, 1944), 37.
18. Ellen A. Wilson to Woodrow Wilson, April 26, 1886, July 17, 24, 1887. *PWW* 5:175,532,538.
19. Ellen A. Wilson to Woodrow Wilson, April 27, 1886. *PWW* 5:175.
20. Ellen A. Wilson to Woodrow Wilson, May 2, 11, 1886. *PWW* 5:191,215.
21. Ellen A. Wilson to Woodrow Wilson, May 15, 18, 1886. *PWW* 5:229,238.
22. Woodrow Wilson to Ellen A. Wilson, May 30, 1886. *PWW* 5:269.
23. On the amount of rent being charged for the Axson house in Rome: Randolph Axson to Ellen A. Wilson, May 9, 1887, *PWW* 5:503; on the suicide of Ellen's Uncle Robert, see Frances W. Saunders, *Ellen Axson Wilson: First Lady Between Two Worlds* (Chapel Hill & London: University of North Carolina Press, 1985), 68.
24. Ellen A. Wilson to Woodrow Wilson, July 17, 1887. *PWW* 5:531.
25. How much Ellen spent on furnishings is unclear. Her uncle Randolph Axson, who took care of her father's estate, sent her a check for $100 and added: "Dont [sic] spend all of your money in furnishing your house." May 9, 1887. *PWW* 5:503.
26. Mary Hoyt to Ellen A. Wilson, May 4, 1887. *PWW* 5:502.
27. McAdoo, ed., *The Priceless Gift*, 159; Janet Wilson to Woodrow Wilson, April 31 [30],[1887], *PWW* 5:500.
28. Eleanor McAdoo mistakenly claimed that her father's new salary was only $1800 per year, McAdoo, ed., *The Priceless Gift*, 159; for Wilson's Bryn Mawr contract, see *PWW* 5:468-469; quote from Ellen, Ellen A. Wilson to Woodrow Wilson, Oct.3, 1887, *Ibid.*, 599; Randolph Axson to Ellen A. Wilson (on the amount of Eddie's income), Oct.1, 1887, *Ibid.*, 597; on Woodrow Wilson's borrowing from his father: Joseph R. Wilson to Woodrow Wilson, March 5, 1888, *Ibid.*, 707.
29. Ellen A. Wilson to Woodrow Wilson, July 24, 1887. *PWW* 5, 538.
30. McAdoo, ed., *The Priceless Gift*, 160.
31. *Ibid.*, 185.
32. *PWW* 5:619; Ellen A. Wilson to Woodrow Wilson, April 20, 1888. *Ibid.*, 721.
33. Axson, 60.
34. Elliott, 25.
35. Ellen A. Wilson to Woodrow Wilson, Feb.19, 1889. *PWW* 6:107.
36. Ellen A. Wilson to Woodrow Wilson, Feb.18, 1889. *PWW* 6:105.
37. *Idem.*
38. Ellen A. Wilson to Woodrow Wilson, March 14, 1890. *PWW* 6:149.
39. Ellen A. Wilson to Woodrow Wilson, Feb.17, 1889. *PWW* 6:102.
40. *Idem.*
41. Woodrow Wilson to Ellen A. Wilson, Feb.24, 1889. *PWW* 6:110.

Young Wife and Mother, 1885-1890

[42] Ellen A. Wilson to Woodrow Wilson, Feb.18, 1889. *PWW* 6:105.; *Ibid.*, Feb.19, 1889, 106-107.

[43] Ellen A. Wilson to Woodrow Wilson, Feb.9, 1889. *PWW* 6:81.

[44] McAdoo, ed., *The Priceless Gift*, 171.

[45] Edwin A. Weinstein, *Woodrow Wilson: A Medical and Psychological Biography* (Princeton: Princeton University Press, 1981), 99; referring to Ellen's albumin problem, Woodrow Wilson to Ellen A. Wilson, Aug.28, Sept.2, 1889, *PWW* 6:374-375, 387.

[46] Ellen A. Wilson to Woodrow Wilson, Feb.19, 1889. *PWW* 6:107.

[47] Woodrow Wilson to Ellen A. Wilson, Feb.20, 1890. *PWW* 6:530-531.

[48] Ellen A. Wilson to Woodrow Wilson, [March 4, 1890]. *PWW* 6:538-539.

[49] Ellen A. Wilson to Woodrow Wilson, March 5, 1890. *PWW* 6:541.

[50] Ellen A. Wilson to Woodrow Wilson, March 10, 1890. *PWW* 6: 548-549.

[51] Ellen A. Wilson to Woodrow Wilson, June 17, 1890. *PWW* 6:672.

[52] Woodrow Wilson to Eugene Schuyler, April 14, 1890, *PWW* 6:615; Marion Wilson Kennedy to Woodrow Wilson, Feb.20, 1890, *PWW* 6:532.

Chapter 4

ELLEN IN PRINCETON, THE 1890'S

*"Woodrow in a letter to me had once remarked that although Ellen was in
bed with a heavy cold, her will power was still unimpaired."*
Margaret (Madge) Axson[1]

"I can do nothing without you."[2]
Woodrow Wilson to his wife, 1892

On May 2, 1890, Woodrow Wilson in Middletown reported to a good friend
that "Mrs. Wilson's foot is almost entirely well at last; but she is now in bed with
an attack of acute tonsillitis" which, he believed, she contracted from daughter
Jessie, only more severely. Although they had a nursemaid for the children, Ellen
was a vigilant mother, and always nursed her children when they fell sick. The
family doctor made the usual house call, but there was no other remedy than bed
rest. Wilson guessed correctly that Ellen had worn herself out nursing Jessie, and
was weakened by her prior convalescence in their cold house during the harsh
New England winter. For most of their two years in Middletown, Ellen had been a
virtual invalid.[3]

Sicknesses spread more rapidly than today, and people's immune systems
were less hardy. No sooner was Ellen recovering from the fever and pain of
tonsillitis, than four year-old Margaret became ill with it, too. "This is a tale of
woe," concluded Wilson. Ill-health in the Wilson household, as in all families in
that period, would be a constant factor. More often than not, doctors were more of
a hindrance than a help.

Few families, however, had the leisure and means of the Wilsons when it came to recovering from their illnesses. Long bed rest was the only remedy. It was quite usual for either Ellen or Wilson or the children to stay in bed all day long for a week, even longer, to recover from a common head cold, or flu. Moreover, once Ellen and Wilson became parents, they would face a gamut of highly contagious childhood diseases. Measles (and more than one variety of measles), whooping cough, scarlet fever and the dreaded diphtheria were common plagues, from which the Wilson children would not be spared.

With the happy certainty that they would be settling down at last, and possibly forever, the Woodrow Wilsons embarked on a real vacation. It would mark the beginning of many summer sojourns at the seaside. Like most denizens of the east coast, they had their favorite beaches. Ellen and her husband preferred Sagaponack, on Long Island's north shore. When it was not possible to get away to relatively remote "dear Sag," New Jersey beaches, less beloved, would do.

Rejuvenated from the strains of illness and moving, the Wilsons were ensconced in their newly-refurbished, commodious rental on Steadman St. (in a few years, re-named Library Place) by September. Ellen and Wilson, including Ellen's sister Margaret (or Madge, who came to live with them in the mid-1890's), became deeply rooted in Princeton, Ellen and Wilson's home for the next 22 years. The next twelve years would be the happiest of their married life.

* * *

Princeton in the 1890's was a far cry from the traffic-clogged, clattering New York suburb of today. Princetonians, students included, referred to it as a village, and a sleepy one at that. The locus of town life was the all-male college, officially named the College of New Jersey--six years' later--re-named Princeton University. Though not as yet a university, Princeton already had a graduate college. At the time of the Wilsons' arrival, the entire student body numbered 597, small by the standards of today, although more than twice the size of Wesleyan in Middletown. On the edge of campus lay Princeton Theological Seminary, the Presbyterian seminary that Wilson's father had attended. It was not part of the college, and its divinity students were nicknamed "Seminoles" and were unpopular with Princeton girls.[4]

Then as well as today, Nassau Street was Princeton's main thoroughfare. However, there were no traffic lights or public transportation, except plodding horse-drawn "hacks," at 25 cents a ride. The railroad (today's "Dinky"), then as now, was located an inconvenient distance from the center of town. There were no restaurants, only a hotel or two, no cafes, and no bookstores. Princetonians--

faculty, students, merchants, and the town's few wealthy families--dined at home, at each other's houses, or in the dining rooms of private clubs. The town offered few services. Wilson's annual lecture visits to Baltimore occasioned more than just lecturing, but necessitated trips to the dry cleaners ("Did you remember dear, to take my waist [blouse] and the little rug to be cleaned?"), to repair shops, "And please, dear, get the toothbrushes and toothpaste," reminded Ellen, since Princeton was bereft of dentists and, apparently, of toothpaste.

It was, however, the "simple" life that Ellen and Wilson liked best. They made friends quickly; Wilson, after all, had been an undergraduate at Princeton and felt at home there.

With her vast array of kin, it comes as no surprise that Ellen discovered one day that she was even related to a founder of Princeton College, Nathaniel Fitz Randolph, who donated the first tract of land, a four and a half acre lot, to the school back in the 1740's. Fitz Randolph's home in Princeton had even stood next to the future official residence of the presidents of Princeton. This may have helped reconcile Ellen to living in the cold splendor of Prospect House in 1902.

While biographers of Wilson always refer to the informality of life in the tiny campus town at that time--people dropping in unexpectedly for visits, or for a meal--by the standards of today, it was anything but. Adult friends often were not on a first-name basis. Despite their weekly teas at Miss Henrietta Ricketts house, and the Wilsons' warm friendship with her, she remained "Miss Ricketts;" and Wilson never addressed the wife of his intimate friend, Jack Hibben, other than "Mrs. Hibben." People dressed up for dinner, even at each other's homes, and according to Madge (Margaret) Axson, women were expected to wear hats in public, unlike in her native Georgia. (Even in the bohemian art colony of Lyme, Connecticut, Wilson could not bring himself to take off his jacket and eat a meal in his shirt sleeves, like the rest.)

When Ellen's teenaged sister Madge came to live with them in 1894, she noticed how far formality had crept into her sister's household: dinner, punctually served at 8 P.M. (Ellen and Wilson never called it "supper"), was elegantly laid out and served by a maid, the same maid who tended to the personal needs of the family. When Ellen asked Madge if she wanted the maid to draw her bath and help her bathe, she blushed deeply, and refused, unaccustomed to "maid service." Yet Woodrow Wilson liked to refer to their highly refined lifestyle as "plain living and high thinking."[5]

There is no doubt that the latter was true of life in that cerebral community of scholars. The Wilsons' best friends--the Hibbens, the Perrys, the Fines, the Westcotts, the Daniels--were professors who lived close by. They socialized with one another daily, and their children played and grew up together. Sometimes they vacationed in the same spot. Each time Wilson, or Ellen and Wilson, set off for Europe, their friends the Hibbens were sure to see them off in New York harbor, and when the Hibbens set off for Europe, the Wilsons' did likewise. It was a close-knit, insular community, seemingly immune to the calamities of the outside world. As in most college towns, there was a division between "town and gown." Madge Axson claimed that Wilson was one of the few academics who made it a point to know the town's tradesmen personally. If so, the Wilsons never socialized with any of them.

Wilson quickly became "the idol of the students; was elected year after year the most popular professor; and was known to them in all of their student councils."[6] Ellen in turn enjoyed the status (and without admitting it, the prestige) of a faculty member's wife, and *mater* to all the students who dropped in "informally," as many of them did in that friendly campus town.

* * *

In the 1890's, Princeton was a large, denominational college, with mandatory chapel every week, and a president, Francis L. Patton, who was still a man of the cloth. The college was rapidly achieving "ivy league" status, thanks to the quality of its faculty, rather than to its students. Admission standards in fact were lower than at Bryn Mawr. Increasingly, students were coming from wealthy families, and upperclass student life coalesced around private clubs, more so than in Woodrow Wilson's student days.

The student body in the 1890's was also not diverse (or "miscellaneous," to use the language of Wilson's day). Besides the exclusion of women, no minorities attended Princeton as undergraduates. Wilson, later as president of Princeton, made sure it stayed that way, pointedly refusing to admit African-Americans.[7] Ellen's brother Stockton, who became a professor of English in the late 1890's, noted that "They [the clubs] and athletics were the really important things to the Princeton undergraduates..." Not only did most students not bother to read their textbooks, recalled Stockton, but they "would do no work whatsoever until a few weeks before the final examination, when they would buy syllabi of the courses, which were prepared by the more intelligent and industrious students and sold at a fixed price."[8]

In 1890, when the Wilsons arrived, cheating on exams was widespread among students. "...men would frankly copy each others' examination papers and get all the assistance they could from each other during examination, even though they had clear notions of honor about other things." Ellen became exposed to this regrettable fact for the second time, first at Wesleyan, now at Princeton. Unlike

Wesleyan, Princeton drew many "lads" from the south. As these "southern lads...were supposed to have high notions of honor, she became a good deal agitated," remembered Stockton.

Ellen heard about the cheating from not a few southern students, among them Wilson's nephew George Howe III. According to Stockton, the Wilsons kept an "open house" for students, "who used to drop in informally in the afternoons and evenings." She lost no time inspiring them to spearhead an honor code system. According to the proposed code, "every student signed a pledge on his examination paper" that he had not cheated. If he had, a student honor committee, and not the faculty, would punish the student.

As a prominent member of the faculty, Wilson was in a position to get the honor system implemented. However, wrote Stockton, "It was really Mrs. Wilson herself"--no doubt thanks to her own "southern code of honor"--"who was the first promulgator of the honor system in this college, a system for which Princeton was supposed to be peculiarly preeminent among the eastern colleges for many years." This marked the first time, but by no means the last, in which Ellen used her husband to implement a social, institutional or even political change that she favored.

Decisiveness and tenacity lay beneath Ellen's unassuming, ladylike exterior. Her brother noted for posterity: "She was always emphatic in a decision." Once conceived, it was "quickly executed."[9]

* * *

Besides socializing with faculty and students, the Wilson home was nearly always brimming with guests, usually out-of-town Wilson or Axson clan. Ellen and her husband liked having people around at all times, especially Ellen.

Ellen's youngest brother Ed (Eddie as a child), sent away to a boarding school in the south after leaving Middletown (private schools were cheaper in Dixie than in New Jersey), returned to attend Princeton as an undergraduate, and lived for years with his sister's family. Ellen's sister Madge settled in with the Wilsons until her marriage in 1910; Stockton lived with them for extended periods, and after her husband died in 1895, so did Annie Wilson Howe, Wilson's sister (the Wilsons would even provide her with an income). Annie's son, George Howe III, also housed at the Wilsons in the 1890's while attending Princeton, as did Wilson's first cousin, Helen Bones, who attended the short-lived Evelyn College for women; finally, in the late 1890's, Wilson's aged father came to live with them "permanently" until he died in 1903.

Madge Axson recalled that neither she nor her other siblings chipped in to help out with the household expenses, although she, Ed and Stockton received a small annuity from their late father. As a result, the expense of feeding such a large extended family grew until, in a few years, it was truly lordly. Ellen's itemization of expenses in late 1896 listed $100 a month merely for food and gas lighting, more than the average American earned in an entire month. Her average monthly expenses totaled just under $200. Only a decade earlier, Ellen and Wilson had made ends meet on Wilson's annual salary of $1500.[10]

Wilson, earning approximately $3500 in 1896 and, according to Ellen, an extra $1500 annually from his lectures at Hopkins and guest-lecturing elsewhere, and royalties besides, could well afford to feed so many. He and Ellen, however, never saved, unless it was for the short-term. Bills still were not being paid on time. In February of 1896, the butcher was "begging" Ellen to pay her over-due bill. "Can you send a check?" she asked her absent husband.[11] In contrast to the early years of their marriage, they began sliding into permanent debt.

One reason they saved little, if at all, is that they rarely scrimped. Despite Ellen's frugal mentality and "cost-cutting" (doing the spring sewing for her children's clothes, for instance, which eventually became such a big project that she had to pay a helper), Ellen shopped at the best stores in New York and Philadelphia--Lord & Taylor's, Wanamaker's, Strawbridge's. Daughter Eleanor's remark that she and her siblings never had store-bought dresses until her father became governor, is belied by Ellen's shopping spree to a New York department store (which became Wanamaker's) in 1895. There she bought each of them a cloak, dresses "of the finest material and beautifully made," and "eight pairs of flannel drawers," over-spending the $40 Wilson had sent her for her shopping, to her chagrin. In 1897, her shopping trip to Lord & Taylor's in New York resulted in the purchase of a "perfectly elegant" gown, on sale for $34. "That is about what my gray dress cost, but this is twice as fine...." Of course, "It was economy to get it now;" however, "I am 'low in my mind' at having spent so much..." Wilson's endearing response was, "But surely, that one gown will not be all you need."[12]

Wilson could not resist the occasional gift of jewelry for his wife (an elegant silver watch, a "pearl and diamond breast-pin," a "necklace and pendant"); he bought books liberally, splurged $75 on a bicycle, while he and Ellen subscribed to all of the popular, high-brow journals and magazines of the day. Despite Eleanor's claim that "there was seldom money then for trips to the seashore," referring to the early Princeton years,[13] the Wilson family spent at least two weeks every summer at an ocean resort, from 1890 onwards. In 1892, Ellen even took a leisurely, three-month vacation with her children to Georgia, and in 1893, she went on a week's pleasure jaunt to the Chicago World's Fair, staying with her cousins at a hotel; a few months later, the whole family spent their summer vacation at Sagaponack, Long Island. As the Wilsons' income (and status) rose, their vacations grew lengthier and more "exotic": to New England, Canada, Europe.

By the standards of today, the Wilsons were not spendthrifts. Ellen budgeted, their children did not receive allowances or go shopping on their own. Moreover, occasionally the Wilsons made good use of their money. The Princeton real estate market was booming in the 1890's. In 1891, when Wilson purchased a lot on Washington St. for $1500, he was able to sell it to the Hibbens four years later for $4500, despite the nation-wide depression.[14] The luxury home which the Wilsons built in 1896 for approximately $15,000 sold, seven years later, for $30,000.

Had they continued investing in Princeton real estate, Ellen and Wilson might have grown rich. Alas, they did not. Unaccountably, by 1910, and for the first time in their married life, they could not even afford to rent a home of their own. By then, Princeton was affordable only to the well-to-do.

The Wilsons' finances were complicated in part by the cumbersome way they paid their bills, at least for most of the 1890's. Wilson handled the family's finances, contrary to Eleanor's assertion that her mother did. Ten years after they married, Wilson still referred to "my checkbook." During his absence at Hopkins in 1895, he even had to instruct Ellen where to find it. He and not she endorsed their checks, which meant that she had to mail them to him during his frequent absences, and he back to her; she in turn handed the endorsed checks to her brother Ed to deposit in the bank, although he was only a minor.[15]

Why this cumbersome arrangement prevailed had something to do with the way Ellen and Wilson viewed marriage. While from the perspective of today, theirs was a partnership of equals, they would not necessarily have viewed it that way. To them, men and women had different, though not unequal, roles to play in life. Men were the providers and bill-payers, even though this turned out to be a troublesome arrangement, especially for Wilson, overburdened with teaching, writing and lecture trips. Nor did this arrangement last. From the time of his first lengthy absence to Europe in 1896, when paying bills was not feasible for him, we see Ellen gradually taking over the family finances, as well as later investments.

* * *

Wilson's pride in his family's "high thinking and plain living," as he expressed it in 1894 (and thereafter), did not alter at the prospect of building their--or rather Ellen's--dream home. She admitted a year later that "it was my idea from the first." Weary of being a renter, Ellen yearned for a roost of her own. Increasingly, complaints about their rental on Library Place (formerly Steadman St.) seeped into their correspondence: the pipes froze in winter; the house was either "full of mice" or flies, which Ellen blamed on the stable behind it, rented out briefly to students.

Ever since Wilson, in 1892, rejected the offer of the presidency of the University of Illinois in Champaign-Urbana, and it appeared that they would be staying in Princeton for good, Ellen began to hatch house plans. By 1894, they were in full swing, despite their lack of capital.

This painful fact did not preclude Ellen from spending many afternoons in the college library, poring over books for design ideas. Her favorite came to be a half-timbered English cottage with "novel features," she noted, such as an "over-hanging" upper story, unusual for Princeton. Consequently, as she was about to discover, it would be more difficult for workmen to build, and hence more costly, than the simple colonial brick or frame homes that prevailed.

While most people in the Wilsons' circumstances might have saved to buy a finished house on the market, Ellen's English-style "small cottage," as she referred to it--although she wanted a minimum of six bedrooms--came at an initial price tag of $7000. And this did not include the architect's fee, nor the price of the lot, situated next door to their rental on Library Place. Ellen and Wilson would be forced to borrow this large sum of money, with not even a down payment to their credit. When they discovered how much this would cost them in terms of re-payment, they balked, though not for long.

For starters, Wilson miscalculated the amount of interest they would have to pay on a $7000 mortgage loan. When he found out that the correct amount of interest due (at an annual 5 1/2 percent) was far higher than he had figured, he concluded that they simply could not afford to build.[16] In a pathetic letter to Ellen from Baltimore in late January, 1895 ("It is only by force of will that I write this letter to you"), an anxious husband informed his wife that, painful as it was for him, they would have to give up their house-building scheme.

Wilson had just discovered that his total annual interest re-payment (including on the loan he borrowed from his father) came to a whopping $495, for a house whose cost had mushroomed, meanwhile, from $7000 to $9000. There was also the principal to re-pay, he reminded Ellen in the same letter, at $425 a year, and the annual "taxes and insurance." What the mortgage terms were on a $7000 loan is unclear, but they were obviously far different from today.

In short, total principal and interest payments, including taxes and insurance, would average out to no less, and probably more, than eighty dollars per month. This was a princely sum for a family who were paying only $42 a month in rent, until the college granted Wilson a housing allowance in 1892, enabling them to live rent-free. Rather than save money, however, they only spent more.

Far from "blasting all your hopes," as Wilson had feared, Ellen took the news gamely. With the $2000 loan from Wilson's father recently deposited in the bank (which Wilson, contrary to his father's wishes, insisted on repaying, with full interest), Ellen asked him: "So if it doesn't make *any* difference perhaps you had better send me a check to be drawn from the $2000 so that I may go to town this week," that is, on a shopping spree to a New York department store, which was having a big sale.[17]

Ellen and Wilson quietly began to save--furiously for the short term, as was their wont--to build the capital they so entirely lacked, and so to dispense with a big loan. "Economizing more fervently than ever," remembered Eleanor, who was only a child at the time, her mother scrimped on the household budget, and "put every dollar not needed for necessary expenses into a savings account, marked 'House,'" (the "savings account" was probably a piggy bank).[18] Ellen also turned to the architect, Edward S. Child, with a simplified version of their "cottage," which her absent husband called "ingenious" and "admirable."

The real burden of earning money to pay for their new home, however, fell squarely on Wilson's shoulders. The alternative to a large mortgage loan, he decided, was to raise some capital of his own. His plan for doing so was sensible, but far from simple. They would have to sell their lot on Washington St., and he in turn would double, even triple, his guest lecturing and teaching load to the point where, throughout all of 1895 and half of 1896, he was off giving lectures as far away as Colorado, and teaching nights for Princeton's university extension, in addition to his regular full-time teaching position.

As a result of his strenuous efforts, Wilson pocketed $4000 from his guest lecturing in a year (including spring lectures at Hopkins), instead of the usual $1500, "and almost killed himself doing it!" remarked Ellen to a friend. Her husband's absences and pre-occupation with work meant that Ellen, from her roost next door, drew up the floor plans (and not Wilson, as Eleanor claimed; as an artist, Ellen was better at this than Wilson), supervised the house-building, dealt with the contractor, the architect, the workmen, as her many letters reveal. She was getting so good at planning a house that she obliged a friend by drawing a plan for *her* new house. Ellen was also getting adept at discovering construction problems. When she saw what the plumber had done to the bathrooms, she exclaimed to her husband: "Several of the joints are leaking, the pipes are slanting instead of vertical, the marbles are put in crooked with bits of wood smeared with cement stuck in to fill out, etc."[19]

The Wilsons also quickly sold their Washington St. lot for $4500. With $8500 in capital, and the $2000 loan from his father, Wilson should have been able to pay for their new house in full. Alas, the cost kept mounting. In a June, 1895 letter to her old school chum from Rome, Anna Harris, Ellen wrote, "We told the architect it must not cost, with the lot, more than $12000.00 *complete*;" but she admitted--it looked like the cost might actually rise to $14,000.[20] When completed, the house actually cost closer to $15,000.

Instead of six, there would be seven bedrooms, two bathrooms, and a spacious enclosed porch on the second floor (with another porch on the first floor). There were three floors instead of two, a "study" on the first floor separate from the library, a butler's pantry, numerous fireplaces, expensive window treatments, and beautiful storm doors. When it was nearly finished in early 1896, Ellen was thrilled: "...the whole house," she wrote her husband, "is getting to look so elegant that it is hard to believe it is really ours!" Far from a small cottage, it was a stately English manor, or, to quote Wilson's father, an "extravagant mansion."[21]

Such a house required new furnishings. In late February, Ellen asked her husband to send her at least a hundred dollars so she could go to New York to buy "curtains for various rooms, your carpet, bed & springs, small rugs, pedestal, lantern, chair, kitchen oil-cloth, stuff for your window-seat, & picture frames."[22]

Moving day that spring of 1896 was relatively painless. In part because they were only moving next door, and also because Ellen hired ten men to move all of their belongings in one day. At day's end, everything down to the pots and pans was in place, and the whole family, led by Wilson's father, knelt in prayerful thanksgiving for their gorgeous new home.

Nowadays, a stroll along untranquil Library Place, lined by stately dwellings in the half-timbered, English "cottage" style, is revealing. Clearly, the Wilson's new house set the tone for the whole--at that time, still undeveloped--neighborhood.

Although Ellen had been the engine driving the house-building plans, Wilson exulted in their new house as much as she did. The sight of his home at the end of a busy day, he was to say, filled him with pride. But Ellen's attachment ran deeper. She designed, planned, furnished and decorated her new home; she knew every brick, stone and windowpane. She would throw herself ardently, down to her muddy boots, into gardening and beautifying the grounds, displaying a talent of which not even her husband was aware. Into her old age, daughter Eleanor, though only six years old at the time, recalled the clay model of their new house that Ellen had fashioned while it was still being built, for family and friends to admire.

At 36, Ellen finally had her own home, the only possession she ever craved. Far from living there permanently, the Wilsons stayed only six and a half years. Her pain at moving away was unfathomable, too deep for words.

* * *

Looking back, Ellen described those brief years in their new home as "the sweet, almost ideal life." Yet it was a time of national depression, and even the Wilsons knew a friend whose father had committed suicide because of "business troubles," wrote Wilson, while Ellen had to sell her stocks in the Southwestern Railroad Co. (which she had inherited) at a total loss. Nonetheless, Wilson wrote to a friend in 1891 that "...we keep busy and grow selfish in this cosey nook of a town," not that relatively remote Princeton was immune to the calamities of the outside world. Ellen for her part, despite her busy life, was far from selfish and complacent. "The social duties during the winter are heavy," she wrote in 1895 to her friend Anna Harris in Rome, "and they have now 'roped' me in for a good deal of regular weekly work in connection with benevolent societies."[23] Wives of faculty, none of whom held outside jobs or careers, devoted much of their spare time to charitable work. One charity in particular would claim much of Ellen's time: the Woman's Employment Provident Charity. None of its records has survived, and despite Ellen's many references to the hours she spent working there, she never described the kind of work she did.

Ellen first mentioned working for the "employment society" in early 1894 when, a day after a snowstorm and "quite a gale," she walked there and back alone. From then on, until the Panic (depression) of 1893 subsided at the turn of the century, she was a dedicated volunteer. There she saw poverty with a human face, and pitied the struggling women seeking to support themselves and even their families.

The clientele she served was without a doubt a mixed one, ethnically and racially. Despite being a well-to-do college town, Princeton had its black ghetto, "African Lane" (along Witherspoon St., where Paul Robeson was born in 1898), and its school system was strictly segregated. Many immigrants, especially from southern Europe, were crowding into the town as well, perhaps working as servants and laborers, there or elsewhere (a railroad connected Princeton to New York, only forty-five miles away). These would have been hardest hit during the depression, and Ellen's reference to "benevolent societies" might well have been to the charities established to alleviate the misery of these poor blacks and immigrants. As late as 1904, a few years after the depression had subsided, Wilson made an oblique reference in his diary to the "degraded poor on John's

St.," and to "all sorts of charitable work," including the Employment Society, to relieve the misery of the poor in Princeton. Ellen's brother Stockton described Ellen's charity as the kind that was entirely personal: she might hear of a needy washer woman or gardener, then don her hat and visit them in person to see how she could help. By contrast, Wilson's experience with poverty and social problems was far from first-hand.[24]

Despite their "idyllic" life in the 1890's, the Wilsons themselves were not free of trouble and worries. Sickness was an all too frequent caller. All three Wilson girls came down with highly-contagious diseases, such as scarlet fever and whooping cough, on a frequent basis, and still more tonsillitis. (In the early 1900's, Jessie and Eleanor would have tubercular glands surgically removed.) Every winter without fail, influenza took its toll on the whole family, including servants. Wilson's year and a half of over-exerting himself, to earn money for their new house, led to his being bedridden for weeks, and suffering a mild stroke, in the spring of 1896. More than one doctor diagnosed it as only a case of "writer's cramp," despite his whole right arm--and hand--being lame for many months.

Ellen's health, too, was far from good. Judging from her and Wilson's correspondence, from at least 1896 until 1898 she suffered from frequent, lengthy periods of nausea and mysterious attacks of abdominal pain and fever that kept her bedridden for days; in 1898, she suffered an inexplicable loss of appetite (as in 1914). As usual, doctors could find nothing organically wrong with her. With regard to her attack of abdominal pain and fever in 1896, Wilson scholar, Doctor Edwin Weinstein, noted: "There is no record of a urine analysis, so it is possible that she had had another attack of pyelonephritis" (that is, inflammation of the pelvic lining and kidney tissue).[25] If a urine analysis was done later, neither Ellen nor Wilson made mention of it.

Stockton's ill health cast a shadow throughout Ellen's adult life. Though a brilliant man and popular professor of English at Princeton (who long out-lived Ellen), Stockton was frequently in and out of sanitoriums, due to nervous breakdowns, depression and hypochondria. Because he never married, Ellen became his surrogate mother, though only seven years his senior. She nursed him during his prolonged periods of unwellness, and rarely complained.

With such a litany of illness (which only touches the surface), it is a wonder that anyone would characterize the Wilsons' life as idyllic. But illness and premature death were far less strange in the 19th century than today, and taken, more or less, as a matter of course.

* * *

When they first moved to Princeton in 1890, Ellen, who had never before been to Princeton, was busy adjusting to life in strange surroundings. A year later Wilson wrote a friend, "...in the morning I write; in the afternoon Mrs. Wilson sketches--and that seems to us to complete the day."[26] In short, even with three small children and a household to run, Ellen still had leisure time. Eventually, at least one live-in maid (who doubled as a nursemaid) and a live-in cook serviced the household, while an outside laundress did the wash for a nominal sum.

With her time not absorbed by a job or career, and with little to no housework to perform, Ellen's life could have drifted into ennui. She did know of southern women who slid into hypochondria and depression, spending most of their married lives lying on a sofa. To her, however, such women merely suffered from laziness.

Ellen was too dutiful and self-disciplined to slide into boredom; besides, she was far too energetic and well-read not to find outlets for her many interests and activities. Intellectual Princeton, as Wilson's sister Marion predicted, was a good match for Ellen. As in Middletown, it also afforded her with a rich social life that her nature seemed to crave.

Before long, Ellen's leisure was filled with visiting and visits, dinner parties and--what passed for entertainment in 1890's Princeton--attending public lectures. To her absent husband, she described her bewildering social calendar in February, 1894:

> I was away all day Thursday 'celebrating,' Friday afternoon there was the lecture, Sat. morn. Mrs. Lewis, and Sat. aft. the Wescotts who made a long visit--spent entirely romping with he children! Tomorrow I must go to a lunch party at Mrs. Fine's, Tuesday morning read with Miss Ricketts & Mrs. Conover, and Tuesday aft. go to the Employment Soc.[27]

At times Ellen noticed a surprising similarity between the Yankee custom of visiting--and hospitality--and the south's. "Mrs. Lewis came in yesterday and 'spent the morning,' southern style." One time when Ellen was feeling unwell, the wealthy "Mrs. Brown," who was very fond of the Wilsons, "sent me this morning three quail and some *delicious* butter. Mrs. Green sent me Sunday a bowl of delightful soup. Quite like the South - isn't it?" referring to the southern custom of bringing food to a sick person. Another wealthy woman gave them an expensive present for Christmas in 1896: "I had a lovely Xmas present today from Mrs. Norris--a beautiful tall jar, or vase, with handles. It is an exquisite shape and in colour would seem to have been *made* for our parlour."[28]

"Calls" had to be reciprocated. "I called on Mrs. Phillips, who receives on Fridays," indicating that visiting, especially when it came to well-to-do women, was not all that informal. On a hot August day in 1894, Ellen wrote, "I went yesterday to see Mrs. Armstrong and, to fulfill my promise, Mrs. Miller's sister. Such a bore [i.e., annoyance] to put on one's best things--and *gloves*--actually! and begin the old business of calling." Ellen could never have foreseen that "the old business of calling," like visiting cards, rug beaters, and horse-drawn hacks, would vanish all too soon.[29]

Ellen, not a member of Princeton's small, wealthy elite, had no formal visiting days, but she and Wilson could not do without their visiting cards. Judging from Wilson's social calendar when he was away, even men left visiting cards and reciprocated visits. "I have not called on Miss Duer and Mrs. Reid...only because my visiting cards have not come yet..." he informed Ellen from Baltimore in 1895. If they could not accept an invitation, such as to a dinner party, Ellen still made a point of sending in her and her husband's visiting cards.[30]

Occasionally, Ellen also received "calls" from male acquaintances. She noted the impromptu visit of a certain "Prof. Smith," probably an aging bachelor, who was not even a close friend of the Wilsons. Yet he "came in just as I had finished with the children and spent the evening!" no doubt drawn to Ellen's friendliness and cultured mind. She could hardly have imagined an age to come when such an unannounced visit--and such a warm welcome--would be unthinkable. An age when people could live lonely and isolated lives in their communities, even in Princeton.

Aside from visits formal and informal, there were constant, usually prolonged visits from southern relatives, and her old school chum, unmarried Anna Harris. Wilson's sister Annie, wrote Ellen in 1892, came up from South Carolina with her baby daughter, and was staying with them for a whole month, one of many such stays. That same year, Anna Harris, traveling up from Rome on her own, visited for several weeks. Writing to her absent husband in June, Ellen gave him an account of her pleasant day. "We [she and Anna] have been loafing most of the day; at about eleven we went to the college library and staid until one; in the afternoon we lay around reading and embroidering, rather used up by the heat." Of course "reading" meant taking turns reading aloud, in this case, Mrs. Gaskell's "delightful 'Cranford.'" Nowadays, when not even close relatives are welcome for long, we can only marvel at such lengthy, and frequent, visiting.[31]

Besides the social institution of visiting and attending each other's dinner parties, not much else took place in the Princeton of the 1890's, aside from college sports, which bored Ellen, with a few exceptions. Dropping by the gym one day with Wilson's young cousin Helen Bones, the student athletes awed them: "There were contests in jumping, wrestling, etc., etc. and the exhibition of

Ellen in Princeton, the 1890's

105

the gymnastic team. We had never seen wrestling before and found it *terribly* exciting."[32] They stayed for several hours.

Princeton students and their activities often provided the stuff of local news and entertainment. During the Spanish-American war, students noisily set fire to an effigy of the king of Spain, causing a stir; they manned the annual, irreverent St. Patrick's Day parade down Nassau St., and held torchlight parades when the occasion demanded, as after an election. In addition, up until the 1930's, there prevailed an "entertaining" custom: a handful of students gathered spontaneously of an evening at the foot of old Nassau Hall, to sing ditties that they made up on the spot (for instance, "Here's to Blank, our Prof retired. Did he quit or was he fired?"). Alas, such clever, innocent rhymes--and the students who sang them-- seem hopelessly inane today.[33]

In early 1895, Wilson whined to his wife, "You have so few pleasures, so little entertainment--so dull a round of life..." as if life in 1890's Princeton could really be dull, even in a town without movie theaters or restaurants. Princeton, after all, was full of dynamic, interesting people, and to this "jet set" of high thinkers and writers, the Wilsons indisputably belonged.[34]

Not surprisingly, public lectures, no matter how cerebral, were popular events, which many women attended. Nor were they always given by men. In 1896, for instance, Ellen attended a series of three lectures ("one Victor Hugo & two Browning") given by a Mrs. Sara Tawney Robson. On another occasion, Ellen fell sound asleep: "Fortunately I was completely hidden from public view by a forest of tall hats and nodding plumes--the appropriate insignia of our bourgeoisie on dress parade," she wrote mockingly.[35]

Ellen was, however, a critical listener. At one point she compared a British scholar's lecture on art to one given by Princeton's Professor Perry. "*His* [Perry's] lecture was really fine, - graceful and delicately beautiful in form--vital in thought. It was *true* criticism of the most serious, penetrating, illuminating sort." On another occasion, a lecture on Martin Luther disappointed her: "He began by stating that Luther & Lessing were the two greatest Germans...but he really gave us no evidence worth mentioning in establishment of that proposition."[36]

When Ellen was not visiting or being visited, volunteering, attending lectures and dinner parties, or teaching her children--she "home-schooled" them daily for four years--she read voraciously and sewed plentifully.

As to the latter, Ellen had a reputation for "exquisite embroidery," according to daughter Eleanor, which she passed on to her daughters; she also sewed her children's clothing as well as her own (including "a stunning new evening gown...at the total cost of 30 cts.!" she exclaimed to her husband). Not because they could not afford to buy clothes. "Can you not buy most of what will be needed? Surely you can," asked her husband.[37] Sewing, like gardening, seemed to be an outlet for Ellen's creativity.

Ellen was not a reader of scientific subjects, nor did she choose to read books that discussed contemporary problems, no doubt because she read about them in her and Wilson's many periodicals. (One exception was the 1888 pamphlet, *The Negro Question*, by George Washington Cable. Would she and Wilson have read this, however, had a friend of Wilson's, James Franklin Jameson, not prevailed on them to read it?) History, biography, memoirs, travelogues are all mentioned in her letters, but her favorite reading was always literature, in which she delved deeply.

Alone with her children at the Belmar, New Jersey seashore in 1894, Ellem informed her husband that she was reading Homer's *Illiad*, as well as Thucydides, Xenophon, and Herodotus. She was a lover of Shakespeare, of whom she could not get enough, and of poetry, especially William Wordsworth and the Brownings, husband and wife. "This morning...I stopped at the library and read poetry until one," she wrote Wilson in the summer of 1899. "Then I brought home Mrs. Browning's general letters, the two vols. published in '97, and read them most of the afternoon; I found them absorbingly interesting."[38]

With the exception of classical writing, literature--fiction and poetry--in the Wilson household was chiefly British, possibly because Ellen had been so narrowly educated (in contrast to her formidably well-educated sister Madge, who introduced her to Henryk Sienkiewicz' novel, *Pan Michael*, in the summer of 1896.) According to daughter Eleanor, Ellen was also the designated reader in the family when reading aloud--a favorite past-time in the Wilson household--as in many others.

* * *

It would be surprising if Ellen--bibliophile, avid reader of newspapers and periodicals, and devotee of public lectures--did not have forceful opinions. "And was there ever such a contemptible hypocrite as Henry C. Lodge," she wrote, referring to Wilson's future nemesis in the Senate, although political opinions rarely intruded into her writing. Regarding President Cleveland's controversial tariff bill in 1894, "For once our legislature too seems to have a dramatic element in it. This trial of strength & endurance between House & Senate is positively exciting." On political issues, she and Wilson were one, Ellen more often than not, taking her cue from her political scientist husband. Being white southerners, they were staunch Democrats.[39]

Ellen in Princeton, the 1890's 107

More often than not, Ellen's strong opinions, at least as expressed in her writing, were reserved for people and their behavior. Referring to the wife of a faculty member in 1894, "Do you know Mrs. Fine is actually going abroad with her brother & Jack, leaving Mr.F. & the baby at home, to stay eight months or more!...A thoroughly selfish woman like that is really a monstrosity." (Ellen would have had little sympathy for the modern-day value of "self-realization.")[40]

Meeting a highly intelligent woman at her boarding house at the shore in 1893, Ellen nonetheless quipped, "but such *aggressive* egotism and selfishness I don't think I ever saw in anyone--except perhaps Miss Graham."[41] At that point, "Miss Graham" (Mary Graham), whom she and Wilson had known back in Middletown as a student, was a doctoral candidate in economics at Yale. She was also an ardent feminist. Feminists (including other radicals, as temperance advocates) continued to receive Ellen's "no holes barred" ire and condemnation.

Lecturing at Johns Hopkins in February of 1895, Wilson told Ellen that he spotted Miss Graham at one of his lectures--unaware that she was taking a break from a conference in Washington, D.C. "I despise her most heartily," he wrote, echoing Ellen's feelings. Ellen shot back: "Its [sic] easy enough to see why Miss Graham was in Washington," having read in the newspaper about the Washington, D.C. convention of the National Council of Women of the United States. "Didnt you know that all the female cranks in the country are there in Congress assembled?"[42] It is unknown whether Ellen or Wilson ever heard that Graham, two years later (Dr. Graham by then), had been committed to an "insane asylum" for the rest of her life.[43]

"The 'new woman' ought certainly to take heart," digressed Ellen to Wilson in a long, chatty letter in August, 1896, when she was 36 years old. "Their cause-- the equality of the sexes--is rapidly gaining ground, among writers of books at least. They are now heartily according her [the "new woman"] many new and *valuable* rights, privileges and immunities." Her sarcasm was biting.

> Du Maurier, their great leader, is getting a brave following in his noble battle for an equal code of morals. Not that they maintain that men should be virtuous. But generously, unselfishly, chivalrously do they contend for the woman's right to be just as bad as the man![44]

Ellen's revulsion at an "equal code of morals" never lessened. One can guess what her reaction to the women's "sexual revolution" would have been, less than a century later.

Of Ellen's own daughters, only Eleanor would be immune from the rising tide of women's liberation, being, as she declared, "a very frivolous" person. Jessie, the only Wilson daughter to graduate from a four-year college, was too religious to succumb wholeheartedly, although she did try in vain to convince her father to support woman's suffrage. Independent Margaret, alone of the Wilson daughters, never married, and it is unknown what opinions she held on women's issues. She was the only Wilson daughter, however, who trained for and sought a career for herself, as an opera singer.

* * *

Marriage and motherhood did seem to put an end to Ellen's career ambitions. Princeton, the school as well as the town, had little to offer in the way of fine arts, that is, until the college opened its small art museum to the public in 1892, a place that Ellen stole away to frequently. If it contained little in the way of art, from time to time, it did display traveling exhibits. The school as yet had no fine arts department, nor were there any private galleries or even artists in town.

Hence when an itinerant English artist visited Princeton in 1896, it was an event, even if his art was, to quote Ellen, "lovely in colour, but terribly-overworked."[45] True, Manhattan was only a train ride away, but if Ellen saw any exhibits there, her letters at this time make no mention of them.

Ellen, moreover, had severed all ties to the Art Students League when she married. Consequently, when First Lady Ellen Wilson met her former art professor, DeForest Brush, at a dinner one evening, he had lost all recollection of her as his student, even though he had constantly praised her work. And whether or not she followed the career of her best friend at the League, Antoinette Farnsworth (Mrs. Drew), is unknown. In the late 1890's, when Ellen was long an obscure housewife, her former friend was exhibiting her work in Paris.

Nonetheless, in Ellen and Wilson's vast correspondence in these years, there are numerous references to Ellen's keeping up with her art work in some form. Nothing could be further from the truth than Stockton's recollection, years later, that Ellen "practically painted nothing until the children were grown."[46]

As already quoted, shortly after moving to Princeton, Wilson wrote to a friend "...in the morning I write; in the afternoon Mrs. Wilson sketches," proving that Ellen, even as a young mother, made time for her art work. It is a testament to her self-discipline and will power that Ellen, during all the years that she was raising her children, produced drawings, portraits, even landscapes (and in 1894, during a busy social "season," she sandwiched in engraving classes taught by a Mr. Frothingham).

Ellen's best friends, Lucy and Mary Smith, testified to Ray Stannard Baker in 1927 that "Mrs. Wilson kept up her art work during vacations and as much as

Ellen in Princeton, the 1890's 109

possible during term times, with much persistence," again contradicting Stockton's claim that "until the girls were well on into their teens, Mrs. Wilson scarcely touched a paint brush..."[47] We have many details of Ellen's work during the summer of 1896 and 1899, when Wilson was traveling in Europe.

"I have been going to the college to draw for the last three days," she wrote in July of 1896. In an era when there were no cheap re-prints in gift shops, Ellen often copied art in the museum that caught her fancy. What she was drawing she kept to herself, perhaps to surprise her husband. Very possibly it was her stunning copy of the "Madonna" by French artist, Adolphe Dagnan-Bouveret (Stockton incorrectly attributed the original to French artist, William Adolphe Bourgereau).

Stockton did make an exception when it came to this masterfully-done painting of his sister's. When she saw the original at the Princeton art museum, "she decided that she must have it...and so she got out her easel and paint brushes and went to the museum and copied it." More than likely, she went there to sketch it, returning home to paint. (Her new house included a studio.) According to Stockton,

I remember Mr. Wilson saying, when it was completed and hung in the little house in Princeton, that one of his colleagues came in one day and seeing it on the wall said: 'Great Scott, have you fallen heir to a fortune that you are able to buy a French masterpiece?' His friend thought this was the original. I also remember Mr. Wilson saying: 'As a matter of fact, the copy is better than the original.'[48]

(Stockton's reference to "the little house in Princeton" might have been to their rental, which would have put her Madonna at an even earlier date. However, the Wilsons typically referred to their homes as small, including the White House. Recalled Stockton, "I think I remember he [WW] stated that the White House did not have such a great number of rooms...")

Wilson, as always, was proud, even in awe, of his wife's artistic talent. In 1919, he confided to a relative "that there were few people in America who could paint better than Ellen could." He kept this portrait in his final home on S Street NW in Washington, D.C., where he died in 1924. Later Ellen's copy of the Madonna was sold and remained in private hands until 2001, the year the house on S Street (the Woodrow Wilson House museum) re-acquired this masterful work.[49]

That summer of 1896 Ellen did indeed apply herself, with much persistence. Besides the Madonna, which she might well have done during this summer, she reported doing "one charcoal at the college"--another copy, and in mid-August, "It was so cool this morning that I went to the college and began my big English landscape," copying one that her husband particularly liked. In addition, she painted (copied) four other landscapes, and "I am trying my hand at water colours." When she was not painting, she added, she was pulling weeds in the yard.[50]

When the Smith sisters spent summer vacation in 1898 with the Wilsons at picturesque Gloucestor Harbour (MA), they remembered that "'Ellen painted and Cousin Woodrow wrote.'" The following summer of 1899 was again fruitful. While Wilson was away in Europe for the second time, Ellen worked continuously, assiduously. "After I finish with the children in the morning, she [her sister Madge] reads the greater part of the day while I sew or paint," indicating, once again, that Ellen liked working with people around. "Do excuse this specially bad scrawl," she scribbled in late June, mindful of the fact that her handwriting was consistently bad. "I have been drawing most of the day and my hand is quite tired," once again vague about her work, which she rarely signed or dated.[51]

At times Ellen would draw or paint something for a friend, or to decorate the house. To decorate the walls of her husband's study, she copied portraits (in crayon) of all the great men whom Wilson most admired (including his father); she tinted her babies' photographs in the family album, and no doubt painted portraits of all of her children. Daughter Eleanor recalled that as a young child, "I remember 'sitting' for her once, hours on end, perched on an improbable dais, very straight and stiff and miserable..."[52]

It seems that it never occurred to Ellen to regard her art work as anything more than a leisure activity, albeit a strenuous one. Freed from household drudgery, and with her daughters finally enrolled in school in the fall of 1898, Ellen had a great deal of time on her hands and much freedom besides, thanks to her marriage to the right partner. At about this time, the late 1890's, she also resumed the study of German, taking classes outside of her home, and practicing with the children's German governess. Alone she visited her old friends from Rome, the Tedcastles, in their new home in Wellesley, Massachusetts, a visit lasting several weeks. Shortly afterwards, in early 1900, she traveled to New Orleans on her own for what was intended to be a two month vacation at the home of her close friends, Lucy and Mary Smith. During both trips, Ellen enjoyed herself enormously.

Hence in lieu of a career in an era when few women had one, Ellen's leisure time was taken up with self-development and self-improvement, and, in the case of volunteering, doing good. The time-consuming custom of "calling" seemed woven into the daily fabric of Ellen's life. Judged by the standards of today, however, visiting, and her habit of spending whole afternoons engaged in leisure

Ellen in Princeton, the 1890's

reading, were a waste of time that would better be filled by a worthwhile job or career. A modern-day Ellen no doubt would have had a job or career of her own-- to feel a sense of self-worth, to fend off boredom, to fulfill herself--apart from her home, children and marriage.

However, no evidence hints at any dissatisfaction in Ellen's life. Quite to the contrary. In 1892 she wrote rhapsodically, "I am like the lark, happiest of living creatures, who 'sings & sings & forever sings he, I love my love & my love loves me;'" six years later she told her husband, "I am simply abashed sometimes at [the] thought of my own happiness; it seems almost too good to be true. Why should *I* have so much more than anyone else?"[53]

ENDNOTES

[1] Margaret Axson Elliott, *My Aunt Louisa and Woodrow Wilson* (Chapel Hill: Univ. of North Carolina Press, 1944), 177.

[2] Woodrow Wilson to Ellen A. Wilson, April 17, 1892. Arthur S. Link, ed., *The Papers of Woodrow Wilson* (Princeton: Princeton University Press, 1966-1996) 7:575. (henceforth: *PWW*)

[3] Woodrow Wilson to John Franklin Jameson, May 2, 1890. *PWW* 6:621-622.

[4] On late 19th century Princeton: Elliott, 131-132, 169-173; Varnum L. Collins, *Princeton, Past and Present* (Princeton: Princeton University Press, [1945]).

[5] Elliott, 98, 154.

[6] Stockton Axson, *Brother Woodrow: A Memoir of Woodrow Wilson* ed. Arthur S. Link (Princeton, Princeton University Press, 1993), 67.

[7] Woodrow Wilson to G. McArthur Sullivan (a young African-American who sought admission to Princeton as an undergraduate), Dec.3, 1909. *PWW* 19:550.

[8] Axson, 129.

[9] Regarding cheating and Ellen's part in the honor system, and her decisiveness, *Ibid.*, 68, 105.

[10] Ellen's itemization appended to Wilson's letter to Frederick Jackson Turner, Dec.15, 1896. *PWW* 10:79.

[11] Ellen A. Wilson to Woodrow Wilson, Feb.12, 1896. *PWW* 9:421.

[12] Ellen A. Wilson to Woodrow Wilson, Feb.2, 1895, Feb.24, 1897.*PWW* 9:165; 10:172. Woodrow Wilson to Ellen A. Wilson, Feb.26, 1897. *PWW* 10:174.

[13] Eleanor Wilson McAdoo, *The Woodrow Wilsons* (New York: Macmillan Co., 1937), 15.

[14] *PWW* 8:198-199, notes 1, 2.

[15] On their "system" of paying bills: *PWW* 8:461,464; 9:174.

[16] Woodrow Wilson to Ellen A. Wilson, Jan.27, 1895. *PWW* 9:133.

[17] Ellen A. Wilson to Woodrow Wilson, Jan.28, 1895. *PWW* 9:140.

[18] Eleanor Wilson McAdoo, ed., *The Priceless Gift: The Love Letters of Woodrow Wilson and Ellen Axson Wilson* (New York: McGraw-Hill, 1962), 192.

[19] Ellen A. Wilson's postscript to Frederick Jackson Turner, Dec.15, 1896. *PWW* 10:80; Ellen A. Wilson to Woodrow Wilson, Feb.26, 1896. *PWW* 9:456. Her drawings of the floor plans (Wilson, with his clear handwriting, might have written the names of the rooms) can be found in the

Presidential Papers, Series 2, Woodrow Wilson Collection, Princeton University Firestone Library.

[20] Ellen A. Wilson to Anna Harris, June 1, 1895. *PWW* 9:281.

[21] Ellen A. Wilson to Woodrow Wilson, Feb.19, 1896. *PWW* 9:434; Joseph R. Wilson, Sr. to Woodrow Wilson, April 16, 1896, *PWW* 9:498.

[22] Ellen A. Wilson to Woodrow Wilson, Feb.24, 1896. *PWW* 9:447.

[23] Woodrow Wilson to James Franklin Jameson, Aug. 14, 1891, *PWW* 7:273; Ellen A. Wilson to Anna Harris, June 1, 1895. *PWW* 9:280.

[24] "Wilson's Diary," Feb.2, 1904, *PWW* 15:154; Axson, 104.

[25] Edwin A. Weinstein, *Woodrow Wilson: A Medical and Psychological Biography* (Princeton: Princeton University Press, 1981), 150.

[26] Woodrow Wilson to James Franklin Jameson, August 14, 1891. *PWW* 7:273

[27] Ellen A. Wilson to Woodrow Wilson, Feb.25, 1894. *PWW* 8:510.

[28] Ellen A. Wilson to Woodrow Wilson, Feb.25, 1894, Feb. 11, 1896, Dec.30, 1896. *PWW* 8:510; 9:417; 10:88.

[29] Ellen A. Wilson to Woodrow Wilson, Feb.25, 1894, Feb.11, 1896. *PWW* 8:510; 9:417.

[30] Woodrow Wilson to Ellen A. Wilson, Jan.26, 1895. *PWW* 9:128.

[31] Ellen A. Wilson to Woodrow Wilson, June 17, 1892. *PWW* 8:4.

[32] Ellen A. Wilson to Woodrow Wilson, Feb.22, 1894. *PWW* 8:503.

[33] Elliott, 182.

[34] Woodrow Wilson to Ellen A. Wilson, Feb.18, 1895. *PWW* 9:205.

[35] Ellen A. Wilson to Woodrow Wilson, March 2, 1897. *PWW* 10:182-183.

[36] Ellen A. Wilson to Woodrow Wilson, Feb.23, 1894, Feb.15, 1895, *PWW* 8:506, 9:199.

[37] Ellen A. Wilson to Woodrow Wilson, Jan.29, 1894. *PWW* 8:440; Woodrow Wilson to Ellen A. Wilson, Feb.4, 1894. *Ibid.*, 453.

[38] Ellen A. Wilson to Woodrow Wilson, June 19, 1899. *PWW* 11:131.

[39] Ellen A. Wilson to Woodrow Wilson, Feb.17, July 31, 1894. *PWW* 8:491, 635.

[40] Ellen A. Wilson to Woodrow Wilson, Feb.26, 1894. *PWW* 8:512.

[41] Ellen A. Wilson to Woodrow Wilson, July 26, 1893. *PWW* 8:292.

[42] Woodrow Wilson to Ellen A. Wilson, Feb.21, 1895. *PWW* 9:213.; Ellen A. Wilson to Woodrow Wilson, Feb.22, 1895. *Ibid.*, 219.

[43] See *PWW* 9: note 2, 220.

[44] Ellen A. Wilson to Woodrow Wilson, Aug.3, 1896. *PWW* 9:558.

[45] Ellen A. Wilson to Woodrow Wilson, Aug.17, 1896. *PWW* 9:571.

[46] Axson, 93.

[47] Axson, 91; Lucy and Mary Smith interview, 1927, Ray Stannard Baker papers, Library of Congress, Washington, D.C.

[48] Axson, 92-93.

[49] *Ibid.*, 93; McAdoo, *The Woodrow Wilsons*, 63.

[50] Ellen A. Wilson to Woodrow Wilson, July 30, Aug.13, 1896. *PWW* 9:553, 567.

[51] Ellen A. Wilson to Woodrow Wilson, June 29, July 20, 1899. *PWW* 11: 139, 183.

[52] McAdoo, *The Woodrow Wilsons*, 13, 19-20.

[53] Ellen A. Wilson to Woodrow Wilson, March 13, 1892, June 21, 1898. *PWW* 7:482; 10:568.

Chapter 5

MATER FAMILIAS

"...you are sweetheart, chum, wife, counsellor, intellectual companion, playmate, as I wish."[1]

Woodrow Wilson to his wife, 1899

"We knew what they [father and mother] expected of us and we wanted to please them and, above all, not to fall short of what we thought they required of us."[2]

Eleanor Wilson McAdoo, The Woodrow Wilsons

As a home-maker, Ellen re-created the kind of home life she had enjoyed as a child: loving and serene. "A distinct rhythm, a deep happy peace permeated the household," remembered Eleanor of her childhood, "... and mother, the center of it all..." she said of her mother, and not of her father, in those years.

> ...her soft Southern voice with its slow drawl, brown eyes so full of changing light, a perfect complexion, great masses of copper hair... She was small, eager, intensely alive.[3]

With admirable efficiency Ellen ran her household, which came to include, besides a cook and a maid, a grounds-keeper and light maintenance man, as well as a governess who taught her children foreign languages. Housekeeping included--what many wives would envy nowadays--a major spring and fall cleaning, from attic to cellar. In Ellen's day, middle class housewives often hired outsiders for such projects. When they were still renting in the spring of 1892,

Ellen mentioned hiring two men and two women to take down all the carpets, beat them thoroughly with rug beaters, and wash all the windows.

Ellen hired and supervised the servants, from whom she expected the same high standards as her own. When Wilson oversaw the household during Ellen's week-long trip to the Chicago World's Fair in 1893, he assured her that "I am not spoiling the servants a bit." Household servants did not come and go over the years. Maggie Foley and "Annie" remained with the Wilsons throughout their years in Princeton, until 1910. The servants were always white, which shocked Madge Axson when she came to live with her sister.

Daughter Eleanor recalled her own fondness for Maggie Foley, an Irishwoman who began as the nursemaid and ended up the family cook. Ellen apparently taught Maggie how to prepare the meals she preferred, which she had learned at Mrs. Rorer's cooking school in her Bryn Mawr days. A glance through one of Rorer's cook books reveals a surprising variety of dishes, not a few of them ethnic and tangy, quite different from the bland meals most Americans were used to. There was her recipe for home-made ice cream (but deliciously flavored), which the Wilsons loved for dessert, and home-made mayonnaise, which they ate with (or on) their chicken. It should be noted that Ellen, more so than Wilson, had grown up on "Georgia broiled chicken," which neither she nor her husband could get enough of. (Hence most winters, as Ellen noted, southern kin mailed her a crate of fresh "young chickens.") Moreover, her husband was easy to please when it came to food, he preferring most of all "chicken and rice" to Yankee men's "meat and potatoes."

The Wilsons could not do without a maid, and Madge Axson remembered well the Wilson maid, known simply as Annie, "one of the most smoothly competent waitresses in Princeton," well-fitted to serve the Wilsons' elegant dinner table.[4]

When Maggie Foley graduated from nursemaid to cook, and before Annie came into their employ, Ellen had the unwelcome task of looking for a nursemaid and all-round servant for her growing household. It was just as hard to find good, stable servants in Princeton as it had been in Connecticut. Perhaps the nearness of New York with its better-paid jobs, or the lack of all social amenities in Princeton, made it difficult to keep servants, who were almost always immigrants.

Down south on a lengthy visit with her children in 1892, Ellen went servant-hunting. Hoping to find a replacement for Maggie Foley as nursemaid, she came to like a certain young black Maggie in Savannah. "She is the genuine African article--very black & very unsophisticated, but apparently kindhearted & faithful, with no nonsense about her." By the time Ellen reached Gainesville weeks later, Maggie was changing her mind about going north, apparently because her sister

Mater Familias

was ill and needed her. To Ellen's Aunt Louisa, however, "'it was a real nigger trick,'" wrote Ellen. By then, Ellen, too, had changed her mind about Maggie.

> I have felt dubious all along about taking her north. Where the negroes are so inconceivably worthless as they are in G. it really seemed impossible that any *one* of them could wholly escape the taint.[5]

Whatever she meant by "taint," her husband must have understood her perfectly. A graduate assistant of his at Bryn Mawr, Jane Bancroft, "'found it a new experience,'" she recalled, "'to meet a Southerner who had no special sympathy for Negroes as human beings.'"[6] Maggie left Ellen's brief employment, reducing Ellen, once more, to only one servant at home.

Their racial prejudice notwithstanding, the Wilsons were not disdainful of their servants, white or black, in Princeton or in the White House. When Ellen overheard that a wealthy Princeton woman always "dropped her clothes on the floor for her maid to pick up and put away," she remarked, "'How disgusting!'"[7]

* * *

Ellen viewed herself first and foremost as a mother. When her traveling husband longed for her to feast her eyes on the Rocky Mountains as he was doing in 1894, she responded,

> How sweet it is in you to be so wild for me to see them too! ...But that particular sort of pleasure--the pleasures of freedom and travel arn't for mothers; --and having bartered them for something better, they certainly have no cause for dissatisfaction.[8]

Madge Axson, only a few years older than her young nieces, found the girls too "tame" and docile for her taste. Their uncle "Stock" had a different view of them, however. "The Wilson girls were docile, not because they lacked spirit, for they were high-spirited above the average, and not through fear of parental displeasure, ...but because they lived in an atmosphere of love..."[9]

As mothers the world over, Ellen was proud of her children. When they were toddlers, Ellen stayed home from church most Sundays to keep an eye on them, since the servants were not allowed to work. However, she would dress them in their best and wheel them to church when the service was ending, ostensibly to meet her husband coming out, but in fact, to show off her little girls. Wilson would tease her about this every time, but he was as proud of them as Ellen, and never betrayed his disappointment at not having a son.

Unsystematic as Ellen was, she had no fixed ideas about raising children. A few of her child-rearing concepts, however, seem odd today. For instance, Ellen insisted that her daughters begin sleeping with the light out while they were still toddlers. Margaret's turn, as the oldest, came first. Even though she cried and cried, the light remained off, while an anxious Ellen spent hours peeking at her through the keyhole. Only Eleanor ("Nellie"), the youngest child, escaped this rite of passage, protesting so fiercely that her parents were forced to give in. Ellen also forbade her children to sit on bare lawn, unless they sat on straw mats, certain that it harmed their circulation. And if a girl was growing "too fast," she believed that her hair should be cut short. In the case of both Margaret and Eleanor, a barber came to their home to give them a "Dutch bob."

Even though Ellen's children were girls and it was the nineteenth century, their upbringing was surprisingly free of restraint. "School was out at one," recalled Eleanor. "And, as we were not required to be home before dark, we ran over the countryside, playing hare and hounds and skating on the brook," completely unsupervised. True, they played with dolls and wore dresses, but unlike today, their free time was spent almost entirely outdoors, in physical activity of one sort or another.

"We hear of nothing but base-ball and tennis with the boys," Ellen wrote of her children in 1896. One day, eight year-old Jessie "...was racing up and down the sidewalk being, as she said, a runner in the Olympian games. She told me with great excitement how many 'other boys' were running too & how she beat them every time." The girls also rode bicycles, skated, hiked, played croquet, learned to ride horseback, and as teenagers, played basketball. Ellen expected her daughters to walk, and later--to ride their bikes--to school, even when it was three miles from home.[10]

Despite their freedom, oldest daughter Margaret "often lamented the fact that she was a girl..." Margaret was the acknowledged tomboy in the family. "Margaret had worn her hair very short for some time," being the first to get her hair bobbed. "She had fought most of the boys, simply and in groups, until they stopped teasing her about it." She did not complain to her mother about her short hair, however. Margaret, like her mother, would remain short in stature, but unlike her, wore eye glasses, which stamped a woman as unattractive.[11]

The children grew up with pets (their cats, "Puff" and "Bunny," and their numerous progeny) and doting relatives. Their young, handsome Uncle Ed, who lived with them for years, was a favorite. He regaled them with "fantastic yarns," taught them to ride bicycles, made snow men for them in winter, and took them sledding. During their father's absences, he was their surrogate father. Their older uncle "Stock," who never married and lived with his sister off and on, loved his nieces blindly. And while Ellen and Wilson tried not to spoil their children, their many relatives had no such reservations. Every Christmas found the girls loaded with presents. The Christmas of 1892 was typical: "The dolls from Anna [Harris] arrived," wrote Ellen, "also beautiful books for them from Sav. & a lovely little ring for each of them from Sister Annie," not to mention what their parents, as well as their live-in uncles, gave them.[12]

In those days, there were few organized activities for children. Ellen mentioned the occasional children's party, and every May 1st, a neighbor would invite children to dance and sing around his Maypole. But there were no playgrounds, gyms, swimming pools, zoos, or children's room in the library. As both Ellen and Wilson were becoming more liberal in their religious views, they took their daughters to dancing lessons (and later, they were permitted to drink wine).

While Ellen and Wilson were mild, they were not permissive parents. As there was not, in those days, any question of "children's rights," they expected obedience from them at all times. (It is surprising to learn that when Jessie was 22 and a college graduate, Ellen still expected her to ask permission.) In those days parents also were expected to, and not censured for, spanking their children. Ellen, never Wilson (according to Eleanor), spanked hers. Afterwards, "Her face always got quite pink and she invariably cried." Quite unlike today, their children were expected to be seen, but never heard, when there were guests at home. And lest they become conceited, "Mother & father never complimented us on our appearance," and were careful to praise them only moderately.[13]

Church-going on Sunday morning, of course, was rigorously enforced. To Eleanor, Sundays were nothing short of gruesome. The whole family walked to the Second Presbyterian Church, about a mile from home (later, to the First Presbyterian Church, a half mile farther). "The long hymns and sermons, of which I understood very little, confused and exhausted me," recalled Eleanor. "The church was plain and uninteresting, the wooden seats cold and hard, and I spent the time in a sort of hopeless stupor..." Of course, the rest of the day there was no play allowed, only Bible study with their mother, and other edifying reading.[14] The day concluded, as most days, with evening prayers, a custom Ellen and Wilson enforced while their children were young.

Neither Eleanor nor Jessie could recall an occasion when their father was angry at them, unlike their mother. As a professor, Wilson was at home more so than most fathers. Unlike many fathers in the nineteenth century, he played with his children from the time they were little, and hugged and kissed them often.

Like any good mother, her children's happiness and needs came before Ellen's own. "...I remember always being able to find her when I needed her," recalled Eleanor. She was, after all, a full-time Mom. Mother and father, however, would both take turns nursing their children when they fell ill, which, by the standards of today, was alarmingly frequent, and would often require isolating both caretaker and patient as much as possible. Falling ill with highly contagious scarlet fever, daughter Eleanor had to be quarantined in her room for days on end...

> At first mother stayed with me, spending every moment in the nursery, with no access to other parts of the house. When she was completely worn out, father relieved her...[15]

Every spring and fall Ellen made new clothes for her daughters, and re-made old ones. When they were little, Ellen loved dressing them in fanciful, matching Kate Greenaway outfits. She was also surprisingly modern in her zeal for her family's dental health. Her children had regular check-ups, and she even saw to it that Eleanor, and possibly her siblings, was fitted with braces by an orthodontist. Ellen herself frequently had teeth that required fillings, ten needed re-filling during one visit alone.

When it came to child-raising, Ellen was a relaxed parent with a sense of humor. One day she discovered some mysterious glop congealed on the ground outside a first floor window. She soon found out that her daughters always, but secretly, tossed out their fish stew whenever they had it for lunch (lunch was the one meal they ate apart from their parents). While many a parent in that era would have given them a scolding or worse, Ellen just burst out laughing. Eleanor's comment was justified, that "...there was no limit to her understanding."

While Ellen, far more than her husband, had first-hand experience with poor, even indigent people, her children grew to adulthood with no such exposure to the real world. In every respect, the lives of Eleanor, Margaret and Jessie were sheltered, snug and secure,"...a time to look back with longing in the years to come."[16]

* * *

On January 31, 1899, Ellen informed her friend Anna Harris,

> I on my part have gone out of the business--of teaching--to some extent. My children are all at school this year for the first time. Until last year I taught them altogether. Then we imported a governess from Germany who proved a great success. The children now speak German as fluently as English, and write it very correctly too.[17]

This sums up her children's education in the 1890s: home-schooling until the fall of 1898, when they enrolled in private school, and in late 1897, the arrival of Fräulein Clara Böhm, thereafter simply called "Fräulein," as their live-in tutor of German and French.

While Ellen had no pre-conceived ideas about her children's education--she regarded home-schooling as a necessity, rather than a preference--there was no question that their education was a very high priority with her and her husband. Despite Wilson's antipathy for "emancipated" women, he expected all three of his girls to get a college education (all three went to college; only one graduated).

Their education was a constant concern throughout the 1890's. Wilson wrote a friend in 1896, "The place is too small to have adequate schools for children, -- at any rate for girls. Boys are fairly well provided for." This statement is surprising in light of the fact that within walking distance of the Wilsons' home, there were not one, but at least two, public elementary schools, and also a public high school. Moreover, Eleanor noted that her father was "a staunch champion of the public school...He believed that the public school developed better habits of study; that it discouraged snobbery and bred confidence in timid people."[18] He said virtually the same to his friend Mrs. Peck years later, when he discovered that she, too, had attended public schools.

When it came to their own daughters, however, Ellen and her husband seemed dead-set against sending them to public school. Eleanor vaguely remembered that the public school in Princeton (there was also a public high school) was "in rather a questionable neighborhood and almost inaccessible, so mother and Fräulein taught us until Mrs. Scott opened a small private school." What Eleanor meant by "questionable" is unclear. Perhaps it was too close to a black neighborhood? The Princeton school system, however, was segregated. Or did it include too many immigrant children? Nor is it believable that the public school was "almost inaccessible." After all, Mrs. Scott's school, when it finally opened, lay three miles from home, and the Wilson girls--before they got bicycles--were expected to walk there and back on their own. Madge Axson's memory is even vaguer, remembering simply that "there was no girls' school in Princeton at that time," saying nothing of public schools.[19]

Ellen, and in particular Wilson, were also opposed to co-education, and public schools were co-ed. In 1894, when Wilson heard that the University of Virginia was considering becoming co-educational, his reaction was bitter.

> It distresses me very deeply that the University of Virginia should think, even through a minority of its Faculty, of admitting women to its courses. I have had just enough experience of co-education to know that, even under the

most favorable circumstances, it is most demoralizing...it *vulgarizes* the whole relationship of men and women.[20]

Wilson's "experience of co-education" harked back to when he taught at Wesleyan, where, out of a student body of over 215, only 15 were women.

Still, when Mrs. Scott's school opened in the fall of 1898, it was co-educational, and the Wilsons sent their girls there anyway. At least it was not a public school. Eleanor recalled that the boys at Mrs. Scotts' were obnoxious. "One little brat who sat behind her [Jessie] tied her braids to an ink well and poor Jessie sent the ink flying when she stood up. She didn't fight and cry as Margaret and I did..." As soon as Miss Fine's school for girls opened a year later, Ellen whisked her daughters away from Mrs. Scotts'. They stayed there through high school.[21]

The reluctance to send her daughters to public school meant that Ellen had to try and instruct them herself, at least at first. As it turned out, the Wilson girls could not have had a better educator.

Ellen was a born teacher who, however, seemed unconscious of her teaching talent. At first she had no clue how or what to teach them, or when to start. "Margaret will soon be eight, you know," she wrote her absent husband in January of 1894, "and I feel that I must be thinking about more systematic instruction." It is unclear whether Margaret could read by then (her father, according to Eleanor,"did not learn to read easily himself until he was twelve.").[22] Jessie was six and a half. Eleanor, at four, was too young for schooling. That month, Ellen made her first hesitant foray into home-schooling. In those days there were no lesson plans, guidelines, or textbooks for home-schoolers or their parents.

With no school books to direct them (and their mother) in their studies, Ellen asked her husband to find suitable text books while he was away in Baltimore; until these arrived, she would make do with "my old 'manual' from 'Parley's' History. They study the maps & pictures half the day. I am also trying to teach them a wee bit about spelling--and finding it rather hard work!" Ellen's regimen was never rigorous. They took a break from lessons while she went into the kitchen, for instance, to make popcorn. "The children are very happy over pop-corn just now," she wrote, noting that they had never had any, and had not known what it was. Ellen made learning fun and relaxing, and her girls learned eagerly under her tutelage. Ellen found that she enjoyed it, too, and was in no hurry to hire anyone else to do it, either, as she and her husband had briefly considered.[23] "School" hours were eventually extended to one o'clock.

Mater Familias   121

In June, 1895, Ellen wrote her friend Anna Harris,

> The 'school,' which takes the morning until twelve, has gone on finely. I feel quite proud of my youngest pupil [Eleanor]. She took her first lesson last Oct. on the day after her fifth birthday, and in four months she could read fluently *anything* she could *understand*...It is very funny to hear that little tot talk about her 'Plato,' -- which she has 'read through.'[24]

After only a year of home-schooling, the Wilson daughters were becoming extremely well-read. Ellen noted that one day they were debating, "Who is the greatest, Shakespeare or Homer, Milton or Dante, Themistocles or Miltiades, Zeus or Odin, Aeschylus or Sophocles, Epaminondas or Washington?" although they were all younger than ten.[25] When they enrolled in school for the first time, they impressed their teacher, who complimented Ellen on her "system;" Ellen laughed and claimed that she hadn't any.

Stockton noted of his sister that "she was always trying to lead them, by easy stages, to appreciation of what is *fine* in thought and letters."[26] Ellen's predilection for literature and fine writing, led her, understandably, to emphasize poetry, which her children memorized in gobs. She taught them the fundamentals of arithmetic, and little, if any, science.

All three daughters were highly intelligent. Eleanor was the least bookish, her real talent running in the direction of acting and dramatics, for which there was little outlet in the Princeton of her day. As to Jessie, perhaps the most gifted of Ellen's daughters, "Jessie's latest exploit is learning yesterday all of Tennyson's 'Brook' by heart," wrote Ellen proudly, soon after commencing her home-schooling. In the summer of 1899, "During the heat of the day they all read Scott devoutly," Sir Walter Scott being still wildly popular in the late nineteenth century, "Jessie has read sixteen of the novels now....", while Margaret was a close runner-up.[27]

Ellen and her daughters so enjoyed learning together that they kept up their studies even during their summer vacations, even after they had started formal day school. Describing a day in July, 1899, when Wilson was on his second trip to Europe

> We have settled into a regular program now; --after breakfast stroll about the 'place,' gather sweet peas, etc.; then we repair to the upper porch and our literary studies(!) in which we sometimes get so interested,--the children begging for more and more--that we go on 'till twelve o'clock. We are going straight through the "English Lands, Letters & Kings," with frequent extracts

from Green and other things, and quantities of poetry, including Shakespeare's historical plays.[28]

Her husband's trip was an occasion to teach them the history and literature of the countries he visited, to great effect.

Notwithstanding their daughters' strides in learning at home, Ellen and her husband continued to be anxious about their future schooling. Ellen was not satisfied with what she gave them, despite her talent as a teacher. Nor was she conscious of, and might not have agreed, that they were receiving far more from her teaching than they would ever have gotten in a formal school setting.

Still reluctant to send them to public school two years after beginning her home-schooling, she and Wilson were ecstatic when they heard that President Grover Cleveland and his family, also consisting of three young girls, were retiring to Princeton after Cleveland's term ended in March (1897) "...their coming may help to solve the question of a school for your girls," wrote Wilson's uncle James, "of which Ellen spoke so anxiously."[29] However, Mrs. Scott opened her private school a year later, at last resolving the problem of their girls' education. The arrival of the Clevelands did have one effect for sure--it drove up real estate prices--though Wilson mistakenly believed that it would not.

While still home-schooling, Ellen scouted for a live-in tutor of foreign languages. Wilson asked a friend of his, who was away in Berlin, to recommend one, and this turned out to be the remarkable Clara Böhm, a Prussian girl in her twenties. She traveled to the States alone, the Wilsons probably paying her ship fare. Arriving in Princeton in the winter of 1896-97, Böhm was no hit with fifteen year-old Madge Axson, "for I didn't like the look of her pale, fishy eyes." According to Madge, but not to Eleanor's more extensive memoirs, Böhm was a bully who took a dislike to daughter Margaret. She would say to Margaret, "'You have the hands of a peasant,' brutal stuff to hand out to a girl who already labored under the disadvantage of having an exquisitely beautiful younger sister," namely Jessie.[30]

Böhm was unusual even for a Prussian. In a day and age when few educated Germans knew English, Böhm's was fluent, and her French was perfect. Although her father was a Prussian officer and a strict German patriarch, he obviously wanted his daughters to be well-educated. Perhaps for that reason, Böhm found herself becoming an "old maid" in a Germany still unfriendly to "emancipated" women. She was glad to leave a home where she "felt in the way;" nonetheless, she told the Wilson girls "that when the ship pulled away from the dock, she was heartbroken and wanted to jump overboard." Wilson's first impression of her, quite unlike Madge's, evoked pity: "Poor thing...she must be feeling very far away from home," he said sympathetically.

She certainly did well for herself. Working for the Wilsons opened doors. Hence when the girls enrolled in Mrs. Scott's school, Scott hired Böhm to teach foreign languages, though she continued living with the Wilsons, "...and for years was an uncomfortable addition to the household," noted Madge Axson. Eleanor, however, claimed that "We loved Fräulein and soon were absorbed in the study of German." Fräulein often admonished her young pupils to appreciate "the American man's consideration for his family, and how different the European attitude was." However, one day when precocious little Eleanor asked her, "'If we had a war with Germany, you would be on our side, wouldn't you?'" Böhm jumped up and declared passionately, "'I would follow my Kaiser.'"[31]

Ellen did not exaggerate when she wrote Anna Harris, less than two years after Böhm's arrival, that her children could read, write and speak German fluently. Had they had any antipathy for Böhm, it is hard to imagine that Jessie would have pursued the study of German as her major in college, long after Böhm had left the Wilsons' orbit.

Even if Ellen had no special preference for home-schooling, she did insist on teaching "Sunday school" at home. Wilson's father, during his career as a pastor, argued "that if they [the parents] couldn't give their own children religious instruction at home, Sunday school wouldn't help much." Ellen, however, distrusted Sunday school for an altogether different reason. Daughter Jessie recalled that her mother had misgivings about Sunday school teachers. They were "'mostly unschooled'" and consequently, "'unable to give a true view of religion.'" Possibly their approach was too simplistic or doctrinal to suit her. For instance, by the 1890's, Ellen and Wilson had ceased to believe in hell (hell was only a "state of mind"), a core Christian belief. They were liberal Christians by then, who took church teachings with a grain of salt, although Wilson's personal faith in God never wavered and he read a chapter of the Bible every day of his life. Ellen's faith did waver, and she tried to find answers to her religious doubts by reading philosophers as Nietzsche (a firm atheist) and Kant, a liberal theist.[32]

Jessie alone of her siblings retained a strong Christian faith. Margaret, and quite likely Eleanor, came to regard all religions as equally valid. Such extreme liberalism, according to Stockton, disturbed Ellen not a little, who was unwilling to go that far. She never lived to see Margaret, in her middle years, embrace a syncretic Hindu mysticism (the cult of Sri Aurobindo), ending her days in an ashram in India.

* * *

Thanks to Ellen's marriage to the right partner, she enjoyed a leisure and opportunities for travel and enjoyment that most women in her day (even today) could only envy. Her marriage also opened doors for her siblings. Thanks to his sister, Stockton was able to give up his dreary job in his uncle's business in Savannah, she and Wilson supporting him while he attended graduate school at Wesleyan, and later at Princeton. He became an English professor at Princeton and afterwards, at Rice University in Texas, where he lived out his life. After graduating from Princeton, Ed Axson went on to a graduate degree in chemical engineering at the Massachusetts Institute of Technology. Madge Axson received private schooling in Brooklyn, paid for by the Wilsons, and afterwards, earned her bachelor's degree from the Baltimore College for Women (today's Goucher College). In an age when women were not pressured to hold a job or career, Madge chose a life of travel and leisure (being the recipient of her late father's legacy), mostly in Italy, before she married in 1910.

Ellen was a devoted and conscientious mother, sister, and wife. As to her sister's deep devotion to her husband, Madge Axson had this to say about it,

> Just as the rest of the world counted for nothing with Ellen in face of her children, so the girls themselves would have been shoved into the background had she been compelled to choose between them and her husband.[33]

A woman choosing her husband--before her own children? Since Madge was far from uncritical of her sister, her assessment, a negative one at heart, is probably untrue. Madge continued,

> Woodrow was not the irritable type for whom the house had to be kept quiet lest 'the master' be disturbed in his work, but had he been, she would have locked her daughters in a dark room without a shadow of compunction.[34]

This claim is too extreme to have been true. To be sure, Wilson was not the "irritable type," for had he been, he would not have been the right partner for Ellen (or for any woman), and consequently, she would have loved him much less.

Ellen and Wilson did in fact love each other passionately, seemingly uncritically, and appeared to have a rock solid marriage. If they were ever angry at each other, they repressed or restrained their anger, in that era when restraint was considered a virtue.

Intense expressions of love were common. From the seaside Ellen wrote one day, "I love you so that it *hurts*! ...What would I not give to clasp you in my arms now," a refrain that she often repeated. "How I *glory* in you! My precious possession!" Her husband's letters "make my heart almost break with love, & longing to be in your arms." Sometimes their love soared to poetic heights, as in Wilson's letters to her from Europe in 1899. After fourteen years of married life, his love for her was as keen as on their wedding day. "*You* are all the world to *me*; you elevate, you stimulate, you delight me: every part of me enjoys you with an infinite ardour." What woman would not be in love with a man like Wilson?[35]

Erotic feelings sometimes surfaced, offering glimpses into their intimate life. In the spring of 1892, when Ellen was away from her husband for several months, Wilson missed her--and her body--terribly.

Ah, my darling, if I could only once a week, when my heart particularly fails me, have just one moment with you--just long enough for one long look into your sweet eyes, one long embrace, straining your sweet body close, close to mine, pressing your lips with a passionate kiss, like an interchange of life, a mixture & union of identities--I could stand this empty room and this empty bed.[36]

This three-month separation, when Ellen and her babies were visiting relatives in Georgia, severely strained Wilson's enforced celibacy. "I have suffered nothing short of torments of desire lately--am suffering them daily now..." Finally, he could stand it no longer. Not one to break his marriage vows, he took the time to translate, from the French, an intensely erotic bedroom scene from a French novel which he obtained from the college library, Théophile Gautier's *Mademoiselle de Maupin*.[37]

Modesty prohibits quoting the graphic lines, which Wilson fluently and gracefully translated, describing a beautiful young virgin's steamy seduction by an older man, and their subsequent love-making, lasting all night long. Surely Stockton's assertion to Ray Stannard Baker that Wilson's French was not very fluent must be taken with a grain of salt. Considering its contents, it is remarkable that this translation, done in the heat of passion, was ever saved for posterity.

Wilson was not alone in suffering "torments of desire" during this, their first lengthy separation. Ellen, too, wrote that "I positively pant & tingle all over with the desire to see you, my own, *my* own love!" Her ardent response was in answer to Wilson's earlier letter, in which he had asked her teasingly, "Do you think you will be able to stand all the kisses, all the involved and various love-making that I shall insist upon[?]."[38]

Three years later, on the eve of his return from his annual lecture trip to Baltimore, he again ended his letter in an erotic undertone, "Are you ready, darling [,] to be kissed breathless by, Your own Woodrow." This is tame compared to what he told her a year later, "Imagine yourself kissed and embraced till forced to fight for breath..." Expressing his feelings in such a vein to his wife hints that Ellen must have been, beneath her demure exterior, far from frigid. "Any woman, young or mature, would seem stale and slow after you," he told her. No wonder that Ellen, who invariably read aloud her husband's letters to her daughters, would suddenly pause and tell them, "'This is too sacred to be read even to you girls'"[39]

The decision to forego having further children meant that Wilson took a step that probably neither his preacher father, nor Ellen's, would ever have condoned. He procured condoms for his use, no doubt via mail order. Since the 1840's, these were made of vulcanized rubber, and not meant for one use, but to be washed and re-used. There are hints that they began using them from the time of Eleanor's birth, in 1889, the year they decided not to have any more children. Nine years later, and probably longer, they were still using condoms. In 1898, as Ellen was preparing to visit Wilson in Baltimore for the weekend, he reminded her, "The other thing I had thought of may occur to you independently: will you not bring the little bundle of *rubbers* in the bottom drawer of the wash stand?"[40]

Contraception did not dispel their fear of unwanted pregnancy. Wilson was always aware of Ellen's "courses," and when she missed a period in the spring of 1892, they were both anxious ("If what we fear should turn out to have happened," hinted Wilson in his letter to her, shortly after she arrived in Georgia). Over a week later, Ellen's "courses" still had not begun, but she was manfully clinging to hope, "for you know, dear, if we have another baby how many heavy expenses it will involve." Having missed one month's period, she was close to the next month's. Wilson wrote five days later, "The courses are due Tuesday, the 22nd, I feel quite sure." If they did come, he wanted her to telegraph him immediately. The next day he again reminded her to telegraph him. "Ah, if *they come!* I do not *dare* to *expect* they will. I only venture a desperate *hope*." Sure enough, on March 23, "When I waked this morning I found that the courses had begun!" and she promptly sent him a telegram. Her husband's relief was almost audible: "...how shall I express the profound joy, the infinite, unspeakable relief I experienced upon receiving that cipher telegram!....I did not realize the dreadful weight of the anxiety that had been making all my days and all their work a wearing struggle." Perhaps it was not so much his fear of another child--which, after all, could turn out to be a son--than wishing to spare his wife (and himself) the prolonged physical misery that seemed to intensify with each pregnancy.[41]

Six years later, when Ellen was experiencing a long spell of nausea, Wilson wrote, "As for what we a little feared, inspite of all likelihood, that ought to be settled this week. It is four weeks today (this afternoon) since your last courses began. They ought to come again within a day or two, if they are coming. But why should I talk of *this*, it is surely quite out of the question!" perhaps because of her age, or perhaps because they had successfully avoided pregnancy for so many years.[42]

Compared to his wife Ellen, wrote Wilson in 1897, "I find other women almost entirely robbed of their charms...They are interesting, and pleasantly feminine, but they are not fascinating in a sufficient degree to give a fellow pleasurable excitement in their presence," to which Ellen responded, "It is simply that I love you with all my heart, and they do not."[43]

By then, after twelve years of marriage, Ellen's faith in her husband's love for her was unwavering. Otherwise, he might not have admitted to her what any other woman, then as now, might have found unsettling:

> I have all the roving, Bohemian impulses the wildest young colt could have. There are a thousand and one things I long to do,--did my purse and my conscience allow: there are scores of ways in which I long to be amused, innocent, questionable, undoubtedly wrong...[44]

He himself marveled at her open-mindedness when it came to expressing his longings so candidly. "I wonder what other wife there is in the world...to whom her husband could make such disclosures of himself as I dare make of myself to you!" Teasingly, he added, "I wonder that you trust me out of your sight!" Remarks like this were sure to be punctuated with protestations of his love, and the assurance that "...I'd rather have a moment with you than all the entertainment and so-called pleasure in the world."[45]

In truth, Wilson relished the company of attractive, intelligent women. To his friend Jack Hibben, he remarked about a new friend of Ellen's "...and one of the friends made a great impression on me; --her brow and eyes would make an impression on any man who had eyes himself; and she proved to have a remarkable and most attractive mind besides..." A Mrs. Harry Reid, whom he met in Baltimore in 1894, and who became deeply attracted to Wilson, was just the type of woman he liked: "She is not at all *intense*, neither is she a bit 'advanced,' except in the power to think and see." At the same time, Wilson saw nothing compromising, as a married man and father, taking out a pretty "Miss Duer" to dinner alone, rather than with another party. Perhaps because he told Ellen about it ("...have seldom enjoyed any woman's talk more than I did hers: it was at once thoroughly intellectual and thoroughly feminine") his conscience seemed clear. One wonders how he would have felt had Ellen done--and said--likewise in his absence.[46]

Ellen's faith in herself as the spouse of so extraordinary a man did waver, however. "If *I* had the chosing [sic] of a wife for you I should not have done you such injustice!" Perhaps this lack of faith in herself explains why Ellen was willing to go to any lengths for him for whom nothing was too good. In her letter to Anna Harris in 1899, she confessed, "I cannot somehow shake off for a moment the weight it [the recent death of her beloved friend Beth] has laid upon my spirits, all the more so perhaps because for Woodrow's sake I must not show it. He is almost terribly dependent on me to keep up his spirits and to 'rest' him as he says...If I am just a little sky-blue he immediately becomes blue-black!"[47] Likewise, though Ellen missed him terribly when he was away for long ("I never really knew what loneliness was before," during his first trip abroad) she prevailed on him to go again to Europe in 1899 for his own good, despite his distress at leaving her behind. (She would not leave her young children.)

Though Wilson's weakness for the opposite sex may well have displeased Ellen (she never seemed to join him, for instance, in his long, heartfelt conversations alone with Jenny Hibbens, attractive wife of his best friend Jack), she repressed her feelings. Surely to please him rather than herself, she encouraged him to go out with interesting women ("I hope you will see a lot of Miss Duer..."). She tolerated his close, unseemly companionship with Jenny Hibben.

Wilson was conscious of his wife's self-abnegation ("giving up your exquisite gifts to the service of others, - of *another*") and could have done nothing about it had he tried. Her will power, as he and others close to her knew, was inflexible.

From the first until the very last, Ellen was more fully her husband's partner than his second wife would ever be. From the very outset, Ellen was helping her husband in decisive ways. Even before their first child was born, she was translating and writing summaries of ponderous German texts for his research; according to Stockton and to Eleanor, she was his most important proofreader. "...though she was the most adoring of wives, there was in her an uncompromising quality which would have made it impossible for her to say to him that something he did was done well if she thought it was not done well."[48]

This made a difference in his career. A case in point was Wilson's public address marking Princeton's Sesquicentennial, when the college turned 150 years old in 1896 and officially adopted the name Princeton University. This was a grand affair, the most important public occasion in Princeton's history.

"It seems a pity to tear up the campus so, just before the Sesqui-centennial" wrote Ellen while Wilson was spending the summer in Europe. This included the demolition of "the old quadrangle." "Indeed the whole town looks torn up, so much building is going on."[49] It was a singular honor, indicative of Wilson's

Mater Familias

129

stature at Princeton, to be chosen the keynote speaker at the upcoming Sesquicentennial. He worked on his speech even while he was traveling abroad that summer.

The speech was not completed until he read it aloud to Ellen. Stockton heard of his sister's criticism from Wilson: "'It does not end well.'" She told him. "'It ends too abruptly. It needs something to lift it and to lift your audience up to the highest plane of vision. It needs a great final paragraph...'" She thought of Milton's "great final paragraph" in his *Areopagitica*. Of course, Ellen could easily quote the lines from memory: "'Methinks, I see her as an eagle mewing her mighty youth and kindling her undazzled eyes at the full midday beam.'" Apparently it took far less to uplift audiences then, than today.[50]

Stockton continued:

> ...he was so easily able to take this suggestion given to him by his wife and frame the sort of paragraph which she in a sense had ordered him to frame on the model which she had suggested....which incidentally is the most famous passage in the address.[51]

There were other changes in the original draft, according to the editors of Wilson's papers: "numerous handwritten emendations and insertions by Wilson and his wife."

Instead of the lead balloon it would be today, Wilson's quaintly Victorian address, "Princeton in the Nation's Service," turned out to be "the most brilliant, *dazzling* success from first to last." Ellen and all three daughters were there on that windy October day, eyes riveted on the podium, as he delivered his oration.[52] Alas, Stockton did not identify "the most famous passage in the address." It might have been Wilson's "uplifting" last lines: Princeton University,

> ...slow to take excitement, its air pure and wholesome with a breath of faith: every eye within it bright in the clear day and quick to look toward heaven for the confirmation of its hope. Who shall show us the way to this place?

whereupon the audience broke into a deafening ovation. "I never imagined anything like it," proudly wrote Ellen to her cousin Mary Hoyt. Unbelievably, "As for the Princeton men some of them simply fell on his neck and wept for joy." The speech was endlessly quoted in the press and re-printed numerous times. Wilson emerged the most important man at Princeton, Ellen having played no small role in his astounding success.[53]

* * *

Wilson admitted to his wife in 1894, "...but such is your husband-hungry-*too* hungry-for reputation and influence." His ambition became hers, even if it was to come at her own expense. This buttresses Jessie Wilson's (Mrs. Sayre's) remark to Ray Stannard Baker: that her mother disapproved of a couple pursuing separate careers; they both should follow the same career.[54]

Wilson seemed to take no professional step without consulting his wife first. Hence in 1892, when he was offered the presidency of the University of Illinois during his wife's absence in Georgia, he acknowledged, "I know that it must have seemed extraordinary to you, darling, that I told you nothing of what I knew of the University of Illinois." He went on to explain. "...but I expected to *see* you before this. I should of course never decide such a matter without detailed conference with you."[55] Over the next two weeks, they discussed this topic endlessly, Wilson drawn to the offer chiefly because of the salary--double what he was receiving at Princeton--whereas Ellen worried that he would have no time for creative work. Her judgment prevailed.

They worked so closely together that Ellen felt free to answer letters from his colleagues and editors when her husband was away. When an editor of a law review reminded Wilson of an article that was due, Ellen informed her absent husband: "'I know you havn't it ready, so I suppose I had better answer it for you.'" A year later, in 1895, she admonished her husband, "....don't forget that you were to strike for better pay there!" referring to Johns Hopkins, with which he had a contract to deliver lectures each spring for six weeks (eventually reduced to five). Wilson was always timid about money matters. Ellen was not so timid.[56]

A remarkable letter of Ellen's to her husband's colleague, Albert Shaw, demonstrated her extensive knowledge of her husband's work. Writing on her husband's behalf--he was in Europe--she informed Shaw not only that her husband would have no time to furnish the article he desired, but she even supplied him with a list of other professors at Princeton, whose work she obviously knew well, who were just as capable of writing the article in question as her husband.[57]

Still more remarkable was her "secret" letter, a year later, to John Bates Clark at Columbia University:

> I am about to do a very odd thing; --I am going to write you a confidential letter; not only without Mr. Wilson's knowledge, but with the full assurance that if he *did* know he would veto it flatly![58]

She proceeded to confide how her husband had made up his mind not to renew his contract at Johns Hopkins, but that he was changing his mind--they needed the money. "And the worst of it is that I am afraid he is right." However, could he not get a contract at Columbia to do the same, instead of lecturing in "distant Baltimore."? Moreover, "...I should like him to give at Columbia some such course as his Princeton one..." and proceeded to describe the kinds of lectures he gave, his areas of expertise, and his audience. She coyly intimated what salary Wilson should obtain: "it is almost like adding another professor for $1,000, or less." but not a lot less. At $1,000, Wilson's pay would be almost double than what he received at Hopkins.[59]

> But I must 'stop this'; --and I am sorely tempted to let it end its career in the waste basket, so much do I fear you will think me foolish and presumptuous. But no, I will not turn coward![60]

Shaw was not only impressed, but he acted immediately, and came up with a scheme to transfer Wilson to Columbia along the lines she suggested, consulting Ellen first, however.

Nothing ever came of the Columbia scheme because Princeton, fearful of losing Wilson altogether, raised his salary that year so that he could dispense with his extracurricular spring lecturing. Had that not happened, Wilson would have found himself better situated at Columbia, if only part-time, at a much better rate of pay, thanks to his partner Ellen's intervention.

In 1899, during Wilson's second trip to Europe, Ellen described her exasperation with a publisher who refused to take her "no" for an answer. He kept bothering her (that is, her husband) for an article.

> But you see he won't take my word for [it]. He seems to be a good sort of a goose, and being a Southerner to boot, perhaps you might write him an amiable little letter telling him what an ass he is.[61]

Apparently, even Ellen indulged in the occasional cuss word, like her husband. By then, Ellen was also in charge of household finances (going to the bank on her own, endorsing checks, paying bills, including taxes).

Ellen was not only Wilson's most trusted advisor, but guardian of his time and health. In her letter to Anna Harris in 1895, Ellen mentioned: "For it is one of my chief occupations to resist people who want him to address articles, make addresses, etc. and so interrupt his life-work..."[62] To her, this was his creative work. Later, it would be his political career.

Wilson's health was nearly always shaky. He was prone to colds, headaches, digestive problems (at one point, he required a ghastly "stomach tube" which

Doctor Weinstein noted was "now happily extinct and "not only scientifically useless but potentially dangerous..."); in 1896, he suffered his "mysterious" paralysis (an undiagnosed stroke). The only treatment available for his paralyzed right arm and hand was a cumbersome electric massage machine, a useless remedy. His health caused Ellen endless worry, though hers was far from good. At one point, during a summer vacation in 1898, after a particularly severe bout of abdominal pain and nausea that spring, Ellen confided in the Smith sisters her fear of imminent death. "'I hope Woodrow would marry again. He cannot live alone.'"[63]

Twelve months later, Ellen nearly became a widow. Her husband and her brother Stockton, who had traveled to Europe together, sailed back in late August on the *City of Rome*. Along the way, the ship hit a massive iceberg "in a thick fog," recalled Stockton. "The ship turned almost over on her side when she ran up on the shelf [of ice] like a sled." Widespread panic ensued, but throughout the disaster, Wilson (unlike Stockton) remained outwardly cool and collected. Miraculously, the vessel righted itself and despite heavy damage, managed to chug its way to New York harbor. Ellen's anxiety, as she read about the calamity in the newspaper, can only be imagined.[64]

Perhaps this test of himself, in the face of extreme peril, gave Wilson a stronger sense than ever of his important destiny. For soon, their lives would be turned upside down.

ENDNOTES

[1] Woodrow Wilson to Ellen A. Wilson, Aug.6, 1899. Arthur S. Link, ed., *The Papers of Woodrow Wilson* (Princeton: Princeton University Press, 1966-1996) 11:210. (henceforth: *PWW*)

[2] Eleanor Wilson McAdoo, *The Woodrow Wilsons* (New York: Macmillan Co., 1937), 45.

[3] McAdoo, *The Woodrow Wilsons*, 13.

[4] Margaret Axson Elliott, *My Aunt Louisa and Woodrow Wilson* (Chapel Hill: Univ. of North Carolina Press, 1944), 134.

[5] Ellen A. Wilson to Woodrow Wilson, March 6, April 26, 1892. *PWW* 7:448, 593.

[6] Quoted in Henry W. Bragdon, *Woodrow Wilson: The Academic Years* (Cambridge: Harvard University Press, 1967), 151.

[7] McAdoo, *The Woodrow Wilsons*, 24.

[8] Ellen A. Wilson to Woodrow Wilson, July 31, 1894. *PWW* 8:634.

[9] Stockton Axson, *Brother Woodrow: A Memoir of Woodrow Wilson* ed. Arthur S. Link (Princeton, Princeton University Press, 1993), 229.

[10] McAdoo, *The Woodrow Wilsons*, 58; Ellen A. Wilson to Woodrow Wilson, Jan.26, 1895, July 2, 1896, *PWW* 9:132, 531.

[11] McAdoo, *The Woodrow Wilsons*, 10-11,45.

Mater Familias   133

[12] Ellen A. Wilson to Woodrow Wilson, Dec.28, 1892. *PWW* 8:74.

[13] McAdoo, *The Woodrow Wilsons*, 9; on expecting 22 year-old Jessie to ask permission, Ellen A. Wilson to Woodrow Wilson, June 2, 1911, *PWW* 23:128.

[14] McAdoo, *The Woodrow Wilsons*, 10-11.

[15] *Ibid.*, 37.

[16] Eleanor Wilson McAdoo, ed., *The Priceless Gift: The Love Letters of Woodrow Wilson and Ellen Axson Wilson* (New York: McGraw-Hill, 1962), 210.

[17] Ellen A. Wilson to Anna Harris, Jan.31, 1899. *PWW* 11:101.

[18] Woodrow Wilson to Frederick Jackson Turner, Nov.15, 1896, *PWW* 10:52; McAdoo, *The Woodrow Wilsons*, 56, on the public schools in 1890's Princeton: Princeton Historical Society, Princeton, New Jersey.

[19] McAdoo, *The Woodrow Wilsons*, 56; Elliott, 108.

[20] Woodrow Wilson to Charles William Kent, May 29, 1894. *PWW* 8:584.

[21] McAdoo, *The Woodrow Wilsons*, 57.

[22] Ellen A. Wilson to Woodrow Wilson, Jan.31, 1894, *PWW* 8:446; McAdoo, *The Woodrow Wilsons*, 40.

[23] Ellen A. Wilson to Woodrow Wilson, Feb.13, 1894. *PWW* 8:481.

[24] Ellen A. Wilson to Anna Harris, June 1, 1895. *PWW* 9:280.

[25] Ellen A. Wilson to Woodrow Wilson, Feb.16, 1895. *PWW* 9:202.

[26] Axson, 107.

[27] Ellen A. Wilson to Woodrow Wilson, Jan.28, 1894, July 10, 1899. *PWW* 8:437; 11:161.

[28] Ellen A. Wilson to Woodrow Wilson, July 10, 1899. *PWW* 11:161.

[29] James Woodrow to Ellen and Woodrow Wilson, Dec.31, 1896. *PWW* 10:89.

[30] Elliott, 108-109.

[31] *Idem*; McAdoo, *The Woodrow Wilsons*, 33-35.

[32] Glimpses of Ellen's and Wilson's religious views in McAdoo, *The Woodrow Wilsons*, 41-42; Jessie Wilson Sayre interview, Dec.1, 1925, Ray Stannard Baker Papers, Library of Congress, Washington, D.C. (henceforth: RSB papers).

[33] Elliott, 161.

[34] *Idem*.

[35] Ellen A. Wilson to Woodrow Wilson, March 7,10, 1892, Feb.25, July 22, 1894, *PWW* 7:451,466; 8:511,621; Woodrow Wilson to Ellen A. Wilson, Aug.14, 1899, *PWW* 11:229.

[36] Woodrow Wilson to Ellen A. Wilson, March 12, 1892. *PWW* 7:481.

[37] Woodrow Wilson to Ellen A. Wilson, March 24, 1892, *PWW* 7:510; "Translation of a Boudoir Scene," *PWW* 7:462-466.

[38] Ellen A. Wilson to Woodrow Wilson, April 25, 1892, *PWW* 7:592; Woodrow Wilson to Ellen A. Wilson, April 23, 1892, *PWW* 7:589.

[39] Woodrow Wilson to Ellen A. Wilson, Feb.25,27, 1895, Jan.27, 1896, *PWW* 9:226, 234, 393; quoted in Stockton Axson's notes on Ray Stannard Baker's manuscript, [undated], RSB papers 53.

[40] Woodrow Wilson to Ellen A. Wilson, Feb.12, 1898. *PWW* 10:389.

[41] Woodrow Wilson to Ellen A. Wilson, March 6, 18-19, 24, 1892, *PWW* 7:447-448,494,496,509; Ellen A. Wilson to Woodrow Wilson, March 15, 23, 1892, *PWW* 7:486,508.

[42] Woodrow Wilson to Ellen A. Wilson, Feb.8, 1898. *PWW* 10:381.

[43] Woodrow Wilson to Ellen A. Wilson, Feb.26, 1897, *PWW* 10:175; Ellen A. Wilson to Woodrow Wilson, Feb.28, 1897, *PWW* 10:178.

[44] Woodrow Wilson to Ellen A. Wilson, Feb.1, 1895. *PWW* 9:148.

[45] Woodrow Wilson to Ellen A. Wilson, Nov.2, 1898. *PWW* 11:66.

[46] Woodrow Wilson to John Grier Hibben, Sept.15, 1899, to Ellen A. Wilson, Feb.19, 24-25, 1894. *PWW* 7:496, 507; 11:240.

[47] Ellen A. Wilson to Woodrow Wilson, Feb.25, 1900, to Anna Harris, Jan.31, 1899. *PWW* 11:102,442.

[48] Axson, 95; McAdoo, *The Woodrow Wilsons*, 13.

[49] Ellen A. Wilson to Woodrow Wilson, Aug.13, 1896. *PWW* 9:568.

[50] Axson, 97.

[51] *Ibid.*, 97-98.

[52] Note 1, *PWW* 10:12; Ellen A. Wilson to Mary Eloise Hoyt, Oct.27, 1896. *PWW* 10:37.

[53] "A Commemorative Address," *PWW* 10:31; Ellen A. Wilson to Mary Eloise Hoyt, Oct.27, 1896. *PWW* 10:37.

[54] Woodrow Wilson to Ellen A. Wilson, July 30, 1894. *PWW* 8:634. "She did not believe in husband and wife following two separate careers; her conception and his was that the two should unite in a single career." Paraphrase of Jessie Wilson Sayre in her husband's letter to Ray Stannard Baker. Francis B. Sayre to Baker, Aug. 5, 1931. RSB papers.

[55] Woodrow Wilson to Ellen A. Wilson, May 5, 1892. *PWW* 7:619.

[56] Ellen A. Wilson to Woodrow Wilson, July 30, 1894, Feb.7, 1895. *PWW* 8:633, 9:178.

[57] Ellen A. Wilson to Albert Shaw, July 22, 1896. *PWW* 9:544.

[58] Ellen A. Wilson to John Bates Clark, June 3, 1897. *PWW* 10:260.

[59] *Ibid.*, 260-261.

[60] *Ibid.*, 261.

[61] Ellen A. Wilson to Woodrow Wilson, July 27, 1899. *PWW* 11:193.

[62] Ellen A. Wilson to Anna Harris, June 1, 1895. *PWW* 9:281.

[63] Edwin A. Weinstein, *Woodrow Wilson: A Medical and Psychological Biography* (Princeton: Princeton University Press, 1981), 127; Helen and Mary Smith interview, 1927, RSB papers.

[64] Axson, 88.

Young Ellie Lou Axson of Rome, Georgia. (Printed with permission, Princeton University Archives.)

Reverend Samuel Edward Axson. 1866-1883 (Courtesy of First Presbyterian Church, Rome, Georgia)

Young mother with baby. According to Eleanor McAdoo's memoir, the infant is Margaret. (Printed with permission, Princeton University Archives.)

At Sea Girt. Ellen surrounded by her husband and daughters (Margaret standing beside her, Eleanor seated, Jessie standing). (Prints and Photographs. Library of Congress.)

First Lady-Elect Ellen Wilson posing in the inaugural ball gown that she never got to wear (the ball was cancelled). Courtesy of the Woodrow Wilson Birthplace, Staunton, Virginia.

The only reminder left of the public housing complex named after First Lady Ellen Wilson. (The complex, along with a statue of her, were demolished in the late 1990's to make room for a mixed-housing development.) 7th & h Streets S.E., Washington, D.C.

Teenage Ellen's sketch of her roommate, most likely Janie Porter. Courtesy of the Woodrow Wilson Birthplace, Staunton, Virginia.

Ellen's portrait of one of her husband's heroes: Joseph R. Wilson, Sr. (Courtesy of the Woodrow Wilson Birthplace, Staunton, Virginia.)

"'The copy is better than the original,'" declared Woodrow Wilson of his wife's copy of Adolphe Dagnan-Bouveret's *Madonna*. ((Courtesy of the Woodrow Wilson House, Washington, D.C.)

Chapter 6

TRAVELS, TRIALS, TRIBULATIONS, AND MRS. PECK, 1900-1910

"Jack Hibben spends part of every day...revising his book on Hegel...I dare say you will find it interesting and helpful."[1]
Woodrow Wilson to his wife, 1902

"I thought of you a thousand times."[2]
Woodrow Wilson to Mrs. Peck, 1909

Gregarious by nature, warm and friendly (unlike her husband), Ellen nevertheless formed not a single close friendship in Princeton in the twenty-two years she lived there, although she had many casual friends. Wilson, on the other hand, was inseparable from his friends Harry Fine and especially, Jack Hibben, both professors, including Jack's wife Jenny. He would spend hours alone with her: "Long walk with Mrs. Hibben in the afternoon. Did not leave the house until nearly seven"--a typical entry in his diary. Wilson's closeness to Jenny may well have bothered Ellen--when he recommended that she use her dressmaker, because he liked Jenny's chic clothes--she never did. It may be that Jenny was just not her type. Professors' wives in Princeton were "Yankee" women and perhaps a tad too "advanced" for Ellen's tastes. For instance, Jenny (who wore her hair "cropped") and her husband Jack, allowed their daughter to call them by their first name, shocking Ellen. Ellen, too, was appalled when Mrs. Harry Fine decided to leave her infant in her husband's care for eight months, while she sailed away to Europe with her brother. Ellen's friendship with Mrs. Purves, wife of the minister of Ellen

146 Sina Dubovoy

and Wilson's church, and mother of five strenuous children, was also not a close one. Everyone except the Wilsons, who were southerners, were Republicans--the "enemy," according to Eleanor. This, too, may have been a subtle cultural barrier for Ellen, who felt most comfortable and at home with her southern kin and old Rome friends, all of them Democrats.

Ellen's sudden, intense friendship with Lucy and Mary Smith, seven years after Ellen had settled in Princeton, attests to a deep need for friendship aside from her husband, kin, and old but distant Rome friends. Nonetheless, her intimacy with the Smiths is surprising. She had less in common with them than, for instance, her lifelong Rome friends, the Tedcastles, who were now living in Massachusetts. The Smiths were neither married, nor mothers, nor otherwise caregivers. Nor were they as intellectual as Ellen, though they certainly were worldly, cultivated women, who spoke French fluently. Yet Ellen's friendship with them ran deeper than with all of her old Rome friends, including the Tedcastles.

These two ladies of leisure, a few years younger than Ellen, lived in their late father's rambling house on Henry Clay Avenue in the heart of New Orleans. They were blessed with a huge number of friends and relations, and were among the few Presbyterians in that overwhelmingly Catholic city and state. Their father had even been a famous man of the cloth.

Lucy and Mary Smith chanced to meet the Wilsons during summer vacation near Front Royal, in Fauquier county, Virginia. They and the Wilsons, including sister Madge, happened to be staying at the same "inn"--a run-down former plantation--of an ex-Confederate officer, Colonel Stribling. Perhaps nostalgia had bestirred ex-patriates Ellen and Wilson to pass late July in the steamy, mosquito-infested old Dominion, where Wilson was born and went to law school. They never tried it again. Next summer would find them, together with the Smiths, enjoying the shore in Gloucester, Massachusetts.

However, there is no question that the Wilsons felt thoroughly at home at the Colonel's. Unlike northerners, they were undisturbed by southern shabbiness. The food was to their liking, too. Daughter Eleanor remembered "mountains of chicken" at breakfast, lunch and dinner, with all the cornbread they could possibly eat. Wilson cut a lordly figure riding horseback, which he seldom got a chance to do in New Jersey. Teenage Madge was thrilled to be "called" on by the young men from church on Sunday evenings. Like Ellen, Madge spoke with a drawl and fit right in; unlike her, she would now and then lapse into dialect ("you was," "we is"), which annoyed Ellen.

It was at this time that Eleanor, the only Wilson daughter not born in the south, became entranced by southern culture and with southerners, who were so relaxed, warm and friendly, and forever calling each other "cousin." She identified so strongly that she began mimicking a southern accent; at too young an age Eleanor even married a southerner, albeit an ex-patriate. William Gibbs McAdoo, a Georgian, was a member of her father's cabinet.

The Wilsons did not seem to mind the swarms of flies and countless mosquitos, in part because of the Smiths, who enthralled them with their "inexhaustible collection of stories and games." Thirty years later, Ray Stannard Baker, too, found the sisters irresistible, "the liveliest-minded, pleasantest, most charming women....full of the zest of life." When Ellen made the fortunate discovery that they had a distant ancestor in common, her friendship was sealed. From then on "Cousin Mary," "Cousin Lucy," and "Cousin Ellen" became more and more inseparable until in 1911, they lived together in Princeton in the house on 25 Cleveland Lane. If they were not as cerebral as Ellen, the Smiths were uncritical friends with a drole sense of humor. Whenever they visited, Wilson could hardly wait to hear their latest "darky" stories. (He was known for his inexhaustible fund of crude "darky" anecdotes, not a few of which he picked up from the Smith sisters, who in turn picked them up from their black cook, Susie.)[3]

In early 1900, Ellen packed her bags for a three month visit with the Smiths, cut in half, however, because of Stockton's sudden illness (he had his appendix removed--a serious operation at the time--right in her home on Library Place). She had never before been to New Orleans, the South's most exotic city. Wilson had felt so guilty enjoying two long trips to Europe, that no doubt he insisted it was her turn to go away. His sister Annie would stay with him and mind the girls.[4]

Ellen nonetheless could not shake off her guilty feelings for leaving home and family. Arriving in New Orleans, however, she was at once entranced by the beauty and charm of the city. A few days later she reported making "a score of calls" with her best friends, who seemed to know everybody. Soon she wrote "My engagements are too numerous to be catalogued, much less described." Not surprisingly, Ellen had kin even here--the Ben Palmers--"native" New Orleaners.

Inspite of her guilty feelings Ellen enjoyed herself to the utmost. During her month with the Smiths, she had her first taste of opera, of the Mardi Gras season ("superb, gorgeous, wonderful"), and her first experience of a Catholic mass, in New Orlean's cathedral. The absence of any criticism of the Catholic church or mass would have surprised her parents, who, like Wilson's parents, had been deeply anti-"Romish." Ellen and Wilson, unlike their parents, were progressively shedding their anti-Catholicism.[5]

While New Jersey was still in the depths of winter, Ellen relished the warm weather, the beautiful flowers, the graceful French quarter; but if the old city throbbed with the rhythms of jazz, Ellen--unable to hold a tune--never mentioned it. She could not get enough of the "Creole" streets, however, with their "old and aristocratic Creole homes in the old Spanish style." One of these palatial homes housed the Jockey Club, whose caretaker impressed her. He was "a truly noble looking old negro, in manners and, I might almost say, in appearance fit to be a duke." She duly noted that his father, a slave in the old days, had been "an African king" before his enslavement. Ellen's atttitude towards blacks, though condescending, was not uniformly negative.

Ellen's racial prejudice, unlike many other southerners, was also tempered by a heavy dose of paternalism--or more aptly, maternalism. She was deeply impressed by Lucy Smith's beau, a Mr. Barton, owner of sugar plantations outside of New Orleans.

> He manages his hundreds of negros perfectly, never any bluster, or apparent sternness. They adore him too, and are perfectly happy and well-cared for, have good houses, a good doctor and from .75 to $1.50 a day *cash* according to the season. His business is tremendous.[6]

That Ellen would admire Barton for his care and concern--rather than for his wealth and worldly success--seemed typical of her. After all, she and not Wilson, had worked with poor black children in Manhatttan; later, at the Woman's Employment Society, she helped many poor women, some undoubtedly black, find jobs.

Assured that Stockton's operation had gone well, Ellen nonetheless cut her trip short to return home, circuitously, via Savannah, Atlanta and Rome, where she briefly visited kin. Unusually somber one day, Ellen wrote Wilson from Savannah,

> To tell the truth it makes me very sad to be here, --and Rome will be worse. Before [in 1892], I had the children to occupy my mind and time, and that made an enormous difference. Now I have too much time to think.[7]

To think--or brood--of what, and why? In two months she would turn forty, and middle-aged. At forty, death no longer seems a remote possibility, and there were numerous dead to remember--her grandparents in Savannah, her parents and Uncle Robert in Rome, and in North Carolina east of Rome, her beloved friend Beth. Her own health was uncertain. In the summer of 1898, she had confided her fears to Lucy and Mary that she might die prematurely.

As yet there was not a strand of gray in Ellen's attractive, coppery hair, and even the faded photographs from this time reveal her blooming complexion. Her husband replied characteristically, "I am afraid that if *I* were with you in Rome now, I should pass all bounds of feeling and *worship* you."[8]

Ellen's nameless dread of returning to Rome, which she had not laid eyes on in eight years, passed the instant she arrived. "They are *so* good to me!" she wrote Wilson joyfully. "Indeed all the dear kinsfolk in Savannah, Atlanta, & here, have treated me like a little princess for whom nothing was quite good enough." Shortly afterwards, she was back in New Jersey, though not in Princeton. Stockton insisted on a long recovery away from Princeton, why or where, nobody could fathom. He finally settled on Atlantic City on the New Jersey coast, windy and frigid in mid-March. Wilson accompanied him there, catching up with Ellen who soon arrived to take care of her brother. Too cold to venture forth, Ellen and Wilson stayed in their hotel for "two days of exquisite happiness," her husband not having laid eyes--or hands--on Ellen for nearly eight weeks.[9]

* * *

In that spring of 1900, Ellen and Wilson appeared to be facing a cloudless future, but for the uncertainties of one's health, Stockton's unending problems, and the rapid pace of change in Princeton, which disturbed them. In ten years the town had ceased to be an isolated village, close-knit and middle-class. Extremely wealthy people were settling down and contributing to the town's "demoralization," as Stockton described it. At the turn-of-the-century, Princeton was "discovered," especially after the Grover Clevelands settled there. Mansions, not to mention the Clevelands' impressive estate, were ever more numerous, as were the tenements that housed the many immigrants from southern Europe. Haves and have-nots were on the increase as hard times gave way to an unparalleled economic boom.[10]

There was another kind of change. In June of 1899, when Wilson was away in Europe, Ellen reported an unheard of incident for Princeton: a burglary in the house behind them. Not one to scare easily, she and her neighbors "have taken it all as rather a joke." But not for long.

The robbery was the start of a series of break-ins, all in Ellen's neighborhood, where, of course, the well-heeled of Princeton lived. She was relieved when her brother Ed came home for the summer. Now he could take charge of her handgun.

> It is a *great* comfort to have him. I havn't been exactly *afraid* of the burglars, still I was quite willing to turn over that pistol to Ed; I have slept with it at my bed-head for some time now. The burglars have been on a perfect rampage for a month, breaking in somewhere almost every night.[11]

Miraculously, her house escaped the "rampage." And the thieves escaped a pistol-wielding Ellen.

If Princeton had a police force, Ellen never once mentioned it. The burglaries subsided, perhaps because the neighbors, including Ellen, paid a "neighborhood watchman" to patrol their street. The college town was increasingly becoming, as Stockton noted, "merely a fashionable suburb for New York City." That year a Princetonian, Mrs. Eleanor Hutton, initiated the Village Improvement Society and became its first president. Wilson is on record as a member, possibly Ellen as well. The society would be dedicated to improving the town "in all its moral, educational, sanitary and artistic aspects."[12]

In 1900 or early in 1901, the trustees of Princeton University, Grover Cleveland among them, granted Wilson a fifteen-month sabbatical on full salary. He planned to spend the academic year, starting in the fall of 1901, with Ellen and the girls in Europe. Financially, they were in better shape than ever. They took it upon themselves to support Wilson's sister Annie, a widow, and sporadically, her son, Wilson Howe III, a graduate of Princeton, who had married, divorced, and was chronically short of cash.

In the summer of 1900, the Wilson family, Madge included, embarked on their most "exotic" summer break. For the first time, they left the United States to spend five weeks in the enchanting Muskoka lake district in distant Ontario, Canada, where they stayed at an inn. The resplendent scenery enamored them. "We have bought a little island, with some mainland adjacent," wrote Wilson to his Uncle James, "and mean as soon as possible to build there." Nothing ever came of the building plan, though they returned there the next summer, and again in 1904.[13]

In the meantime, a growing dissatisfaction with President Patton was becoming a tidal wave. Both faculty and trustees wanted nothing less than to sweep this relic of the past out of office. Who was better qualified--especially after his unforgettable Sesquicentennial oration--to lead Princeton University into the new century, than Woodrow Wilson, Princeton's most reputable, popular professor?

With foreboding Ellen sensed what lay ahead. If the inevitable occurred, their lives would turn upside-down. They would have to leave their beloved home in Library Place, their private lives becoming suddenly quite public. At age forty, drastic change is far less welcome than when young. Though she dreaded what lay ahead, not for an instant would Ellen discourage this dazzling career advance for her husband.

Uncertainty was only part of the stress and strain of 1901.

Jessie's serious bout with tubercular glands that spring, and President William McKinley's assassination in September, were sadly upsetting events. In early April, 1901, Jessie underwent what was then a three hour, dangerous operation to have her tubercular glands removed. Consequently, Stockton Axson went alone to his brother Ed's wedding in Cambridge. Afterwards he hurried to the hospital in Philadelphia, where he found Ellen glum and unable to converse, dreading the outcome. All went well, although the same operation would be repeated on daughter Eleanor a few years later.

The terroristic assault on McKinley, the popular Republican president who had led America to victory against Spain, unnerved even Democrats. Eleanor accompanied her father to the train station in Princeton Junction to view McKinley's funeral train as it slowly conveyed his body back to its final resting place. Wondering aloud why anyone would kill a president in cold blood, her father, for once, had no answer.

Ellen and Wilson gave up their plan to spend a year in Europe. Too much was happening at home. The summer of 1901 passed without even a family vacation. Neither Ellen nor her husband dared leave the ailing senior Wilson alone, who had been living with them since the late 1890's. They took turns caring for him as now Wilson, now Ellen, went away on brief vacations that summer.

The following spring of 1902, Ellen's worst fears materialized--tempered by elation for her husband--when President Patton gave in to the mounting pressure, and resigned. The trustees, without a vote of dissent, elected Wilson in his place. In a few months, the whole family would have to move into the fortress-like mansion of Prospect House, official residence of Princeton presidents.

* * *

The new U.S. president, Teddy Roosevelt, upon hearing of Wilson's appointment, wrote "'Woodrow Wilson is a perfect trump.'" Although it may not sound like it, this was an accolade, and "T.R." had every intention of attending Wilson's inaugural that fall. Himself a Harvard man, his coming was a confirmation of Princeton University's status as an ivy league school. (In the end, he was too busy to attend, but he read Wilson's inaugural speech and invited him to "spend a night with me at the White House this winter.")[14]

Everyone in the family listened with pride to Wilson's inaugural oration, as Princeton's 13th president. On yet another brisk fall day six years earlier, Wilson had delivered his maiden public speech before the university assembled. The success of that address resonated for years. Now Wilson, inaugurated as the new president, clad in flowing academic robes, marched at the head of the parade down Nassau Street, daughter Eleanor failing to catch his attention as she waved to him from the crowded sidewalk. Afterwards, they celebrated with a party in their new home, to which Wilson even invited African-American educator, Booker T. Washington. Wilson and Axson clansmen were horrified to hear of it, but since Wilson greatly admired Washington (probably as much for his tacit approval of segregation as for his emphasis on self-reliance), his word was law, as far as Ellen was concerned.

The Wilson girls, all of them teenagers, including twenty-one year old Madge Axson, were thrilled in anticipation of all the "balls" and parties they would attend in the years ahead. Despite their sadness at leaving Library Place, they greeted change with enthusiasm.

Ellen, however, was inconsolable. They would be moving into "that great, stately troublesome 'Prospect,' and be forever giving huge receptions, state dinners, etc. etc." and thus would end "the sweet, almost ideal life" they had enjoyed, she confessed to her cousin Florence Hoyt. "Broken-hearted" was her apt description of how she and Wilson felt "about this side of it," though Ellen surely felt the loss more deeply than her ambitious husband.

Privately Ellen despaired about her ability to be a public person, a "president's wife." She even despaired a little for her husband, for the sake of whom nothing was too good. "It is enough to frighten a man to death to have people love and believe in him so and *expect* so much."[15]

Once again Ellen put herself in charge of all the moving, a complicated, burdensome task that fully distracted her during the summer and fall of 1902. This move would be the worst of their many moves. Not since she and Stockton had packed up their parents' belongings in Rome did Ellen abhor possessions as deeply as she did now. Moreover, Prospect House was partially furnished, so many of their belongings would be stowed in the attic, and they remained in storage, in one place or other, forever. She and Wilson never again had a home of their own.

The thirty-five room, cavernous Prospect House had been built as a private home before the Civil War, and later, donated to the college. In 1879, the university exchanged the simple, attractive, two story colonial residence of Princeton presidents--situated on Nassau Street, next to Nassau Hall--for this monstrosity of a building, a fake Italianate villa crowned by an improbable tower. Originally the view, clear down to the hills bordering the ocean thirty miles away, was panoramic, no doubt why it was nicknamed Prospect. By the early twentieth century, the campus, especially surrounding dormitories full of high-spirited young men, was intruding on the residence. After football games, excited students overran the lawns, and the din was intolerable. If they leaned out of their dorm windows far enough, students could see into the private rooms of the president's house. More than one student tried in this way to catch glimpses of alluring Jessie and her aunt Madge.

On an inspection visit to Prospect House shortly after Wilson's appointment was announced, Ellen had liked nothing about it. Then and there she determined to re-decorate and refurbish the mansion inside out. She insisted on putting herself solely in charge and "spare" her husband, and Wilson reluctantly acquiesced. Weeks later she informed him that "Plumbing, heating, lighting, painting, papering, carpets, shades, bedding, hangings, upholstering, refinishing are all settled in *detail* and contracted for..." Eleanor remembered that "at the end of a long day's struggle with plumbers, painters or carpenters, or an exhausting shopping trip, she was never too tired to tell us of the progress she had made..."[16]

Indeed Ellen spent the summer of 1902 in a perfect frenzy of activity, while Wilson went away on a five-week summer break with his friends the Hibbens, for which he felt "deeply, abominably selfish." Ellen quickly retorted, "You know you have frequently observed that running about, going to the city, etc. agrees with me better than sitting at home sewing..."[17] She besieged antique shops, even auction houses, for furnishings and decorations that suited her taste. Ellen disliked the cluttered, heavily draped Victorian interiors of her day. Flowered chintz (heavy cotton) sofas and chairs, windows that actually let in light, and no clutter (with the exception of books), were Ellen's simple rules of decor. The result was gratifying. The high-ceilinged, palatial first floor rooms now invited the outdoors in, were filled with books and tastefully furnished with her many new antiques. In the coming years the walls of Prospect House would be filled with Ellen's collection of original American art, including her own paintings.

The glory of the interior, as Eleanor recalled, was the magnificent and "huge stained-glass, Tiffany window, the gift of two of the trustees," situated midway above the staircase. Ellen created the design--choosing as her subject the philosopher Aristotle holding his book on ethics--while two women artists executed the design in glass. The Tiffany eventually was removed in the 1930's, replaced by an inconspicuous plain glass window. According to Frances Saunders' tracing in the late 1970's, Ellen's window was adorning a restaurant in New Jersey (which is still in operation and still displays Ellen's window).[18]

The experience of re-doing Prospect House turned out to be a blessing in disguise, and temporarily eased Ellen's pain at leaving her home. Health-wise she never felt better, reported forty-two year old Ellen from Library Place late that summer.

I am just as well as possible, never felt better... In the morning I wake rather early and, --having nothing better to do!--take a hot bath and go back to bed and read for awhile. Then I get up and do my exercises in a leisurly [sic] & exhaustive manner and come down to breakfast feeling *fine*.[19]

Both she and Wilson, fastidious about personal cleanliness and daily bathers, liked the fact that there were at least a half dozen bathrooms at Prospect House. Telephones were coming into general use. They got one installed at Library Place in 1899, but the one at Prospect House had extensions in more than one room. While the university paid for all the refurbishing, it was surprisingly stingy when it came to providing Wilson with a secretary--he had none--or with an automobile, at a time when even students were beginning to have them. In fact, Wilson never bothered to learn to drive (unlike his future second wife Edith, who was buying her own car around this time, the first woman to drive a car in Washington, D.C.).

What to do with their Library Place house was a matter of concern. Regrettably, by late August, they decided to part with it for good, instead of renting it. Their realtor, John Fielder, recommended a price tag of $30,000, which seemed exorbitant to Ellen and Wilson. Once on the market, however, the house was snatched up within days for the full asking price. The Wilsons apparently deposited the money in the bank, and added the interest--at least $1500 a year--to their personal income, which was considerable. Wilson would be paid an annual salary of $8,000 and, as usual, earned additional monies from guest lectures and royalties. (In 1903, Ellen noted the receipt of a royalty check of $7,000 for Wilson's *History of the American People*.)[20] Every penny of income, moreover, was their own. The "progressive" income tax, which Wilson firmly supported, did not go into effect until 1913. They could in fact afford to invest in lucrative Princeton real estate, or save a good deal. In the eight years they spent in Prospect House, they did neither.

Madge Axson admitted that during their eight years at Prospect House, the Wilsons had enough money for many of the "graces" of life. (A car was one "grace" they willingly did without.) They could now afford to live and dress well, and travel often. What drained Wilson's income, it seems, was supporting various relatives. Annie, Wilson's sister and a widow with an underage daughter, received a regular annual income from him (yet this did not stop her from asking her brother, at one point, for several thousand dollars to build a new house). Ellen and her husband even supported her adult son Wilson, who, too, seemed unable to support himself. In 1902, Ellen received disturbing news concerning the children of her late friend Beth. "This miserable story of a broken household...," she wrote her husband. "Think of *three* children dead, and the rest scattered; --and, worst of

Travels, Trials, Tribulations, and Mrs. Peck, 1900-1910

all, none of them getting any education, and sinking down even in the social scale" thanks to their irresponsible, indifferent clergyman father, for whom she had long felt contempt.[21] Beth's fifteen-year old daughter Ellie (Ellen's namesake) caused her the greatest concern. Ellen quickly saw to it that the girl was enrolled in a private boarding school, for which the Wilsons paid--including all of her personal expenses. In the coming years they educated other unfortunates, and their list of charitable contributions increased greatly.

Moving day for the Wilsons was a nightmare, and delayed until mid-October. Ellen's admirable system of moving (by then she had much practice) called for every item to be in place in short order. This time, however, there were no family prayers at day's end giving thanks. The mood was somber. Eleanor never forgot overhearing her mother sobbing that night, behind closed doors--and her father, blaming himself, trying to soothe her--a break-down that was truly out of character for Ellen.

Thanks to her loving family, Ellen recovered her good spirits and adjusted to her new life. But woe followed upon woe. In early November, teenaged Jessie Wilson, who sustained the painful operation the year before, and Wilson's young niece Annie, who was visiting them, were stricken with highly contagious scarlet fever. Normal life halted at once--no visitors to the house, and strict quarantine of the patients--until the girls recovered; Jessie recovered fully, but the fever left niece Annie with a heart ailment. Then Wilson's father's death agony commenced. His screams of pain filled the house for weeks on end. "It is simply harrowing," wrote Ellen to her cousin Mary Hoyt. "...I regret to say I have developed a habit of lying in bed awake half the night and holding myself."[22] He died at Prospect House on Jan. 21, 1903, at age 78. Inauspicious beginnings for their new life in Prospect House.

* * *

Though lacking confidence in her public role as "first lady" of Princeton, Ellen came to enjoy her "official" duties, giving dinners, parties, receptions for faculty, trustees and students. Her first social foray was a great success. She decided to hold ten formal, but intimate dinners for several faculty members and their wives at a time, almost all of whom she knew well. She even bought a new dress, sea green trimmed with white lace. This she wore to all ten dinners, proof of her frugality, to Eleanor. Perhaps the clothes-horse Mrs. Peck, who got to know Ellen quite well, was closer to the truth when she observed that Ellen was simply uninterested in clothes.

As the guests at Prospect House, more often than not, were official guests of the university, they tended to be personages rather than faculty members or students. One famous couple was Sidney and Beatrice Webb from England; another, Sir Gilbert and Lady Mary Murray. In the case of the latter, Ellen served for dinner a classic Rorer meal: clear soup as the first course, followed by sweetbreads, and for the third course, broiled squabs. (Only to discover, by the third course, that the Murrays were vegetarians. They had to settle for scrambled eggs.)

Life for Ellen settled into a routine of social functions, visiting, and, as Madge noted, weekly shopping trips to New York or Philadelphia and in the summer of 1903, a wonderful nine-week vacation trip with her husband to England, Scotland, France and Switzerland. With the $7,000 royalty check that year, they could well afford exotic travel. Their expenses for this trip, as itemized minutely by Wilson, came to $1,200, a lordly sum for those days, considering that it did not include their round-trip, overseas fare.[23]

For the first time, Ellen would feast her eyes on all the sights in the British Isles that her husband had longed for her to see. In particular, Edinburgh, John Knox's house, Wilson's beloved Lake district, Wordsworth's grave, Shakespeare's home, the cathedral at Durham, the National Portrait Gallery in London (which apparently Ellen visited alone). In Paris, there beckoned the immense Louvre, the world's greatest art museum, and imperial Versailles, to which a world-renowned Wilson would return sixteen years later. In Switzerland, they limited themselves to the French-speaking cantons. Surprisingly, they never set foot in nearby Germany, despite Wilson's intellectual debt to that country's scholars.

Wilson's itemized list of daily expenditures showed that together, they donated between 60 cents and a dollar to Sunday church collection plates, five dollars went to a "Surgeon, Ellen's leg" in England, indicating that she might have sustained some kind of injury--or perhaps it was her old injury, her burned leg-- although it did not impair their trip. Wilson spent the same amount, five dollars, on a fine top hat, $33 on "waterproof coats" for both him and Ellen, a few dollars for cheap art re-prints, $12 on silk scarves and $27 on jewelry; they only bought a few books. Aside from a few pairs of gloves and 5 dollars on some necklaces, they bought nothing in either France or Switzerland. Altogether, their purchases were extremely modest for a well-to-do couple spending two months in Europe, with an army of relatives back in the States. This may have been due to their frugality, or to the high import duty that awaited them on their return. In short, they would have to declare everything that they had purchased abroad, and pay a hefty tax, in that age of high tariffs on practically every foreign-made item.

Ellen and Wilson consequently frittered away much of their money, as tourists do today, on cabs, buses and trains, tips for porters, waiters and waitresses, admission fees to museums, and eating out. Back in the U.S., the import duty on their modest purchases abroad, as noted by Wilson, came to a not inconsiderable $23.75.

Wilson's cut-and-dried list of expenses in no way reveals whether he and his wife were enjoying themselves on this, their first trip alone since their honeymoon. Apparently they did, so much so that Ellen wrote wistfully a week after they returned, "I am perfectly spoiled by this summer when we were always together."[24]

Back in Princeton in late September--Wilson's second academic year as president--life returned to its now familiar routines, including more illness. On January 7, 1904, Wilson noted the tragic death of Ruth Cleveland, Grover Cleveland's young teenaged daughter, from diphtheria. She was friends with the Wilson daughters, who as children often played in the Cleveland's luxurious estate, Westland. The Clevelands, too, were among the few Democrats in town and attended the same Presbyterian church as the Wilsons. There, every Sunday, the lovely young Mrs. Cleveland drew everyone's attention with her costly and fashionable apparel. In fact, Wilson was greatly attracted to Mrs. Cleveland. After an evening spent at Westland--"I literally sat at her feet, --where every man of sense and taste must feel that he belongs. She is so fine, unusual, beautiful and delightful."[25] Consequently, the Clevelands' cruel loss was felt deeply by the Wilsons. Shortly after the funeral and the burial in the bitter cold winter weather, Ellen took sick and lay in bed for days with a heavy cold.

Daughter Jessie, who had made a slow recovery from scarlet fever only the year before, was still in such frail health that she was kept out of school. Although Ellen had some misgivings, she made up her mind to bring her along on yet another two-month jaunt to Europe in early spring, surprisingly, since she had only just been there six months before. This time she planned to spend the whole time in warm, sunny Italy, where presumably they could leave illness and the sad memory of Ruth Cleveland's death behind them. Besides Jessie, her travel companions would be Lucy and Mary Smith. Once in Rome, they would get in touch with Ellen's young cousin Mary Hoyt, fluent in Italian.

Jessie Wilson was 16 years old that spring, and already a gorgeous young woman, outwardly unrelated to her father, mother and siblings. With her dark blond tresses, classical features, beautiful eyes and figure, she was a madonna, if one adds to her physical beauty a deep piety, modesty and high intelligence. Alone of the Wilson daughters she would earn a bachelor's degree (from the Baltimore College for Women, today's Goucher College), and became a member of Phi Beta Kappa. When her aim in life--to be a missionary--was disappointed, she became a full-time, live-in social worker at the settlement house of the University of Pennsylvania in Philadelphia. While living in the White House, she actively promoted the Young Women's Christian Association (YWCA)--at a time when it still had a strong Christian identity--traveling all across the country on its behalf.

On March 21, 1904, Wilson saw them off--Ellen, Jessie and the Smiths--at the pier in New York harbor, where they set sail on the *Hohenzollern*, a German liner. Later that afternoon, circus tickets in hand, he and 14 year-old daughter Eleanor "consoled" themselves with the pleasure of a marvelous Barnum & Bailey circus performance, "and the extraordinary show,--*truly* extraordinary and full of wonder, --proved the best tonic I could have taken," wrote Wilson to his absent wife. For Eleanor, alas, the "tonic" turned out to be a poison. A little over a week later, she discovered a rash on her chest. It was measles, and Wilson was sure she had contracted it at the circus show. Still, he thought, it was "most unlikely" that Margaret, home on a holiday break from college, would come down with it, too. He soon proved wrong. Wilson--now father, mother and nurse to his two stricken daughters--could only be thankful that Jessie was spared.[26]

Though her husband tried to minimize the bad news, guilt pangs stabbed Ellen, as usual ("Something always happens when I leave home! I'll never do it again.") The illness at least was not serious, her one consolation. Frail Jessie was turning out to be a tough travel companion and knowledgeable beyond her years. (Later at the Roman forum she even served as their tour guide, "the rest of us...followed her about like school-children," noted Ellen).[27]

To Ellen, Italy's beauty was incomparable--its art treasures traumatized, its gardens bewitched. The overwhelming Catholic culture vanquished the last vestiges of anti-"Romish" prejudice in her Presbyterian heart.

Ellen, Jessie, Lucy and Mary Smith were stalwart, uncomplaining tourists. Even during their brief layover in Gibralter, their penultimate stop before Italy, they trooped about the "Moorish" market for several hours. The "Moors"--Ellen's first exposure to Muslims--fascinated her. They stared at one Moor in particular, a "superb fellow" from a portraitist's perspective, "...we stood solemnly around gazing fixedly at *him*..."[28]

Ellen's power of expression would rise to new heights in the coming days and weeks. Their first stop in Italy was Naples, where they lodged at a convent that rented guest rooms. One of the guests was a southern woman and "of course the Smiths and she have thousands of acquaintances in common," wrote a bemused Ellen. The nuns were "kindness itself" and helped them plan their tour and engage a tour guide. When it came to art and architecture, Ellen knew more than the guide. Their whole first day turned out to be "a debauch of beauty from early morning to night. We went to bed perfectly drunken." Yet neither she nor her husband ever owned a Kodak or took pictures.

In Rome, where they planned to spend most of their trip, they hooked up with Ellen's cousin Mary Hoyt--from Rome's namesake in Georgia. Mary, along with her sister Florence, were graduates of Bryn Mawr College, and neither one ever married. Ellen soon discovered that this scion of Presbyterian divines was attending Mass regularly; a worshipper on the altar of Italian culture, Mary Hoyt also spoke the language fluently. Ellen accompanied her to a "great papal function"--it was Easter season--and Ellen was struck by the visage of Pope Pius X, which she studied intently. His face was "very beautiful and noble..." However, "I can't say as much for the cardinals and bishops."

When it came to the Sistine chapel, Ellen was not about to miss the smallest detail. Baedeker advised bringing "opera-glasses & *mirror!*" and Ellen, no opera buff, was forced to purchase the small binoculars for the enormous sum of ten dollars--"..and I am trembling over the duty." The four of them managed to detach the sizable mirror from one of their bedroom bureaus (and escape the notice of the hotel management?). Thus armed, they entered the Sistine chapel ready to begin their study of Michelangelo's glorious ceiling. "It was a grand success; we could see the whole ceiling at once in it and study it in perfect ease and comfort. We were the envy of the whole crowd in the chaple [sic]," perhaps in more ways than one.

Seventeen churches and ten art galleries later, including whole days spent in the Vatican ("it was pretty hard to turn my back on it forever! I could scarcely keep from crying"), they were ready to leave Rome. These native southerners (except Jessie) could tell that malaria season was upon them; they were retreating indoors at sunset, and sleeping sensibly with windows shut tightly. "I am glad to be leaving Rome, for there is doubtless less danger of illness in Florence than in either Rome or Naples, & I have, of course, had all the time more or less dread of Jessie's getting ill, for she has never before been exposed to a malarial climate." Ellen's vague foreboding proved sadly correct, but it was not malarial mosquitos that attacked Jessie, but deadly diphtheria.

Only three and a half months earlier, diphtheria had killed the Clevelands' eldest daughter. Even if one escaped death, serious heart complications could follow. When they arrived in Assisi, en route to Florence, a horrified Ellen took note of the "huge solid white patch" in Jessie's throat, and nearly fainted.

Jessie, more so than Ellen, had longed to visit Assisi en route to Florence--St. Francis having fascinated her ever since early childhood. Now the girl could not have been more badly situated to overcome a life-threatening illness, than in this backward, dirty village, far from home, without a hospital, trained nurse or English-speaking doctor. Ellen deeply regretted leaving Rome, ironically, to spare Jessie from falling ill. Guilt over-whelmed her. "I am certainly being bitterly punished for my selfishness in leaving home," she wrote in despair.

Ellen telegraphed the American embassy in Rome at once in the hope that an English-speaking doctor would be willing to come to their aid. To her immense relief, a Dr. Ball arrived and immediately administered an unspecified "anti-toxin" (to use Ellen's term). It was an antidote rather than a cure; doubtful indeed was his other prescription: "a little cognac or whiskey in *hot* milk several times daily & during the night," which Ellen nonetheless dutifully administered. Ellen kept Jessie immobile in bed so as "not to raise her head from the pillow for a week more, to guard against heart trouble," that is, heart failure. If it came to that, the nurse (a nun whom Ellen also procured from Rome) was nearby with a strychnine injection.

While most Italian mothers would have crawled up the stairs of the nearest church on bended knee, in prayer and supplication, Ellen made not the slightest reference to turning to a higher power, as she waited, hour after hour, for a sign of her daughter's fate. Not that she did not pray. However, previous tragedies--her mother's and father's deaths--had left her feeling numb with anger. Anger, at herself and at her Maker, may well have overwhelmed her now.

Remarkably, given Jessie's weakened immune system that had no doubt invited the disease, and her none-too-competent doctor, she recovered without complications; it was her mother who needed recuperating from the trauma and stress. Did she ever recall the time in her youth when she mocked a woman who was obsessed with the fear of diphtheria? Now Ellen, like that mother in Savannah, imagined diphtheria germs lurking in the most unsuspecting places. The very letter she was writing her husband, she warned him, was probably infected. She was sure that diphtheria was in the very layers of her clothes, so before venturing outside, she elaborately wrapped clean cloth around her skirt and avoided human contact, including her kind inn keepers; the hapless Smiths had long ago been persuaded to leave that place of contagion.

All the while Ellen had refrained from writing her husband of Jessie's condition, at least until she knew the outcome. Besides, she had no time for writing. When she finally did, on May 1, she downplayed the trauma, wrote only of Jessie's "short, sharp attack" of diphtheria and the "extraordinarily short duration" of her illness, though the danger was still far from over. Two weeks later, with her daughter recovering, Ellen finally admitted that Jessie's illness "was far from being a mild case" and that her throat had in fact been "the most dreadful looking throat I ever saw."

Travels, Trials, Tribulations, and Mrs. Peck, 1900-1910

All told they spent four weeks in Assisi. When Jessie finally was able to venture out, they made a short trip to Raphael's home town of Perugia. Assisi, too, was well worth looking at, as Ellen finally discovered. It was full of Giottos, and the scenery, after all, was glorious.

For what was probably the first time in her life, Jessie clashed with her mother. Should they return to the States immediately, or visit Florence? Ellen adamantly insisted on leaving Assisi for home; she dreaded a relapse, not uncommon with diphtheria victims. Jessie knew how much her mother had looked forward to Florence, and vehemently insisted on staying. Surprisingly, Jessie's will turned out to be stronger than her mother's (she was a lot like Ellen--soft and sweet without--tough within). Torn between her concern for Jessie yet fearful that her daughter's disappointment would make her ill, they headed for Florence. Their week-long stay would forever be one of the highlights of Ellen's eventful life.

Upon arriving in Florence, it dumbfounds one to read of the relief they felt at staying at their first American inn, which served "the very best of *American* cooking," though "cuisine" was hardly the word one would use to describe it. Where was all the Italian pasta and pizza? Ellen, much as she took cooking seriously and enjoyed good food, never once mentioned them in her letters. Now and then they had eaten unsavory "boiled kid," an Italian dish which she and Jessie did not miss. Pasta and pizza must simply have been far less common then, than today.

Despite being glad to be in an American inn, Ellen was far from homesick. Indeed, Florence then as now cast its typical spell on art lovers: it stunned her. For a week her senses reeled, she went about dazed, tearful, semi-comatose. Her letters were a running commentary on art.

The galleries "are simply inexhaustible! I am left gasping, overwhelmed, -- almost dismayed at the feast spread before me."

> Everywhere I turn there is some masterpiece that I have longed to see all my life, and I rush from one to another and am so overcome with rapture and excitement that I end by holding my head with both hands in a sort of despair.[29]

In the end, "there is no other place to *compare* with Florence--from the artists standpoint--not even Rome."

Ellen and Jessie sailed back in mid-June, returning in time for Ellen and Wilson's 19th wedding anniversary. This trip had cost even more than her previous one, with Jessie's illness alone running up a tab of $550. Ellen knew that

162 Sina Dubovoy

Jessie would have to be treated "like glass" for months to come, despite her seeming recovery. Wilson greeted them, in particular Jessie, with utter relief. For her sake the whole family headed for Ontario, their favorite, enchanting Muskoka lake, for a lengthy vacation. But the angel of death caught up with them even here.

Ellen and her husband loved to row across the lake, disembark, and spend hours in the woods alone together, strolling, talking, reading to each other. One afternoon, noticing an approaching storm, they started back earlier than usual, but the storm rapidly caught up with them. Wilson rowed desperately (neither one could swim). While the winds lashed their boat and their children looked on in amazement, the two stared death in the face as their boat struggled against the swirling waters. Luckily, they made it ashore. Unable to shake off their harrowing experience, "That night they made a will and explained it to us."[30] For the second time in exactly five years, Woodrow Wilson had escaped death by drowning. It was their last trip to Muskoka lake.

Eleanor vaguely recalled this incident as taking place in either 1904 or 1905, during their "second summer" at the lake, which in fact would have been 1901. As they never returned to the lake after 1904, the incident occurred either right after Ellen and Jessie's ill-fated trip abroad, or several years before.

* * *

Their two costly European junkets notwithstanding, the following summer Jessie, her sister Eleanor and once again, the Smiths, embarked on yet another European tour, this time, including Germany. Jessie was so radiantly beautiful that "Some dapper Frenchman was sure to stroll back and forth, staring at her. I thought it thrilling and romantic, but it embarrassed Jessie and she always pulled me away quickly."[31]

Meanwhile Ellen's duties as "first lady" of Princeton seemed to leave no time for sketching and painting. Besides, with three teenaged daughters and an unmarried sister living at home, Ellen was perpetually chaperoning them to dances, balls and dinner parties, in that era when chaperones were a must. As Madge noted, there were many more young men in Princeton than young women, who consequently were much sought after as dance partners. When "Brother Woodrow" hired fifty new faculty members to serve as "preceptors" (tutors) at Princeton, his educational innovation impressed the whole country, but positively dazzled Madge and her nieces. "Fifty new men at one whack! *Fifty*." True, reasoned Madge sagely, some of them would be married. But not all of them. To be sure, not her future husband, "preceptor" Edward Elliott.[32]

Travels, Trials, Tribulations, and Mrs. Peck, 1900-1910   163

If Ellen and Wilson thought that they were putting the trials and tribulations of 1904 behind them, what they would face in 1905 was infinitely worse. But 1904 was not over yet.

Barely a month after the family's return from Canada, students vandalized a dormitory, '79 Hall. Described as an "attack," this unheard of violence--breaking windows, smashing a chandelier and "chipping the steps in one of the entries from top to bottom"-- came on the heels of the annual student "horse peerade," akin to a Halloween parade. But what may have precipitated it was Wilson's recent order to erect a gated fence around the Prospect House grounds, for privacy's sake. No Princeton president had ever done such a thing before. The unpopularity of this act is as puzzling as it is astonishing. Enraged students, shut out of Prospect House grounds (which were "their" college grounds), took out their anger at a dormitory named after--and funded by--Woodrow Wilson's 1879 graduating class. The students might have taken their cue from some drunken alumni earlier in June, who during the commencement festivities, had proceeded to tear down the fence. (Wilson had it restored.) "That fence was the cause of more bitterness than the most drastic reform he instituted at the college," according to Eleanor. Wilson stood his ground, although the following year, students made yet another attempt to tear down the fence. (It remains to this day.) The furor over the fence was ominous, provoking not a little suffering and humiliation for Wilson's entire family. It is noteworthy that Ellen later painted a hauntingly lovely impressionist landscape, *Prospect Gate*, depicting a gate that was wide open, rather than closed.[33]

The shock and ugliness of this student rebellion may have caused an old hernia problem of Wilson's to flare up, worsening his other old enemy--phlebitis-- in his leg. A hernia operation became unavoidable, and altogether Ellen spent five weeks at her husband's side in the hospital in Manhattan, missing Christmas and New Year's with the family. The "fence incident" may also have taken its toll on her own health. Accompanying her husband to Palm Beach, Florida for several weeks, Ellen returned in late January looking "very thin and pale," a few months shy of her 45th birthday.[34]

Ellen's brother Stockton was back in a mental hospital, having suffered a nervous breakdown that fall. He was a popular professor of English at Princeton, a stodgy, phlegmatic man, but a sensitive soul who did not weather personal storms--or problems--lightly. Having given up the hope of marriage, Stockton lived alone in a studio apartment on Prospect Avenue. His nieces would often drop in, lugging a cooked meal or hot soup, to comfort their uncle who seemed to be forever ailing. On March 11, 1905, Ellen wrote her old Rome chum, Anna Harris, in detail about her exasperating, but lovable brother Stock. For the past three months, unable to teach, he lay in his hospital room in Philadelphia--"in *bed*...with complete nervous exhaustion, and melancholia." The previous fall "he was struggling desperately to keep out of that pit [a nervous breakdown], yet slipping steadily down inch by inch...It was *terrible*. I hardly know how either of us lived through it." Stockton, of course, depended on his sister for all of his needs--a fact never mentioned in his memoir--and she, perhaps out of long habit, rushed to his side whenever he called. As the president's brother-in-law, Stockton, too, may have been more indulged than might otherwise have been the case. In the fall of 1904, when Stockton had his breakdown, the trustees granted him a full year's absence from teaching, on full salary.[35]

On April 28, 1905, it was Wilson's turn to convey to an old school chum, "Bobby" Bridges, the profoundly tragic news of Ed Axson's death, along with his wife of three years, Florence, and their infant son, only two days before. The whole family had drowned in a river near the town of Creighton, Georgia. Ed was only 28 years old.[36]

The tall, blond young Ed, handsome and athletic, had baffled his sister and relatives by insisting on moving back to the south after graduating from M.I.T. and marrying his housemate, Florence, in Cambridge. Ed had turned out to be one of Thomas Edison's most brilliant research assistants. Yet he chose to settle in Tennessee, and shortly afterward, in the backwoods town of Creighton, Georgia, where he was manager of the Franklin Gold Mining Company. Despite his responsible position, Ellen was so dissatisfied with Ed's living in a southern backwater that she made up her mind to send Stockton (Ellen's trouble-shooter) to Creighton that spring, to persuade Ed to leave. By then it was too late. Ed had taken his wife and child (Edward, Jr.) in their horse-drawn buggy on a Sunday outing. Just as they were about to mount a flat-bottomed ferry, to convey them across the Etowah river, his team of horses suddenly became unmanageable. What happened next was witnessed by at least two men, unable to swim, who watched in horror as the tragedy unfolded.

Why the horses panicked and plunged into the deep, swift-flowing river, the buggy crashing and sinking into the rolling water, is unknown. In that tangle of horses hooves, heads, bodies and carriage wheels, Ed struggled fiercely to save his wife and son. Without them--he being an excellent swimmer--he might have saved himself. Instead he died heroically, using every sinew and ounce of strength to extricate them, trapped and drowning in a carriage, in the midst of a river swollen with spring rains.

Had Stockton been the one who had died, Ellen might have mourned him and recovered. To lose Ed was to lose a surrogate son, the young boy whom she nursed through childhood illnesses, whose clothes she had sewn and mended,

Travels, Trials, Tribulations, and Mrs. Peck, 1900-1910 165

whose severe stuttering had caused her endless concern as she sought the best treatment for him. Ed's cruel death, and that of his whole family, was the greatest tragedy of Ellen's life.

Whether she met the railroad car in Princeton, conveying the coffins of her beloved young brother and his family, is unknown; unknown, too, is whether she attended their funeral and burial in Princeton. Ellen found herself sliding into an abyss, as her father before her. She withdrew from life altogether; for many weeks she ate and slept little, spoke to no one, could not concentrate on what anyone said. But Ellen's reserves of strength, or courage, ran deeper than her father's. Perhaps sheer will power enabled her to draw strength from the memories of her father's demise. Not for her would be a life of drugged-induced sleep, of mental and emotional breakdown.

By early summer, having forced herself to emerge from death's shadow, she again took interest in those around her, to her family's immense relief. Without her constant support, Wilson might never have realized the great destiny that lay before him.

When her recovery was still far from certain, Wilson made a decision that would affect her life profoundly. That spring he happened to hear from friends of his, one of whom was Jack Hibben, of a summer art colony in Old Lyme, Connecticut and of the boarding house where the artists lived, owned by an eccentric spinster, Florence Griswold (1850-1937). In short order he reserved a room for himself and Ellen---and surprised her with the announcement in late spring. Rather than return to Muskoka lake, they would instead wade deep in art in the most unlikely of habitats, Florence Griswold's grimy headquarters, whose denizens became some of the most important names in American landscape art. And by the way, you took turns making breakfast.[37]

* * *

Madge Axson, just returned from Europe, was touched by how eagerly a broken-hearted Ellen looked forward to painting again. Not just cramming it into her family vacation, but working alongside professional artists, all day, in a place where she finally could get some grounding in landscape painting, a genre she had wanted to learn, years ago, at the Art Students League. Unfortunately, Madge underrated Ellen's talent for art as well as gardening. "...she could get effect with plants as she did with her paints on canvas," remarked Madge.[38] That she could do no better than "get effect" was as cutting as it was condescending. Ellen, perhaps a little in awe of her brilliant sibling, just as her daughters were, took Madge seriously, her own confidence suffering in consequence.

As a young teen only five years older than her oldest niece, Madge had nagged her nieces into calling her "aunt," which embittered them. To "keep the peace," they finally submitted. "When she grew up, we admired her tremendously," noted Eleanor, but did not say that they loved her. "She was aloof, languid, almost mysterious," but it seems, not lovable.[39] Wilson was the only person Madge never criticized. They seemed to enjoy a special bond, not hard for Wilson who was in awe of the kind of feminine beauty that Madge possessed. Proud, haughty and brilliant, Madge stayed in Griswold's grubby quarters at least one summer, and saw nothing unique about it or its inhabitants.

Perhaps the beauty of Lyme (that is, Old Lyme, where Lyme disease got its name) situated in southern Connecticut, close to the Long Island Sound, and its nearness to New York, as well as Florence Griswold's indigency--left alone with a huge, cluttered house that she could ill-afford to maintain--combined to make this spot an artist's haven. Charging little--at times reluctant to charge at all-- Griswold took in itinerant or homeless artists, who sometimes paid their bill by offering her a painting. Such was the case of Willard Metcalf, a notable artist of American Impressionism, which predominated in late 19th, early 20th century American art. He offered to give her his *May Night*, which she refused; an astute amateur critic and unselfish besides, Griswold would not take his best work from him. Shortly afterward, the Corcoran Gallery in Washington, D.C. bought the painting and awarded Metcalf its gold medal. Another famous denizen of Griswold's establishment, Childe Hassam, who arrived in the summer of 1903, beautifully painted the wall panels and door of the dining room as his gift to her (which can still be seen today, at what is now the Florence Griswold Museum).

When Ellen and Wilson arrived in the summer of 1905, Griswold had housed the colony of artists for at least a half dozen years. Lyme was not the first summer art colony. That distinction belonged to Southampton, Long Island, where artist William Merritt Chase established a summer art school in 1891. But it was the most enduring, lasting until the end of Griswold's life in the 1930's.

Madge Axson had vivid memories of her first summer in Lyme (most likely, 1908)--not all of them to her liking.

How Ellen, with her exquisite sense of order, endured 'Miss Florence's' where we boarded is still an unexplained mystery. The house was literally tumbling about our ears; from month's end to month's end no scrubbing brush touched the wide boards of the century-old floors; the two bathrooms were old enough to be rated archeological specimens; the food was awful beyond words; and service was non-existent.[40]

The beds and floors creaked, the roof leaked, cats clawed the dilapidated furniture and overran the dinner table, but Griswold was too impoverished to repair or renovate anything. Townsmen looked askance at her "boarding house" and some of its scruffy residents, even though Griswold single-handedly did more to put the town of Old Lyme "on the map" than anyone else. Every summer the artists-in-residence organized an exhibit of their work, which drew increasing numbers of tourists and art lovers to Lyme, and spread its fame. Though Ellen purchased art work from her fellow artists, she never exhibited any of her own in the five summers she spent there. Many of her landscapes still adorn Woodrow Wilson's last home on S Street in Washington, D.C.

There were no rules, no fixed meal times, sometimes not even enough food in the larder to satisfy hungry guests; Griswold left her guests to forage on their own for breakfast. But there was no lack of "studios" on her property, small shacks in the orchard, or on the banks of the little Lieutenant River. In one of these Ellen set up her easel and paints, and painted all morning long, while Wilson wrote on his typewriter, or played golf on the nearby links. Everyone, that is, except Griswold and Wilson, painted the whole morning, criticized each other's work, and offered instruction if needed. Daughter Eleanor remembered one summer in Lyme, when all the artists vied to paint beautiful Jessie and alluring Madge. Each morning Wilson would carry his wife's easel and paintbox to her "studio," and her daughters would take turns rubbing her with "citronella" to ward off insects, "but when we went back for her we invariably found her smudged with paint and bitten by mosquitos."[41]

Ellen, a gifted portraitist, did an about-face that year, switching to landscape painting, which she had never done on a major scale before. Oddly, she never returned to portraiture. Her fellow artists gave her the grounding she lacked--and for someone with her shaky confidence--encouragement. Two instructors whom she mentioned in these years were Frank Vincent DuMond, and A.T. van Laer. In 1907, when Ellen introduced herself in a letter to art collector William Macbeth, she scribbed after her name, "studied with A.T. Van Laer."[42] Van Laer, a famous landscape artist and art professor, offered instruction during Ellen's first summer in Lyme in 1905. DuMond, a full-time professor at the Art Students League, was among the first gathering of artists to arrive at Lyme in 1899. In 1908, he held an informal summer school in which Ellen, and possibly Eleanor--the most artistically gifted Wilson daughter--were students. Other artists with whom she rubbed shoulders were the already-mentioned Metcalf and Hassam, Robert Vonnah and his wife (who became Ellen's good friends when she became First Lady), and Chauncey Ryder, whom she admired greatly.

Ellen did more than just "endure" Lyme, she loved it, and they all loved Griswold. In 1910, when she was absent, the artists who came back year after year conspired together to restore and refurbish her whole house, from rooftop to cellar, and everything in it, at their expense, and thus surprise their proprietress (surprise is an understatement). Ellen chipped in with the rest, asking via letter to pay for re-decorating and furnishing "two of the largest bedrooms," which probably cost the Wilsons a small fortune.[43] Hence daughter Eleanor best remembered Griswold's abode not as the dump it had been for years, but as a "beautiful old house" which it has remained to this day.

The significance of her first summer in Lyme cannot be over-rated. Ellen recovered from her great sorrow, sprang back to life and art, returning to the stimulating environment of Lyme for four more summers (1908-1911). Shortly after her last summer there, she got up the courage to make her first foray into the world of professional art. Had death not overtaken her several years later, she would have ranked among America's foremost women artists.

* * *

By the time Ellen and Wilson returned to Princeton at summer's end, everyone noticed how well and even happy Ellen looked. From then on she made time to paint, although once again, painting was compressed into her other duties. She liked particularly to stand outdoors in good weather and paint "her" garden, the garden at Prospect that is, which she re-designed from formal French to lush Italian (based on her memories of Italy's beautiful gardens), with "hidden" nooks, statuary, and benches. Madge Axson, with her noted gift for words, described what Ellen's garden looked like.

> The terrace where Woodrow and I sat on these spring afternoons overlooked Ellen's south garden with its backdrop of clipped cedars against which rose tall columns of *Rosa hugonis*, the small-petalled, exquisite golden Rose of China. In the center of the garden was a pool bordered by purple iris. Above us, purple wisteria frothed against the iron grill that supported the roof at that end of the terrace. From the low hedge near by came the tangy fragrance of sweetbriar.[44]

"Paths were boarded with masses of multicolor flowers," remembered Eleanor.[45] Two beautiful paintings that capture the luxuriance of Ellen's garden are her *Prospect Garden* and *Garden at Prospect*, mirroring, in pastel oils and in loose brush strokes typical of impressionism, a Prospect garden so different from what it is today

Travels, Trials, Tribulations, and Mrs. Peck, 1900-1910 169

* * *

Restored and revived in health and spirits, Ellen resumed her normal life. A major challenge (for a discriminating hostess as Ellen) was the arrival in November of President Teddy Roosevelt, who, this time true to his word, visited Princeton to attend the Army-Navy football game. Prospect House was crammed with guests as T.R. arrived for lunch (that is, "luncheon"), planned to perfection by Ellen. The whole time, however, he had eyes only for ravishing Madge Axson, just turned 24, whom he shamelessly ogled and teased. "I felt myself turning tomato-red up to the roots of my hair, and that apparently was just what Mr. Roosevelt wanted. He shouted with delight and pounded the table until the plates all down its length danced a crazy jig," and so it continued until the meal ended. As to Eleanor and her siblings--and probably Ellen as well--"We decided that he was undignified, much too noisy and not to be compared with father."[46]

Eleanor, the youngest daughter, was of an age for college and went, unwillingly, after hard persuasion on her father's part (but not on her mother's) to a two-year college in Raleigh, North Carolina, run by Ellen's best friend in the old days, Rosalie and her husband, Reverend DuBose. Connecticut-born Eleanor made a point of acquiring a heavy southern drawl, prompting Wilson to joke about his daughter's "educated nigger" accent.[47] Both he and Ellen laughed when this least bookish of daughters was voted "most intellectual" in her school, which to them, spoke volumes about southern girls' intellects in general. Cerebral Ellen, however, had once been a southern girl herself, while Eleanor had more depth and intelligence than people gave her credit for.

That summer of 1906 did not bring a return to Lyme. A wholly unexpected, terrible event gripped the family once more. In early May, Wilson woke up one morning, completely blind in one eye, while his right arm was lame. This, his second stroke, was more serious than the one ten years before.

An anxious Ellen traveled with him to Philadelphia to consult specialists. One doctor concluded that Wilson was suffering from arteriosclerosis, the same disease that supposedly killed his own father. The pressure from his arteries had caused a blood vessel to rupture in his eye. Though what Wilson had suffered was more than likely a stroke, the word was not used, and possibly the diagnose, too, was inaccurate. Ellen left Philadelphia none the wiser about what really ailed her husband. "All sorts of tests were made to determine the cause, --it is something wrong with the circulation due entirely to a general condition of overstrain," she wrote her cousin Mary Hoyt, although later she was informed of his hardening of the arteries.[48] No special diet was prescribed in those days; fortunately, Wilson was an abstemious eater and a fan of exercise.

According to Doctor Edwin Weinstein, Wilson's stroke of 1906 may have been caused by a "blocked" ophthalmic artery, a branch of the carotid artery, that supplies blood to the brain, a blockage that might have been due to arteriosclerosis.[49] His right hand again was weak, his arm lame, and he never recovered full vision in his left eye. His doctors were not inaccurate about the seriousness of his illness. "The doctors said he must stop *all* work at once," continued Ellen, "that it was impossible to exaggerate the critical nature of the situation."[50] It is noteworthy that, as Eleanor remembered it, this news had a shattering effect on her mother rather than on her father, who returned from Philadelphia, cheerful and even joking.

Had Wilson heeded the physicians' advice to cease all work and go into full retirement, he might well have lived into ripe old age. But was retirement even an option? Princeton University offered no pension plan for retired professors, and judging by the Wilsons' shaky finances several years later, they would have had little income to live on beyond the interest on their savings: about $2000 a year. He was earning at least four times that much.

Meanwhile Ellen's health, too, had suffered a setback. A few weeks before his own stroke, Wilson informed her friends, the Tedcastles, that for that whole year--hence at least four months--she had been ailing from a mysterious, "painful stiffness in the back and limbs, which has made constant massaging necessary and has held her off from a great many of her ordinary activities." Still, "there is no ground for real anxiety," which sounded more like Ellen talking than her husband.[51]

For the time being, however, Wilson did take the doctor's advice seriously. With his eyesight improving, he and Ellen made plans to spend the whole summer in England, along with their daughters, where they would rent a cottage in Wilson's beloved lake district. In nearby Edinburgh, Scotland, he would consult other doctors.

The Wilsons set sail in late June for a lengthy holiday that proved to be a tonic for the family of five. While the Wilsons were celebrities in Princeton, away from home they were private persons and as such, attracted no attention, exactly how Ellen liked it best. They settled down, in Ellen's words, "in a picturesque rose-bowered cottage on the banks of the Rothay," in the serene village of Rydal, in the heart of England's lake district in northern England. The grave of Wordsworth, Ellen's beloved poet, lay only a stone's throw away from their cottage, and Matthew Arnold had once lived nearby. Adhering to her regimen at Lyme, Ellen spent every morning at her easel and "painted to her heart's content." But even in ideal surroundings, illness was never far behind. For the second time, Eleanor succumbed to measles, only this time, it was German measles.

Travels, Trials, Tribulations, and Mrs. Peck, 1900-1910   171

Fortunately, no one else caught them, although her illness cast a slight pall over the family vacation.[52]

Wilson's soon-to-be favorite friend and neighbor, Frederic Yates, was a poor but well-established portrait and landscape painter, who sketched portraits of all the Wilsons that summer. His drawing of 46-year old Ellen captured her looks and spirit, according to daughter Eleanor, more closely than any other rendering of her. An unmistakable, haunting quality permeates the portrait, for which she posed while listening, engrossed, to Wilson's reading of Browning's "Saul." While the eyes look weary and sad, her face is composed and serene, in stark contrast to Yates' portrait of a tense, gloomy Wilson. When Wilson himself lay dying in 1924, he would wake often in the night and flick on a small flashlight, pointing at Ellen's portrait, contemplating it intently. Yates' sketch of Ellen can still be seen in Wilson's last home on S Street, in northwest Washington.

Mother, father and daughters spent every minute of every day together in a close-knit, harmonious family life. This was no less true when Ellen took Eleanor and Jessie with her on a two-week tour of England, leaving Margaret "in charge" of her recovering father. The family kept in touch every day. Wilson's letters, the only ones to survive, are touching memorials of his deep love for his family. Addressing his absent wife in the familiar "My own darling," they tell often of his daughter Margaret's devotion and sweetness. The two took long walks together, did the laundry in their small cottage (for once, their house really was small), and played whist in the evening. When Wilson returned from his day trip to Edinburgh to consult doctors, Margaret stood waiting for him in the rain.[53]

The girls--20, 19, and almost 17 years old--were neither bored nor rebellious, nor addicted to movie stars, loud music, or boyfriends. In the absence of radio, television and a private automobile, the family socialized often with their neighbors, especially Fred and Emily Yates (she was American-born) and their teenaged daughter Mary, or enjoyed themselves alone. They hiked every day, Wilson covering as much as fourteen miles on his own. For the first time in her life, daughter Margaret had a chance to ride in a "motorcar." Fred Yates often mentored Ellen in her work. Thanks to the Wilsons, Yates visited the States in 1907, where he found work painting portraits of the rich and famous, including the not-so-rich but celebrated Woodrow Wilson (the full-length portrait of Wilson, in flowing academic robes, still hangs at Princeton University. Wilson's future second wife Edith described it as "awful.") Yates attended Wilson's inauguration as U.S. president, and remained friends with him until he died in England in 1919.

An Edinburgh doctor pronounced Wilson recovered--possibly a misdiagnosis--encouraging him to return to active life, but to work only in "moderation." A relieved Wilson and family reluctantly took leave of their idyllic retreat in tranquil Rydal, in that heyday of Edwardian England and "rule Britannia." Though afterwards he and Ellen often spoke about retiring there someday, they never returned together.

* * *

Far from working only moderately, Wilson worked at a frenzied pace that fall of 1906. Ellen was not too far behind, as she informed her old Rome friend, Anna Harris. "There is simply no end to the 'functions' I am called upon to have...Then there are guests constantly coming to a meal or overnight..."[54] In winter, Wilson succumbed to a heavy cold, and took the advice of his doctor to go on a prolonged winter vacation to a warm climate. Rather than choosing Florida again, in mid-January he sailed for Bermuda, his first of several trips to the bewitching isles.

This time Ellen would not accompany him--"it was always hard to budge Ellen"--according to Madge. Young Eleanor had only recently undergone a serious operation for the removal of tubercular glands in her neck, a "frightfully severe case," wrote Ellen to her friend Anna Harris.[55] She slowly recuperated at home. So Wilson departed alone, without his wife and children, remaining a whole month; his many letters hid his growing fascination with another fellow vacationer, Mrs. Mary Peck.

The archipelago of Bermuda, then as now, was a British colony. Its capital, Hamilton, lies on the main island; at that time, its shores were dotted with the colonial villas of the well-to-do, and the odd hotel or two. There were no automobiles on the island until the Second World War, nor did Wilson ever experience, in his four lengthy stays there, any of the hurricanes or other horrendous storms of today. Calm gorgeous weather seemed to be the norm, as were dinner parties, swimming (that is, "bathing"), croquet and lounging. No one seemed to wear sun-tan lotion or sun-bathe on the beach. Women visitors to the island, like the well-to-do Mrs. Peck, wore the ridiculous, over-sized hats of that era even in the hottest weather, as well as the perennial long-sleeved blouse (or "shirt-waist"), ankle-length skirts, and buttoned shoes.

Wilson immediately fell under the spell of that enchanting island. He stayed at a beach front hotel and eventually met--and became friends with--Mark Twain, by then an embittered, misanthropic old man. He rubbed shoulders with the colonial administrators and British officers who ran and "protected" the colony; although blacks were three-quarters of Bermuda's population, Wilson never once mentioned seeing any. Nor do his many letters ever breathe a word of crime, or drugs. For the jaded and well-to-do, Bermuda was a safe, segregated paradise, an easy boat ride to and from New York.

Wilson's ethnic background was Scotch-Irish, and he was wont to say that when his passionate Irish side got the better of him, his other half, the "dour Scots" side, was sure to rein him in. That formula did not seem to work in Bermuda. Here his passions reigned free and seemingly un-checked. Here he fell in love with the remarkable Mrs. Mary Peck, either on this first trip, or the next. If his Scots side came to his rescue, it was to prevent him from sleeping with Peck, which probably never happened.

Wilson had turned fifty on December 28. Women admired the slim, fit, tall and masculine man, and he them. Even during his recent vacation in the British Isles, he had a memorable encounter with a Scottish nurse in an Edinburgh hospital: "The only thing that disquieted me at the Infirmary," he wrote an absent Ellen, "was a charming young nurse whom I met in the corridor and of whom I asked my way. Her smile and her bewitching Scots speech nearly stole my heart away. I had to hurry on out of danger."[56] Wilson never seemed to feel guilty writing Ellen in this vein; Ellen, on the surface at least, took his weakness for the opposite sex in stride. So sure was she of his love for her.

Peck was a youthful-looking, worldly and well-traveled 44 year-old when she met Wilson for the first time in Bermuda, at a dinner party in her home. Born and raised in Michigan, she began smoking after an operation (upon the advice of her doctor) and never stopped; unlike Ellen, Peck loved to swim and dance, and like Ellen, had an "interesting mind," which was important to Wilson. Wilson frequently referred to her as a "child of nature" and a woman with a "free Western manner." She lived none-too-happily with her second husband--her first had died suddenly after six years of marriage--and candidly admitted that it had been a marriage of convenience. Though Thomas Dowse Peck was a wealthy woolen manufacturer, she was, quite plainly, bored living in Pittsfield, Massachusetts. Her son from her first marriage was her idol. Peck had been an only child of doting, middle class parents, and seemed to have no close relatives other than her aged mother and only child.[57]

In the 1930's Peck, long divorced and impoverished, wrote an engaging memoir that revealed her as a woman of strong opinions, quite emancipated, who never went to church. Photographs do not reveal a beautiful woman, but when Wilson met her she certainly was slender, tall, coolly attractive. Addicted to fashion--he had a weakness for chic women--she wore clothes and jewelry extremely well.

Although during this first trip Wilson was meeting Peck daily--for meals or long walks--he never once mentioned her to Ellen. The following year, when their paths crossed again, he never stopped seeing or writing her until Ellen died, in the summer of 1914.

Upon his return to Princeton after his first trip to Bermuda, Wilson again so over-worked himself that he suffered another stroke--misdiagnosed once again--this time as neuritis. Again he lost the feel of his right arm and hand, although this time his whole right shoulder was affected. Again he sailed to Bermuda alone in January of 1908, to recuperate, where he knew he would find Peck vacationing in her beautiful beach home. He no sooner arrived in Hamilton on January 25th when she invited him to dinner. His reply to her invitation breathed suppressed feeling and excitement, and began with, "My dear Mrs. Peck."[58]

The next day, for the first time, Wilson wrote Ellen of Peck, devoting most of his long letter to her. In his second letter, three days later, he admitted that "Of course I am seeing a great deal of Mrs. Peck. She is fine and dear," an unwelcome remark to most wives, especially when the woman in question lives far from her husband. He mentioned that he had shown Peck photographs of her, and that she had insisted on keeping one on display. He lovingly described her mother and son Allen. Did he feel that such assurances were in order, were in fact necessary to justify his time with her? After all, Peck *was* married. Yet this fact probably was cold comfort to Ellen, in view of Peck's long absence from her husband.

On February 1, barely a week in Bermuda, he began a letter or note to Peck, "My precious one, my beloved Mary." He got no further, and for some reason, never discarded the unfinished note. For someone like Wilson, who always addressed his best friend's wife as "Mrs. Hibben," despite his close friendship with her, who reserved such intimate terms solely for his wife, clearly something had transpired between Wilson and Peck. Three and a half years later, in a letter to Peck, he lovingly reminded her of their time together in that sultry spring of 1908. They had taken "delectable walks to the South Shore,--when you were like a gay child of Nature, released into its native element, and I felt every quickened impulse of the blood communicated to me."

Peck was vulnerable: unhappy in her marriage, subject to depressions (her reason for going to Bermuda), lonely. Though few of her letters to Wilson survive, those that do reflect an intensity of feeling unsuitable for a married woman. As to Wilson, when he returned to Princeton a month later, his marriage for the first time seemed to be undergoing a strain.[59]

Ellen and Wilson's marriage seemed to be changing. In his painfully honest memoir, Stockton Axson made the remarkable comment that after Wilson became president of Princeton, the romance of his marriage cooled, though he added--never the love that was at its core.[60] Madge's comment that it was hard to "budge"

Ellen away from home must be taken with a grain of salt. When Wilson left for Bermuda for the second time, Ellen took off on a long visit to Georgia.

According to Stockton (who, despite being an English professor, had no gift for words), Wilson's relationship with Peck "was scarcely beer and skittles" to Ellen.[61] He knew more about his sister's feelings than anyone else, but commented no further about Wilson's feelings for Peck, perhaps out of loyalty. Madge's and Eleanor's comments are even scantier.

Something clearly was wrong when Wilson, in the summer of 1908, returned to England and the lake district alone. Ellen spent the summer in Lyme. None of his daughters accompanied him either, preferring to be with their mother. Ellen's letters to him are not extant; his to her hint at an estrangement between them. Had she inadvertently found his scribbled words, "My own, my precious Mary"? Or did she open an incriminating letter? At any rate, Ellen was now paying a heavy price for her tolerance--even encouragement--of Wilson's friendships with other women. Henceforth, Wilson's letters to Ellen never mention other women and his attraction to them.

As to Wilson, his trip to Rydal was marred by emotional suffering, despite an interesting stay at Andrew Carnegie's estate in Scotland. Unlike all of his previous correspondence with Ellen when he was away, his letters now were pleading and anxious. Aboard ship, in his first letter, he asked anxiously, "Do you love me? Are you sure?" He felt unworthy, "...teach me how, in some worthy way, to satisfy you..." A week later, comfortably ensconced in a hotel near Rydal, he continued along the same vein. "I know I do not give you satisfactory proof of it, my darling, but it [his love] is there as the greatest force of my life. Try to believe it and realize it and accept it with a *little* joy!"-- perhaps anticipating that it would not have the desired effect.[62]

In his July 20th missive to Ellen, Wilson alluded to a comment of hers in a previous letter: "'Emotional love,'-ah, dearest, that was a cutting and cruel judgment and utterly false;" but was it? He was suffering, "-am suffering still, ah, how deeply!...Suffering and thinking over here by myself..." Several weeks later he again wrote, "I only know that I am glad to have you have a vacation from my selfishness and subtle exactions..."[63] A month later, he was back in Princeton.

Perhaps Ellen's emotional pain eased during her delightful summer spent at Griswold's in Lyme; or perhaps Wilson's suffering and non-stop declarations of his love for her had the desired effect. His letters hint that he was trying to convince her, and ultimately must have, of the harmlessness of his feelings for Peck. That way, he could go on seeing her.

Why Wilson continued to see and write Peck boggles the mind. (One wonders what his reaction would have been had Ellen done the same with a male friend.)

That fall, Wilson, despite how busy he was, arranged to visit Peck in her home, all the way in Pittsfield, persuading Ellen to come along with him. She went, perhaps to size up Peck for herself, perhaps to impress on her that she was very much married to her husband. Afterwards he mailed Peck a photo of himself (not of himself and Ellen), and went so far as to persuade Jessie, who could not possibly have had an interest in Peck, to visit her in Pittsfield as well. This charade maintained the fiction that his relationship with Peck was innocent.

Peck of course was flattered by his unceasing attention and affection, his fatuous claim that it was a "privilege" to see and hear from her. It seems that her friendship with Wilson gave her the courage to break up her marriage. In 1909, nineteen years after she married him, she began divorce proceedings against her husband. While to her, her husband had many faults, stinginess and marital infidelity were not among them.

Years later, as U.S. president, Wilson expressed remorse and "deep shame" at his relationship with Peck. By then, he feared that she might even blackmail him on account of the scores of personal letters she possessed. In the late 1920's, Ray Stannard Baker purchased Wilson's letters from an impoverished Peck (Hulbert by then).[64] Her memoir, published in 1933, was an attempt to quash the rumors, still circulating, of a liaison with Woodrow Wilson.

There is little to indicate that Ellen ever warmed up to Peck. She did drop in to visit her in her apartment in New York, not once, but several times. By then, Wilson was a public figure and she was bent on making the world see that his relationship with Peck was above-board. How Ellen really felt is hinted at in a confidence she once shared with young Doctor Carey Grayson--her and Wilson's personal friend in the White House. The only pain Wilson had ever caused her in their marriage, she told him, was over the "Peck affair." How long did that pain last, however? Did it begin and end in 1908? Or did it follow her all the way to the White House?

* * *

To her old friend from Rome, Anna Harris, Ellen confided the ordeals of recent years in mournful cadences uncharacteristic of her. Referring to that bleak year, April, 1904-April, 1905, she wrote,

> In that one year Jessie had diphtheria, Margaret nervous collapse, Nellie tubercular glands, Madge severe malarial fever in Italy; Woodrow was operated on for hernia in New York and had phlebitis after it...Stockton was

Travels, Trials, Tribulations, and Mrs. Peck, 1900-1910   177

almost hopelessly ill the whole year, and I lost my darling boy and his little family.[65]

Daughter Margaret's "nervous collapse" had ominous implications for the Wilsons, who feared that she might be taking after her maternal grandfather and uncle. Her parents took her out of college--she never returned--but she did recover fully, enrolling for a year in the Peabody Institute of Music in Baltimore. Stockton, who had a nervous breakdown in the fall of 1904 followed by months of hospitalization, had another breakdown upon hearing of his brother Ed's death. Ellen conveyed the tragic tidings to him in person. They were both traumatized, but Stockton's collapse deprived Ellen of the support she needed from her closest relative, and deepened her own despair.

Ellen ended her tale of woe with characteristic self-reproach: "But such a summing up savors too much of self-pity, --a contemptible vice." There were other sorrows that went unmentioned, that she might have been reluctant to divulge. These had to do with her husband's growing--and to Ellen, exceedingly painful--unpopularity at Princeton.[66]

The trustees' unanimous choice of Wilson as a successor to the aging Patton gave Wilson a powerful mandate for change.

He made a promising beginning by tightening admissions and course requirements. "It began to be hard to enter Princeton, and moderately hard to stay in..." noted Stockton.[67] In his quest to make Princeton the greatest university in the nation, Wilson put an end to Princeton's identity as a Christian, denominational school, which he viewed as a stumbling block. (In the 1890's, Wilson's candidate for a history position, Frederick Jackson Turner, was rejected by the faculty because he was not a Christian; Wilson criticized Dean West's opposition in particular as a "stubborn prejudice.")[68] Wilson's next reform, the introduction of a "preceptorial" system of undergraduate education ("an adaptation of Oxford's tutorial system," as Stockton described it) was widely hailed as an important innovation. Yet by the time he left Princeton in 1910, Wilson was a disaster as university president; worse, he alienated almost every friend that he and Ellen ever had. Most painfully for Wilson, these included his closest friends, Jack and Jenny Hibben.

Wilson's new, revolutionary system of preceptorial education was soon developing problems. The colleges that hailed this reform could not adopt it because of its costliness. Princeton's fifty new preceptors were all paid professors' salaries; fortunately, Patton had left Princeton, as Wilson himself admitted, in excellent financial shape. Two years later, however, there was some grumbling: there were too many preceptors and it was costing the university too much.

Perhaps Wilson should have done a more careful "feasibility" study of this expensive reform. Over time, preceptors became, as they are today, little more than teaching assistants.

Infinitely worse was Wilson's "quad" plan of 1907 to rid the campus of private eating clubs. Student life was increasingly dominated by the popularity of upperclass eating clubs--who would be accepted, who rejected mattered to most if not all lower classmen. Housed in elaborate buildings that lined Prospect Avenue, upperclass eating clubs had proliferated since Wilson's undergraduate days. Club members ate their meals and socialized there, and had their own membership rules. Students from wealthy families invariably got to join the clubs. Club members enjoyed the camaraderie of eating and socializing together, and, according to Stockton, disdained non-club members. To Wilson, their chief evil lay in eroding Princeton's "democracy."

Princeton, with 1500 students in 1907, was a much larger school than in Wilson's day. Wilson attended Princeton in the 1870's when the school was one big family, and the president's wife herself ministered to sick students in their dorm rooms. It grated on Wilson that clubs were destroying that collegial atmosphere, although they had nothing to do with academics. True, club members did seem to care more about their clubs than their education, a sad fact acknowledged by most if not all of the faculty members, including Stockton. And because so many club members were sons of wealthy families, it seemed, to Wilson at least, that Princeton was catering to the well-heeled.

Not that anyone had complained about the clubs, not even faculty. When Wilson in late 1906 announced to the startled trustees his plan of putting an end to the clubs, there had been no backlash against them, no simmering discontent. Without taking a "straw poll" to see how students and faculty really felt about the clubs, Wilson decided on his own that they must go. Wrote Stockton, "From the beginning of his presidency of Princeton, Mr. Wilson had been too much inclined to rely on a few, too little inclined to listen at length to what others had to say," a style of leadership he would carry over to the U.S. presidency.[69]

Wilson introduced a plan whereby all undergraduates would be organized into "quadrangles," similar to British colleges, where upper-and lower classmen would live, study and eat together, whether they wished to or not. The new quads would absorb the clubs, radically altering campus life. To make his plan more palatable, Wilson insisted that the students would benefit academically from this arrangement--as they did at Oxford and Cambridge--by studying and discussing together.

The reaction to his quad plan was similar to the "fence incident," when Wilson suddenly erected a fence on college property without consulting anyone: it enraged people, especially wealthy alumni (former club members) who so often bankrolled major building projects. But eventually, even faculty came to criticize his quad plan. Were not Cambridge and Oxford, Wilson's models for his quad plan, among the most class-ridden, elitist institutions in the world? Alas, Wilson goes on record as brooking not the slightest modification of his plan. Those who opposed it--most notably, Dean West and Grover Cleveland ("West's dupe and tool," noted Wilson[70]), became his enemies, even his beloved friend, Jack Hibben. When Cleveland died of heart failure in the summer of 1908, Wilson scarcely hid his relief.

Academic squabbles being what they are, they soon over-shadowed everything else in Princeton. People--even the children of faculty members--took sides, and refused to speak to one another. Eleanor recalled that painful year. "The whole town was taking sides, even the children. My friends were divided and we spent much of our time arguing fiercely."[71] One by one, friends ceased visiting the Wilson household; Sunday afternoons, which for years had been spent socializing with the Hibbens, were now spent at home, where a depressed, angry Wilson, far from reconciling himself to the discontent and withdrawing--or modifying--his plan, discussed resigning. But where would they go, and what would they do? Without his Princeton income, the family would be reduced to living off the interest of their savings, only $2000 a year. Nor could they sell off any property-- since they had not invested in any--or move back to their house on Library Place. Wilson vaguely talked about "starting over as a practicing lawyer," and moving his family "back" to Virginia, where they had never lived.[72]

Ellen found herself taking her cue from her husband, shunning those who shunned him, criticizing his (but not her) detractors behind their backs. Her brother Stockton's candid memoir noted that "I doubt if she ever knew what hatred was until these [the Princeton controversies] arose. She really hated some of the Princeton opponents, had scurvy names for them..." He made the remarkable comment that "Doubtless it would have been better if she had advised mollification and less fighting--but she didn't--a principle at stake." In his interview with Ray Stannard Baker in 1927, Stockton re-affirmed that: "Mrs. Wilson was more bitter than Wilson himself." Understandably, the whole family rallied around Wilson. Privately, however, Stockton could see that "Wilson pressed too hard at this time, asked too much of human nature." Young Eleanor, too, kept her mixed feelings to herself. The "small exclusive club dances," after all, were "the most exciting of all," and privately, she was sorry to see the clubs go.[73]

In July, 1908, nine months after the trustees had soundly defeated the quad project, Wilson wrote Ellen from Rydal, probably facetiously, how he wished the

Democratic National Convention would nominate him for something, anything, just to get him away from "troublesome Princeton."

Ellen, concentrating on her painting in Lyme that summer, was also trying hard to relax. Last year there had been the oppressive fall-out from the quad controversy, this year she was facing marital unhappiness. The year before, she, Wilson, the girls and Madge had summered in the Adirondacks, close to Princeton faculty, especially, near the Hibbens. With Hibben bringing up the painful topic of the quads nearly every day, neither Ellen nor Wilson could fully be off their guard. This year she had returned to Old Lyme, where she would return for three more summers. More than ever, Lyme became Ellen's personal refuge, her private paradise, where she felt free from care and fully alive. "Ellen is never so happy as when she is here," wrote Wilson.[74]

Rather than become more accommodating after his quad defeat, Wilson forged ahead with yet another major "reform," thereby unleashing, in hindsight, what appears to have been the silliest academic squabble in the annals of academia.

It is astonishing how highly-educated, perfectly sane people--faculty, alumni, and trustees--and their wives, even children, became locked into bitter factions over whether the new graduate college should be built on-campus, or off. To both Wilson and the dean of the graduate college, Andrew F. West, and to their respective factions, it appeared to be a life-and-death issue. Wilson insisted that graduate students, who would be living and learning in the new facility, would be better off in the heart of campus, while West, their dean, believed they would benefit from a more secluded location, away from noisy undergraduates. To Wilson, West was malevolently intent on building a luxurious facility that catered exclusively to rich students, an accusation that West angrily denied.

According to Wilson scholar Arthur S. Link, "the greatest crisis in Wilson's career" was over the on-campus or off-campus location of the graduate college. Madge would have concurred. "The quad wrangles were almost forgotten in this new and much greater battle." Eleanor recalled the conflict over location--as a conflict over control. Her father "believed, moreover, that it [the graduate college] should be controlled by the head of the university, not run separately by the dean and the College graduate committee." (Nearly thirty years later, Eleanor had a contrary recollection: West sought personal control versus control by "university authorities.") Possibly this issue would have been less divisive had not West been the graduate dean. He had locked horns with Wilson over the quad issue, and Wilson never forgave him. To West, Wilson was an autocrat. "'Heaven knows I hated Wilson like poison.'"[75]

Wilson, an all-or-nothing idealist by temperament, rejected a compromise solution to the problem offered by the trustees. The feud finally resolved itself, as one of Wilson's enemies gleefully noted in a letter, by the bequest of a wealthy widow, Mrs. Wyman. Her husband had left upwards of ten million dollars for the building of the graduate college according to West's plan. This second defeat for Wilson left him, and Ellen, deeply embittered for the remainder of their lives.

At the height of the crisis over the graduate school, in the spring of 1909, Wilson still found time to write Peck long letters. In fact, he admitted to his "preoccupation" with her *happiness or unhappiness*. He mentioned buying her a "little ornament" for her birthday and was "deeply excited with impatience to hear everything that concerns you" on his forthcoming visit to New York. (Peck had separated from her husband and was living in Manhattan.) A week later, he wrote, "It was a deep pleasure to see you," alone, without Ellen.[76]

Meanwhile rumors and tales of Wilson's brave struggle against wealth and privilege were circulating in the press nation-wide, including an editorial in *The New York Times*. With Ellen's support and encouragement, Wilson began casting a wider net in his public speeches and talks which, from 1908 onwards, began focusing on political issues. "It has been suggested that I run for Governor of the State in the approaching campaign..." he informed Peck in mid-July.[77] It was well that Ellen, the most influential person in Wilson's life, had not been a moderating influence on him at Princeton. He might never have launched his political career otherwise.

ENDNOTES

[1] Woodrow Wilson to Ellen A. Wilson, August 24, 1902. Arthur S. Link, ed., *The Papers of Woodrow Wilson* (Princeton: Princeton University Press, 1966-1996) 14:104. (henceforth: *PWW*)

[2] Woodrow Wilson to Mary Allen Hulbert Peck, July 18, 1909. *PWW* 19:312.

[3] On the Smith sisters and the summer of 1897, Margaret Axson Elliott, *My Aunt Louisa and Woodrow Wilson* (Chapel Hill: Univ. of North Carolina Press, 1944), 145-151; Stockton Axson, *Brother Woodrow: A Memoir of Woodrow Wilson* ed. Arthur S. Link (Princeton, Princeton University Press, 1993), 168; Eleanor Wilson McAdoo, *The Woodrow Wilsons* (New York: Macmillan Co., 1937), 32-33; Mary and Lucy Smith interview, March 12-13, 1927, Ray Stannard Baker Papers, Library of Congress, Washington, D.C. (henceforth: RSB papers); on Wilson's borrowing "darky" stories from the Smiths, McAdoo, *The Woodrow Wilsons*, 271.

[4] Ellen's letters from New Orleans, *PWW* 11:430-458.

[5] Sina Dubovoy, "The Spirituality of Woodrow Wilson." Unpublished paper, 1997.

[6] Ellen A. Wilson to Woodrow Wilson, Feb.24, 1900. *PWW* 11:438.

[7] Ellen A. Wilson to Woodrow Wilson, March 7, 1900. *PWW* 11:490.

[8] Woodrow Wilson to Ellen A. Wilson, March 11, 1900. *PWW* 11:502.

[9] Ellen A. Wilson to Woodrow Wilson, March 15, 1900, *PWW* 11:514; Woodrow Wilson to Ellen A. Wilson, March 25, 1900, *Ibid.*, 526.

[10] McAdoo, *The Woodrow Wilsons*, 58; Axson, 112-114.

[11] Ellen A. Wilson to Woodrow Wilson, June 26, July 24, 1899. *PWW* 11:135, 187.

[12] *PWW* 12:384, note 1.; Axson, 112.

[13] Woodrow Wilson to James Woodrow, Feb.4, 1901. *PWW* 12:89.

[14] Quoted by Moses Taylor Pyne to Woodrow Wilson, June 19, 1902, *PWW* 12:441; Theodore Roosevelt to Woodrow Wilson, Dec.6, 1902, *PWW* 14:265.

[15] Ellen A. Wilson to Florence S. Hoyt, June 28, 1902. *PWW* 12:464.

[16] Ellen A. Wilson to Woodrow Wilson, Aug.25, 1902. *PWW* 14:107; McAdoo, *The Woodrow Wilsons*, 62.

[17] Ellen A. Wilson to Woodrow Wilson, Aug.25, 1902. *PWW* 14:107.

[18] McAdoo, *The Woodrow Wilsons*, 63; Frank J. Aucella, Patricia A. Piorkowski Hobbs with Frances Wright Saunders, *Ellen Axson Wilson: First Lady & Artist* (Washington, D.C., 1993), 6; Frances W. Saunders, *Ellen Axson Wilson: First Lady Between Two Worlds* (Chapel Hill, 1985), note 16, p.312. The restaurant, "Charley's Other Brother," in Mount Holly, New Jersey, still (as of 2003) displays Ellen's Tiffany window.

[19] Ellen A. Wilson to Woodrow Wilson, Aug.15, 1902. *PWW* 14:88.

[20] On the sale of their home, Ellen A. Wilson to Woodrow Wilson, Aug.15, 1902, Woodrow Wilson to Ellen A. Wilson, Aug.19, 1902, John W. Fielder to Woodrow Wilson, Sept.5, 1902, *PWW* 14:88, 93, 123; on Wilson's salary as PU president and the $7,000 royalty check, Ellen A. Wilson to Woodrow Wilson, April 30, 1903, *PWW* 14:438 and "A News Report," Dec.5, 1911, *PWW* 23:564.

[21] Ellen A. Wilson to Woodrow Wilson, Aug.26, 1902. *PWW* 14:110, 118, note 2.

[22] Ellen A. Wilson to Mary E. Hoyt, Dec.15, 1902. *PWW* 14:294.

[23] "A Record of a European Trip," *PWW* 14:521-543.

[24] Ellen A. Wilson to Woodrow Wilson, Sept.29, 1903. *PWW* 15:8.

[25] Woodrow Wilson to John Greer Hibben, Nov.27, 1902. *PWW* 14:224.

[26] Woodrow Wilson to Ellen A. Wilson, March 21, April 4, 1904. *PWW* 15:201,231.

[27] Ellen A. Wilson to Woodrow Wilson, April 20, 1904. *PWW* 15:269.

[28] Ellen A. Wilson to Woodrow Wilson, March 26, 1904. *PWW* 15:211; On Ellen's correspon-dence from Italy, see *PWW* 15:211-360.

[29] Ellen A. Wilson to Woodrow Wilson, May 25, 1904. *PWW* 15:348-349.

[30] McAdoo, *The Woodrow Wilsons*, 83.

[31] *Ibid.*, 88.

[32] Elliott, 159, 185.

[33] On the "fence incident," *PWW* 15:507-509; McAdoo, *The Woodrow Wilsons*, 78.

[34] McAdoo, *The Woodrow Wilsons*, 84.

[35] Ellen A. Wilson to Anna Harris, March 11, 1905. *PWW* 16:28-29.

[36] Woodrow Wilson to Robert Bridges, April 28, 1905. *PWW* 16:86 and note 1. Note 1 in *PWW* gives a slightly different version of Edward Axson's death than Eleanor in *The Woodrow Wilsons*, 87 and in *The Priceless Gift* (New York: McGraw-Hill, 1962), 240. I have followed the more detailed, *PWW* version.

[37] Ellen and Wilson stayed at a different boarding house in the summer of 1905. Presented here is a composite of Ellen and Wilson's experiences at Griswold's in the summers of 1909-1911.

[38] Elliott, 164.

[39] McAdoo, *The Woodrow Wilsons*, 46.

Travels, Trials, Tribulations, and Mrs. Peck, 1900-1910   183

40 Elliott, 248.

41 McAdoo, *The Woodrow Wilsons*, 105.

42 Ellen A. Wilson to William Macbeth, March 16, 1907. Macbeth Gallery Records. Smithsonian Institution Archives of American Art, Washington, D.C.

43 Arthur Heming, *Miss Florence and the Artists of Old Lyme* (Essex, Conn.: Pequot Press, 1971), 34-35.

44 Elliott, 220.

45 McAdoo, *The Woodrow Wilsons*, 66.

46 Elliott, 222; McAdoo, *The Woodrow Wilsons*, 82.

47 McAdoo, *The Woodrow Wilsons*, 90.

48 Ellen A. Wilson to Mary E. Hoyt, June 12, 1906 and to Florence Hoyt, June 27, 1906. *PWW* 16:423, 429-430.

49 Edwin A. Weinstein, *Woodrow Wilson: A Medical and Psychological Biography* (Princeton University Press, 1981), 164.

50 Ellen A. Wilson to Mary E. Hoyt, June 12, 1906. *PWW* 16:423.

51 Woodrow Wilson to Arthur Tedcastle, April 10, 1906. *PWW* 16:357.

52 On their vacation in Rydal: Ellen A. Wilson to Anna Harris, Dec.1, 1906, *PWW* 16:494; Woodrow Wilson to Annie Wilson Howe, Aug.2, 1906, *PWW* 16:432, and McAdoo, *The Woodrow Wilsons*, 94-96.

53 Wilson's letters from Rydal to Ellen, *PWW* 16:436-451; see also Eleanor's account in *The Woodrow Wilsons*, 94-96.

54 Ellen A. Wilson to Anna Harris, Dec.1, 1906. *PWW* 16:493.

55 Ellen A. Wilson to Anna Harris, Jan.12, 1907. *PWW* 17:33.

56 Woodrow Wilson to Ellen A. Wilson, Sept.2, 1906. *PWW* 16:446.

57 Mary Allen Hulbert, *The Story of Mrs. Peck* (New York: Minton, Balch & Co., 1933)

58 Woodrow Wilson's letters during his second trip to Bermuda in *PWW* 17:606-616.

59 *PWW* 17:611; Woodrow Wilson to Mary Allen Hulbert Peck (henceforth: Peck), July 24, 1911, *PWW* 23:224.

60 Axson, 104.

61 *Ibid.*, 103.

62 Woodrow Wilson to Ellen A. Wilson, July 2, 1908. *PWW* 18:350.

63 Woodrow Wilson to Ellen A. Wilson, July 20, Aug.3, 1908. *PWW* 18:372,387.

64 Hulbert, 283.

65 Ellen A. Wilson to Anna Harris, Feb.12, 1907. *PWW* 17:34.

66 About the Princeton controversies, Stockton Axson had a great deal to say in his memoir, 112-150.

67 *Ibid.*, 123.

68 "From the Diary of Woodrow Wilson," *PWW* 10:120.

69 Axson, 145.

70 Woodrow Wilson to Ellen A. Wilson, June 26, 1908. *PWW* 18:346.

71 McAdoo, *The Woodrow Wilsons*, 99.

72 Axson, 130.

73 *Ibid.*, 106; also Stockton Axson interview, March 15,16, 1927, Ray Stannard Baker Papers, Library of Congress, Washington, D.C.; McAdoo, *The Woodrow Wilsons*, 80.

74 Woodrow Wilson to Peck, Sept.5, 1909. *PWW* 19:358.

75 *PWW* 19:viii; Elliott, 240; McAdoo,*The Woodrow Wilsons*, 101 and *The Priceless Gift*, 246; West's comment quoted in Elliott, 202.

[76] Woodrow Wilson to Peck, May 25, 31, 1909. *PWW* 19:214, 229.
[77] Woodrow Wilson to Peck, July 11, 1909. *PWW* 19:309.

Chapter 7

POLITICIAN'S WIFE, 1910-1912

"Surely you must be a man of destiny."[1]
Ellen to her husband, May, 1911

"...she went on to promote his cause in every way she could."[2]
Stockton Axson of his sister

The controversies at Princeton, over the quads and the graduate college, were becoming known throughout the nation, thanks to Wilson. If he could not make his case popular in Princeton, then he would travel around the country presenting the issues--his fight "to free Princeton from the influence of money and privilege"--to audiences of well-heeled alumni. In the spring of 1910, Wilson once again rested in Bermuda, *sans* Mrs. Peck. His letters to Ellen were heartfelt and loving. "ah! how unspeakably I love you and long for you, my darling," his first letter ran. "You are all the world to me. I have never known it so clearly as during the past few weeks!" Now more than ever, he knew her true worth. She emerged from the ugly academic frays a proven partner, unquestionably loyal and dedicated to him. That she suffered in consequence was painful to him. "It makes me feel deeply selfish to think of having left you there...in the midst of all the talk that must be distressing you, or the silence that may be puzzling you." The social isolation, the ostracism, cut deeply. One by one, her Princeton friends deserted her, her social life constricted until it was centered almost wholly on her family, not even on church and family.[3]

For years Wilson had been an ordained elder, a position almost on a par with a pastor. Wilson and Jack Hibben had attended the same church, and switched to the same church--from Second Presbyterian to First Presbyterian--after they failed to merge the two. Now that Hibben was, to Wilson (but not to Hibben), a bitter foe, church attendance must have been awkward and going to church, less comforting. The pastor, Dr. Beach, and even substitute pastors took sides. "Mr. Kirk preached yesterday...," wrote Ellen to her husband in Bermuda. "He is a tremendous partisan of yours." His evening sermon--the Wilsons still attended two church services on Sundays--was "avowedly suggested by the situation here..."[4]

Although still a devoted church-goer, Ellen was increasingly subject to religious doubts. Daughter Jessie referred to her as being "often much disturbed" and Stockton to her being "plagued with doubt" when it came to religious belief. She devoted more and more time to books on philosophy, seeking answers to life's enigmas. Her brother Stockton noted that Ellen "mastered Kant, Hegel, Fichte, etc., "although this must be taken with a grain of salt. This was in contrast to her husband, who remarked once, "I do not have to be satisfied intellectually to be satisfied spiritually." Yet except for their observance of "Sabbath day," Ellen and Wilson became over the years less orthodox in their religious beliefs and wholly secular in their style of life. Having both grown up in teetotaling families who eschewed dancing and card-playing, they made sure that their daughters learned to dance; they limited their drinking to social functions, and loved to play cards. Wilson, as an ordained elder and Peck's most influential friend, could have counseled Peck in her marital trouble, instead of abetting her desire for a divorce.[5]

While Wilson's letters to Ellen from Bermuda resounded with love and feeling, wholly unbeknown to her, his epistles to Peck were no less loving and intense. Peck, now separated from her husband and living in New York, could no longer afford to spend part of every year in Bermuda. She and not Ellen saw Wilson off from the pier in New York. Shortly after his ship departed, she wrote him, "I've had no thought apart from you the whole day through." As to Wilson, there were all too many "haunting associations" in Bermuda, at every turn and corner, that reminded him of Peck. "I cannot dissociate any part of it from you...and am lonely whenever I go because you are not there!" In her next letter Peck called him "Best Beloved," and he in turn called her his "Dearest, sweetest Friend." Peck wrote of her longing to be in Bermuda, "...I am homesick for it ...the life I *love* - and with *you* there. I could not sleep last night for the tormenting thought of it." Wilson withheld any mention of Peck in his letters to Ellen, when in fact he was obsessed by thoughts of her. "As for my missing you," he wrote Peck, "I have a sense of loneliness and loss from morning to night because you are not here."[6]

With her husband away in Bermuda for two weeks, Ellen kept herself busy as usual. An avid lecture-goer, she attended a talk on "American Women" given by none other than Ida B. Tarbell. This firebrand critic of John D. Rockefeller's petroleum empire was notably conservative on women's issues. Even to conservative Ellen, "You can hardly imagine anything more conservative" than Tarbell's views on American women. For once, Ellen could not have agreed more. "Indeed it was largely a demonstration of the fact that the grandmothers were incomparably superior to us...they respected their work in the order of society..."[7]

Ellen, too, was glad to get away from Princeton, if only to Camden. On her own she attended the convention of "Associated Charities," which "I thoroughly enjoyed...several of the papers both by men and women were most able and interesting." She also spent time in New York interviewing prospective maids. Faithful Annie apparently left her employ, succeeded by a German immigrant, who soon quit. "I have no one in her place yet--am expecting a coloured girl to 'fill in.'" She and daughter Eleanor attended "several small picture shows" in New York--Ellen's first mention of motion pictures. Afterwards, they dropped by Peck's apartment for a "little visit," more to please her husband than herself. Wilson, referring to Ellen's visit in his last letter to Peck, mentioned the "two ladies whom I love"--and he did not mean Ellen and his young daughter ("my darling baby")--his first admission of loving Peck.[8]

As Wilson was preparing to return home, he wrote Peck of his deep desire, on the morning of his disembarkation, to see her, "my dear, dear friend before I must start for Princeton. It would be heartbreaking to have to wait still longer, when my thought has been waiting, waiting, waiting for the happy moment when I should be in your presence again and have one of the hours with you that means so much to me!" To Ellen on the same day, he touched lightly on his upcoming return: there would be delays at quarantine and at customs, he feared, and hence, "at best I may miss the morning trains." He hid his intention to be with Peck, and lied when he ended with, "My thought is wholly of you." In his letter to Peck he admitted, "I am with you in imagination all the time."[9]

* * *

After a two-year absence from Lyme, Ellen returned to the art colony in the summer of 1908. Madge and the girls joined her. Writing to Emily Yates afterwards--wife of artist Fred Yates in Rydal--Ellen paid tribute to Yates' talent as a landscape artist. "In my humble opinion he outranks every other American landscape artist, --and that is saying a great deal, for we undoubtedly have a noble school of landscape over here now." Ellen had the highest regard for her fellow artists at Griswold's, even if their private lives were not always above reproach. Regarding Willard Metcalf--who had once offered Griswold his best painting in lieu of paying his bill--it was obvious that her moral code was as conservative as ever: "After years of dissipation he finally turned over a new leaf some five years ago, and, very bravely, married a young woman with whom he had been living. But she of course was utterly worthless and last year went off with another, --young--artist." Ellen had never met Metcalf in Lyme, rather, at his studio in New York. Thanks to her summers in Lyme, she was now visiting artists in their private studios, cultivating a professional interest in art and its creators as she had while an art student at the League. Very likely she dropped in at William Macbeth's prominent art gallery on Fifth Avenue. Writing to the art dealer for the first time in 1907, Ellen tried to get him interested in Yates' paintings, and identified herself as an artist.[10]

The following summer of 1909, Wilson and the whole family joined Ellen at Griswold's. The house's antiquity--a year before its renovation--coupled with the slow pace of life, heightened the feeling of time standing still. Wilson wrote Peck that summer—

> Lyme is certainly a haven. We have the sound of trains often in our ears and motor cars whirr by on the road at our door; but the world which passes by us does not notice us: we are side-tracked at a very quiet rural station where life has hardly changed its pace since the thirties.[11]

As in 1905, Wilson again spent his days at the typewriter, or playing golf, resting his nerves for what was bound to be another grueling academic year. Sundays he devoted to writing Peck. "... I set apart Sunday for a letter to you. That makes it a day of release and pleasure: a red-letter day." (Five months later his brother Joseph, who worked as a reporter in Tennessee, "was overjoyed to hear from you a few days ago after fully fifteen months of silence.")[12]

Wilson confessed what his letters to her really meant.

> Do you recognize what these letters are? They are merely a poor attempt on my part to have the pleasure of an imaginary conversation with you...It is thus that we keep vividly conscious of one another throughout long separations and keep alive the delightful impression of travelling the road of life together, not losing sight of one another...[13]

In this love letter, he made not a single reference to his wife. In another letter he wrote, "How happy it would make him could a lady he knows who is made for good company and good fellowship look in upon this little world and complete it." No longer did Ellen complete his world, as she used to. He ended this letter, "All join in affectionate messages"--which is very doubtful. [14]

During that pleasant summer Eleanor took lessons from artist Frank DuMond, while her mother, "free from all household cares, and knowing that we were all busy and enjoying ourselves, went with an easy mind to spend entire days alone at the work she loved." Meanwhile there was a certain artist, a Mr. Robinson, staying with his wife at Griswold's. Mrs. Robinson, wrote Wilson to Peck, was a "slave" to her husband, following him around everywhere, solicitous, submissive to his every beck and call. "Mrs. Wilson says it is all right: that Mrs. Robinson is doing what she ought to do: 'They have no children and that is her whole duty, and chief pleasure. That is what a woman ought to do.'" Then why had Ellen never done so? Wilson thought Ellen's view was "debatable."[15]

By summer's end, the artists at Lyme once more held their annual exhibition, and again Ellen preferred not to submit anything. Wilson hoped Peck would consider visiting Lyme for a few hours to see the exhibit. "I am afraid it would mean only a glimpse of you; but a glimpse is better than nothing, --how much better than nothing!" He chided her for not writing more often. "I can think of nothing that would give me so much pleasure, of nothing that my spirits at this moment need more," which sounded as though he needed Peck more than Ellen. Peck stayed away.[16]

The following summer of 1910 was more than usually exciting. Back in Lyme, Wilson was formally asked to become his party's candidate for governor, a possibility he had been turning over in his mind for months. Before he accepted the offer he went straight to Ellen to ask her advice. "What, he asked Ellen, did she want him to do?" Though for years he had fantasized about a career in politics, now that the opportunity presented itself--he hesitated. According to Eleanor, "he was still reluctant to take the final plunge, reluctant to give up his work at Princeton," contradicting what Stockton and others remembered, of Wilson's desire to resign right after his defeat over the quad controversy, and again after the graduate school fiasco. Yet even in her old age, Eleanor maintained that her father "was pushed--and pulled--into public life."[17]

If Wilson vacillated, Ellen did not. Sacrificing her own personal interests--she who loathed publicity and living in the public's glare--Ellen wholly supported his career move. Back in February she had referred to the possibility of his cutting himself loose from Princeton, "that is to accept the nomination for governor and go into politics." Now, with a formal invitation in hand to run as a candidate, she urged him to accept. "Many times in the evening we could hear him in the next room talking with mother for hours at a time." Wilson at last took the step of accepting the offer, and running for governor. Stockton recalled another incident, years before, which seemed to prefigure the summer of 1910. He and Wilson could not decide on undertaking a trip together. Ellen stepped in and said, "'*Now* you *must* go, for you are both getting paralysis of will.'"[18]

While all of this was going on at Griswold's, to the backdrop of telephone calls to and from Trenton and visits from New Jersey politicos, "The jolly irresponsible artists knew nothing..." They all knew, however, of Madge's impending wedding, which would take place in Lyme. No one in the family could believe it--not even Ellen--when the haughty Miss Axson, almost an old maid, consented to marry Princeton preceptor, Edward Elliott, a friend of her late brother Edward. That whole summer prior to her wedding Madge was strangely aloof and hateful to everybody, wrote a bemused Ellen.

Presumably not to her brother-in-law. He and his wife's beautiful sister had always had a close relationship. Madge's bedroom at Prospect was in the tower, away from the rest of the family, beneath Wilson's office, where she could hear him ceaselessly typing away. He was the one who allowed her to go away to college in her mid-teens, overriding Ellen's objections; who tolerated her leaving the dinner table to answer the phone, when no one else in the family was permitted to do likewise; who most comforted her after the death of her beloved brother. Now he would be giving her away in lieu of the father she never knew. Wilson was father and brother to Madge, whose memoir of him reveals the enormous crush she had on her brother-in-law. Her wedding that September, in the historic Congregational church in Lyme, would have been the highlight of that summer but for Wilson's plunge into politics.

* * *

The gubernatorial election was slated for the following November. That meant that at age fifty, Ellen's life was less settled and secure than ever. After eight years in Prospect House--the longest they had ever lived anywhere--they might have to move again. Despite her initial misgivings, Ellen had grown fond of Prospect and loved her garden. In the event of an election victory, where would they live? New Jersey governors were not provided with an executive mansion. Election victory would entail moving out at the last moment, a gruesome prospect. And this time they would have no luxurious home--no home at all--to move into. Ellen surely must have had misgivings and apprehensions, which she kept to herself. Outwardly she evinced nothing but cheerfulness and pride in her husband.

Wilson meanwhile campaigned hard. According to Stockton, who followed his campaign with all-consuming interest, Wilson "spoke in every county in the state, and in several counties more than once," thereby making his speeches "connected," as he put it. New Jersey's corrupt Democratic party machine was controlled by the likes of "Boss" Jim Smith, "Big Fellow" Jim Nugent, and "Colonel" Harvey. Smith, who fancied himself the real power in the Democratic party, had only desired Wilson to run because a more winnable alternative was not forthcoming. He felt sure to control any inept wannabe, despite his solemn promise to Wilson that he--Wilson--would be left free to run his own show as governor. According to Eleanor, Wilson extracted this promise before he would even consider running for office.[19]

After the campaign ended on election day, Stockton suffered another nervous breakdown. "...We are all very anxious about him," wrote Wilson to his friend Yates, "and it has quite upset Mrs. Wilson."[20]

Peck meanwhile was nothing if not well-informed. Pre-occupied as he was that summer, Wilson found time to write Peck a long, chatty letter. "I miss you dreadfully," he wrote. Peck was away in Minnesota. "I hate to go near New York: it is so empty and forlorn." He was crestfallen when she failed to answer his letter. "My anxiety deepens with every day...I am unhappy with suspense and conjecture." When he left Lyme abruptly to attend a Democratic dinner meeting in New York, Peck was back in the city, and Wilson was anxious to meet her. "I hope to drop in to see you some time after three o'clock. If I do not find you, I will try again later." She knew he accepted the nomination for governor before some of his best friends and close relatives did. The whole time he was campaigning for governor, Wilson had Peck on his mind. His correspondence during the campaign slowed down to a trickle, but resumed after his election victory in November. By then Peck had enough money to go away to her beloved Bermuda. Governor-elect Wilson saw her off at the pier in New York. Immediately afterward he wrote disconsolately, "I am desperately lonely, --as lonely as I was when I walked away from Pier 47 the day you sailed,"--and evidently for the same reason. "My dear friend is not here...."[21]

* * *

Not only had Ellen not accompanied him on his campaign trips, but Wilson refused to allow his family to be present at any of his rallies, even in Princeton. He feared that being a political rookie would show, to his embarrassment. Although Ellen stayed home during his campaign, day after day she pored over newspapers, and, according to Ray Stannard Baker, "clipped out everything relating to the campaign. She would go over the assortment with Mr. Wilson every day, often giving him suggestions as to people to see, Mr. Wilson making memoranda in the little book he carried always in his vest pocket." On election day, "he had swept the state in a tremendous victory," said Eleanor. It was later in the day that it dawned on Ellen and her daughters: "We would have to leave Prospect! Library Place had been sold and we had no home!"[22]

Wilson had tendered his resignation as president of Princeton in late October, burning all of his bridges in the event that he lost the election. (This further throws doubt on Eleanor's claim that he was reluctant to relinquish Princeton in the summer of 1910.) The Board of Trustees voted to continue his salary until February 9th, when Wilson technically would have ended his academic term, and just when he would begin receiving his salary as governor. But Wilson refused to accept a penny of what was due him. The chairman of the finance committee tried hard to persuade him. "Continuing the salary of a retiring officer until the conclusion of the current period of service," he wrote Wilson, in fact "followed a well established custom." Wilson was still unconvinced. Yet money was so tight that friends of Wilson's sent him a hand-out, which he gratefully accepted. Christmas was around the corner, and it would be a lean one. Ellen invited artist Fred Yates, who was in the States, to spend Christmas with them. "In fact we do not propose to make any 'fuss' over it at all this year; we havn't either the time or the money." Painful as it was, she supported her husband's decision to refuse any further income from Princeton, valued his "independence," and was glad that he was finally cutting himself loose from a school that no longer wanted him.[23]

Wilson did accept the trustees' offer to remain at Prospect House until the new year. His and Ellen's finances were at such a low ebb that even renting a house was unthinkable--even in view of Wilson's future earnings as governor--at a salary $2,000 higher than what he earned at Princeton. (That even his governor's salary would be insufficient to live on is implied by his application for a private Carnegie pension, which was awarded to distinguished educators. He did not, however, receive the pension, because of his expected income as governor.) After eight years of living rent-free in Prospect House, in ease and comfort, how had it come to this?[24]

Writing in the 1930's, Eleanor was vague about her family's "post-election" financial troubles. "The problem of meeting new and increasing expenses became serious. Mother kept it from father as much as she could." In the 1960's, she hinted that her father "had refused to use any campaign funds for his own expenses." These, as it turned out, were hotel bills, meals and transportation, as Wilson noted in a letter to a friend in 1910. Perhaps he wished to make a show of his incorruptibility and honesty. In that case, did he have to borrow money to cover his personal expenditures, and incur serious debt? Along with refusing the rest of his salary, it would certainly explain the deep financial strain of the family at the end of his campaign.[25]

It would explain why he and his family had no choice but to move into a four-room apartment suite in the Princeton Inn on Nassau Street. It was unfurnished, without a dining room or kitchen, because meals were served in a common dining room. Gone were expenses for servants, dinners, or socializing. To go from a thirty-five room mansion to lodging in four rooms, even if it was in an elegant hotel, was a painful transition. The Wilsons' only comfort was that they could remain in Princeton, their home for the past twenty years. Wilson would commute between Princeton and Trenton. As governor he was entitled to a car, but he preferred to take the train.

Moving out of Prospect House in the second week of January, 1911, proved "a difficult ordeal," recalled Eleanor and her siblings. Their mother took it especially hard. "Day after day she came down from the attic or up from the cellar, tired and dusty and a little sad..." Only this time, most of their belongings were put in storage. As on other occasions, she would not permit her husband to help. When it was all over and they were re-settled, "The first evening we sat and looked at one another in despair. No fireplace, no garden, and meals in a hotel dining room surrounded by other people. How could we bear it?" Selling their Library Place home had turned out to be an unwise decision. The money from its sale may have given them a false sense of security and prosperity, discouraging them from saving and investing. All it took was a short, low-budget political campaign to wipe them out financially. In his long letter to Peck on January 13, Wilson bemoaned the loss of his accustomed life and surroundings, but not a word about how Ellen was taking it. How he longed to be in Bermuda, where Peck was at the moment, "sitting by my dear friend, for a long, intimate chat that would get my thoughts and my spirits into perfect fettle again."[26] What *was* the hold that Peck had on him?

The life of the governor of New Jersey and his spouse in that era was quite different from today. Strangest of all, the governor's wife remained a nonentity, as no role was expected of her. As "first lady" of Princeton, Ellen had had important social responsibilities. Now, however, with her daughters grown and more or less independent (but not financially), Ellen foresaw spending her days in the apartment, doing little besides reading and writing letters. For the first time in over twenty-five years of married life, she had no household to manage. Gone from her life was this prerogative of a woman that claimed so much of her time and talents. Lacking her own studio and living in tight quarters, Ellen could hardly pursue her career. In short, she must have been far from happy. But she, as well as

Wilson, had been brought up in an age when to complain and sulk were considered bad manners. Besides, her nature dictated looking on the bright side. "We are settled at the Inn now in a charming little suite," she wrote a cousin," with our own furniture, books and pictures about us."[27]

The governor's role, too, had its peculiarites. Every weekday morning Wilson calmly boarded the train in Princeton for Trenton (necessitating changing trains at Princeton Junction--a car would have been less hasseling) and at day's end, calmly boarded the same train during rush hour for the 15-mile trek back to Princeton. Any commuter could sit next to the governor. Sometimes no one picked him up when he returned home, in time for dinner, so he walked home alone. "Monday nights I sit up with the legislature to all hours...but most other nights I get home to dinner," he wrote Peck in late February, shortly after his inauguration. Dinner at home meant eating in the common dining room.[28]

Eleanor was the only daughter living at home. Because she commuted to and from her studies at the Academy of Fine Arts in Philadelphia, she was gone all day; Jessie lived in Philadelphia, and Margaret in New York, although they usually came home on weekends. Four months after moving into the Inn, cost-conscious Ellen compared weekly rates with another hotel in Princeton, the Peacock Inn, and was relieved that the Peacock charged more. Evidently times were still lean for the family. "I was afraid that if it was much cheaper we ought to go there." Thank goodness, "that is off my mind." Shortly afterward Ellen described attending a four-hour breakfast of the Women's Club in Princeton, punctuated by speeches. "...I was bored almost to extinction," wrote Ellen to her absent husband. Despite being the wife of a governor, she had little to do with her time. Worst of all, with her husband away on frequent speaking engagements, she was left all alone. Not once did she complain or hint at her unhappiness, although it was probably the loneliest time of her life.[29]

That summer New Jerseyans were startled to learn that Governor Wilson not only intended to undertake an inspection tour through the state, but that Mrs. Wilson would accompany him. It was rare for governors to go on personal inspection tours of state-supported facilities--mental institutions, orphanages and prisons--where the "wards of the state" were warehoused. The whole idea of such a tour, focusing on society's most marginalized, was so thoroughly "vintage Ellen" that it is hard to imagine it coming from Wilson at all. In contrast to Ellen, social concerns had always been peripheral to him. The forthcoming tour created such a sensation that a reporter badgered Ellen, not Wilson, for an interview.

For some time Ellen had stubbornly refused to give personal interviews. Southern women just didn't do such things, she insisted. Later, when she was asked to give speeches during the presidential campaign, she was adamant.

"Southern women, she told her friends and her family, knew better than to show off in public." Show off or no, Ellen broke her resolution about not giving interviews when she felt called upon that summer to come out against women smoking. The ex-wife of a cousin of Wilson's, a Mrs. Wilson Woodrow, was a writer who was being confused with Ellen, the governor's wife. When Mrs. Woodrow wrote an article defending the right of women to smoke and it appeared that Ellen was taking such a stand, Ellen had to set the record straight. In her first interview ever, she let it be known that she was not Wilson Woodrow's Ex, and was unalterably opposed to women smoking because, well, because it was unfeminine.[30]

Now, with her husband's inspection tour before her and the public's curiosity aroused to a high pitch, Ellen consented to another interview. This time she did not feel goaded to going public, as she had with regard to women smoking. Again one suspects that this trip was planned to be, besides a tour, a publicity coup. Wilson would benefit by showing off his wife, whose interest in charities was, unlike his, true and tried. Meanwhile, it also did not hurt to highlight that he had a daughter, Jessie, who was a social worker at the University of Pennsylvania's settlement house in Philadelphia. She, too, would accompany her father and mother. The trio would be traveling around the state, at last, in a car.

"The Main Object of Tour of Institutions is to Plan Better Way to Spend Money," according to a newspaper article that featured Ellen.[31] "Mrs. Wilson's presence on the trip is altogether such an exceptional thing that she was asked about it." Ellen was her usual understated, coy self. "'I am getting interested, that is all'' was her quiet reply." But the reporter was impressed with Ellen. He paraphrased her when she said that her husband's life "'has broadened, to these bigger things.'" The reporter went so far as to refer to her as the "inspector," rather than her husband, who seemed to be just tagging along.

They stopped first at the "State Home for Women" in Vineland, where "they witnessed an opera rendered by the feeble-minded inmates." Then on to the "State Home for Soldiers, Sailors or Marines and Their Wives," followed by a visit to "the famous Training School for Feeble-Minded Children." Later, and for the first time in their lives, Ellen and her husband stepped into penal institutions, where they found young boys imprisoned side by side with hardened criminals and the mentally ill. Wherever they went they found over-crowding, but no signs of either squalor or mismanagement. New Jersey was ahead of many other states in its care for the indigent, mentally ill and imprisoned. In the end Wilson was convinced that the best way to improve conditions was not more money, but greater government oversight and regulation.

As so many people who met Ellen, the reporter was smitten by her charm. He wrote admiringly and with insight, "One soon comes to think...that she is being guided in what she is doing by strong common sense and her characteristic broad motherhood for every one, especially unfortunates." By then Ellen was quite voluble. "No one knows what good I might be able to do or what help I could give him by having broad enough knowledge of the big questions of charities and correction with which he will have to deal."

Characteristically, Ellen did not focus on herself, never mentioned her avid participation, without her husband, in the convention of "Associated Charities" in Camden the year before, or any of her other charitable work or interests. She did tell the reporter, in his paraphrase, that "Mrs. Wilson's determination to go along grew out of what she had heard" from a Mrs. Alexander--a friend or acquaintance--who first informed Ellen of conditions in state institutions. Ellen would have related to her husband what she had learned. At the very least Ellen inspired the inspection tour, or even came up with the idea. Wilson, if not Ellen, saw the publicity value of such a trip.

Ellen had truthfully admitted to the reporter that her life had changed. "'My family cares have diminished, and there is a bigger family awaiting me.'" It was to become her leitmotif.

* * *

Only a few months after moving into their apartment, Ellen was counting the days until spring. Early May, when it was still cold at the shore, she departed for Sea Girt. A stone's throw from the ocean, forty miles from Princeton, Sea Girt was a sparkling white mansion that once served as the New Jersey exhibition at the Chicago World's Fair in 1893, the very event Ellen had visited on her own with friends all those many years ago. (It was a replica of the stately home that George Washington had once inhabited during his New Jersey campaign, and Ellen, a New Jersey resident, could not have missed seeing it at the World's Fair.) Not knowing what to do with it after the fair ended, the state turned the mansion into a summer retreat for the governor and his family, and had it moved, in pieces, to Sea Girt. Living once again in a spacious home with a wide veranda and a garden, was deeply refreshing for the whole family. Wrote Ellen to her absent husband in early May, from Sea Girt, "The house is really most attractive, and the surroundings all that could be desired, --great stretches of well kept grass, and a few good trees."[32]

Yet Ellen spent only a few weeks there with her daughters--Wilson was on a speaking tour--before abruptly leaving for Lyme on her own. He soon joined her there at the now renovated establishment of Florence Griswold's. Again Ellen plunged into landscape painting with zest, and even judged her work better than the year before. This time the all too brief summer weeks at Lyme were marred by her worry over Stockton's continuous ill health. Having suffered a nervous breakdown after the gubernatorial election, Stockton was still ailing and unable to work. By late May, Ellen, writing from Lyme, confided in Wilson that "It seems quite certain now that he will never take up his work in Princeton again:--...his latest idea is to 'go into a monastery.' He insists upon having a priest sent for with whom he can confer on the subject." No priest was forthcoming, and Stockton did return to teaching. But the bitter controversies at Princeton had stressed him to the breaking point, and he soon left Princeton--but not teaching--for good.[33]

Late July found the family, including Wilson, once more assembled at Sea Girt. Ellen had enjoyed her few weeks there in May. Only this time, peace and quiet were noticeably absent. Crowds now descended on the shore, and strangers strolled up and down the ungated, unfenced front yard, occasionally peering into windows. A little boy, wearing only his bathing suit, even walked straight into the house, looking for Governor Wilson (the front door was kept unlocked). When a surprised Ellen discovered him, she promptly took him by the hand, led him into the kitchen for a treat, and handed him over to his anxious mother at the door; later the youngster told his father--a reporter--that he'd met the governor herself. As if crowds of strangers were not bad enough, the New Jersey National Guard commenced its noisy summer exercises, marching past the house every day.

Sea Girt was still better than apartment living. The family ate their meals in a screened porch overlooking the yard, and the Wilson daughters were enthralled with the young New Jersey National Guardsmen who invited them to a continuous round of dances and balls. The noise and distractions were unconducive to painting, however. There was besides a constant stream of reporters and visitors, one of whom was Mrs. Peck.

Even now that he was a busy governor--and a politician with big ambitions-- Wilson could not get Peck off of his mind. As always, his letters to her followed like clockwork: every single week without fail, in January, February ("I think about you at all times"), March, April. On a speaking tour out west in early May, he still wrote her long, heartfelt letters, his communiques to Ellen limited to short telegrams. Meanwhile Ellen, clueless about his letters to Peck, assumed he had no time to read long letters, much less write them. "I am hungry for all sorts of particulars," she wrote him. From Seattle Wilson wrote Peck how he looked forward to her visit to Trenton. "How I hope I will find you there!" upon his return in early June. "It is inexpressibly delightful to think of seeing you."[34]

Peck did indeed stop in Trenton for a brief visit (Ellen was already in Lyme). Ellen, of course, was informed of Peck's tour of her husband's office in the state house. "She sends you her love," wrote Wilson to Peck afterwards, unbelievably. A week later he again wrote Peck, that is, "...my dear friend Mrs. Peck, of whom I think so often and upon whom I depend to keep me in spirits...," apparently Ellen no longer did the same. When Peck returned to Pittsfield that summer, Wilson could not understand it. "Why perversely go back to the place that nearly starved the life out of you?" instead of hoping that she might reconcile herself with her husband. "Such a flower cannot grow in New England air," he had written a few days before. "A life of suppression, of *self*-suppression, is deadly to it." A week later, writing from Sea Girt, Wilson invited Peck for a visit of no less than five days ("...the 18th and stay through the 23rd") which she gladly accepted. She was in an ebullient mood. "I am just beginning to realize to the full my blessed freedom. It is *wonderful*," although her divorce would not be finalized for a year. "You are the larger part of my life," she added. "...I am the proudest woman in the world to feel that you find me worthy of calling me yours." Shortly afterward she wrote, "Do you think I would like a home in England? Would *you*?"[35]

When Peck cancelled her visit because of illness, Wilson was afraid that she might not come at all. "We *must* see you. I shall not be fit for the autumn campaign otherwise." Peck finally arrived for a two-day stay in late September. The whole family was cordial to her, but daughter Eleanor found her especially fascinating. "Watching her daintily puffing one cigarette after another, I decided that it was a mistake to think it wrong for women to smoke..." (Later in life, Eleanor came to resemble Peck: chic, divorced, and a chain smoker). Peck never asked if she could smoke, and Ellen was too polite to let her know how intensely it bothered her. By the second day of her visit Peck had grown tiresome, although she did not know it."...her constant suggestions about improving our appearance got on our nerves at last." Peck seemed insensitive, or just oblivious, to people's feelings about her. The final straw came when she insisted that lovely Jessie "would be more attractive with a sleek coiffure and long dangling earrings."[36] No one, except Wilson, was sorry to see her leave. "...those delightful hours at Sea Girt seem already months ago...I have missed you so much..." he wrote her two weeks later. A month later he informed Peck that he bought three theater tickets in New York--two for himself and Ellen, and one for her--insisting that she join them for dinner afterwards. As he was frequently absent on speaking trips, he might have indulged Ellen with an evening out of town, alone, just the two of them.[37]

The Wilsons stretched their summer break until it was fully five months since they left their apartment in Princeton. Thanks to Eleanor, they never returned to it.

All along she had felt her mother's misery, shut up in her lonely suite of rooms, with no outlet for her creative energy. More than just commiserate, Eleanor, in her words, "positively brooded" over the lack of a house. Six months into his governorship, Wilson still could not afford to rent one, in what was now pricy Princeton. Gone were the days when a young professor could expect to rent a house for his family--on a salary of only $3000 a year.

Against all odds, Eleanor was determined to get a house. This youngest Wilson daughter, 21 years old and living at home, had pleased her mother "that I had chosen the vocation she had dreamed of for herself..." But after her thrilling summer at Sea Girt, Eleanor was sure "that an utterly frivolous life was infinitely more attractive than the career of the most successful artist." Her duty-conscious parents, however, expected their daughters to make something of their lives, even if they married (and marriage, after all, was also a "vocation"); hence she could not, in good conscience, drop her art studies, although they now bored her. Meanwhile her sister Margaret took her voice studies seriously, while Jessie "was the humanitarian in the family" (Ellen's words), bent on making the world a better place.[38]

Eleanor lost no time deciding what had be done. If they could not afford to rent a house on their own, why not write the Smith sisters in New Orleans, suggesting that they go into housekeeping together? They were, after all, Ellen's best friends and good companions besides. "...I suggested to mother that she write and ask them if they would like to have a house with us, sharing expenses...the Smiths replied immediately that they would be delighted and it was agreed that we should move in the fall." Now that they could afford a rental, Eleanor, on her own, scoured Princeton until she found a suitable house. In early October, Wilson wrote Peck delightedly, "and here we are ensconced in as pretty and comfortable a little house as you would wish to see. (It is No.25 Cleveland Lane, please note, and our telephone number is 98.)" He omitted the fact that Eleanor had found the house, and that two other women, the Smiths, were living with them and sharing the rent.[39]

Cleveland Lane, then as now, was a pleasant, shady residential street, and the house, fully furnished, was built in the half-timbered English cottage style, reminding them of their beloved former home on Library Place, just a few blocks away. The owner was an absentee artist, Parker Mann, whose paintings ("quite indifferent affairs," according to Wilson) now graced the walls of their rental. The "cottage" came complete with a garden, fire places, and best of all, a well-lighted studio. An African-American, whom they dubbed "Black Sam," became their servant. This time the move was painless--all they needed was their suitcases. Ellen took immediate possession of her studio and started painting again, working day after day, while Lucy and Mary Smith kept her company, taking turns reading aloud as she stood at her easel. From then on, the threesome was inseparable.

The house's only drawback, as far as Wilson was concerned, was that it stood next door to his former best friends, now his enemies, Jack and Jenny Hibben. Although Wilson had extricated himself at last from Princeton affairs, hostility to him still ran deep. Out on a walk one afternoon "to see the changes in the old town...They are many, and all make the dear old place more beautiful," Wilson wrote Peck afterwards,

> ...but my walk has left me sad, --all the more in need of a chat with you! For I am somehow made aware at every turn of how the University...has turned away from me, and of how full the place is of spiteful hostility to me...It sickens the heart and makes life very hard.[40]

Worse was to come. A horrified Wilson heard the rumor from Ellen, that Hibben was being considered as Princeton's next president. In vain did he try to preclude Hibben's advance. When the trustees elected Hibben anyway, Wilson was so bitter that he refused to attend the inaugural, even though, as governor, it was expected of him. It was Ellen who wrote Hibben, "to offer my congratulations on your recent success," a letter that was both polite and politic. "All who know you will feel that you have fully earned it, and that you are ideally fitted for what is expected of you." Hibben, whom Wilson criticized for being "hopelessly weak," for the next twenty-one years was a popular, successful leader of Princeton, a moderate and above all, a team player.[41]

* * *

Presidential possibilities were budding in the spring of 1911, shortly after Wilson took his oath as governor. He made a speaking trip out west; Ellen wrote him that she talked politics all evening long over dinner with friends. Ostensibly Wilson was traveling to Denver only to speak on behalf of the Bible Society. Yet when 12,000 people showed up, he was amazed and gratified. That any ambitious politician in his right mind would say out loud--to a crowd that size--that "America was born to exemplify that devotion to the elements of righteousness which are derived from the revelations of Holy Scripture"--shows how times have changed since then. That night, finding it hard to unwind, an exhausted Wilson described that strenuous but "wonderful meeting" to Peck, expressing his conviction, in no uncertain terms, that "The Bible...is undoubtedly the book that has made democracy and been the source of all progress." Inspite of his success,

Wilson could not quite commit himself to running for president, prompting far-off Ellen to chide him, "By-the-way, *please* don't say again that you 'are not thinking' about the presidency."[42]

Even before his trip to Denver, Ellen had intervened resolutely on her husband's behalf. Learning that the wildly popular William Jennings Bryan ("the Great Commoner") would be coming to Princeton to give a speech in March, she at once sent him a telegram, inviting him to dinner to meet her husband. When Bryan accepted, she quickly telegrammed Wilson, who was away in Atlanta, to hurry home. Wilson lost no time in heeding her in what would mark a decisive turn in his political fortunes.

Wilson had never liked the bombastic Bryan, had even poked fun at him and his weird money theories. But this was a golden opportunity to try and woo this popular politician, and two-time presidential candidate, to his side, which might eventually swing voters Wilson's way. Bryan for his part had never heard of Wilson until he was elected governor, but since then, he was more and more impressed with him. He had even written Wilson in January letting him know how much he would like to meet him someday.

Consequently Ellen had seized the first opportunity that came her, that is, her husband's way, to arrange a meeting with this living legend. Without a dining room or kitchen in their apartment, the dinner would have to take place in a private dining room of the Princeton Inn. Daughters Eleanor and Jessie were also present on March 12, after Bryan had finished delivering his address in Alexander Hall. While he and Wilson took an instant personal liking to each other, Ellen positively "captivated" him, he said afterwards. That night a deeply exhausted Wilson ("...I can scarcely see the type I am hammering") wrote Peck a long letter, in which he described the meeting, without giving his wife credit for arranging it. Several weeks later he and Bryan appeared on the same speaking platform for the first, but by no means last, time.[43]

When Governor Wilson's excitable young secretary, Irish-American Joseph Tumulty, heard what Ellen accomplished, he was awestruck. "'You have nominated your husband, Mrs. Wilson!'" In her soft southern drawl Ellen replied, "'My dear, it was only good manners.'"[44]

That winter of 1911 Governor Wilson announced his bid for the presidency. When rumors circulated in an influential weekly shortly afterwards, in January, that Wilson had turned "violently against" New Jersey strong man Colonel Harvey during a confrontation in the Manhattan Club, had even verbally abused him (Harvey was disenchanted with the new governor's "radicalism," while "bossism" disgusted Wilson), Ellen once again intervened. "At Woodrow's suggestion," according to her, she wrote Judge Robert Ewing, a cousin of a close ally of Harvey's. It was a powerfully persuasive letter which she penned in order to set the record straight about the alleged confrontation between her husband and the popular politician and "boss," Colonel Harvey. Most likely she did not write at her husband's behest (though doubtless with his knowledge). Wilson did not leave it to Ellen to do "damage control," but he did turn to her for advice, and her letter was the result.

And set the record straight she did. In her letter to Judge Ewing she claimed that while her husband may have said things "so badly," as a result of a certain "stiffness," he never, as *Harper's Weekly* claimed, "hysterically denounced" Harvey, "....and no one in the world needs less than Col. Harvey to have things elaborately explained to him, for you know what an extraordinary mind he has," concluded Ellen, with the utmost tact. Judge Ewing at once adopted Ellen's "true" account of the confrontation between Wilson and Harvey in an article which appeared, shortly afterwards, in several newspapers. Wrote Joseph Tumulty years later, "Suddenly, as if over night, a reaction in favour of Governor Wilson began to set in," without Tumulty in the least crediting--or even mentioning--Ellen's timely intervention.[45]

A few weeks later, *The Boston Globe*, in an article on Governor Wilson, described Ellen as "a very pretty woman with a sweet, motherly sort of voice," who was, moreover, "a great companion of the Governor."[46]

Wilson's presidential campaign that spring of 1912, before the primaries took place, was a strenuous one. In mid-April, he took Ellen on his campaign to Georgia, where the press--and the public--could not get enough of her. "It was at Gainesville," reported the *Atlanta Journal*, "that Mrs. Wilson vied with her distinguished husband in the popular eye. She was besieged by ladies, and numbers of bouquets were sent aboard to her and delivered on behalf of Georgia women," none of whom could vote; otherwise they might have voted for Wilson in the upcoming primary, which he lost instead to his rival.[47]

Their summer vacation that year was later than usual. This time Ellen chose not go to Lyme. With the decisive Democratic national convention looming in late June, a nerve-wracking prospect, she would have enjoyed little peace and seclusion. By mid-June the whole family, minus Eleanor, was assembled once again at Sea Girt. With the convention only ten days away, no one could relax except Wilson, sphinx-like in his calm, playing golf day after day. Soon Eleanor, fresh from her trip to Mexico, re-joined her family, shocking her father and mother by announcing her engagement to a prepossessing young engineer, Ben King, whom they had never even met. Outwardly they took the news calmly, although Wilson looked grim. Secretly Ellen made up her mind to send her brother Stockton--recovered, and teaching in California--to meet the man with whom her daughter had fallen head-over-heels in love, to size him up, and report back to her. (His report was very positive, to her and Wilson's relief.)

In those days neither the presidential contender nor his family was permitted to make speeches at nominating conventions. It was considered in bad taste, and mercifully spared audiences the heartfelt testimonials of wife and children on behalf of the candidate's good character. Wilson believed that even appearing at the convention was unseemly, so the Wilsons stayed on at Sea Girt, much to Eleanor's disgruntlement. When she objected on the grounds that other candidates' families were at the convention, her father coolly replied, "Does it follow that you should?" Later, when Wilson heard that one of the contender's wives, Genevieve Clark, was grabbed, wrapped in an American flag and carried around the convention hall, he felt justified. "How would you like something of that sort to happen to you?" although Eleanor was not so sure she would have minded.[48]

With no T.V. or radio to keep the family in Sea Girt informed, they kept in touch via telephone, which never stopped ringing. Making matters worse, reporters did not even bother to ring the doorbell as they "dashed in and out all day...bringing us the latest news..."

For the first four days of the convention, matters went badly for Wilson. Other Democratic rivals--notably Oscar Underwood of Alabama, Judson Harmon of Ohio and possibly the strongest candidate of all, "Champ" Clark of Missouri, Speaker of the House of Representatives--were far ahead of Wilson in the race for nomination, for which a two-thirds majority was required. New Jersey's powerful political bosses--Joe Smith and Colonel Harvey--disenchanted with a governor they considered extreme, were not supporting Wilson, either, although New Jersey voters favored him. Powerful Bryan led a Nebraska delegation that ostensibly supported the likely winner, Clark, although Bryan privately hoped that he himself would be nominated.

It had not helped Wilson that newspaper publisher William Randolph Hearst had launched a scurrilous anti-Wilson campaign that spring, portraying him as anti-immigration, which was only partly true (Wilson was adamantly opposed to Asian immigration, but not to immigrants from southern and eastern Europe), and anti-labor, which was untrue. The voice of African-Americans, expressed in *The New York Age*, also was anti-Wilson. "'THE NEW YORK AGE does not see how it will be possible for a single self-respecting Negro...to vote for Woodrow Wilson. He was born in Virginia and lived a good part of his life in Georgia and Alabama. Both by inheritance and absorption, he has most of the prejudices of the narrowest type of Southern white people against the Negro.'" It went on to note that "'As governor, Wilson had 'not by the turn of the finger recognized a single Negro in New Jersey,' though he owed his election to black votes.'"[49]

Wilson passed his first and possibly most important hurdle--over who would be selected as convention chairman--with flying colors, thanks to Ellen. When it appeared that conservative Alton B. Parker would become chairman, liberal Bryan was outraged. At once Bryan had his supporters telegram all the presidential contenders, "asking them to state their position in the matter at once, by wire." No presidential hopeful, Wilson included, wanted to offend the mighty Bryan by supporting Parker. Yet neither did any one wish to alienate Parker, and hence his powerful Tammany constituency. Campaign managers astutely counseled their respective candidates to send replies to Bryan--that were evasive. Wilson's campaign manager, William F. McCombs, did likewise.

This did not sit well with Wilson. Yet he hesitated as to what he should do. "Woodrow, as usual, sought Ellen's counsel," remembered Eleanor, who witnessed what happened next. He went into their bedroom at Sea Girt to discuss the matter of Bryan's telegram. "We thought we knew what he would do, but it was mother who first said firmly, "'There must be no hedging.' He smiled at her and said, 'You are right, of course.'" Right there on the bed, he proceeded to write his reply, firmly rejecting the conservative Parker as chairman. According to Ray Stannard Baker, however, Wilson at first favored an evasive answer, but Ellen and his secretary, Tumulty, persuaded him otherwise. Daughter Eleanor, however, gave credit entirely to her mother--and none to Tumulty, whom Wilson, in her version, did not even consult.[50]

Writing a half-century after the event, Eleanor wrote

> There are often times in the affairs of men, especially men in politics, when a decision is made which changes the whole course of their lives, although its significance is not always recognized at the time...Woodrow Wilson's unequivocal stand united the progressives behind him, satisfied Mr. Bryan and, in the final analysis, won him the nomination.[51]

The balloting for a presidential nominee began soon afterward. Wilson's support seemed thin indeed. By the tenth ballot, on the fourth day of the convention, Speaker Clark of Missouri appeared to have a decisive (the necessary two-thirds) majority. Wilson's campaign manager, McCombs, even phoned Sea Girt at one o'clock in the morning, conveying the sad news to Tumulty.

There are radically different accounts of what happened next.[52] In Eleanor's 1937 memoir, the whole family was awake when McCombs, in the wee hours of the morning, telephoned the bad news to Tumulty. They, though not Wilson, went to bed heavy-hearted. When they arose later that morning, Wilson was on the phone with McCombs, promising to wire his withdrawal and release his supporters. "When we realized that father was ready to send the telegram, we were speechless...We sat down to breakfast with heavy hearts--all except father." Yet mysteriously--because Eleanor offered no explanation--after breakfast, "later in the morning," Wilson still had not sent the telegram. In her compressed account of that morning written in the 1960's, Eleanor recalled that when "McCombs telephoned from Baltimore to tell Woodrow that the battle was lost," asking him to telegram his withdrawal, "Woodrow...said that he would send the release by wire" and then "went to tell Ellen." She in turn insisted that he send the telegram-- only after he had breakfasted.

In both of Eleanor's versions, Wilson, after breakfast, still had not sent the telegram. What was he waiting for? He had no idea that his adviser, William G. McAdoo, would call him "later in the morning" (in the 1930's version) with a very different prognosis, urging him to hang on.

Stockton Axson's handwritten account (for the benefit of Ray Stannard Baker), was based on what Joseph Tumulty had told him happened that morning. "Governor Wilson wrote out [the] message of withdrawal [and] showed it to Mrs. Wilson. She immediately flashed back, 'What do you gain by doing this[?]. You must *not* send it.' After some argument he deferred to her opinion." To Stockton, "it was like her." To Eleanor, "All the faculties of her mind were dedicated to his service, but they were not under his control." It would certainly explain why Wilson deferred sending the telegram.

According to Tumulty's 1921 version of that morning, "...as the Governor put down the telephone, she [Ellen] walked over to him and in the most tender way put her arms around his neck, saying: 'My dear Woodrow, I am sorry, indeed, that you have failed.'" Ray Stannard Baker rejected both Stockton's and Tumulty's version of that morning, preferring one closer to Eleanor's recollection.

Why had Eleanor not recalled her parents' "argument" over the telegram? Either there had been none, or it could have taken place away from her and her sisters' hearing. Highly unlikely was Tumulty's recollection of her defeatist remark to her husband.

In fact, more transpired on that fateful morning--from one a.m. until "later in the morning" after breakfast--than anyone could recall, years later.

A draft of Wilson's message to Bryan, via telephone, on that critical morning, June 29, has survived. That morning Bryan telephoned Wilson from Baltimore, unconvinced that all hope for Wilson was lost. He asked Wilson to assure him in writing that he, Wilson, would reject the help of Tammany--which, to Bryan, was synonymous with corruption--if New York's delegates decided to switch their votes from Clark to Wilson. Again Wilson consulted Ellen, with Tumulty present.

Tumulty advised Wilson to go along with Bryan and not antagonize him. Ellen, however, was of the opposite opinion. "...at Mrs. Wilson's urging, Tumulty recalled that 'her idea was that Mr. Bryan was not playing fair'" in urging Wilson to reject Tammany's support, which could prove critical. Ellen's "urging"--to use Tumulty's word--to reject Bryan's bidding and keep his options open, persuaded Wilson to amend his message to Bryan with a statement asserting his independence. Could anyone like Ellen believe her husband could really fail?[53]

It proves that more was going on at Sea Girt than met Eleanor's eyes, or ears. Ellen was indeed playing a decisive, behind-the-scenes role during that fateful week of the convention. Stockton's recollection of his conversation with Tumulty was remarkably consistent with Tumulty's remark about Ellen and her "urging" her husband to remain independent. "If it is true," continued Stockton, that Ellen had urged her husband not to send a telegram of withdrawal--

> and nothing but documentary criteria to [the] contrary could convince me that it was untrue (and it was like her, and what earthly reason had Tumulty to manufacture the story with all sorts of detail for me?) then she quite literally as well as spiritually made him president. And yet she didn't want this thing for herself. Tumulty once said she was 'one of the best politicians' he knew.[54]

Tumulty, however, virtually ignored Ellen in his memoir.

In the meantime, in Baltimore on that fateful morning, William McAdoo, ex-patriate Georgian, lawyer and Wilson loyalist, found out that McCombs had urged Wilson to withdraw, and was furious with him. McCombs had acted on his own when he urged Wilson to quit, ignoring Wilson's other advisers. After another frantic phone call--this time urging Wilson to hang on ("We'll stick till hell freezes over")--it was now McAdoo's turn to go behind-the-scene and wear down Wilson's opposition. Bryan, by then resigned to the fact that he would not be nominated himself, soon switched his delegation's votes from Clark to Wilson. Once this happened, it was only a matter of time before other delegations followed suit. By the forty-sixth ballot, the Democratic nomination at last went to Woodrow Wilson. Ellen's timely interventions had saved the day for her husband.

Daughter Margaret and secretary Tumulty were not the only "sleepless wonders" at Sea Girt, who had stayed up night after night during the convention. The Wilsons' servant, "Black Sam," did likewise "...sitting in a straight chair at a respectful distance," from both Margaret and Tumulty; it was proof of his "worship" for her father, according to Eleanor.[55]

Not for a moment did Wilson lose his equanimity at the news of his nomination. For the first time in a week, "That night we slept like the dead." In the morning, the Wilson daughters served their mother breakfast in bed. She looked happy as she ate and chatted, by nature an optimist, accustomed to looking on the bright side. But things were far from bright for Ellen. The weeks ahead, until the November election, would prove a gruesome strain on her. By then it was noticeable to her daughters, the Smiths, and her husband, that there was something very wrong with Ellen.

* * *

Even during the tense days right before the convention, Wilson had taken time to write Peck, complaining that he had not heard from *her* in a long time. "...I am afraid that you are ill." He continued, "You are a wonderful person, physically as well as every other way. Mind and body, you are one of the most wonderfully *vital* persons I have ever known." During the week-long convention, he thought of her "hour after hour," he wrote her, "wondering what *she* was thinking about and doing and feeling." Peck's divorce was finalizing. She was still living in her Manhattan apartment with her unmarried son, an unsuccessful businessman; together, they lived off of their modest investments. Writing soon after the convention, Wilson lamented, "It was hard, *very* hard, to know, last week, that you were in New York and not only not come to see you but not even send you a message." Was he, as a presidential candidate, at last becoming more cautious? He proceeded to describe the hectic days of the convention, his nomination ("My nomination was a sort of political miracle"), and the aftermath ("bushels of mail now pouring in upon us"), without so much as a mention of Ellen. "I think of you with a great solicitude. Please write." Peck's letters to him, of course, are nearly all missing. However, to have a man of such prominence and distinction lavish so much loving, if not ardent, attention, would make any woman's head spin.[56]

Shortly afterward, in his July 14th missive, Wilson hinted that Peck's reply had been anything but satisfying. "And now tell me what has happened. You sign that pitiful little note 'M.A. Hulbert.'" Her divorce was granted, and she was reverting to the name of her first husband, Hulbert. "I hope with all my heart that the dreaded trial is entirely over, and that there was less hateful talk and publicity than you feared there would be. I am very, very anxious to hear all about it." Was his anxiety so deep because his name might just be implicated?[57]

Easy "no-fault" divorces were still in the future. In Wilson's day, reasons had to be furnished, and divorces were long, drawn-out, and public. People certainly had seen him and Peck together, alone. ("Often he was recognized by some official..." wrote Peck of Wilson, when he and Peck would be out walking together in Manhattan.) On one recent occasion, when Peck returned early from her Bermuda vacation, she had asked Wilson to pick her up in New York. Unbeknowns to her and Wilson, her husband, too, showed up at the pier. So the two, her husband and her "friend" Wilson, stood uncomfortably side-by-side, waiting for her to arrive. What might her husband have been thinking?[58]

Wilson ended his missive with "Ellen begged me to thank you most warmly for your letter to her." So Ellen chose not to write Peck even a short reply, not so much as a few lines appended to her husband's letter.

Hulbert's (Peck's) memoir makes it obvious that she, Peck, surfaced like a bad coin every time Ellen visited New York with her husband to go to the theater, or shopping, or to view the latest art exhibit. No longer was Ellen's company enough, Wilson needed Peck's. Hulbert recalled one occasion when Ellen and Wilson, then governor, visited Manhattan to view an art exhibit. Although Ellen was keen on seeing the paintings (according to Hulbert), Peck managed to persuade Wilson--with Ellen reluctantly acquiescing--to attend a dance performance of the famous Isadora Duncan instead. Peck raved about her dancing, convinced that Ellen and Wilson would enjoy her, too. Nor was it enough for Peck to see them off to the theater; she, of course, would join them. So away they went, the threesome, and Ellen missed the exhibit. (Ellen and Wilson had even lunched that day at Peck's.)[59]

Peck would join the two at restaurants for a meal, or on a stroll; it seemed never to occur to her to decline Wilson's polite invitations to join them, so that Ellen might enjoy herself alone with her husband. Was Peck always insensitive to people's feelings in general, or just to their feelings for her in particular, the spoiled only child of doting parents? Despite Ellen and Peck being thrown together often, as her memoir attests, they never became friends. Yet Ellen tolerated Peck's intrusions for the sake of her husband, whose strange weakness for her "friendship" she had come to accept. Then again, throughout their marriage he had shown a conspicuous weakness for women and this, too, she had accepted, never once doubting his marriage vows to her. And as long as he was technically faithful to those vows, Wilson must have rationalized that there was nothing wrong in his obsessive "friendship" with Peck.

If Wilson feared the effect of Peck's divorce on his reputation, his fears were justified. Five weeks before the election, an exhausted Wilson wrote Hulbert (her name henceforth):

> You may imagine how I was affected by the report that a scandal was being fabricated against me. Exactly what I heard was this, that Mr. Elihu Root, the Senator from New York [,] had recently said to some one who was sitting next to him at dinner that he understood that a judge in Pittsfield had in his

possession, or had been shown a letter, in connection with an action for divorce, which showed me in some way implicated in the matter...It at once came into my mind that this might be an attempt to set gossip afloat, if nothing more, which would, no matter how completely discredited later, abundantly suffice, just at his juncture, to ruin me utterly.[60]

Not only ruin him, but "all connected with me." Wilson implored Hulbert to find out about the incriminating letter (Hulbert had no knowledge of it). He found out afterwards that the author of the letter had in fact been her husband (referred to as "T.D."--Thomas Dowse) who "had alleged certain things to *him* [the judge in Pittsfield]." Although the letter still was not publicized (and never would be), Wilson nonetheless was still anxious. "By the way, do you know where that young Lawrence is who was Allen's tutor in Bermuda, and what he is doing. Is he, too, inclined to lie vindictively?" Did Wilson fear that the tutor had noticed him and Peck together? Or that he might try to blackmail him? Surprisingly, the "whispering campaign" of an affair between Wilson and Hulbert during that summer of 1912 never escalated beyond a whisper, compared to what would happen today. Yet rather than taking the precaution of breaking his ties with Hulbert once and for all, Wilson continued writing her long, at times compromising, letters.[61]

To the Wilsons at least, it seemed that publicity and public prying, now that Wilson was a presidential candidate, were worse than ever. "We had become accustomed to reporters, but now the human interest variety descended upon us in full force...They did not hesitate to question us about any and every detail of our lives."[62] To question them yes, but not to investigate. The reporters did not go snooping on their own, in contrast to today. Otherwise they might have unearthed many a tantalizing tidbit: Eleanor's secret engagement to Ben King, Wilson's relationship to Peck, Peck's recent divorce, and other divorces in the family (a nephew, a cousin), Jessie's romance with Frank Sayre, Margaret's nervous breakdown of 1904, not to mention Stockton's prolonged stays in mental hospitals and Ellen's father's (and uncle's) suicides. Such revelations, which would routinely surface nowadays, might well have ruined Wilson. Then again his rivals--Teddy Roosevelt and incumbent President Taft--would not have been spared, either.

One potentially damaging revelation that could easily have surfaced, concerned Wilson's health. Soon after his nomination Ellen took pains to quash any possible rumors on that subject. Printed in the *St.Louis Post-Dispatch*, one month after his nomination, was a lengthy description of her husband's constitution--and stamina--which read as if she had written it herself. It was probably transcribed, indicating that once again she felt called on to go public.

After providing his physical measurements ("5 feet 10 1/2 inches in height, chest measurement 39, collar 16, size of hat 7 3/8, weight 170 pounds"), Ellen proceeded to declare that "He is in much better physical condition than when he was a young man." As to his previous strokes, not to mention his serious attack in 1906 that left him blind in one eye, she was entirely silent. How it was possible for a man of fifty-five to be in better health than a man in his twenties also went unexplained, other than his living "under more wholesome conditions" than when he was a student.[63]

Privately, Ellen expressed deep anxiety about her husband's health. Earlier in the year she had written a mutual friend, "Of course my own anxiety, though concealed from him, is constant and intense...", admitting, however, that doctors had given him a clean bill of health. As to Eleanor, she feared that the presidency would kill her father. Nine weeks before the election, Wilson confided to Hulbert that he suffered from intense fatigue and from a "wretched sick headache" that he could not get rid of.[64]

As to his campaign, Wilson wrote Hulbert on August 25 that "The contest is between him [Teddy Roosevelt] and me, not between Taft and me." A split Republican party, with two official candidates, was sure to play in Wilson's favor. But Wilson saw it differently. Former president "T.R." was still a formidable rival. "He is a real, vivid person, whom they have seen and shouted themselves hoarse over and voted for, millions strong; I am a vague, conjectural personality."[65]

Not for the world would Ellen give a speech or make herself conspicuous in public, although her vow against granting interviews was getting harder to keep. Right after the Democratic convention, reporters besieged Sea Girt, seeking Wilson. Discovering that he was away, they cornered Ellen instead. A reporter for *The New York Times* expressed surprise at what happened next, "For Mrs. Wilson to talk to reporters, knowing that they were taking notes, was an entirely new experience." Not for her but for them. "Throughout the week they had coaxed for an interview in vain." But with her husband away, Ellen changed her mind. "Mrs. Wilson was in a confidential mood, and she confided things that the colony of reporters stationed here through all the period of stress had not guessed." Ellen was far from disclosing some "skeleton in the closet," however. It amounted to nothing more than "She confided that her husband had abandoned hope last Friday, and had begun to plan with her for a summer trip to Europe."[66]

Ellen also gave in to "a particularly persistent woman reporter" who pestered her that summer. This time, the reporter wished to know, to the point of prying, why neither Ellen nor her daughters wore jewelry. "'Have you some sort of moral prejudice against wearing jewelry, Mrs. Wilson?'" Ellen replied smilingly, "'No, I

Politician's Wife, 1910-1912   211

have no prejudice against it; we just haven't any.'" Writing years later, Eleanor, who was with her mother in Sea Girt on that day, recalled her distaste for that prying eye. "I realized how impossible it would be for her to understand why mother had no jewelry...I thought of her rigid economy, her perennial brown dress and hat..." Then there were her mother's many sacrifices, "so that father might have the books he needed, the vacations; that we might study art and singing..." as though Ellen had been the family breadwinner, and not Wilson.[67]

Yet Ellen and Wilson's correspondence over the years do mention jewelry-- he had given her a "pearl and diamond brooch," a "necklace and pendant," a handsome silver watch--and that was only what came up in their correspondence. At least one photo of Ellen, already middle-aged, reveals her wearing a pearl necklace (or was it just beads?). During her trip to Europe with Wilson in 1903, they purchased numerous jewelry items, although perhaps these were intended as gifts. Had she in the meantime given away her jewelry--little as it might have been--or lost it? In 1911, daughter Margaret returned to her Manhattan apartment to discover that her watch and "trinkets" had been stolen.

Perhaps what Ellen understood by "jewelry" was something above and beyond what she owned. At any rate, the interview on the porch at Sea Girt that day certainly caught Ellen at her most politic, discreet self. Eleanor, too, was learning to be wary, lying to reporters that she was engaged, "I trembled for fear my secret engagement would be exposed to this pitiless light," admitting, however, that she had been asked.[68]

Not wearing jewelry may have enhanced the puritanical image of Wilson's campaign. It was important to him to give the impression that it was being run on a high moral plane. Wilson did indeed refuse to accept a penny, according to Ray Stannard Baker, from any corporate giver or other extremely wealthy donor. As a result, Wilson could not afford to stump in as many states and places as he desired. In the end, this did not hurt him, or his vice-presidential running mate, Thomas R. Marshall. (Marshall has disappeared into history's dustbin. Few remember that he once said: what this country needed most was a good five-cent cigar.) Right after election day, however, Ellen ran out to buy jewelry and furs.

During Wilson's presidential campaign Ellen stayed at home, in their rental on Cleveland Lane. This was in contrast to his spring campaign, when she accompanied him on a trip to Georgia. Cleveland Lane, where the family returned in early October, seemed to Wilson, at least, to be a haven of serenity. "The quiet and freedom of Princeton are delightful and healing," he wrote Hulbert a few weeks before the campaign. Whether Ellen found it to be likewise is unknown, since none of her correspondence from this period--if she had time to write at all-- has survived. Her husband was seldom at home. The Wilsons had no budget for secretarial help, and the whole family, Ellen included--as well as Wilson's brother Joseph--pitched in to answer the ever-ringing phone and take care of the massive mail that poured in daily. Unexpected guests also stopped by frequently, while reporters and photographers made themselves a nuisance. One photo, of the Wilsons posing on their back yard patio, showed a gray, grim-faced Wilson and an aged, worn-out Ellen.

At one point during the campaign Jessie noticed that there was something amiss with her mother, who had turned fifty-two that May. Recalled her sister Eleanor,

> Jessie told me that mother was looking very badly and a few days later, going home from the station at Princeton, I saw a little figure walking slowly ahead of me. I was shocked when I realized that it was mother, whose movements had always been so eager and quick. When I talked to the Smiths about it, I found that they, too, were greatly disturbed...[69]

And so was her father, which explains why Ellen stayed home during his campaign. There is no evidence that Ellen went to the doctor for a check-up, although this might have made no difference. (When Ellen was dying two years later, the doctors still could find nothing wrong with her.) Though spared the pitiless glare of television, the tension and stress of the campaign on Ellen and the family was at times more than they, than Ellen, could bear. What it must have been like for Ellen to be one of the star attractions at a pro-Wilson rally in Madison Square that October, with 16,000 shouting, stomping onlookers staring at her, can only be guessed. "They were on their feet, roaring and stamping, cheering and waving flags..." Although she was staying at home, in "peaceful" Princeton, it is no wonder that "Mother reached the end of each day utterly exhausted."[70]

Nor did ceaseless worry for her husband's health--and safety--help matters. On October 14, in Milwaukee, a would-be assassin shot and wounded presidential candidate Teddy Roosevelt in the chest. Ellen's terror can only be imagined. Wilson, however, refused to have a bodyguard. "'It seems to me that police and secret service guards are useless if a madman attempts to attack a man in public life.'" It was Ellen rather than her husband who sent a telegram of condolence to Mrs. Roosevelt. "Mr. Wilson and I have been shocked beyond expression and await each item of news with deep solicitude." Solicitude, however, was all on Ellen's part. Wilson was quick to see the political advantage of the assassination attempt for "T.R." But out of deference to his recovering rival, he postponed campaigning for awhile. Meanwhile Wilson's principal adviser, Texan "Colonel" House (not to be confused with New Jersey politician Colonel Harvey), went behind Wilson's back and secured a bodyguard, a Texas Ranger named Bill McDonald, who protected Wilson until election day.[71]

The frenzy of a presidential campaign notwithstanding, Wilson found time to write Hulbert a long letter, just three and a half weeks before election day. Despite the embarrassing loss of his voice in front of a crowd of 35,000 people, and his exhaustion, "it is wonderful how tough I have turned out to be." Hulbert meanwhile was living on Nantucket Island in a house she recently inherited. She would, however, be dropping in on her apartment in New York from time to time. "Please telephone if you come in before Thursday," wrote Wilson," --for I expect to be at home...and should so like to run in with Ellen to see you."[72]

* * *

Election day found the Wilsons at home on Cleveland Lane. As usual, reporters were camped outside. The womenfolk--Ellen and daughters, sisters Lucy and Mary Smith--stayed behind while Wilson went out to vote (he still was opposed to woman suffrage). As the day progressed tension mounted, although Wilson was as unflappable as ever. He insisted on reading poetry aloud to the family after dinner, for which they had not the least appetite. Suddenly the bell began ringing madly in old Nassau Hall. Outside the reporters were shouting, "'He's elected!'"[73] Pandemonium broke out as Princeton students began besieging Cleveland Lane, serenading Wilson with the college song.

As it turned out, Wilson did not receive a majority of the popular vote, split among three candidates. Despite the dire warning of the *The New York Age*, Wilson calmed the fears of African-American voters at the prospect of a southerner being elected to the presidency--the first southerner since Zachary Taylor of Louisiana became president, in 1848. "My sympathy with them [blacks] is of long standing," wrote Wilson to African-American Bishop Alexander Walters, right before the election, "and I want to assure them through you that should I become President of the United States they may count upon me for absolute fair dealing and for everything by which I could assist in advancing the interests of their race in the United States." A year later, Wilson would become the first president in U.S. history to approve segregation in the federal government.[74]

All eyes that day, including those of his daughter Eleanor, were now focused on Wilson. One can only guess how Ellen--in the background, as usual--must have felt. Awe and wonder for her husband to be sure, but "...she didn't want this thing for herself," as her brother Stockton remembered. She dreaded it.

ENDNOTES

[1] Ellen A. Wilson to Woodrow Wilson, May 22, 1911. Arthur S. Link, ed., *The Papers of Woodrow Wilson* (Princeton: Princeton University Press, 1966-1996) 23:81. (henceforth: *PWW*)

[2] Stockton Axson, *Brother Woodrow: A Memoir of Woodrow Wilson* ed. Arthur S. Link (Pinceton: Princeton University Press, 1993), 107.

[3] Eleanor Wilson McAdoo, *The Woodrow Wilsons* (New York: Macmillan Co., 1937), 106-107; Woodrow Wilson to Ellen A. Wilson, Feb.14, 20, 1910, *PWW* 20:126,146.

[4] Ellen A. Wilson to Woodrow Wilson, Feb.21, 1910. *PWW* 20:152.

[5] Jessie Wilson Sayre interview, 1925, and "Memorandum of conversations with Stockton Axson," Feb.8,10-11, 1925, Ray Stannard Baker Papers, Library of Congress, Washington, D.C. (henceforth: RSB papers); Axson, 105; on the religious life and opinions of Woodrow Wilson in particular, John M. Mulder, *Woodrow Wilson: The Years of Preparation* (Princeton: Princeton University Press, 1978); Wilson's remark quoted from *PWW* 6:462.

[6] Woodrow Wilson to Peck, Feb.18,25,1910, *PWW* 20:138,180; Peck to Woodrow Wilson, Feb.10,22, 1910, *PWW* 20:118,155.

[7] Ellen A. Wilson to Woodrow Wilson, Feb.17, 1910. *PWW* 20:135.

[8] Ellen A. Wilson to Woodrow Wilson, Feb.21, 1910. *PWW* 20:153; Woodrow Wilson to Peck, Feb.28, 1910. *PWW* 20:187.

[9] Woodrow Wilson to Peck, Feb.28, 1910, *PWW* 20:185,188; Woodrow Wilson to Ellen A. Wilson, *Ibid.*, 184-185.

[10] Ellen A. Wilson to Emily Yates, Feb.15, 1909 in Presidential Papers, Series 2, Woodrow Wilson Collection, Princeton University Firestone Library; on Willard Metcalf, *idem*; for Ellen's correspondence with Macbeth, see "endnotes, chapter 8."

[11] Woodrow Wilson to Peck, July 18, 1909. *PWW* 19:312.

[12] Woodrow Wilson to Peck, Aug.22, 1909, *PWW* 19:351; Joseph R. Wilson, Jr. to Woodrow Wilson, Jan.24, 1910, *PWW* 20:49.

[13] Woodrow Wilson to Peck, Aug.5, 1909. *PWW* 19:332.

[14] Woodrow Wilson to Peck, July 18, 1909. *PWW* 19:314.

[15] McAdoo, *The Woodrow Wilsons*, 104-105; Woodrow Wilson to Peck, July 18, 1909, *PWW* 19:313.

[16] Woodrow Wilson to Peck, Aug.29, 1909. *PWW* 19:356.

[17] On his desire to resign, see Wilson's note to Jack Hibben, Feb.10, 1910, *PWW* 20:92; Eleanor Wilson McAdoo, ed., *The Priceless Gift* (New York: McGraw-Hill, 1962), 263.

[18] Ellen A. Wilson to Woodrow Wilson, Feb.28, 1910, *PWW* 20:189; McAdoo, *The Woodrow Wilsons*, 107; Axson, 103.

[19] McAdoo, *The Woodrow Wilsons*, 109; Axson, 161.

[20] Woodrow Wilson to Frederic Yates, Dec.14, 1910. *PWW* 21:187.

[21] Woodrow Wilson to Peck, June 1,17, July 11, Dec.7, 1910. *PWW* 20:493,535,575; 21:141.

[22] McAdoo, *The Woodrow Wilsons*, 114-115; Ray Stannard Baker, *Woodrow Wilson, Life and Letters* (New York: Greenwood Press, 1927,1968), v.3:114.

[23] Edward Wright Sheldon to Woodrow Wilson, Dec.9, 1910, and Wilson's thank-you note to Robert Bridges for check, Jan.14, 1911, and Ellen A. Wilson to Frederic Yates, Dec.20, 1910: *PWW* 22:165,234,333.

[24] On his salary as governor, and his application for a Carnegie pension, see: "A News Report About Wilson's Application for a Carnegie Pension," *PWW* 23:564.

Politician's Wife, 1910-1912

215

[25] McAdoo, *The Woodrow Wilsons*, 117 and *The Priceless Gift*, 264; Wilson on his personal expenses during the campaign, to David Benton Jones, Sept.25, 1910, *PWW* 21:162-163.

[26] McAdoo, *The Woodrow Wilsons*, 116-117; Woodrow Wilson to Peck, Jan.13, 1910, *PWW* 22:329-330.

[27] Ellen A. Wilson to Mary Celestine Mitchell, Feb.8, 1911. Presidential Papers, Series 2.

[28] Woodrow Wilson to Peck, Feb.26, 1911. *PWW* 22:454.

[29] Ellen A. Wilson to Woodrow Wilson, May 6,15, 1911. *PWW* 23:10,52.

[30] McAdoo, *The Priceless Gift*, 267 and *The Woodrow Wilsons*, 131.

[31] *PWW* 23:300-302 and a follow-up report, *Ibid.*, 304-305.

[32] Ellen A. Wilson to Woodrow Wilson, May 11, 1911. *PWW* 23:30.

[33] Ellen A. Wilson to Woodrow Wilson, May 22, 1911. *PWW* 23:82.

[34] Woodrow Wilson to Peck, Feb.26, May 21, 1911, *PWW* 23:81,453; Ellen A. Wilson to Woodrow Wilson, May 11, 1911, *PWW* 23:30.

[35] Woodrow Wilson to Peck, June 25, July 2, July 5, Aug.11, 1911, *PWW* 23:174,184-185,190,257; Peck to Woodrow Wilson, July 22, July 30, 1911, *PWW* 23:223-224,241.

[36] Woodrow Wilson to Peck, Aug.11, 1911. *PWW* 23:257; McAdoo, *The Woodrow Wilsons*, 131.

[37] Woodrow Wilson to Peck, Oct.10, Nov.11, 1911. *PWW* 23:424,559.

[38] McAdoo, *The Woodrow Wilsons*, 134,149.

[39] McAdoo, *The Woodrow Wilsons*, 127-128; Woodrow Wilson to Peck, Oct.8, 1911. *PWW* 23:424.

[40] Woodrow Wilson to Peck, Oct.8, 1911. *PWW* 23:425.

[41] Ellen A. Wilson to John Grier Hibben, Feb.10, 1912. *PWW* 24:149.

[42] "An Address in Denver on the Bible," May 7, 1911, and Woodrow Wilson to Peck, *PWW* 23:11, 20; Ellen A. Wilson to Woodrow Wilson, May 11, 1911. *Ibid.*, 30.

[43] Woodrow Wilson to Peck, March 12, 1911, *PWW* 22:501; on this dinner and Bryan's reaction to Ellen, Baker, *Woodrow Wilson: Life and Letters*, v.3:209-210.

[44] Baker, *Woodrow Wilson*, v.3:210; McAdoo, *The Woodrow Wilsons*, 123-124.

[45] Ellen A. Wilson to Judge Robert Ewing, Jan.12, 1912, *PWW* 24:41-42; Joseph P. Tumulty, *Woodrow Wilson As I Knew Him* (New York: AMS Press, 1921),88.

[46] "An Interview," Jan.27, 1912. *PWW* 24:77.

[47] "A News Report," April 17, 1912. *PWW* 24:333.

[48] McAdoo, *The Woodrow Wilsons*, 153,158.

[49] Quoted in *PWW* 24:559, note 2.

[50] McAdoo, *The Woodrow Wilsons*, 155 and *The Priceless Gift*, 271.

[51] McAdoo, ed., *The Priceless Gift*, 271.

[52] For Eleanor's version: McAdoo, *The Woodrow Wilsons*, 160-162 and *The Priceless Gift*, 272-273; Axson, 106; Tumulty, *Woodrow Wilson*, 120-121.

[53] "Two telephonic messages to William Jennings Bryan," June 29, 1912. *PWW* 24:508-509 & note 1.

[54] Axson, 106.

[55] McAdoo, *The Woodrow Wilsons*, 163.

[56] Woodrow Wilson to Peck, June 23, July 6, 1912. *PWW* 24:495, 541-542.

[57] Wilson to Peck, July 14, 1912. *PWW* 24:551.

[58] Mary Allen Hulbert, *The Story of Mrs. Peck* (New York: Minton, Balch & Co., 1933), 219-220, 230.

[59] *Ibid.*, 225-226.

[60] Woodrow Wilson to Hulbert, Sept.29, 1912. *PWW* 25:285.

[61] Woodrow Wilson to Hulbert, Oct.27, 1912. *PWW* 25:461.

[62] McAdoo, *The Woodrow Wilsons*, 166.

[63] "Ellen Axson Wilson's Description of her Husband," July 28, 1912. *PWW* 24:573.

[64] Ellen A. Wilson to John Wesley Westcott, Feb.23, 1912, *PWW* 24:190; Woodrow Wilson to Hulbert, Sept.1, 1912, *PWW* 25:67; McAdoo, *The Woodrow Wilsons*, 119.

[65] Woodrow Wilson to Hulbert, August 25, 1912. *PWW* 25:55-56.

[66] "News Report," July 3, 1912. *PWW* 24:523.

[67] McAdoo, *The Woodrow Wilsons*, 167.

[68] *Ibid.*, 168.

[69] *Ibid.*, 149.

[70] *Ibid,*, 176,179.

[71] "News Reports," Oct.15, 1912. *PWW* 25:418.

[72] Woodrow Wilson to Hulbert, Oct.13, 1912. *PWW* 25:416.

[73] McAdoo, *The Woodrow Wilsons*, 180.

[74] Woodrow Wilson to Alexander Walters, Oct.21, 1912. *PWW* 25:449.

Chapter 8

FIRST LADY AND ARTIST

*"She proved to be one of the soundest and most influential of his advisers.
Perhaps it would not be too much to say that she was the soundest and most
influential of them all."[1]*
William Gibbs McAdoo, Secretary of the Treasury under President Wilson

"I painted all morning, standing of course..."[2]
Ellen to her husband, August, 1913

The president-elect and soon-to-be first lady, family and staff could barely breathe a collective sigh of relief before the publicity and mail--fifteen thousand pieces a day--reached intolerable proportions. Wilson had complained to Hulbert that summer that a minimum of sixteen reporters tailed him wherever he went; including his bodyguard, seventeen men never left him alone for an instant. Now, thanks to the addition of Secret Service men, that number was even greater, and privacy was a thing of the past.

The first weekend after the election, Hulbert descended on Cleveland Lane for a visit. Reporters could not have failed to notice her going about with the Wilsons, and marching to church with them on Sunday. "Sunday morning we walked to church, the President-elect, Mrs. Wilson and I." Flanked by Wilson on one side and the about-to-be first lady on the other, she who never went to church would not miss this Sunday service for the world. According to Hulbert, Wilson had phoned her on election day, as the returns were trickling in. Even on that most stressful, distracting of all days, he could not get her off of his mind.[3]

Apparently his fear and anxiety--that his relationship to Hulbert might be exposed and "distorted"--were past him, now that he was elected, although he owed his election above all to the split Republican ticket. Or perhaps he hoped that by letting the world see him with Hulbert that weekend, he could quash rumors, once and for all, of a clandestine liaison. After all, his wife would be seen with them.

She was in Princeton, ostensibly, to help the Wilsons finalize their plan to spend a month in her rented cottage in Bermuda, *sans* Hulbert. A post-election getaway had long been planned, as to where, was undecided. Had Wilson lost either the Democratic nomination or the presidential election, he and Ellen intended to go back to the English lake district. Now that he was elected, a shorter, closer getaway was desired. Wilson turned down the offer of a friend of his to spend a few weeks in Lake George in New York state, on account of the cold. He and Ellen desired something warmer, above all, he wrote, Ellen did. They could have returned to Florida--they had once enjoyed Palm Beach--instead of picking Bermuda. But Hulbert was insistent. The previous January, she had even invited Ellen to stay with her, just the two of them. Ellen emphatically declined, "...indeed it is quite impossible for me to leave home for even a *short* stay," without giving a reason. Why indeed would Hulbert think that Ellen would stay with her, a divorcée who was neither a relative, or a family friend?[4]

Again one suspects that their choice of Bermuda was calculated not only to serve their need for a vacation, but to impress on the public that Wilson's connection to Hulbert was innocent. Just as Wilson was able to persuade Ellen to give up an art exhibit for a dance performance instead, he persuaded her to go to Bermuda, so long as it was without Hulbert. One can easily imagine Hulbert's pride and elation at the thought of joining her most valued friends on their vacation--had Wilson only asked her. For in fact, she set off for Bermuda on the same steamer that brought the Wilsons back to the States.

Daughter Margaret, a budding opera singer, declined to go with the family to Glen Cove, Hulbert's rented cottage overlooking the sea; Ellen and Wilson, Eleanor and Jessie, arrived in mid-November and stayed until mid-December.

Eleanor remembered their sojourn in Bermuda as a lovely interlude before the onrush of events, in particular the trauma of packing up and leaving Princeton for good. She was not planning to marry her fiancé for another year or two; a month earlier Jessie had announced her engagement to a lawyer, Francis Sayre, a pale, thin young man from Bethlehem, Pennsylvania, who was working in New York. They, too, planned a long engagement. Jessie, Eleanor and even Margaret, who was still pursuing a career, had vowed to live in the White House for a full year to lend moral support to their parents, and partly for the thrill and excitement.

Glen Cove was a lovely old villa, situated on a bay and enclosed by a high wall. It was filled with beautiful antiques, purchased in the days when Hulbert was married to Mr. Peck and could afford to furnish her house tastefully. Her husband, who had provided her with a generous, two hundred dollar a month allowance when she was away, stubbornly refused to purchase the house that he never laid eyes on. Judging from Hulbert's memoir, she never once invited him there.

A chance photograph taken of Ellen and Wilson in a horse-drawn carriage-- photographers were omnipresent, even in Bermuda--showed a middle-aged, well-dressed couple seated primly, side by side. Neither one smiles nor appears relaxed. Yet the two sit close together. Ellen looks plump and unattractive in an unbecoming hat and tight-fitting, long-sleeved, high-necked suit, as if she were off to a business meeting. She leans on his arm as she turns to speak to her grim-faced husband, who seems lost in thought. Fashion-conscious Eleanor sits across from them, dwarfed by her monstrous plumed hat. Secret Service men watch their every move. One wonders whether Ellen was having a good time.

Was Ellen interrupting her husband while he sat fantasizing about Hulbert? Only eight weeks earlier he had written her suggestively, "*I* made you unveil your real self, quit the masquerade and show me the whole of your great, your lovely nature." Living in the very abode of his "dearest friend" ensured that Wilson would experience even more "haunting associations" than on his previous visit, two and a half years before. Indeed, he wrote her that he was "constantly conscious of you...the whole place seems so like you--so pervaded by you...." thoughts that he no doubt kept from Ellen.[5]

What were Ellen's feelings as she dwelled in the house of the woman who had caused her such pain a few years back, and perhaps was still causing it? Her health, which had so concerned her family and close friends, was far from robust. Did her old fears of dying prematurely come back to haunt her? Did Hulbert, now a divorcée, occur to her as her likely successor? Hulbert recalled a cutting comment of Ellen's to her husband, made in her presence. Upon returning to New York from Bermuda, Hulbert met them and handed Wilson a present of some handkerchiefs (she had nothing for Ellen), irritating Ellen enough to remark: "These must be for *your* trousseau, Woodrow," adding "for the White House," that is.[6]

The interlude in Bermuda was a much-needed respite for a family that had undergone little but uninterrupted tension and stress that year. Nor would Ellen again have leisure and a measure of privacy until she left on an extended vacation for New Hampshire, seven months later. Wilson, who during his campaign had feared public exposure of his infatuation with Hulbert, recklessly continued writing her regularly, adding to her growing horde of letters with which she could, he feared later, blackmail him.

* * *

With the inauguration and move to Washington slated for early March, only ten weeks remained to pull up their stakes and leave their home--Princeton--of the last twenty-two years, perhaps never to return. They had no real home to call their own, and more enemies than friends in town. In fact Wilson stayed on in the nation's capital when he left office, the first former president to settle in Washington, D.C.

Ellen's correspondence and duties were now so overwhelming that she had to hire a personal secretary. (A social secretary would begin working for Ellen after the inauguration.) This was an extremely sensitive position that only the most trustworthy person could fill. It was filled by none other than Wilson's favorite cousin, Helen Bones, of Rome, Georgia, where Wilson had kin. Unmarried, in her late thirties, Bones was a graduate of the short-lived Evelyn College in Princeton, which she attended while living with the Wilsons. Afterwards, she never went back to live in Rome. She remained a favorite with the Wilson family, though it is hard to say why. Very little is known of her, while her correspondence reveals a commonplace woman with a rabid prejudice against people of color, and a worshipful, obsessive love for Woodrow Wilson (her "Cousin Woodrow"). The latter made her ideal as Ellen's personal secretary, despite her lack of skill in typing, dictation and short-hand.

Bones moved in with the Wilsons on Cleveland Lane (the Smith sisters returned to New Orleans), and soon was put in charge of paying their mounting bills. This time, unlike the aftermath of the gubernatorial election, belt-tightening was out of the question. Wilson at once took out a $5,000 bank loan, and afterwards, borrowed thousands more. In view of his anticipated $50,000 annual salary as president--compared to only $12,000 as governor--they could easily re-pay this sum, and start saving real money: $2,000 a month in 1913 alone, according to Ellen, who took charge of his pay and their investments ("Don't forget to deposit your salary, for I am going to invest some of it at once. So it should be in bank."). In late September Ellen would note, "We have $142,000 in all invested bringing an income of about $6400." The money from the 1903 sale of their house, combined with their savings, was finally yielding handsome dividends. Meanwhile, $5,000 went to various relatives during Wilson's first year as president.[7]

Right after the election, everyone went shopping. "For the first time in our lives we bought what we wanted without having to dwell too carefully on the price." Trailed by reporters and photographers, onlookers gawking at them, daughters and mother nonetheless managed to purchase a "complete wardrobe" apiece. To Eleanor at least, "a complete wardrobe was simply my idea of heaven." For Ellen, a wardrobe was not complete without furs, which she had never bought in her life. Hulbert, nothing if not a clothes horse, stepped in to advise her. "We went to Gunther's where I had always bought my furs," that is, in the days when she was still Mrs. Peck. Ellen, instead of lingering in the shop to select furs, purchased only a "modest neckpiece of mink." Yet a photo of Ellen walking away from her Cleveland Lane home on her last day in Princeton shows her draped in a luxurious fur stole with a matching fur muff. Had she bought these, too, at Gunther's? Ellen also bought her daughters "the first jewelry that we had ever had," seed pearl necklaces for Jessie and Margaret, a "bar pin" set in diamonds for Eleanor.[8]

In honor of the soon-to-be First Lady, the Patterson silk mill of New Jersey presented Ellen with a bolt of lovely silk for her inaugural ball gown. Should she accept this, she naively asked Colonel House, Wilson's closest advisor? (Unlike today, the president and family members could keep costly gifts.) When House assured her that it was appropriate, Ellen had it made into a stunning dress: short-sleeved, low neckline, lace draping elegantly from the waist downward, with a long, elegant train. (The gown is now the property of the Woodrow Wilson birthplace museum in Staunton, Virginia.)

Christmas came and went--with no opportunity for a break--Ellen and Wilson spending their days in a perfect frenzy of activity. On Wilson's birthday, December 28th, they left for Staunton, Virginia, his birthplace, where Wilson was due to give a speech at Mary Baldwin Seminary. Assembled outdoors on the college steps, Wilson, already formally introduced, had commenced speaking when Ellen called out to him from the audience, "Put on your hat!" Others picked up her command, and cried out likewise, "Put on your hat!" Wilson with a cheerful mien, exclaimed "That was a suggestion from in front and a command from behind," and continued. That she would embarrass him in public, in the midst of a speech, was unheard of behavior for the normally shy, ladylike Ellen. Was her concern for his health so overriding that she forgot her tact and good manners?[9]

That Ellen was not her normal self that winter seems the only explanation for what appeared to be a break in her friendship with Wilson's secretary, the young Joseph Tumulty. Like so many people, Tumulty had been charmed by Ellen's warm friendliness and unassuming manners. She was equally fond of him. With

Wilson's election, it was not a given that he would remain his secretary. He did not accompany Wilson to Bermuda. Charles Swem did instead, renowned as the fastest stenographer in the nation. Since their return from Bermuda, letters began pouring into Cleveland Lane, urging Wilson not to appoint a practicing Roman Catholic to such a visible role. Tumulty, who opened the mail, was aware of the complaints and understandably agitated. However, he did not open mail addressed to Ellen and other family members. Ellen, too, was being deluged by mail-- complaining about Tumulty's religion. "...the writers were afraid to send them to Governor Wilson because they thought that Tumulty would intercept them and that they would never reach them." Both Ellen and Wilson had long ceased to be anti-Catholics. Surprisingly, instead of standing up for him staunchly as her husband did (who did at last appoint him), Ellen had doubts. During the Princeton controversies, she had sided against her husband's detractors, and firmly with her husband's friends. Now, her strange about-face could not have gone unnoticed by Tumulty. The old friendliness between the two seemed to disappear, and perhaps for this reason, too, Tumulty all but ignored her in his memoirs.[10]

Ellen partook conspicuously in these and other discussions of appointments that her husband would make. When Wilson was unsure whether to appoint William Jennings Bryan secretary of state, "mother felt that there was no alternative and finally he made up his mind." Of Wilson's new cabinet of ten men, five were southerners, ex-patriates, as he and Ellen.[11]

As the days to the inauguration drew near, Wilson wrote Hulbert, "Our trial draws nearer and nearer, and we dread it-- especially Ellen." A week later, Helen Bones confided in a cousin, "Every minute of every day is taken with 'business' and sometimes I wonder if the poor darling will ever again have any time she can call her own." In January, Wilson canceled the inaugural ball, in all likelihood out of his concern for Ellen's frail well-being. Wilson the politician gave a different view to the newspapers, however. "For the reason that it entails unnecessary expense upon the Government, President-elect Wilson has come out strongly in opposition to the Inaugural ball, the time-honored institution...the balls have in recent years become mere feminine clothes shows, sometimes not much to show, either." Once he made up his mind to cancel the ball, Wilson saw no harm in gaining a little political mileage from doing so.[12]

Daughter Eleanor, who had just purchased the perfect ball gown, was crestfallen. Two years before, when her father was elected governor, "mother and I spent hours planning what we would wear," and there had been no cancellation of the inaugural ball. Eleanor, however, preferred to give her father's official version of why the ball was cancelled in 1913.[13]

Among Ellen's many distractions that winter was learning all that she could about housekeeping matters in the White House. Out-going President Taft and his spouse began corresponding with her and Wilson, even mailing them a chart, probably a lay-out, of the executive mansion. Ellen warmly thanked President Taft in writing for his helpfulness, candidly admitting that "...life in the White House has no attractions for me!"[14]

* * *

Writing to Hulbert on March 2, the day before their departure from Princeton, Wilson lamented, "This is our last evening in this little house, and we find our hearts very heavy." The next day arrived all too soon. Photographers were ready when Ellen and Wilson emerged from the house on Cleveland Lane, their home for less than two years. Wilson walked ahead of Ellen, looking grimly, Ellen smiling bravely, wearing her new fur stole, fur muff, tailored suit (probably brown, the color she usually wore) and a shapely feathered hat. Deciding to forego a car, they walked to the train station instead, deliberately choosing a route that took them past their beloved former home (and their former rental that stood next to it) on Library Place. It was a walk down memory lane for the two of them, one that Ellen, with less than two years to live, was not destined to repeat. (Wilson repeated it two years later, with his new wife-to-be).[15]

Nearly a hundred Princeton students crowded on the train heading for the capital, where they would cheer the president on inauguration day. As the noisy train slowly left the station, Ellen took final leave of Princeton, her home for the past twenty-two years, longer than she had lived in Rome.

According to Eleanor's vivid memories of that day, it was a terrible one. Despite Ellen's broad smile for the photographers that morning, inwardly she was feeling traumatized. Arriving in Washington's Union Station, Ellen was overwhelmed by the enormity of the occasion--the crowds, especially women, calling her and her daughters by their first names, the huge Shoreham hotel where they would spend the night, the heavy public functions that lay ahead. Confusion and noise were the order of the day. An hour after arriving at their hotel Eleanor grew alarmed, "mother looked so white and so tiny." A few hours later, as Eleanor was arranging her mother's hair, Ellen suddenly burst out sobbing. "There was almost despair in her sudden break, something I had never seen before." Eleanor comforted her and led her to her father's room. Wilson had been wise in canceling the inaugural ball.[16]

Her mother's break-down set off alarm bells in Eleanor. With her parents gone, she locked herself in her mother's hotel room and "went to pieces." She ended up, reminiscent of her Uncle Stockton, giving way to a break down, crawling under the bed and "pounding on the floor with my hands and crying in black despair, "'It will kill them--it will kill them both.'" Despair, however, was not second nature to Eleanor. A few hours later, recovered and dressed in her best, she was back in action: dancing the fox trot at a party, and flirting with her male admirers.[17]

Recovering her composure, Ellen set off with her husband for the traditional formal visit to the out-going president and his spouse on this, their last day in the White House. There they had their first tour of the mansion, and kindly Mrs. Taft "told her many housekeeping secrets." Ellen took a particular liking to a painting hanging over a mantelpiece: "Love and Life," by English painter George Watts. It depicted "two beautiful, naked figures," and had been the artist's personal gift to President Rutherford B. Hayes. Later, when the inaugural festivites were over and life began to settle down, Ellen noticed that the painting was gone. Upon inquiring, she discovered that when the Tafts were moving out, they had it returned to the Corcoran Gallery, a stone's throw from the White House. Ellen and her daughters thought it was hilarious that the nudity had so disturbed the pious First Lady, Lucy Hayes, that she had gotten rid of it; since then the painting kept bouncing back and forth, between the White House and art galleries. Ellen ordered it returned.

The next day, March 4, was the day of Wilson's inauguration and his address, which he had gone over carefully with Ellen. On this, Wilson's great day, an army of relatives had converged on the White House; the only invited guests who were not relatives were Lucy and Mary Smith, who were like family, and family friend, artist Fred Yates, once again visiting the States. Wilson's "dearest friend" was notably absent, never having been invited. Conveniently, Hulbert was away in Bermuda. Not that she would have hesitated rushing back to the States, if she had only been asked. Ellen did not invite her, and Wilson obviously respected her feelings. (However, soon after the inauguration, she was invited to spend the night in the White House.)

Hardly anyone noticed Ellen on this day, as much hers as it was her husband's. Although she practically knew his speech by heart, when he began to deliver it, she left her seat to stand where she could get a full view of his face. Her diminutive figure is barely visible from photographs, engulfed as she was in an over-sized hat and fur stole. (Wilson, Taft and other dignitaries were hatless on that cloudy winter day.) One wonders what Ellen was thinking. Stockton never forgot what she told him once. "She witnessed in New York an impressive performance of *Macbeth*--said, 'It makes one pause to consider whether a wife should encourage her husband to have everything to which ambition prompts

First Lady and Artist

him.'" Nevertheless, "But having considered, she went on to promote his cause in every way she could." Standing there, gazing up at her husband on that triumphant day, she was not unconscious of her role in shaping and making him president.[18]

After the formal luncheon and parade that followed (during which Ellen stood next to her husband for four hours, "waving a little lace handkerchief" at the marchers), the day ended on a serene note. Not with the daunting social event of the season--the inaugural ball--but with an intimate tea party in the bosom of the family, the victrola properly cranked up, softly playing music in the background. Earlier in the day, Eleanor had overheard ex-president Taft remark to her father, "'I'm glad to be going--this is the loneliest place in the world.'" Privately, Eleanor disagreed, "but we wouldn't be lonely--we had each other--no one could take that away from us."[19]

The day was not without its odd happenings. Ellen's handicapped cousin Florence Hoyt, who had lost her leg to tuberculosis some years back, had no sooner arrived at the White House when Ellen and Wilson's greetings were interrupted by a guest tumbling down the staircase, "giving her back a bad twist." Small, young Doctor Cary Grayson attended the victim. The Wilsons were meeting Grayson for the first time that day, whom Taft introduced with a "I regret to say that he is a Democrat..." That evening Florence Hoyt regaled everyone with her own story. Arriving late at Union Station, unable to find a cab, a black driver of a grubby hot dog cart drawn by a "scarecrow" horse took pity on her and offered her a ride; lifting her up on to the seat, Hoyt addressed him as "uncle" (which to southerners, was the "polite" term of address for a black man) and directed him to drive her to the White House. Thinking her out of her mind, he refused. Finally, after hard persuasion on her part, they set off. Arriving at 1600 Pennsylvania Ave., he rolled his eyes in disbelief when she ordered him to drive right up to the White House instead of to the servants' entrance in back. Reluctantly, he did as she commanded. On a day that should have been bristling with security, the sight of a well-dressed white woman being carried off a shabby cart by a poor black man did not arouse suspicion. Identifying herself (without presenting identification) as a cousin of the First Lady, she was ushered in.[20]

The following day, head usher "Ike" Hoover led them on a tour of the White House. As the Wilson daughters discovered, "With the exception of the chauffeur, the cook and the ladies' maids, all the servants were colored." Helen Bones disdained the blacks. "...the head usher, and two colored doormen, perform all sorts of imaginary offices, bowing and scraping." The Wilsons liked all of them, and were in awe of head usher Hoover, "the most quietly efficient person I have ever known," noted Eleanor.[21]

The days when the public was free to wander unescorted into the very living quarters of the president and his family were long past. By 1913, only the basement rooms, fitted up as museums rooms, were open to the public. As to the rest of the mansion, Ellen was surprised and grateful for the elevator that lifted one with ease from basement to attic. She had as much of their Princeton furniture, paintings and rugs as could fit into their private quarters, taken out of storage and carted to the White House. When they arrived and were put into place, Ellen began to unwind at last, even delighting in her beautiful new surroundings. The exception was the historic Red Room, "one of the ugliest I had ever seen," according to Eleanor. "It was gloomy beyond words." Her mother selected this room, in late March, to receive two dozen women reporters invited to a White House tea.[22]

At last Ellen could garden to her heart's content. Not since moving out of Prospect House over two years ago had Ellen's green thumb had an outlet. On their first day in the White House Ellen described her gardening plan to her daughters. Pointing out the formal garden below her bedroom window: this, she told them, she intended to change from formal to informal, with "a suggestion of Italy, a lovely illusion of vistas;" its centerpiece would be a rose garden. The soon-to-be famed rose garden became Ellen's enduring legacy to the White House grounds.

Wilson referred to the White House as not having very many rooms, and Ellen no doubt concurred. In his correspondence with the Wilsons in January, Taft had mentioned that the vast attic on the third floor could be divided into bedrooms, and Ellen set about doing so. Delighted to find an attic chamber with a skylight, she had it turned into a studio, though she never found time to use it. Aside from the attic, Ellen altered little in the White House. Her bedroom suite on the second floor, consisting of a bedroom, dressing room and bath, she decorated with her favorite flowered chintz furnishings, including flowered lampshades; it adjoined her husband's (although each had a separate bath and bedroom, his with the historic Lincoln bed), in which little was altered. Their conjoined suites were situated on the sunny south side of the mansion, with its impressive view of the Washington Monument and Ellipse.

Her family marveled at Ellen's "swift adaptation to the new life." Once the tension of the election and the trauma of moving subsided, she actually relished her new career as First Lady, and no wonder. After all, she once told her husband, "You know you have frequently observed that running about, going to the city, etc. agrees with me better than sitting at home sewing..."[23] Just as she came to enjoy being first lady of Princeton--despite her initial misgivings--she now adapted easily to this far more demanding role. In time Ellen would make this full-time, highly-visible position even more visible.

The rotund, jolly Belle Hagner, Mrs. Taft's former social secretary (a professional, who could type and do short hand), was pleased to remain in the White House to work for Ellen, and as it turned out, for her three live-in daughters. Unlike Helen Bones, who lived with the Wilsons, Hagner commuted to and from the White House. Every morning after the family breakfasted, Ellen and daughters would go to Hagner's office "to settle plans for the day and go over our colossal mail." Ellen's social schedule was always packed with "dinners, receptions and musicals," not to mention "two or three tea parties a week" as well as receiving the inevitable "callers," not one day a week, but every week day afternoon. Then as now it was prestigious to receive an invitation to a White House social event. After awhile the observant Eleanor concluded of Washington society that "Jealousy was the prevailing note, for the place was seething with ambitious people, and the gossips were busy from morning to night." Wilson echoed her feelings...."'there are a lot of people here who get on your nerves.'" It was these same people--Washington's intelligentsia--who were in the habit of making off with "silver spoons, napkins, even small dishes" after every White House event.[24]

Never was Ellen too busy to assist her husband who never ceased to be first, but discreetly, behind-the-scene. Treasury secretary William McAdoo pronounced her "the soundest and most influential" of all of his advisers, although in what way, he did not say. Surely not when it came to matters of state or foreign policy, areas in which Ellen consistently followed her husband's lead. At the very least, however, she kept abreast of all of Wilson's activities and appointments, proofed his speeches ("Often she suggested an idea which he invariably used," recalled Eleanor) and as in their Bryn Mawr days, frequently made digests of reading material for him whose own schedule was filled to the brim.

* * *

Had Ellen confined herself to the traditional roles of social hostess and housekeeper of the White House, nothing would have distinguished her from other first ladies. True, she was also her husband's confidante and adviser, unlike some first ladies, notably Mary Todd Lincoln; but this was a behind-the-scenes role of which the public was unaware. If Ellen today is remembered at all, it is as an activist, a social crusader for the betterment of people's working and living conditions.

That Ellen would take on the conspicuous role of social crusader indicates that she was far from shy and, though ladylike, far from docile. She knew how to pull political strings as well as her husband, and influence people even better than he. Just as she had joined her husband on his inspection trip through New Jersey in 1911, now she went out on inspection tours, without him. (This further persuades one to believe that Governor Wilson's 1911 tour was more Ellen's idea than his.) What and where she chose to investigate came from tips she received from Washington, D.C.'s vast underground of humanitarians and social workers, chiefly middle and upper-class, educated women. These she could have politely ignored, as did the second Mrs. Wilson, Edith Bolling Galt. Despite her five years as first lady (compared to Ellen's year and a half), tramping through slums and inspecting government facilities, day after wearying day, was not for Edith.

One humanitarian tipster, unnamed, was still vivid in Eleanor's mind, twenty-five years later. "I grew to hate the sight of...a tall angular woman who was constantly arriving at the White House, and pounding at mother, tearing her tender heart with tales of woe." She was in all likelihood Mrs. Archibald Hopkins, a dedicated advocate of slum clearance and decent public housing for poor blacks. (To this day, the public housing project at 12th and K Streets SE is known as Hopkins Place.) She and the other "philanthropic women" whom Eleanor disdained, could tell that they had in Ellen an ally, someone who had walked in their shoes. As Stockton noted, his sister's concept of charity meant reaching out in person, someone who was "less given to reforms than to quietly performed acts of mercy..." And as First Lady, she could not help but reach out.[25]

Barely three weeks after the inauguration, Ellen, prefiguring Eleanor Roosevelt, began going out on personal inspection trips. In some public buildings, she found no bathrooms for the low-paid clerks who worked there; by bringing this matter to the attention of the relevant cabinet secretary--and following through--bathrooms were installed. Ellen's crusading efforts were most tireless, however, when it came to aiding the poorest and most marginalized, the anonymous mass of poor black slum dwellers. She did not intellectualize too deeply about the causes of their plight; to blame it on segregation or discrimination would have been alien to her who saw misery not at all from an intellectual standpoint, but from the heart. Few would give her credit today for seeking out this unenviable crusade, and choosing to see the human face of degradation and poverty at first hand, and not once, but over and over again. Meanwhile, she faced a barrage of criticism from southern lawmakers and their spouses that all but killed her efforts for improvement.

Eleanor, who never accompanied her mother on any of her forays into the slums (or for that matter, into public buildings), nonetheless was an interested, intelligent observer. She along with many others took note of the squalid neighborhoods surrounding the White House and Capitol. Through her mother she learned, "There were ninety-six thousand Negroes in Washington, one-third of the population, and philanthropists had tried for years to get Congress to do something about improving and rebuilding the places where they lived."[26] In fact, Washington, D.C.'s black citizens numbered 64,000 at this time and constituted at least half of the population, many of whom were far from poor. In no American city did they have more schools and a larger, better-educated middle class; but the majority barely made headway in a city ahead of many others in its policy of enforced discrimination in employment, education and housing; though attempts had been made in the 19th century to introduce a system of self-government in the city, the large number of black voters intimidated middle-class whites, who had no wish to be governed by blacks. Hence the federal government oversaw the District of Columbia, and did nothing for the well-being of the city's black residents.

It may not have occurred to Ellen to fraternize with any of the numerous well-educated, middle class black men who were judges, doctors, lawyers and businessmen in the city, who might have given her a deeper understanding of the city's problems. Except for the annual children's Easter egg roll on the White House grounds, White House social events were not open to blacks. In this respect, however, the Wilsons were no different from their predecessors. Certainly none of them ever repeated the "Negro ball" initiated by President Andrew Jackson, who in holding it in the executive mansion, incurred the wrath of the city's most powerful whites.

However, in that spring of 1913, Ellen did rub shoulders with the poor black slum dwellers of Washington, D.C.; she very bravely walked the filthy, fetid slum streets on Capitol Hill. These were the notorious alleyways, lined with run-down row houses and converted stables, built after the Civil War when the population of Washington exploded. Their picturesque names, "Louse Alley" and "Slop Bucket Row," spoke volumes of their horrible conditions. Here Ellen entered the third world: run-down shacks teeming with tuberculosis and lice, wretched communal outhouses, and little children with swollen bellies. (Yet 11% of the city's entire population lived in these alleys, which took up 237 blocks.) Here she entered the shacks and talked to the slum dwellers in person; and here she would return, not once but many times, always after charming a reluctant congressman into going along with her. Neither did Ellen neglect to pay a visit to the Colored Social Settlement, run by dedicated social workers who gave her a tour and gratefully accepted her donation. These women ended up idolizing Ellen. She, however, felt deeply undeserving. "The women are so grateful that it is embarrassing. How they have worked years & years and could get nothing. I have done so little--only been interested," she remarked to her cousin, Florence Hoyt. As always, Ellen had a poem for every predicament. "'Do you remember Wordsworth's 'Simon Lee'? I think of that line, 'The gratitude of man hath oftener left me mourning.'" There was nothing sanctimonious about Ellen.[27]

No simple appeals would do this time. Something far more potent was needed to inaugurate change, along with a plan for the revitalization of the slums. That Ellen was involved in the renewal plan itself was evident from a letter written by Hopkins herself, after Ellen's death. Writing to Wilson in June, 1915, she reminded him of his wife's plan for creating playgrounds, a library, coop stores, a common laundry and decent public housing, one block at a time. "Mrs. Wilson never made any secret to any of the men she took in the alleys that the work she was trying to do in passing the bill was to improve the conditions of the negroes..."[28]

Miraculously, Ellen accomplished what no one ever had, despite the many public outcries against the slums over the years, even from Teddy Roosevelt. Thanks to her ceaseless, behind-the-scenes lobbying, on May 26, 1913, her bill (which later became the Alley Dwelling Act, 1914) was introduced by Congressman Julius Kahn. Without Ellen's vigilance, however, the new bill would have died a certain death. Resistance to it was fierce, notably from Southern congressmen, senators and their wives. It probably would not have passed at all had it not been for Wilson's last ditch (and only) effort to get it passed, when his wife lay dying. Wilson's support of the bill all along had been tepid. After her death, despite the fact that the bill had become law, he ignored it altogether. It remained a dead letter until the late 1930's, when the slums began to be cleared, one block at a time.

* * *

It escaped no one's notice that spring that Ellen was taxing her strength to the limit, "Day after day she came home worn and white," recalled Eleanor.[29] After her bill was born, she could at last afford to take a rest, although her struggle to get it passed had just begun. Nonetheless, with summer beckoning, she looked forward to a long break away from Washington's frying summer heat. Hulbert had insisted that they make her house in beautiful Nantucket their summer retreat. After all, they had stayed in her home in Bermuda, so why not Nantucket? Yet this time Wilson rejected her offer, with lame excuses: they were "half-way" into renting a vacation home (at a hefty rent of $2,000 a year; Hulbert would have charged them nothing), and "we have felt all along that if we did take a house by the sea it must be in old New Jersey, which would not easily forgive us if we went elsewhere." After this awkward refusal his letter took on the tones of deep affection, even passion. "They [her weekly letters to him] make my heart ache! For I know what they mean coming from a person of such extraordinary vitality and natural high spirits as you are...You may be sure that the sympathy they excite, and the comprehension, is quick and deep, and lasts through every day and hour of the week!" This time Ellen must have been dead-set against staying anywhere near her husband's "dearest friend," which makes one wonder whether Bermuda had been quite the idyll that Eleanor had described it to be, at least for her mother.[30]

Returning to Griswold's and her jolly fellow artists, which Ellen had so eagerly looked forward to in the past, did not seem to tempt her this time. Perhaps because she was curious about another famous art colony that she had been hearing about, this one in relatively remote Cornish, New Hampshire. Unlike Lyme, the Cornish area was surrounded by primitive roads barely traversible by car, which added to its charm. However, Cornish itself was far from primitive: its cultivated surroundings were dotted with the stately homes and magnificent gardens of successful, sophisticated New York artists, writers, and sculptors, who had abandoned the city years before in search of the simple life.

In early March, Ellen's good old friends from the past, the Tedcastles, had heard of a house for rent just outside of Cornish with an enchanting view of Mt. Ascutney in nearby Vermont. The black and white photos ("Kodaks") which the Tedcastles sent them of this queenly estate, called Harlakenden House, captivated Ellen. ("Harlakenden" was the middle name of the owner's beautiful British wife). The then famous--but now forgotten--American writer, playwright and art dabbler, Winston Churchill, was renting his Cornish home fully furnished. (Needless to say, the house had no burglar alarm or security system of any kind. The fact that Harlakenden was going to be the summer White House raised no security concerns whatever.)

Edith Bolling Galt described Harlakenden as it looked in June, 1915, ten months after Ellen's death, when she was Wilson's chosen sweetheart:

> ...I wandered through the big house by myself and found it very lovely and comfortable. It was like an English country house, long and low, with a charming out-of-doors dining room at one end...which was architecturally balanced on the opposite side by a sunny terrace overlooking the Connecticut River. There was a long music room opening on the terrace, with many deep-set windows and a great fireplace.[31]

Ellen and Wilson rented Harlakenden, sight unseen. On warm sunny days the terrace became Ellen's studio, where she stood at her easel for hours on end, painting some of her finest landscapes. (Ten years later, long after it ceased being the "summer White House," Harlakenden burned down in a tragic fire.)

Washington was already sizzling by the time Ellen agreed to leave for Cornish, without her husband. Week after week she kept delaying her departure, refusing to leave unless her overburdened husband came with her. The crisis in Mexico kept delaying him: in early spring, the legitimate government of Francisco Madero had been forcibly overthrown by the brutish Victoriano Huerta. Huerta then murdered Madero and seized power. While American interests were not threatened by the regime change, Wilson, as a matter of principle, refused to recognize the new dictatorship; in fact he was contemplating sending in American forces to restore democracy to the beleaguered Mexicans (which he eventually did). Privately, Helen Bones sided with the non-interventionists. "I say let those lying, sneaking Mexicans kill one another, for they certainly aren't good for much; it seems too wicked that our splendid men should be sacrificed to them..." The Mexican situation grew more critical as the summer advanced.[32]

Ellen therefore left Washington late, at June's end, feeling unusually dejected. Although her daughters came with her (neither she nor her daughters were guarded by Secret Service men), Ellen nonetheless shut herself up in her railroad suite, refused to eat, and cried herself to sleep. Yet this was the same Ellen who had frequently traveled on her own, enjoying herself quite apart from her husband. Now, however, she could not stop herself from worrying about him, fearing for his health, when her own health was far from robust.

Her husband took her departure less tragically. Several weeks earlier, on June 9, he had written Hulbert suggestively, "I shall envy you at Nantucket only because I should love to have such company as you are..." When his family arrived in Cornish, Wilson set off for Gettysburg to preside over the 50th anniversary of the famous battle. "Duty wears a by no means intolerable aspect," he wrote Ellen from Gettysburg, clearly enjoying himself. Unlike his predecessor Taft, Wilson relished his work and was loathe to part from it. "Ah, but it's grand being President and running the Government," he had written to Hulbert on that same day, in an even longer, chattier letter. Again he reminded Hulbert of how "dependent" he was on her letters, "which I wish for more and more."[33]

Meanwhile the rolling beauty of Cornish--or rather, the Cornish area--dotted with tiny villages beyond which lay Mt. Ascutney and the lush hills of Vermont; the splendid gardens of the Cornish residents, the dignified loveliness of Harlakenden and the opportunity to paint every day, sent Ellen into the kind of raptures she had not experienced since Italy. "...the beauty everywhere is thrilling.

First Lady and Artist
233

I really believe this is the lovliest country I have ever seen," which is what she had said of Italy. She quickly recovered her spirits and wrote her husband every day, sounding her old, cheery self. "Our days keep rather full in one way or another for of course I paint every morning." These, the twilight years preceding world war and revolution, were the golden age of the Cornish art colony. In August, Ellen was delighted to have the Smith sisters with her again. They stayed with her at Cornish and followed her to the White House afterwards.[34]

Ellen set to work every morning. She invariably sat when she sketched, but painted while standing. Her productivity was impressive that summer, as it typically was in the summer months. The previous summer at Sea Girt, despite the extreme tension and distractions of the national convention, was no exception. Thanks to articles by women reporters, we have glimpses of Ellen's artistic life at Sea Girt in the summer of 1912. Reporter Cloe Arnold could not resist mentioning that when the governor's wife went out in the morning to paint in the woods, she wore "'short skirts'," which had been creeping into vogue in recent years. Mabel Daggett, writing in *Good Housekeeping* magazine, noted that Ellen at Sea Girt "'spent many days sketching along the Rumson Road, toward Red Bank, and among the sand dunes at Barnegat.'" Resulting from this summer were her four paintings of sands, dunes and sky, in soft rose-hued tones. (They are on display at the Woodrow Wilson House in Washington.) Although they are far from her best work, she nonetheless included them, along with forty-six of her other landscapes, in a solo exhibit of her work in February, 1913.[35]

As a landscape painter, which was not the genre Ellen felt strong in, her progress varied. Perhaps for this reason she never entered her work into the annual exhibitions at Lyme. By the time she did enter a painting, it was in 1911, several months after her last Lyme summer. By then, even Ellen felt some confidence in her work. Fellow artists at Lyme, those who returned year after year as did Ellen, noted her progress and duly praised her. Writing to her husband in 1911, she said, "My rock picture is done and is rather stunning, Mr. Van Laer thinks."[36]

Nonetheless it is a pity that Ellen relinquished the more difficult art of portraiture in which she had excelled since girlhood. In her student days at the Art Students League she had once declared, "I must paint from life," referring to live models. Now she painted only from nature, preferring nature scenes that were static (i.e."peaceful"), devoid of human beings, animals, even birds. Her particular genre of landscape painting was indeed undemanding and relaxing, a form of escapism for a woman who, since her brother's tragic death in 1905--when she switched to landscape painting--had her fill of tension and sadness.

In mid-October, when she was ready to leave Cornish for Washington, she wrote her agent William Macbeth "...I am having expressed to you *two* boxes of canvasses--four large ones which I would be obliged if you would have framed for me." Of these four, she considered "'The Old Road' the best of the four." Macbeth wrote her back, frankly stating his opinion. "I have very much enjoyed seeing these pictures and I think that they are decidedly better in quality than the earlier ones." Regarding her choice of colors, "...I think you would find others that would be more brilliant and transparent."[37]

Thanks to Macbeth, doors now opened to Ellen. She could not have chosen a more able and reputable agent. Macbeth was a remarkable man of great intuition, resourcefulness, and devoutly religious. A native of Northern Ireland, the twenty-one year old Macbeth got his first job in New York in 1873 working for five dollars a week as a clerk and errand boy in an art gallery. In 1892 he was ready to open his own, the Macbeth Gallery on 250 5th Avenue, the first gallery devoted to furthering American art. Fifteen years later, Ellen introduced herself in a letter to the now reputable Macbeth--penned in an effort to get him interested in Frederic Yates' paintings--signing it "Ellen A. Wilson" and scribbling underneath her signature, "also an artist" and in the corner,"tutored with A.T. Van Laer." (She met Van Laer, a famous American artist in his day, in Lyme, and tremendously admired his work.) By now she had been active in art for two years, yet she refrained from putting her own work forward, and consequently Macbeth showed no interest in her. In the spring of 1910, when the Princeton controversies were forcing Wilson to go into politics, she wrote him again, indicating that she wished to purchase a painting. "It is rather crazy in me to buy $600.00 pictures, but I *must* have it"--that is, "In the Valley at Assisi"--by Chauncey F. Ryder, one of her favorite Lyme artists. (She later re-sold it, doubtless for a profit.)[38]

When Ellen finally got around to putting her work forward, in late 1911, she was so terribly self-conscious that she sent her un-signed painting to Macbeth under an alias, "W. Wilson," the first and only time she would ever resort to another name (although she rarely signed her paintings). When a New York exhibition selected it for viewing--no small thing for any artist--Ellen at last had the courage to "come out of the closet." The following May she wrote Macbeth shyly, but eagerly, "My friends have been urging me for some time to send my pictures for exhibition to the Penna. Academy." This was the Pennsylvania Academy of Fine Arts, the oldest art school in the nation, which was going to hold its 108th Annual Exhibition in the following February, 1913. ("My friends" were probably a euphemism for her daughter, enrolled in the academy, her husband and the Smith sisters, the people who showed the keenest interest in her career.) Since she was so "exceedingly shy" about submitting any of her work, she wondered whether he could assess some of her paintings. "I work so entirely alone that it

First Lady and Artist 235

would be quite a help to me..."*Please look at them under glass*. I have never varnished my pictures at all."[39]

Evidently Macbeth was impressed by her work, sending her best paintings to various upcoming exhibitions, besides the one in Philadelphia. In this keenly competitive process, Ellen's work was selected for the Chicago Institute of Art's exhibition in November and the December exhibit at the art institute in Indianapolis, followed at last by the Pennsylvania Academy's exhibit in February, 1913. As a result of these high-profile exhibits of her work, the Arts and Crafts Guild in Philadelphia offered her an opportunity that many artists could only dream of: a solo exhibition of her paintings. This, too, would take place in February. Gone were the days when Ellen could write, as she had to Macbeth only the summer before, "I am so exceedingly shy about my work that I should have probably gone on forever endeavoring to conceal the fact that I painted at all." At age 52, Ellen had at last "arrived" as a professional artist in her own right. Ellen's self-discipline and dedication over the years were admirable, and were now paying off; alas, her example failed to inspire her artistically-gifted daughter Eleanor, the reluctant art student. "Neither of my sisters gave herself up to frivolity as I did," she admitted, who gave up any consideration of a career.[40]

February 9th, barely a month before Wilson's inauguration, heralded the opening of the prestigious annual exhibition of the Pennsylvania Academy of Fine Arts. Here again, Ellen's paintings had survived the highly competitive process of selection. Her two most beautiful landscapes, *Autumn* and *The Old Lane*, no doubt scenes from around Princeton, were selected for display. These she executed on small canvasses, typical for her paintings ("...almost all that I have done are *small*, 12 x 16...of which I have a large number," she wrote Macbeth.) The exhibition was impressive in its all-encompassing range of genres and its scores of entries-- everyone who was anyone in American art vied to get their work displayed. The full-page *New York Times* review of it, however, was surprisingly scathing. "The proportion of very good pictures in this year's exhibition at the Pennsylvania Academy is, of course, small," proceeding to give a detailed run-down of dozens of pictures, missing Ellen's entirely, which were no doubt unsigned, and perhaps fortunately for her. It is possible that the art critic simply disliked the traditional selections of art displayed by an academy known for its conservative leanings. In Manhattan that month, the huge "Exhibition of Modern Art" opened in the Armory, the first time that modernist art was ever featured in an exhibit. Macbeth's review was equally scathing. Writing in *Art Notes* in April, Macbeth found scores of entries to be "utterly absurd" and having "no relation to art..."[41]

Somewhat kinder in tone was *The New York Times* brief, unsigned review of Ellen's solo exhibit in Philadelphia a few weeks later. Fifty of Ellen's landscapes, done over a period of years and ranging in quality from very fine to passing, were the featured display at the annual Arts & Crafts Exhibition. "In her landscapes, most of which represent scenes about Trenton, she has striven for substance rather than symbol...The peace and quiet of her scenes are marked by subdued color and a sacrifice of detail," with the exception of "two charming sketches of old-fashioned flower gardens" (one wonders what the critic, probably a man, meant by "old-fashioned"). Her landscapes depicted Princeton rather than Trenton, and it is noteworthy that Ellen's deliberate choice of peaceful, quiet (i.e. static) landscape scenes did not escape the reviewer's notice. His ambiguous assessment notwithstanding, he credited Ellen for being "a real lover of nature and the possessor of a fine faculty for interpreting it."[42]

Later that spring, the popular *Ladies Home Journal* devoted a full-length article to Ellen's, that is, the new First Lady's, art work, which now was drawing nation-wide attention. Macbeth was kept busy as her agent, and Ellen's work was being shown at several other upcoming locales, including Manhattan, the mecca of American art. (This was the November, 1913 exhibition of the Association of Women Painters and Sculptors). By the time Ellen arrived in Cornish at the end of June, she could finally look forward to having her works displayed, and even purchased. Half of her paintings had been snatched up at the Arts and Crafts Exhibition. Some paintings, however, Ellen was loathe to part with. One of these, *The Terrace*, displayed the view from her terrace "studio" in Harlakenden, a lush scene not at all "subdued in color" and bereft of detail. (This painting is in private hands. Many of Ellen's other landscapes can be viewed at the Woodrow Wilson birthplace in Staunton, Virginia and at the Woodrow Wilson House in Washington, D.C.)

Ellen's four paintings of that summer turned out to be larger than her usual ones. She kept in touch with Macbeth, proposing to submit two of her four paintings to the upcoming, 1914 exhibition of the Pennsylvania Academy of Fine Arts. Unlike the year before, however, Macbeth now advised against it. "It is unlikely that it will be a dignified show," perhaps alluding to the approaching invasion of modernist art. Ellen heeded his advice; there were plenty of other venues for her work.[43]

Selling her paintings was a new experience for Ellen, who had not sold anything since she had been single and earning a living, with the single exception of a landscape she had painted in 1910 at Lyme, and sold for $100. Initially she was unsure what to charge, except that it would be a lot lower than the $600 she paid in 1910 for one of Chauncy Ryder's works. Regarding a particular painting of hers ("The *other* Autumn one...with the little Lyme view") she proposed selling it for $250. Some of her other paintings, "Light & Shade" and "Autumn Fields," sold for $100 a piece, and "Ascutney" for $150 (at the November, 1913 exhibit of Women Painters and Sculptors.) A "Mr. Bittinger" of the New York Academy suggested a price of $250 for her painting entitled "Princeton," and "$300 for the other," unnamed one.[44]

Ellen donated the thousands of dollars she earned in 1913 and 1914 to charity. According to the art critic who had reviewed her solo exhibition in Philadelphia, the proceeds from her sales were going to the "Georgia School," referring to the two schools for impoverished children established by a remarkable Georgian humanitarian, Martha Berry.

Because of the dearth of public schools in Georgia, the children of "Crackers" were growing up as ignorant and illiterate as their parents. The resourceful, well-to-do Berry founded a school for these children, a boy's school in 1902, followed in 1909 by her school for girls, both located outside of Rome. (Ellen had no doubt met Berry during her trips back to Rome.) In addition to donating the proceeds of her paintings to the Berry schools, Ellen also set up an endowment in memory of her brother Edward, and supported several students there. From then on, Ellen saw it as her mission to help destitute children in the south--where the need for education was greatest--to achieve at least a basic education. Nor were Ellen's efforts limited to the Berry schools. As First Lady she supported and chaired the Southern Industrial Educational Association, and paid for the education of several students in the Nacoochee Institute for mountain children in Sautee, Georgia.

Today Ellen might be criticized for limiting her concern to poor white children only. But in the south of Ellen's day, a white woman who championed education for blacks would have faced ostracism and ridicule, negating her efforts.

* * *

All summer long Ellen worked in her beautiful home in Cornish (actually in Windsor, across the river from Vermont) with her usual discipline and dedication. She was loathe to leave her paradise even when autumn arrived, delaying her return to Washington until mid-October. She was feeling remarkably fit and well, nor did she complain of so much as a headache in her daily letters to her absent husband (but then, she would not have wished to worry him). It would have been a perfect summer had Wilson only managed to get up to Cornish and spend some time with her. Except for one or two brief visits, he was too pre-occupied to give Cornish much thought. In contrast to Ellen's daily letters, he found time to write her only once a week. Two years later, when he was courting Edith, she marveled

238 Sina Dubovoy

at how this busy president found time to write her every day, what with a world war going on.

From the White House that summer Wilson was corresponding with Hulbert as regularly as when he was president of Princeton and later, governor of New Jersey. While she was in Bermuda in early 1913, he wrote her emotional, feeling letters. "My thoughts are every day over the water with you," he wrote her in January. His letters to Hulbert in Bermuda more than hint at her depressed state of mind. Was she feeling hurt and dejected that Wilson had not invited her, his "dearest friend," to attend his inauguration? Four days after the inauguration he wrote her tenderly, "...at last, with the comparative quiet of Sunday, has come the opportunity...to write my dear, dear friend of whom I have thought so often the days through..." A week later, he complained about not hearing from her; when he did, it was about how lonely and useless she felt. For the first time, she was eager to leave Bermuda. After receiving yet another pathetic letter from her, Wilson wrote, "You are to come here, straight, just as soon as you set foot on this continent again....," an invitation he repeated a month later. "It is delightful to think that you will be at hand, at least, *obtainable*. My mental (spiritual) barometer goes up with a great leap when I think of it." Ellen, it seems, was powerless to erect an impenetrable wall between herself and her husband's "dearest friend," even in the White House. It is extraordinary that Hulbert's memoir, which gushes about her visits to Princeton and Sea Girt, makes no allusion to her overnight stay at the White House. Yet stay she did, for at least one night. Wilson alluded to the White House room "you occupied" in a letter of his to Hulbert in July. [45]

At about the same time, up in Cornish, Ellen had already finished a large landscape. "...it is rather stunning colour, -- deep blues and strong sunlight and shadow. I rather like it now, but I may be utterly disgusted tomorrow night." By ten or eleven o'clock, she was ready to read her sizeable mail. Afterwards, "I have engagements for every afternoon this week," and every week thereafter. By late September she was writing, "Another glorious day but spoiled for us by the necessity for going to luncheon and an afternoon tea--and also for me by having to settle down to desk work [her correspondence] instead of painting." On the whole, however, she was enjoying herself so much that she could write: "Ah but the world is a beautiful place in spite of all drawbacks." [46]

Besides painting, Ellen sat for hours being painted, that is, along with Eleanor, Jessie and Margaret, "fortunately we do not all have to pose at once." Her friends from her Lyme days, artist Robert Vonnah and his wife, had settled in Cornish and he now wished to paint a large canvas of her and her daughters, dressed up and sitting in a parlor having tea. Ellen did not mind the frequent long

First Lady and Artist

sittings in the Vonnoh's beautiful house, although she did not think the painting was worth the trouble, rightly so. "It bids fair to be a nice thing of the sunny impressionist sort." Wilson's response was: "I hope the picture will be a success, even if it must be impressionistic." Vonnah gave her the painting when it was finished, and it now hangs in the Woodrow Wilson House in Washington.[47]

"I have just escaped--I hope--a visitation from the suffragists..." wrote Ellen to her husband at the end of July. Suffragists, who were strenuously lobbying Congress and the White House, wanted Ellen on their side. Ellen, however, did not want to put herself "on record" that she had even received them, much less supported them. Fortunately for her, she was not pressured as she would have been today, to come out publicly for or against women's suffrage. Other unwanted visitors that summer were reporters. Ellen barricaded herself from them as best as she could. "There was not a word of truth in the story about the old ladies tea...Really, I believe the reporters up here are the worst we have yet encountered, the most shameless liers [sic]." One person who was also kept at arm's length was Hulbert. In an interesting allusion to her Ellen remarked, "I met piles of New England spinsters--and I must say I like them, Mrs. Peck notwithstanding!"(who had a well-known distaste for spinsters). Hulbert, divorced for over a year, disliked being called "Mrs. Peck." Wilson, by contrast, carefully adhered to her changed name.[48]

In July, Jessie and Frank officially announced their engagement--kept hidden from the public since October. The two, however, could be seen together often and when queried, Wilson passed Frank off as a family relation. The couple was together as often as Frank's schedule permitted during those long summer weeks of perfect weather, and Frank would typically stay overnight at Harlakenden. There is no question that Ellen trusted her daughters implicitly, and consequently, had nothing to fear when Jessie and her fiancé went horseback riding for hours on their own. Her greatest fear was that the horses--Jessie's in particular--might suddenly, inexplicably, become uncontrollable. When her other daughters insisted on riding horseback, too, she again was uneasy. "...Margaret and Nell gave me a fright this morning by going *riding* at ten & staying until nearly two. I was really in a panic for half an hour." Her brother's death still haunted her deeply.[49]

Jessie and Frank's obvious passion for one another seemed contagious. After Wilson's quick one week visit to Cornish in mid-July, Ellen wrote with deep feeling, "We were so close to each other that I hardly feel even yet as if we are really separated. I am with you in spirit constantly." Wilson reciprocated her feelings, "What shall I say to a little girl whom I love with all my heart and yearn for almost more than I can stand who *asks me if I would like a daily letter;* saying that she had hesitated to write every day because she was afraid I was too busy to be 'bothered' with a daily letter now!" Nonetheless, he and Ellen slept in separate bedrooms at Harlakenden, connected by a common bathroom, as they did in the White House.[50]

While Wilson wrote Ellen that summer that "I have had many, many tender thoughts about you, my darling," he did not mention that he also had many tender thoughts about Hulbert. On that same day he penned Hulbert an even longer letter. "Meanwhile, how is my dear friend faring? I need not tell her how often I think of her..." He then waxed rhapsodic: "You have a positive genius, not only for being delightful yourself, but also for drawing others out and making them appear at their best." Yet the following Sunday, he again wrote passionately to Ellen, "It seems to me that I never loved you as I do now!" only to write to his "dearest friend" on the same day--in the third person—

> You need not be told that one of his chiefest solaces is to think of the friend who has stimulated and delighted him so much...the priestess of Democracy who yet seems, to those who see only the surface, to have been meant for gayety and light intercourse and the circles where interesting talk is the law of life and pleasure. How delightful her talk is, in fact...The present leader of the Democratic party would be deeply indebted to the priestess of Democracy for frequent messages of sympathy and inspiration, Your devoted friend, Woodrow Wilson

Why in the world was he so devoted to this "priestess of Democracy"? She, who seemingly was worthier than his closest friends and relatives to receive lengthy, heartfelt letters from him. Yet Sunday upon Sunday, he kept writing her long, loving letters. In early fall, he even longed to see her again. "How it would brighten everything if some day the friend who has been so much to me might happen this way!"[51]

Cornish society was nothing if not high class. One afternoon, Ellen attended tea at the Goodyears. "They are the rubber tire people," explained Ellen to her husband. When Eleanor was offered a part in a "masque" ("in the interests of some society for bird conservation," noted Ellen vaguely), Ellen was not at all displeased. "You know of course that this colony is rather famous for its 'high class' pageants and such things." The artists who lived there year-round, like the Vonnohs and the Maxfield Parrishes, and the writer Winston Churchill, were extremely successful people and lived in beautiful homes with splendid gardens. Ellen reveled in their company. As to her daughters' company, "There seems to be a very nice crowd of young people here; much superior to the Lyme set!" It is hard to imagine her returning to the unpretentious surroundings--and people--of Old Lyme.[52]

First Lady and Artist 241

* * *

Despite her heavy social engagements and her painting, by vacation's end, Ellen looked rested and refreshed, and felt energetic. She was even eager to resume her campaign on behalf of slum dwellers, and was looking forward to Jessie's elaborate White House wedding in late November. Close to her departure from Cornish in mid-October, Ellen and Jessie immersed themselves for hours as they compiled a guest list for the wedding. Did it ever cross their minds to invite the president's "dearest friend," divorcée Hulbert? After all, Jessie had once visited her in Pittsfield when she was still Mrs. Peck; recently, Hulbert had even spent the night in the White House. Moreover, Hulbert expected to be invited. In late October Hulbert even mailed Jessie a wedding gift, a "beautiful table," as Wilson described it. Yet she was pointedly excluded. A week before the wedding, Wilson's excuses for not inviting her (he had had nothing to do with the invitation list) were so transparent that they must have hurt more than helped:

> I wish with all my heart that we had known that there was even a possibility that you could come to the wedding. We would have kept a place open for you in the house as well as in our hearts. But we knew how you have felt ever since your dear one went [Hulbert's mother had died nearly a year ago], and how far from well you have been lately, and sadly took it for granted that you could not and would not venture upon the excitements and fatigues involved.[53]

Hulbert, however, seemed to like nothing better than "excitements and fatigues." (She was shortly to embark on an exotic trip to Egypt as the guest of a woman friend.) Had there been a word of truth in Wilson's apology, then Ellen could easily have sent Hulbert an invitation on the assumption that she would decline it--a chance that Ellen was not about to take.

When Ellen at last returned to Washington, after an absence of nearly four months, her social calendar was, as usual, full to the brim. She could easily have subordinated her social work and lobbying on behalf of her slum clearance bill--to her social engagements and her daughter's upcoming wedding, the most glamorous, high-profile event of the season. But from the time she arrived back in Washington, Ellen was lobbying for her bill: courting politicians, even speaking publicly for the first time in her life--though only to small select groups.

Two weeks after leaving Cornish Ellen went on an inspection of the main post office building. There she saw the many women clerks handling filthy mail bags, and was appalled. Aware that there was an abnormally high rate of tuberculosis among these mail handlers, she appealed to postal secretary Albert

242   Sina Dubovoy

Burleson to have these bags disinfected regularly. Colonel House, Wilson's most trusted adviser, promised to convey her appeal to the postal secretary, a southerner. Burleson's bibulous response to her appeal was, in House's paraphrase, that "he did not fear microbes, that during the day he killed them with tobacco and at night he killed the tobacco microbes with whiskey."[54]

It was one of the few occasions when Ellen's crusading impulses got nowhere. That spring Burleson had been the first cabinet secretary to institute segregation in the federal government, a move which the other secretaries watched closely, who would soon follow suit. Segregation had Wilson's wholehearted approval, in contrast to President Taft before him, who had pointedly refused to segregate government departments. By the time Ellen observed working conditions in the post office, postal workers and facilities were already segregated in Washington. Hence it is unlikely that Ellen voiced "shocked disapproval...at seeing colored men and white women working in the same room in the Post Office Department," as historian Constance Green asserted, implying that she may somehow have helped to usher in segregation.[55] Segregation of government departments was a high-level, complex undertaking in which Ellen would have had no part. However, she certainly would have seen nothing objectionable about her husband's policy.

Jessie and Frank's much-anticipated wedding occurred in the East Room on November 25. It was in stark contrast to Ellen and Wilson's humble wedding nearly thirty years ago. The Marine Band played soft music, congressmen, senators, the entire Diplomatic Corps and other dignitaries were invited, along with the inevitable Smith sisters; the couple was deluged with presents, including a costly, "massive silver service from the Senate and a magnificent diamond pendant from the House," gifts paid by the American taxpayer, and which Jessie declared she neither needed nor wanted. Here Wilson did not object, as with the inaugural ball, to the "unnecessary expense upon the Government," even when similar gifts appeared for Eleanor's wedding the following year. Eleanor was kept busy designing the four bridesmaids' dresses, complete with "head-dresses too-- little rose velvet caps...wired and standing up in the Russian manner." Her mother not only desired photographs of the wedding--her own wedding went without so much as a snapshot--but hired famed photographer Arnold Genthe to take pictures of the bridal party in color. Genthe recalled meeting Ellen for the first time in Cornish, "at the dedication of the Bird Sanctuary." The Berlin-born photographer observed with the critical eye of an artist, including Ellen's landscapes, which he deemed merely "creditable." At the White House that November, he no doubt missed Ellen's stunning copy of the Dagnan-Boveret "Madonna," hanging over a mantelpiece. As to the alcohol-free punch served at the wedding reception--a

First Lady and Artist

grape juice concoction of Secretary of State Bryan's--it appalled the worldly Genthe as much as it did the European diplomats.[56]

There would be no honeymoon in the North Carolina woods for these sophisticated newlyweds, who would spend theirs in London, relaxing in the abode of the U.S. ambassador. Then it was off to their home in Massachusetts and the start of an idyllic marriage, cut cruelly short by Jessie's sudden death from peritonitis at age 45, leaving motherless her three young children.

For the first time Ellen and Wilson faced the holidays without Jessie, a depressing blow to both parents. Treasury secretary William McAdoo, a Georgia native, highly recommended the Beaulieu plantation in Pass Christian, Mississippi for their Christmas sojourn. Then as now, Pass Christian was a popular vacation spot, situated on the Gulf, warm and pleasant, with plenty of golf links nearby. Even in this remote spot, however, reporters and photographers shadowed the family day and night, and there was little privacy. Consequently, the Wilsons refrained from attending church on "Sabbath" days. This was an omission so uncharacteristic of Wilson and his family that he felt compelled to write the pastor of Pass Christian Presbyterian Church to explain why. (He was afraid of the "spectacle" that would ensue if his family went to church.) Military intervention in Mexico, too, was all but certain, casting a cloud over their festivities.

On New Year's Eve, at the stroke of midnight, the Wilsons--including their family friends, the Smiths and Helen Bones--promptly mounted the dining room chairs and, arms entwined in the Scottish style, lustily sang in the tragic new year of 1914 to "Auld Lang Syne." Two weeks later, back in Washington, Ellen began shedding weight rapidly.

ENDNOTES

[1] William G. McAdoo, *Crowded Years: the Reminiscences of William G. McAdoo* (Boston: Houghton Miflin Co., 1931), 285.

[2] Ellen A. Wilson to Woodrow Wilson, Aug.4, 1913. Arthur S. Link, ed., *The Papers of Woodrow Wilson* (Princeton: Princeton University Press, 1966-1996) 28:112. (henceforth: *PWW*)

[3] Mary Allen Hulbert, *The Story of Mrs. Peck* (New York: Minton, Balch & Co., 1933), 234,236.

[4] Ellen A. Wilson to Hulbert, Jan.10, 1912. *PWW* 24:27.

[5] Woodrow Wilson to Hulbert, Sept. 22, Nov.22, 1912. *PWW* 25:220, 556.

[6] Hulbert, 228.

[7] On the Wilsons' finances, "From the Diary of Colonel House," Dec.22, 1913, April 28, 1914, *PWW* 29:56,58,531; Ellen A. Wilson to Woodrow Wilson, Aug.1, Sept. 25, 1913, *PWW* 28:103,328.

[8] Eleanor Wilson McAdoo, *The Woodrow Wilsons* (New York: Macmillan, 1937), 184; Hulbert, 235.

9 "An Address at Mary Baldwin Seminary," *PWW* 25:627.

10 "From the Diary of Colonel House," Jan. 15, 1913. *PWW* 27:57.

11 McAdoo, *The Woodrow Wilsons*, 196.

12 Woodrow Wilson to Hulbert, Feb.9, 1913, *PWW* 27:106; Helen Bones to Margaret C. Axson, Feb.15, 1913, Box 50, f.25 (Woodrow Wilson Collection, Princeton University, Mudd Manuscript Library); "A News Report," Jan.17, 1913, *PWW* 27:59; Ray Stannard Baker, *Woodrow Wilson: Life and Letters* (New York: Greenwood Press, 1931, 1968), v.4:5.

13 McAdoo, *The Woodrow Wilsons*,118.

14 Ellen A. Wilson to William Howard Taft, Jan.10, 1913. *PWW* 27:28.

15 Woodrow Wilson to Hulbert, March 2, 1913. *PWW* 27:146.

16 McAdoo, *The Woodrow Wilsons*, 201-202.

17 *Ibid.*, 202.

18 Stockton Axson, *Brother Woodrow: A Memoir of Woodrow Wilson* ed. Arthur S. Link (Princeton: Princeton University Press, 1993), 107.

19 McAdoo, *The Woodrow Wilsons*, 208; Frederic Yates to Emily Chapman Yates, March 5, 1913. *PWW* 27:155.

20 McAdoo, *The Woodrow Wilsons*, 210-211.

21 *Ibid.*, 215, 223; Helen Bones to her sister, June 1, 1913. *PWW* 29:559.

22 McAdoo, *The Woodrow Wilsons*, 215; on inviting women reporters to the White House, see brief article in *The New York Times*, March 28, 1913, sect.15:4.

23 Ellen A. Wilson to Woodrow Wilson, Aug.25, 1902. *PWW* 14:107.

24 McAdoo, *The Woodrow Wilsons*, 216, 233, 255-256.

25 *Ibid.*, 237; Axson, 104.

26 McAdoo, *The Woodrow Wilsons*, 236.

27 "From Florence Stevens Hoyt...," Sept. 12, 1914. *PWW* 31:29; "Mrs. Wilson Slumming," *The New York Times*, May 16, 1913; Sandra Fitzpatrick, Maria R. Goodwin, *The Guide to Black Washington: Places & Events of Historical and Cultural Significance in the Nations's Capital* (New York: Hippocrene Books, 1993), 66-67.

28 Charlotte Everett Wise Hopkins to Woodrow Wilson, June 21, 1915. *PWW* 33:430.

29 McAdoo, *The Woodrow Wilsons*, 236.

30 Ellen A. Wilson to Woodrow Wilson, March 16, 1913. *PWW* 27:189-190.

31 Edith Bolling Wilson, *My Memoir* (New York: Bobbs-Merrill, 1939), 70.

32 Helen Bones to her sister, Feb. 23, 1913. *PWW* 29:554.

33 Woodrow Wilson to Hulbert, June 9, 29, 1913, *PWW* 27:506, 28:14; Woodrow Wilson to Ellen A. Wilson, June 29, 1913, *PWW* 28:11.

34 Ellen A. Wilson to Woodrow Wilson, July 18, Oct.8, 1913. *PWW* 28:43, 375.

35 Frank J. Aucella, et al, *Ellen Axson Wilson: First Lady--Artist* (Washington, D.C., 1993), 20.

36 Ellen A. Wilson to Woodrow Wilson, May 6, 1911. *PWW* 23:10.

37 Ellen A. Wilson to Macbeth, Oct.12, 1913, Macbeth Gallery Records, Archives of American Art, Smithsonian Museum, Washington, D.C.; Helen Bones to Macbeth, Jan.15, 1914, *Ibid.*; Macbeth to Ellen A. Wilson, Oct.18, 1913, *Ibid.*

38 Ellen A. Wilson to Macbeth, March 16, 1907, April 11, 1910. Macbeth Gallery Records.

39 Aucella, et al, *First Lady--Artist*, 7; Ellen A. Wilson to Macbeth, May 25, 1912, Macbeth Gallery Records;

40 Ellen A. Wilson to Macbeth, June 21, 1912, Macbeth Gallery Records; McAdoo, *The Woodrow Wilsons*, 235.

First Lady and Artist   245

[41] Ellen A. Wilson to Macbeth, Oct.11, 1912, Macbeth Gallery Records; "Art at Home & Abroad," *The New York Times*, Feb.16, 1913.

[42] "Mrs. Wilson's Art on View," *The New York Times*, Feb.20, 1913.

[43] Macbeth to Isabelle Hagner, Jan.21, 1914. Macbeth Gallery Records.

[44] Aucella, et al, *First Lady--Artist*, 13; Ellen A. Wilson to Macbeth, Oct.11,19, 1912, Dec. 19, 1913; Helen Bones to Macbeth, Nov.8, 1913. Macbeth Gallery Records.

[45] Woodrow Wilson to Hulbert, Jan.19, March 9, 30, April 21, July 27, 1913. *PWW* 27:65,166,242,343; 28:86.

[46] Ellen A. Wilson to Woodrow Wilson, July 22, Aug. 5, Sept. 25, 1913. *PWW* 28:63,120,327.

[47] Ellen A. Wilson to Woodrow Wilson, July 18, 1913, *PWW* 28:43; Woodrow Wilson to Ellen A. Wilson, July 30, 1913, *PWW* 28:45.

[48] Ellen A. Wilson to Woodrow Wilson, July 23, 28, Aug.2, 1913. *PWW* 28:67,92,103.

[49] Ellen A. Wilson to Woodrow Wilson, Oct.8, 1913. *PWW* 28:376.

[50] Ellen A. Wilson to Woodrow Wilson, July 21, 1913, *PWW* 28:55; Woodrow Wilson to Ellen A. Wilson, July 20, 1913, *PWW* 28:44.

[51] Woodrow Wilson to Hulbert, July 20, September 7, 1913. *PWW* 28:46-47, 264.

[52] Ellen A. Wilson to Woodrow Wilson, July 24, Aug. 5, 1913. *PWW* 28:81,120.

[53] Woodrow Wilson to Hulbert, Nov.19, 1913. *PWW* 28:565.

[54] "From the Diary of Colonel House," Oct. 30, 1913. *PWW* 28:476.

[55] Constance McLaughlin Green, *The Secret City* (Princeton: Princeton University Press, 1967), 172-173.

[56] McAdoo, *The Woodrow Wilsons*, 260-261; Arnold Genthe, *As I Remember* (New York: Reynal & Hitchcock, 1936), 128-130.

Chapter 9

1914

"The trouble centers in her kidneys..."
August 6, 1914

"I never understood before what a broken heart meant, and did for a man."[1]
Woodrow Wilson, August 23, 1914

No one had a clue about what actually ailed Ellen until almost the day she died. Her family, her friends the Smith sisters and Helen Bones, Wilson's close adviser Colonel House and Wilson's personal physician, naval officer Doctor Cary Grayson, concluded that she suffered from the strain of over-work. Recalled Eleanor, as late as July, "...the doctors kept reassuring him." Nine days before Ellen died of kidney failure on August 6, Wilson wrote, still puzzled, "...yet it still seems certain that there is nothing organic the matter and we are hoping and believing that it is only the weather that holds her back."[2]

Despite her sudden weight loss in January, Ellen plunged into a whirlwind of White House functions. Wilson described that winter as a "social season of all sorts of functions and exacting duties." On the day of their return, January 13, "that evening we have the diplomatic reception (some three thousand guests invited) and on three other evenings of that week we are to give or attend dinners...None of us relishes these things...," he lamented to Hulbert.[3] Ellen was not about to neglect her lobbying on behalf of her alley bill, either; though introduced the previous May, the bill was arousing little enthusiasm in Congress.

In her 1962 memoir, Eleanor recalled that after an evening reception spent "shaking hands with 3,000 people," her mother fainted in her room. "She insisted, afterwards, that it was nothing. 'This goose," she said, smiling at Woodrow, 'is worrying about me for no reason at all!'" Referring to Ellen's "very bad fall" in a letter to Hulbert, Wilson blamed it on the highly polished floor in her room, causing her to slip, but not on any fainting spell; Helen Bones, too, blamed the slippery floor. In his medical and psychological biography of Woodrow Wilson, Doctor Edwin Weinstein took a different view: "Mrs. Wilson may have already been in kidney failure when she fell heavily in her room on March 1, 1914. It is probable that a fainting spell was the cause of Mrs. Wilson's fall. She stayed in bed for several weeks recovering from the soreness and stiffness; but she remained weak, lethargic, and anorexic, a triad of symptoms typical of chronic nephritis," that is, inflammation of the kidneys.[4]

The collapse in her room did more than weaken Ellen, it apparently "aggravated a trouble she has had for some time," Helen Bones informed a mutual cousin.[5] This was a long-standing gynecological problem that resulted in a minor operation in the White House. (Doctor Weinstein presupposed that Ellen's third pregnancy had caused the kidney damage that resulted in her death, years later; could it also have caused the problem for which she now underwent surgery?)

Six weeks later, Ellen was well enough to travel on a family Easter vacation to White Sulphur Springs in West Virginia; at the last minute, Wilson hired a personal nurse to care for her. Beautiful surroundings were like a tonic to Ellen, doing much, as had Cornish, to restore her health. Eleanor described this last family vacation as a "lovely interlude," with everyone remarking at how well her mother was looking. Nonetheless, she had not managed to re-gain her weight.

That spring Eleanor had became engaged to Treasury Secretary William G. McAdoo, the man who had done so much to help Wilson win the presidential nomination the year before. "Mac" was more than twice Eleanor's age, a recent widower and father of six children, his oldest daughter only a few years younger than his blooming, twenty-four year old fiancée. He had begun to woo Eleanor soon after Wilson's inauguration; the determined ex-patriate Georgian had no trouble sweeping Eleanor off her feet and crumbling her secret engagement to Ben King. Surprisingly, her parents had no reservations about their daughter breaking her engagement to a promising young man of her own age, to marry the senescent widower. Wrote Wilson to Hulbert, "The dear little girl is the apple of my eye; no man is good enough for her," that is, with the exception of "Mac;" he seemed to offer her "such prospects of happiness."[6] A wedding photo of the bride and groom reveals a tall, jaded McAdoo standing arm-in-arm with the fresh-faced, bright-eyed Eleanor. (His own presidential ambitions would be crushed when he became implicated in the "Teapot Dome" scandal in the early 1920's, compelling him and

Eleanor to settle in faraway California. A decade later she divorced him, but one might surmise that their marriage had long been an unhappy one.)

Eleanor and her fiancé planned a small-scale wedding to spare Ellen unnecessary strain. When the day arrived, May 7, only family intimates and a few officials were present. Once again the taxpayer footed the bill for several of the bride's wedding gifts, to which Eleanor, in contrast to Jessie, did not in the least object: "Again a huge silver service, complete with enormous candelabra," from the House of Representatives, and "an exquisite pearl and diamond bracelet" from the Senate. Hulbert, too, felt obliged to send the newlyweds a gift ("little embroideries"), and a necktie for the father of the bride, for which Wilson, soon after the wedding, thanked her profusely. He added a curious remark: "Ah! how desperately my heart aches that she is gone. She was simply part of me, the only delightful part," a statement it is hard to imagine him making a decade ago, when he was still in love with Ellen.[7]

Eleanor recalled what her mother looked like on her wedding day:

Her dress was made of creamy lace, with a little bunch of violets on the shoulder, and she wore a set of amethysts that father had given her. She looked so radiantly pretty...[8]

By contrast, Stockton Axson, who had come all the way from his new teaching post in Oregon, was shocked at how thin and slow his sister had become.

Ellen's decline swiftly followed. After returning from her two-week honeymoon in Harlakenden, Eleanor was alarmed to find her mother bedridden. "...my heart sank when I looked at her. She had changed--she looked very small and white, and all her lovely color was gone." Her father arrived, confessing to Eleanor that he was "terribly worried" but that "the doctors had told him that it wasn't too serious." Helen Bones wrote a mutual cousin that soon after the wedding, Ellen began having "nervous indigestion almost constantly." As a result, "All sorts of examinations have been made and have shown that her stomach was absolutely all right. The chief trouble comes from tired nerves." Yet by early June, Ellen's symptoms deepened. Wrote a crestfallen Wilson to Hulbert: "My dear one absolutely wore herself out last winter and this spring and has not even started to come up hill again yet. She can eat and retain almost nothing, and grows weaker and weaker...There is nothing at all the matter with her organically...and the doctors assure us that all will come out right." For the first time he referred to her condition as a "nervous breakdown." He was beginning to suspect that her illness was mental, redolent of her father and similar to her brother Stockton's breakdowns. With her "rest cure" prohibiting all work and activity, Ellen was indeed growing despondent.[9]

Characteristic of her brother's past breakdowns, Ellen, too, seemed all at once to rally. "The dear lady here is at last beginning to come up hill..." he wrote Hulbert on June 21. A few days later, on June 25, Helen Bones also noted that "She is improving steadily and the doctor is no longer worried about her." Craving activity, Ellen directed the planting of trees and shrubs from her wheelchair, and the placing of a large ornamental stone in her rose garden. She insisted on making digests of newspaper articles that her husband was too busy to read, as in the old days. The ever-faithful Smith sisters arrived in June, their cheerful company lifting her despondency. Doctor Grayson, Wilson's private physician, even suggested that she go off to Harlakenden for the summer, where, however, she would have been far from any medical care. But she refused to leave her over-burdened husband alone, solicitous as always about his health and well-being. In the meantime Wilson wrote Hulbert, "I am well, absolutely well," having remembered, as always, to send her a beautiful, touching birthday letter. "I know that I myself am more deeply in your debt than I can ever hope to pay," he wrote fatuously.[10]

Ellen's recovery soon ground to a halt. "I wish Ellen were making more rapid progress," Wilson wrote his brother on July 24th, two weeks before she died, still clueless about what was ailing her. How was it possible that at this late stage, her doctors failed to detect her mortal illness, and kept reassuring the family that she would recover?

It is difficult to discern who "the doctors" were who attended Ellen, and what if any treatment she was receiving. First and foremost there was Doctor Cary Grayson, a young Virginian who was assigned to be the president's personal physician. Wilson had taken an instant liking to the personable Grayson, whom Eleanor described as "a charming man with a handsome aristocratic face, speaking 'educated nigger' in a soft attractive voice..." This unpretentious man "became the family physician and later held the official position of Medical Adviser to the White House. He was one of the dearest and most loyal friends that father or any of us ever had."[11]

Grayson became the family doctor by default: his main duty was to serve the president. Ellen therefore was not his prime concern. The fact that he soon became intimate with the family--he was the only person to whom Ellen ever confided her unhappiness over Hulbert, he also served as Eleanor's best man at her wedding--made him less fit to be Ellen's doctor, according to Weinstein. "Grayson's status as a virtual member of the family...made it difficult for him to act with professional detachment."[12]

That Grayson kept misdiagnosing Ellen's fatal illness and feeding false hope to the Wilson family is no where to be found in his own, posthumously published memoir, penned in the mid-1920's (Grayson died young, in 1938). Wrote Grayson,

But in the following spring [of 1914] Mrs. Wilson again showed signs of debility. As my uneasiness about her condition increased I felt it necessary to inform the President.[13]

"'I am sorry to say, Mr. President, that I cannot report any improvement,'" without telling him what was wrong with her. "...for he wanted the truth, not false consolations." Yet what was the truth? As late as July, going by Wilson's and Helen Bones' correspondence and Eleanor's memoirs, "the doctors" were still holding out false hopes for Ellen's recovery. Who were these other doctors? Grayson credits himself for bringing "into consultation Dr. Francis X. Dercum and Dr. E.P. Davis of Philadelphia, and Dr. Thomas R. Brown of Baltimore," but not until July, when "Mrs. Wilson's condition grew so much worse." One can safely assume that between March and July, Grayson was the only one attending Ellen, the one who recommended, during her brief rally in late June, that she go off to vacation in Harlakenden. As late as July 25 Helen Bones wrote, "She has her ups and downs, as the doctor [singular] said she would; but the rest cure is working." Three days later and nine days before Ellen died, Wilson wrote his friend, Doctor Davis, "...it still seems certain that there is nothing organic the matter and we are hoping and believing that it is only the weather that holds her back."[14]

Grayson claimed that the doctors he called to the White House in July "confirmed my diagnosis and my hopelessness of the patient's recovery. It was Bright's disease with complications," although he never indicated when he made this diagnosis. A diagnosis, moreover, which no member of the Wilson family ever received in July, or earlier. If Grayson had known all along that Ellen suffered from Bright's disease, he would not, judging from his memoirs, have kept it to himself, "...he [Wilson] wanted the truth, not false consolations." However, if Grayson had known the truth all along, but could not muster the courage to tell the president, he did not thereby "spare" Wilson and his family. There are numerous references to what Wilson referred to as his "unspeakable distress that my dear one gets no better." Eleanor remembered that despite "the doctors" assurances, "...in my heart I knew. The old fear had caught up with us at last."[15]

Why had the other doctors who had ministered to Ellen in March failed to detect Bright's disease? As far back as the 1880's, President Chester A. Arthur had been diagnosed with Bright's disease long before he died, his reason for not seeking re-election. Yet Ellen, who showed all the signs of the disease only five months before she died, had been given a clean bill of health.

Whether it was medical malpractice or Grayson's intimate connection to the family--making it difficult for him to probe Ellen's condition, or to admit it--a correct diagnosis would have done nothing to save Ellen's life. Prolonged bed rest and drugs to dull the pain--the traditional mainstays of medical treatment--would still have been advised. Nor did the Wilson family, when they at last found out what was wrong with Ellen, ever blame Grayson for his inability to diagnose (or disclose) Ellen's illness. Quite the contrary. On the day she died, Wilson credited him for his "noble work" in trying to "save" Ellen, although what he meant by "noble work" is far from clear. By then Grayson had become a kind of surrogate son of Wilson's, who could find no fault in him.

As late as August 2, four days before Ellen died, Wilson wrote Hulbert, "She is struggling through deep waters of utter nervous prostration...," still unknowing of her real illness. The next day he wrote Colonel House, "Mrs. Wilson is so weak and suffering so much that I cannot find it in my heart to be away overnight," cancelling his speaking engagement. Either on that day or the next, Eleanor arrived at the White House from a brief trip to New York. Her sister Margaret greeted her with the news that "Doctor Davis, father's old friend and classmate, was on his way from Philadelphia for a consultation. We sat all day waiting." It was the same Doctor Davis whom Wilson had reassured just a week earlier that Ellen's problems were due to the weather, who now came to Washington not on Grayson's, but more likely, upon Wilson's request, to examine Ellen and offer a second opinion. It was he, and not Grayson, who soon made the diagnosis of Bright's disease, giving Ellen only hours to live. "It was Doctor Davis who told us the truth at last--that mother could not live." Writing in 1962, Eleanor had a different version of her mother's end: "In July, two other physicians, called in for consultation, found that she had tuberculosis of the kidneys, so far advanced that it was incurable," contradicting her first memoir, written twenty-five years earlier. (Had this indeed been the diagnosis in July, why would Wilson have written Doctor Davis as late as July 28, that "it still seems certain that there is nothing organic the matter..." with Ellen?) As death certificates were not the rule in that era, one can only accept Grayson's account of what Ellen actually died of: incurable Bright's disease "with complications."[16]

On August 5, Wilson sent a curt telegram to Stockton in Oregon indicating, at last, that "Ellen is seriously ill," and requesting that he come to the White House.

Wilson hastened to gather the rest of the family to Ellen's bedside. Neither he nor his daughters thought of summoning a clergyman. Consequently, Ellen would die without the solace of prayers or benediction.

Neither in her 1937 or 1962 memoirs did Eleanor, who visited her mother daily, mention that her mother suffered a painful end. By contrast Stockton Axson, who was out West the whole time Ellen was ill, noted that she suffered great pain, which is indeed characteristic of kidney disease. On the day that Ellen died, however, perhaps because potent drugs had dulled her pain, she was peaceful, lucid and brave. Her one anxious worry--the fate of her alley bill--had been allayed, thanks to Wilson's last minute lobbying. Earlier on that day she expressed her final, most deeply felt wishes to Grayson, who for days had rarely left her side: to take care of her husband, and the other, which Grayson failed to mention in his memoirs, that he tell the president, not now, but "'later, when he will listen,' that she wanted him to marry again."[17]

During her last hours, Ellen lay holding her husband's hand, surrounded by her daughters and Grayson. Jessie had told her mother only a few weeks earlier that she was pregnant with her first child. Now Ellen endured the pain of knowing that she would never lay eyes on her grandchild (Francis B. Sayre, Jr., future Dean of the National Cathedral in Washington, D.C., where Woodrow Wilson would be laid to rest.)

From the day that Ellen became engaged to Woodrow Wilson until the final moments of her life, "her heart and mind were filled only with deep concern for him." When Ellen drew her last breath, Wilson folded her hands on her breast, stood up and walked to a nearby window, and broke down sobbing. Even without Ellen's death, for which he had been so ill-prepared--thanks to physicans' incompetence or their pusillanimity--he would have been over-burdened enough. Only three days earlier, to Wilson's horror, "the incredible European catastrophe" had at last been unleashed. "'Don't tell your mother anything about it,'" he warned Eleanor, to spare his wife even more worry on his behalf. This tragic turn of events came when the deepening Mexican crisis was still unresolved. It is no wonder that the day after Ellen's death he could say truthfully, without self-pity, "God has stricken me almost beyond what I can bear."[18]

On August 8, a small, private funeral took place in the East Room. By then, Wilson and his daughters had decided that Ellen ought to be laid to rest next to her parents in Rome. Ironically, that fall she was scheduled to pay a visit to her "dear old town." In preparation for her visit, Romans worked hard to spruce up their city, laying a beautiful flower garden in her honor. Now she was coming home for good.

Because no first lady had ever before died in the White House, the public's curiosity was aroused to a high degree. Crowds of strangers paid their respects, lining Pennsylvania Avenue as her hearse slowly made its way to Union Station. There a grieving president and deeply bereaved family boarded the train for the long journey to Rome, the city of Ellen's youth. The whole town turned out on that rainy day when her funeral train drove into the station, the day her second funeral took place in her father's old church, where Wilson first laid eyes on Ellen, thirty-one years before.

The only time anyone had ever seen Woodrow Wilson break down publicly occurred when her coffin was lowered into its somber grave. Nearly two years later, a beautiful tombstone would be placed there. It depicted, in the art nouveau style of the day, a kneeling woman with her right arm outstretched, "reaching out to the flower, suggesting the way she always reached out to people," wrote Margaret Wilson to her father.[19]

ENDNOTES

[1] Woodrow Wilson to Hulbert, Aug.23, 1914. Arthur S. Link, ed., *The Papers of Woodrow Wilson* (Princeton: Princeton University Press, 1966-1996) 30:437. (henceforth: *PWW*)

[2] Eleanor Wilson McAdoo, *The Woodrow Wilsons* (New York: Macmillan, 1937), 296-297; Woodrow Wilson to Edward Parker Davis, July 28, 1914, *PWW* 30:312.

[3] Woodrow Wilson to Hulbert, Jan.9, March 15, 1914. *PWW* 29:114,346.

[4] Eleanor Wilson McAdoo, ed., *The Priceless Gift: the Love Letters of Woodrow Wilson and Ellen Axson Wilson* (New York: McGraw-Hill, 1962), 314; Woodrow Wilson to Hulbert, March 15, 1914, *PWW* 29:346; Edwin A. Weinstein, *Woodrow Wilson: A Medical and Psychological Biography* (Princeton: Princeton University Press, 1981), 255.

[5] Helen Bones to Margaret C. Axson, June 25, 1914. Box 50, f.25. Woodrow Wilson Collection, Princeton University, Mudd Manuscript Library. (henceforth: WWColl.)

[6] Woodrow Wilson to Hulbert, March 15, 1914. *PWW* 29:346-347.

[7] McAdoo, *The Woodrow Wilsons*, 284; Woodrow Wilson to Hulbert, May 10, 1914, *PWW* 30:13.

[8] McAdoo, *The Woodrow Wilsons*, 285-286.

[9] *Ibid.*, 290; Helen Bones to Margaret C. Axson, June 25, 1914, WWColl.; Woodrow Wilson to Hulbert, June 7, 1914, *PWW* 30:158.

[10] Woodrow Wilson to Hulbert, May 25, June 21, 1914, *PWW* 30:72-73, 196; Helen Bones to Margaret C. Axson, June 25, 1914, WWColl.

[11] McAdoo, *The Woodrow Wilsons*, 211.

[12] Weinstein, 256.

[13] Cary T. Grayson, *Woodrow Wilson: An Intimate Memoir* (Washington, D.C.: Potomac Books, 1977), 32.

[14] Grayson, 32-33; Helen Bones to Margaret C. Axson, July 25, 1914, Box 50, f.25, WWColl.

[15] Grayson, 33; Woodrow Wilson to Hulbert, Aug.2, 1914, *PWW* 30:328; McAdoo, *The Woodrow Wilsons*, 296-297

1914 255

16 Woodrow Wilson to Hulbert, Aug.2, 1914, *PWW* 30:328; Woodrow Wilson to Edward M. House, Aug.3, 1914, *PWW* 30:336; McAdoo, *The Woodrow Wilsons*, 299 and *The Priceless Gift*, 315.
17 McAdoo, ed., *The Priceless Gift*, 315.
18 McAdoo, *The Woodrow Wilsons*, 299-300; Woodrow Wilson to Hulbert, Aug.7, 1914, *PWW* 30:357.
19 Margaret Wilson to Woodrow Wilson, June 17, 1916. *PWW* 37:247.

Chapter 10

EPILOGUE

"You are my very life."[1]
Ellen to her husband, 1913

"He could not live without love..."[2]
Eleanor of her father

"I have thought ever so often about what you said yesterday and I cannot think that your career killed her," wrote Ellen's cousin Mary Hoyt to Wilson, five days after Ellen died. As is common with people who lose loved ones prematurely, feelings of guilt now tortured Wilson. Mary Hoyt's letter was meant to soothe: "in the first place, her family on both sides is rather short-lived;" true, although Ellen's sickly brother Stockton and sister Madge lived into their seventies. Secondly, wrote Hoyt, there was the constant giving of herself that took its toll: "Don't you remember how, when she was studying here at the Art League, she could not keep herself away from some kind of social work. 'The need is so great,' she said; and she would always have found the need great, wherever she was," she concluded. It is true that neither rain, gales nor snow kept Ellen from plodding back and forth on foot to the Women's Employment Society during her years in Princeton; and in the White House, when her illness became pronounced in the spring of 1914, she still gave of herself unstintingly, too unstintingly as far as Eleanor and Helen Bones were concerned. One night in March, shortly after her mother's fall in her room, "I raged against the social workers who were demanding too much of her, but Helen said that there was nothing to be done about it; that mother had her heart set on getting the bill for better housing conditions in Washington passed by Congress, and that she would not spare herself."[3]

Wilson, however, may not have been misguided in his belief that his career had been a factor in "killing" Ellen. Unknown in his day but a scientific fact in our own, is the role that stress plays in aggravating, even causing illness. While stress did not cause Ellen's disease, it is not hard to see how it may have accelerated it. Ellen was never settled in one place for more than eight years. Each move from familiar, well-liked surroundings--Bryn Mawr, Middletown, her beloved Library Place home, Prospect House, Cleveland Lane and, finally, Princeton--was a painful, wrenching pulling up of roots followed by a stressful re-adjustment. Frequent moves affected Wilson as well, but his distress was always mitigated by the satisfaction that comes from rising rapidly in one's career.

Besides moving, there was the emotional and psychological strain of Wilson's presidency of Princeton. Almost from the outset, starting with the ruckus caused by erecting a fence around Prospect House, growing opposition to Wilson's radical reforms became enormously stressful for the whole family. Just when the horror and trauma of her brother Ed's death (and that of his whole family) nearly killed Ellen emotionally, the crises at Princeton deepened. It is no wonder that Ellen's illness began to manifest itself shortly after leaving Prospect House. From 1910 onwards, when Wilson entered the political fray as candidate for governor of New Jersey, Ellen's life to all intents and purposes was lived in a pressure cooker. Add to this her constant anxiety for her husband's health and safety, and one need not be an expert to discern how her husband's career could have aggravated her disease and hastened her end. It is also noteworthy that no sooner did Ellen find herself in peaceful, stress-free surroundings--Old Lyme, Harlakenden, even in White Sulphur Springs as late as April, 1914--her health improved dramatically.

While Wilson's career may have hastened Ellen's end, she had, after all, encouraged and abetted it, was proud of his every advance, and gladly sacrificed her needs for his, out of her love for him. "I would give my life, ah! how freely to make life happier for you," she had declared to him in 1910. Nevertheless, guilt continued to dog Wilson. Three months after Ellen died, Colonel House reported that Wilson had no wish to live, was even having suicidal thoughts. Perhaps his tortured conscience had another source. Perhaps, at last, he was beginning to regret his infidelity to Ellen: that is, his emotional attachment to Hulbert. Although this may technically have been platonic, there is little doubt that he loved the bewitching Hulbert right up to Ellen's death.[4]

Ellen had once confided in the young Cary Grayson that "'the Peck affair was the only unhappiness he had caused her during their whole married life.'" This quote is actually a paraphrase of a conversation that Breckinridge Long had with Grayson in 1924, hence that Grayson himself was paraphrasing--of what Ellen had shared with him ten or eleven years before. Consequently, we will never know if what followed this quote were her words as well:"'...not that there was anything wrong--or improper--about it for there was not, but just that a brilliant mind and an attractive woman had somehow fascinated--temporarily--Mr. Wilson's mind--and she (Mrs. Wilson) did not want to share his confidence or his inner mind with any one."[5] Or was this editorializing on Long's, or on Grayson's part? After all, could Ellen really have minded that her husband shared his "inner mind" with Colonel House and the young Doctor Grayson? Hence no one will ever know exactly what Ellen told Grayson, probably as she lay dying in 1914, when he was at her bedside every day.

If "the Peck affair" were Ellen's words, was she alluding to something that was already over, or to something that was still on-going? If it was short-lived, what marked its end? Peck, or rather, Hulbert, was very much alive in Wilson's thoughts and affections even as late as 1914. What with her continuous stream of letters and her overnight stay in the White House, Hulbert was still an intrusive presence in Ellen's life even after she became First Lady. Helen Bones caught Ellen by surprise one day while she was burning papers, to Ellen's evident displeasure. Could these have been Hulbert's letters, almost all of which have disappeared?

In September, 1915, right after Wilson became engaged to Edith Bolling Galt, an event that triggered his fear that Hulbert would publicize his correspondence, he wrote a statement of confession. "These letters disclose a passage of folly and gross impertinance in my life," he admitted. Since the correspondence began in earnest in 1908 and lasted until Ellen's death in 1914, the "passage of folly" lasted six years. Yet in his letter to Edith that accompanied or followed his written confession, Wilson gave the impression that the time was a much shorter one, "...the contemptible error and madness of a few months..."[6] His confession began:

> Even while it lasted I knew and made explicit what it *did not* mean. It did not last, but friendship and genuine admiration ensued.[7]

So "it" had been a short-lived relationship of a few months, exceeding in intensity the "friendship and genuine admiration" that followed. Wilson never explains to Edith why he never ended all contact with Peck once "it" ended, considering that "it" had been such a "contemptible error and madness" on his part. (Yet in 1908, he denied to Ellen that his feelings for Peck had been "romantic love" and convinced her that his relationship was innocent.) Nor does he disclose to Edith how much this woman dominated his thoughts and feelings for years: throughout his two-year governorship, even into the White House; of how often he continued to seek out her company, either alone or with a reluctant Ellen in tow, nor of how often she visited him: in Trenton, Princeton, Sea Girt, and even the White House, nor of the gifts he sent her, the tender birthday letters which he wrote her every year. In short, "it" was far from short-lived.

His confession continued,

> "...I did not have the moral right to offer her the ardent affection which they [his letters to her] express,"

admitting, at least, how unmistakenly ardent his correspondence to her had been. As to his wife Ellen:

> "She, too, knew and understood and has forgiven, little as I deserved the generous indulgence."

That she knew all along about her husband's infatuation with Peck there is no doubt. One wonders, however, what exactly Ellen "understood."[8]

Wilson's sole comfort now was "the recollection that nothing associated with this correspondence could even in the least degree affect the honor of the noble lady to whom I then had the distinction and happiness to be married." Perhaps not Ellen's honor, but obviously, according to Grayson's paraphrase, her personal happiness. While Ellen was quite willing to die for her husband's happiness, he was unwilling to sacrifice his infatuation for a woman who continually imposed herself on Ellen and her family. Even at the risk of losing his presidential bid in 1912. (When he feared that his relationship with Hulbert would be publicly disclosed, which would "ruin me utterly, and all connected with me...," including Ellen.[9])

After Colonel House read Wilson's confession, he declared in his diary, "To illustrate how honest he is, he had told Mrs. Galt every detail concerning the matter."[10] Every detail?

The "deep humiliating grief and shame" which Wilson expressed in 1915 may have been at the root of his intense feelings of guilt and deep depression following Ellen's death. By resigning herself to her husband's "friendship and genuine admiration" for Hulbert, Ellen had indeed sacrificed her happiness for the sake of her husbaand's. Although he did not admit it to Edith, perhaps he at last came to realize the magnitude of her sacrifice.

If Hulbert dared to entertain any hope that Wilson might marry her after Ellen's death, her hopes were crushed when she visited him in the White House,

Epilogue   261

sometime in early 1915. So important an event went unmentioned in her memoirs. Was it because the outcome was so humiliating? Wilson would not now, when he was free, dishonor his late wife's memory and do that which she might have, while she lived, half-expected him to do: marry Hulbert after her death. Nor was Wilson's "confession" ever publicized, since no negative backlash--either on the public's part or on Hulbert's--followed the announcement of his engagement to Edith, as he feared it would. He and Edith were married shortly afterward, on December 18, 1915, just fifteen months after Ellen died.

Wilson's correspondence with Hulbert continued after a fashion. Aware that she possessed hundreds of incriminating letters from him, he could not very well put an abrupt end to his "friendship" with Hulbert. Following her son's catastrophic losses on the stock market in late 1914, which wiped out his and his mother's modest fortune, her son's health broke down in early January. To recuperate, Hulbert and her son re-located to California, but not before Wilson paid off two of her mortgages on property she and her son were unable to sell. (According to her memoir, she had no one else to appeal to for help. And Wilson might have feared the consequences of a refusal.) This transaction, which leaked to the public, fueled even more rumors of a liaison with her. But at least Wilson now, with Hulbert so far away, had an excuse to stop writing her altogether. "The man I used to know...became more remote than the physical distance then separating us," her memoir recalls. She would not hear from him or see him again until 1919, shortly before his stroke, when he was lobbying in California on behalf of his League of Nations covenant. "I was arrayed in the same gown in which I had last appeared in the President's household in 1915." A four-year old gown? Unthinkable for the once fashion-conscious Mrs. Peck.[11]

As to her cache of Wilson letters, Hulbert's memoir tells of an almost cloak-and-dagger conspiracy on the part of Republican enemies of Wilson's, and possibly even German agents--who shadowed and dogged her throughout the war, and even afterwards--offering her huge sums of money for them. To her credit, Hulbert refused to part with even a single one, despite her deepening penury. Not until after Wilson's death did she agree to sell them to Ray Stannard Baker. Because so many family intimates of Wilson's were still living while Baker was writing his official biography, he refrained from making full use of Wilson's heartfelt letters to his "dearest friend."

* * *

As is common with people who lose loved ones, Wilson began to idealize Ellen as soon as she died. After her burial, he sought peace and solace in

262   Sina Dubovoy

Harlakenden, where every room and every view reminded him of his dead wife. At one point Colonel House joined him. He noted in his diary in late August, "I was surprised at his desire to discuss Mrs. Wilson. He showed me photographs of her, read poems written about her, and talked of her as freely as if she were alive."[12]

As war in Europe raged on that year and the next, Wilson confided to Stockton and to Grayson, "'I feel that I ought for her sake to devote myself more entirely to alleviating the suffering of the world,'" feeling deeply how much Ellen had tried, on her part, to do the same.[13] He became increasingly a crusader, as Ellen in the end had become, devoting himself to world peace and unity. He drew closer to his Maker, and began to remind people of the prophets of old. "We have got to save society, so far as it is saved, by the instrumentality of Christianity in the world," a theme he would intone time and again. Stockton was right when he noted that Ellen had made Wilson president "literally as well as spiritually," only the latter came upon her death.

Even after Wilson became engaged to Edith, Colonel House noted, "...I believe the President's affection for Mrs. Wilson has not lessened..."[14] They were indeed very different, Edith and Ellen. Where Ellen had been diminutive, fragile (until her weight gain in middle age), and moon-faced, Edith was only an inch shorter than Wilson, and, though only in her forties, had a hefty figure, a perfect heart-shaped face, and quite unlike Ellen, was addicted to fashion and fine jewelry. With less than a year of formal education behind her, Edith was less well-read than Ellen by far; nonetheless, she had wit where Ellen had none, and was, like Ellen, a fluent writer and an engaging speaker. A southerner (from Virginia) as Ellen, Edith, too, was less religious than her husband-to-be. She would out-live Wilson by nearly four decades.

Wilson never recovered fully from the massive stroke he suffered in 1919, during his second term. Consequently, he did not seek re-election. Even after he left the White House, settling in a townhouse on S Street in northwest Washington, Doctor Grayson continued to minister to him and was by his side on the day he died, on February 3, 1924. During Wilson's last months, he reminisced constantly of Ellen, especially when his daughters visited him. During one such visit he told Eleanor, who had come all the way from her new home in California to be with him,

> I was back on the island at Muskoka, he said, softly. Do you remember our picnics there, and your mother reading poetry under the pines? I wish I could hear her voice.[15]

"'I owe everything to your mother--you know that, don't you?' and he began to talk about their life together...how she had devoted her life to him and to us, with no thought of herself--how she had never failed him." Eleanor sat listening, finally expressing her wish to "'hand her torch on to my own children.'" Her father replied, "'You can--tell them about her. That is enough.'"[16] But it was not enough for Eleanor. Besides her own children, she would tell the whole world.

ENDNOTES

[1] Ellen A. Wilson to Woodrow Wilson, Sept. 8, 1913. Arthur S. Link, ed., *The Papers of Woodrow Wilson* (Princeton: Princeton University Press, 1966-1996) 28:267. (henceforth: *PWW*).

[2] Eleanor Wilson McAdoo, ed., *The Priceless Gift:the Love Letters of Woodrow Wilson and Ellen Axson Wilson* (New York: McGraw-Hill, 1962), 315.

[3] Mary E. Hoyt to Woodrow Wilson, Aug.11, 1914, *PWW* 30:375; Eleanor Wilson McAdoo, *The Woodrow Wilsons* (New York: McMillan, 1937), 276.

[4] Ellen A. Wilson to Woodrow Wilson, Feb.28, 1910, *PWW* 20:190; "From the Diary of Colonel House," Nov.14, 1914, *PWW* 31:320.

[5] "From the Diary of Breckinridge Long," Jan.11, 1924. *PWW* 68:527.

[6] Woodrow Wilson to Edith Bolling Galt, Sept.21, 1915, *PWW* 34:500.

[7] "An Outline and Two Drafts of Statements," Sept.20, 1915, *PWW* 34:496-497.

[8] *Idem.*

[9] Woodrow Wilson to Hulbert, Sept.29, 1912. *PWW* 25:285.

[10] "From the Diary of Colonel House," Sept. 22, 1915, *PWW* 34:507.

[11] Mary Allen Hulbert, *The Story of Mrs. Peck* (New York: Minton, Balch & Co., 1933), 249-269.

[12] "From the Diary of Colonel House," Aug.30, 1914, *PWW* 30:465.

[13] Stockton Axson, *Brother Woodrow: A Memoir of Woodrow Wilson* ed. Arthur S. Link (Princeton: Princeton University Press, 1993), 226.

[14] "From the Diary of Colonel House," Sept.22, 1915. *PWW* 34:508.

[15] McAdoo, *The Woodrow Wilsons*, 300.

[16] *Ibid.*, 301.

INDEX

A

Alley Dwelling Act, 236
alma mater, 15, 46, 77, 86
alumni, 167, 183-184, 189
American Women, 191
Art Students League, 48, 50-54, 59, 65, 108, 169, 171, 239
Atlanta Journal, 206
Atlanta University, 9
Austen, Jane, 22, 31
Axson, Edward, 2, 4-8, 10, 12, 22, 24, 27-29, 39-40, 42-44, 46-48, 64, 140, 187
Axson, Randolph, 41, 88
Axson, Robert, 75
Axson, Stockton, v, xii, 2, 27-28, 35, 46, 63, 67, 79, 87, 111, 135-136, 155, 178, 185, 188-189, 209, 218, 250, 255, 259, 269

B

Baker, Ray Stannard, v, 11-12, 28, 63, 87, 108, 113, 127, 132, 135-136, 151, 180, 183, 185, 188, 195, 208-209, 215, 218-219, 250, 267
Baltimore College for Women, 126, 161
Beech Island, 7
Benton, Thomas Hart, 52
Berry, Martha, 243
Bible Society, 204

Bible study, 119
birds, 239
Blaine, James G., 54
Board of Trustees, 196
Bones, Helen, 56, 95, 104, 226, 228, 231, 233, 238, 249-251, 253-257, 260-261, 263, 265
Boston Globe, The, 206
British colony, 176
British Isles, 160, 177
Brower, Jessie Bones, 32, 35
Brown, Thomas R., 257
Brush, George DeForest, 52
Bryan, William Jennings, 205, 220, 228

C

Carlyle, Thomas, 38
Carnegie, Andrew, 9, 179
Cherokee Baptist, 15
Chester A. Arthur, 258
Chicago World's Fair, 96, 116, 200
Child, Edward S., 99
Christianity, 268
Churchill, Winston, 237, 246
Civil War, 2, 9, 15, 38, 40-41, 52, 80, 156, 235
Clark, Genevieve, 207
Clark, John Bates, 132, 136
Cleveland, Grover, 54, 124, 153-154, 161, 183
Cleveland, Ruth, 161

Index

Columbia Theological Seminary, 2, 4, 49
Columbia University, 132
Congressional Government, 49, 54
Corcoran Gallery, 50, 170, 230
Cox, Kenyon, 52

D

Daggett, Mabel, 239
Darwin, Charles, 49
Davis, E.P., 257
democracy, 182, 204, 238
Democrat, 54, 231
Democratic National Convention, 184
Dercum, Francis X., 257
DuMond, Frank, 193
Duncan, Isadora, 212

E

Eakins, Thomas, 52
Edison, Thomas, 168
Edwardian England, 176
Eliot, George, 38, 69
Elliot, Edward, 166, 194
employment society, 101
energy, 10, 203
Equal Rights Amendment, 70
Erwin, Beth, 69
Evelyn College, 95, 226
Ewing, Robert, 205, 220

F

Fielder, John, 158
Fine, Harry, 149
Florence Taft, 83
Foley, Maggie, 116
Franklin Gold Mining Company, 168
Freer, F.W., 52
Freud, Sigmund, 39
Front Royal, 150
function, 163

G

Galt, Edith Bolling, 234, 237, 265, 269
Garden at Prospect, 172
Gaudens, Augustus St., 52
Gettysburg, 238
Good Housekeeping, 239
Goucher College, 126, 161
Graham, Mary, 107
Greensboro Female College, 2, 5-6, 15

H

Hagner, Belle, 233
Harlakenden House, 237
Harmon, Judson, 207
Harris, Anna, 17, 100-101, 104, 112, 120, 123, 125, 130, 133, 135-137, 167, 176, 180, 187-188
Hayes, Lucy, 230
Hayes, Rutherford B., 230
Hibben, Jack, 93, 129, 149, 169, 183, 189, 218
Hopkins, Archibald, 234
Howe, Annie Wilson, 95, 187
Hoyt, Mary Eloise, 77, 136
Hoyt, William, 27, 47
Hulbert, M.A., 211

I

inaugural ball, 143, 227-229, 231, 248

J

Jackson, Andrew, 235
Jameson, James Franklin, 106, 112
Johns Hopkins University, 34-35

K

Kahn, Julius, 236

Index 267

Kennedy, Marion Wilson, 75, 89
King, Ben, 206, 213, 254

L

Lane, Cleveland, 151, 203, 215, 217, 223, 226-229, 264
League of Nations, 267
Library of Congress, xii, 28, 63, 87, 113, 135, 142, 185, 188, 218
Library Place, 92, 98, 100, 151, 154, 156-158, 183, 196-197, 203, 229, 264

M

Macbeth Gallery, 55, 187, 240, 251
Macbeth, William, 171, 187, 192, 239
Madero, Francisco, 238
Manhattan Club, 205
Mann, Parker, 203
Mardi Gras, 151
Marshall, Thomas R., 215
Mary Baldwin Seminary, 227, 250
Massachusetts Institute of Technology, 126
Mawr, Bryn, 10, 56-57, 60, 69-82, 87-88, 94, 116-117, 163, 233
Mayrant, Katie, 36
McAdoo, William Gibbs, 64, 151, 223
McCombs, William F., 208
McKinley, William, 155
medicine, 43
Metcalf, Willard, 170, 192, 218
Methodists, 80
Metropolitan Museum of Art, 51, 55
Mexicans, 238

N

Nassau Street, 92, 156, 197
National Academy of Design, 16, 52
National Cathedral, 259
National Portrait Gallery, 160
New York Age; The, 207, 217
New York Times, 185, 214, 241, 250-251

Nietzsche, 125
Nugent, Jim, 195

P

Palmers, Ben, 151
Paris International Exposition, 18
Park, Arden, 62, 67-69
Pasteur, Louis, 25
Patton, Francis L., 94
Peck, Thomas Dowse, 177
Phi Beta Kappa, 162
Philadelphia Academy of the Fine Arts, 52
Pollock, Jackson, 52
Pope Pius X, 163
Presbyterian Church, xii, 2, 8, 10, 28, 35, 41, 119, 140, 249
Presbyterian seminary, 92
Presbyterians, 3, 5, 12-13, 15, 32, 35, 61, 150
Princeton Historical Society, xii, 135
Princeton in the Nation's Service, 131
Princeton Theological Seminary, 92
Princeton University, v, xii, 27-28, 63-64, 87, 89, 92, 111-112, 130-131, 134-135, 137, 139, 141, 154-155, 174-175, 185, 187, 218, 249-251, 260, 269
Princeton, v, ix, xii, 11, 27-28, 31, 34, 63-64, 70, 81, 86-87, 89, 91-99, 101-105, 108-109, 111-112, 116-117, 121, 123-124, 126, 130-135, 137, 139, 141, 149-151, 153-156, 158-159, 161, 166-167, 169, 172-175, 178-179, 181-185, 187-189, 191, 193-198, 200-205, 215-218, 224, 226-229, 232, 240-244, 249-251, 260, 263-264, 266, 269

Q

Quakers, 70

R

Randolph, Nathaniel Fitz, 93
Republican president, 155
Rice University in Texas, 126

268 Index

Rockefeller, John D., 191
Roman Catholics, 41
Rome Female College, 15-18, 70
Roosevelt, Eleanor, 234
Roosevelt, Teddy, 155, 173, 214, 216, 236
Ruskin, John, 38, 45
Ryder, Chauncey F., 240

S

Secret Service, 223, 225, 238
segregation, 56, 156, 217, 234, 248
Smith, Jim, 195
Society for Ethical Culture, 58
Southern Industrial Educational Association, 243
Southern Presbyterian Review, 49
Southwestern Railroad Co., 101
Spring Street Mission School, 58
stress, 44, 46, 154, 164, 214, 216, 225, 264

T

Tarbell, Ida B., 191
Taylor, Zachary, 217
Thomas, Martha Carey, 60, 69, 72
tobacco, 21, 248
Tumulty, Joseph, 205-206, 209, 227

U

Underwood, Oscar, 207
Union troops, 10
United States, v, xi, 52, 107, 154, 217
University of Illinois, 98, 132
University of Leipzig, 76
University of Michigan, 79
University of Pennsylvania, 162, 199

V

Van Laer, A.T., 171, 240
Village Improvement Society, 154
Vonnah, Robert, 171, 244

W

Washington, George, 106, 200
Wesleyan College, 80
Wesleyan University, 79
White House, 109, 117, 155, 162, 180, 224-225, 229-235, 237-239, 244-248, 250, 253-254, 256-258, 260, 263, 265-266, 268
White Sulphur Springs, 254, 264
Wilson, Joseph R., 24, 29, 33, 38, 89, 112, 146, 218
Wilson, Thomas Woodrow, v, xi-xii, 1-4, 6, 9-10, 12-14, 16, 22, 24, 27-29, 31-32, 36, 38, 44, 54, 56, 59, 62-67, 73, 77-79, 87-89, 91-94, 109, 111-113, 115, 134-137, 143, 145-147, 149, 154-155, 166, 171, 175, 180, 185-188, 207-208, 210, 218-221, 226-227, 239, 242, 245-246, 249-251, 253-254, 259-261, 269
Woodrow Wilson House, 109, 147, 239, 242, 245
Woodrow, Hattie, 35
Woodrow, James, 49, 135, 186
world war, 239, 244

Y

Yale, 107
Yates, Frederic, 175, 219, 240, 250
YWCA, 162